Stress Management
FOR
DUMMIES
A Wiley Brand

2nd Edition

by Allen Elkin, PhD

FOR
DUMMIES
A Wiley Brand

Stress Management For Dummies®, 2nd Edition

Published by
John Wiley & Sons, Inc.
111 River St.
Hoboken, NJ 07030-5774
www.wiley.com

About the Author

Allen Elkin, PhD, is a clinical psychologist, a certified sex therapist, and the director of the Stress Management & Counseling Center in New York City. Nationally known for his expertise in the field of stress and emotional disorders, he has appeared frequently on *Today, Good Morning America,* and *Good Day New York*, as well as programs on PBS, CNN, FNN, Fox 5, and National Public Radio. He has been quoted in *The New York Times, The Wall Street Journal, The Washington Post, Newsweek, Men's Health, Fitness, Cosmopolitan, Glamour, Redbook, Woman's Day, Self, Mademoiselle, McCall's, Parents*, and other publications. Dr. Elkin holds workshops and presentations for professional organizations and corporations, including the American Society of Contemporary Medicine, Surgery, and Ophthalmology; the U.S. Drug Enforcement Administration; Morgan Stanley; IBM; PepsiCo; and the New York Stock Exchange.

He is the author of two other books on stress, *Urban Ease: Stress-Free Living in the Big City* (Penguin Books), and *Relax in the City Week by Week,* (Duncan Baird). He is also a coauthor of *Thriving in the Workplace All-in-One For Dummies* (Wiley).

When he's not talking about stress, you can probably find him at his home on the Upper West Side of Manhattan, where he lives with his wife, Beth, their two children, Josh and Katy, and their cat, Smokey.

Dedication

To my wife, Beth, my best friend, and our children, Josh and Katy, who bring us great joy.

Acknowledgments

First, and certainly foremost, I would like to thank my wife, Beth, who not only tolerated all the stress and tension that came with writing this book but also helped me edit the manuscript and kept me on track when I got lost. Her caring patience and sense of humor made writing this book much less stressful than it might have been.

I would also like to thank the many wonderful people at Wiley for their attention and care in turning an idea into a book. Special thanks are due to my editors, Lindsay Lefevere, Chrissy Guthrie, and Ashley Petry, and technical reviewer Matthew Grant for their support and encouragement and enormous help in making this a much better book than it might have been.

Finally, thank you to all my teachers and mentors whose thoughts, ideas, and insights are blended in these pages. I owe a special debt to my patients, who daily show me that there is still much more to learn.

Publisher's Acknowledgments

We're proud of this book; please send us your comments at http://dummies.custhelp.com. For other comments, please contact our Customer Care Department within the U.S. at 877-762-2974, outside the U.S. at 317-572-3993, or fax 317-572-4002.

Some of the people who helped bring this book to market include the following:

Acquisitions, Editorial, and Vertical Websites

Senior Project Editor: Christina Guthrie
 (Previous Edition: Tim Gallan, Brian Kramer)

Executive Editor: Lindsay Sandman Lefevere

Copy Editor: Ashley Petry

Assistant Editor: David Lutton

Editorial Program Coordinator: Joe Niesen

Technical Editor: Matthew Grant, PsyD, HSPP

Vertical Websites: Rachel Mills

Editorial Manager: Christine Meloy Beck

Editorial Assistants: Rachelle Amick,
 Alexa Koschier

Cover Photos: © TommL / iStockphoto.com

Art Coordinator: Alicia B. South

Composition Services

Project Coordinator: Patrick Redmond

Layout and Graphics: Jennifer Creasey,
 Joyce Haughey

Proofreaders: Jessica Kramer,
 Evelyn C. Welborn

Indexer: Potomac Indexing, LLC

Illustrator: Pam Tanzey

Special Help: Megan Knoll

Publishing and Editorial for Consumer Dummies

 Kathleen Nebenhaus, Vice President and Executive Publisher

 David Palmer, Associate Publisher

 Kristin Ferguson-Wagstaffe, Product Development Director

Publishing for Technology Dummies

 Andy Cummings, Vice President and Publisher

Composition Services

 Debbie Stailey, Director of Composition Services

Contents at a Glance

Introduction 1

Part I: Getting Started with Stress Management............. 7
Chapter 1: Stressed Out? Welcome to the Club!...9
Chapter 2: Stress Explained (In Surprisingly Few Pages).............................23
Chapter 3: Getting Started: Gathering Your Tools 35

Part II: Mastering the Basics 49
Chapter 4: Relaxing Your Body...51
Chapter 5: Quieting Your Mind 73
Chapter 6: Cultivating Mindfulness 97
Chapter 7: Stress-Reducing Organizational Skills.......................................117
Chapter 8: Finding More Time...139
Chapter 9: Eating, Exercising, and Getting Your Zzzs 161

Part III: The Secrets of Stress-Effective Thinking 185
Chapter 10: Understanding How Your Thinking Stresses You Out........................187
Chapter 11: Stress-Resilient Values, Goals, and Attitudes.............................211

Part IV: Managing Your Stress in Real Life 231
Chapter 12: Overcoming Your Anger 233
Chapter 13: Worrying Less 249
Chapter 14: Reducing Interpersonal Stress 271
Chapter 15: De-Stress at Work (And Still Keep Your Job) 295
Chapter 16: Maintaining a Stress-Resilient Lifestyle 315

Part V: The Part of Tens 337
Chapter 17: Ten Habits of Highly Effective Stress Managers 339
Chapter 18: Ten Events That Trigger Stress 343

Index 347

Table of Contents

Introduction 1

    About This Book 1
    Conventions Used in This Book 2
    What You're Not to Read 3
    Foolish Assumptions 3
    How This Book Is Organized 3
        Part I: Getting Started with Stress Management 4
        Part II: Mastering the Basics 4
        Part III: The Secrets of Stress-Effective Thinking 4
        Part IV: Managing Your Stress in Real Life 4
        Part V: The Part of Tens 5
    Icons Used in This Book 5
    Where to Go from Here 6

Part 1: Getting Started with Stress Management 7

    Chapter 1: Stressed Out? Welcome to the Club! 9
    Experiencing a Stress Epidemic? 9
    Understanding Where All This Stress Is Coming From 10
        Struggling in a struggling economy 11
        Getting frazzled at work 11
        Feeling frazzled at home 12
        Piling on new stresses with technology 13
        Dealing with daily hassles (the little things add up) 14
    Looking at the Signs and Symptoms of Stress 15
    Understanding How Stress Can Make You Sick 16
        Understanding how stress can be a pain
          in the neck (and other places) 17
        Taking stress to heart 17
        Hitting below the belt 18
        Compromising your immune system 18
        The cold facts: Connecting stress and the sniffles 19
        "Not tonight, dear. I have a (stress) headache." 20
    Stressing Out Your Family 20
        Your relationships 21
        Your kids 21
    Stress Can Be Good? 22

    Chapter 2: Stress Explained (In Surprisingly Few Pages) 23
    So What Is Stress Anyhow? 23
        "Sorry, but I really need a definition" 24
        Stress causes stress? 25

How This Whole Stress Thing Got Started 25
    Imagining you're a cave person 25
    Surviving the modern jungle 26
Understanding the Signs of Stress 27
    Your body reacts 27
    Your feelings and behavior change 29
Understanding Stress Is as Simple as ABC 30
Managing Stress: A Three-Pronged Approach 32
    1. Managing your stressors 32
    2. Changing your thoughts 33
    3. Managing your stress responses 34
Tuning Your Strings: Finding the Right Balance 34

Chapter 3: Getting Started: Gathering Your Tools **35**
How Stressed Are You? Finding Ways
    to Measure Your Stress Level 36
    Starting with a simple gut check 36
    Using a stress gauge 36
    Measuring your stress in other ways 37
Monitoring Your Stress with a Stress Journal 41
    Knowing how to record your stress 41
    Knowing when to record your stress 44
Facing Roadblocks 45
    Take it a step at a time 45
    Give it a try 46
    Accept your different strokes 46
    Practice to make perfect 46
    Find a quiet place 46
    Link up 47
    Get a stress buddy 47
    Don't expect overnight results 47

Part II: Mastering the Basics **49**

Chapter 4: Relaxing Your Body **51**
Stress Can Be a Pain in the Neck (And That's Just for Starters) 52
    Funny, I don't feel tense 53
    Invasion of the body scan 53
Breathing Away Your Tension 54
    Your breath is fine. It's your breathing that's bad. 55
    "Why change now? I've been breathing for years." 55
    Evaluating your breathing 56
    Cutting yourself some slack 56
    Changing the way you breathe, changing the way you feel 57
    The yawn that refreshes 60
Tensing Your Way to Relaxation 61
    Exploring how progressive relaxation works 61
    Scrunching up like a pretzel 64

Mind over Body: Using the Power of Suggestion......................65
Stretching Away Your Stress...67
Massage? Ah, There's the Rub!.....................................68
    Massaging yourself 68
    Becoming the massage-er or massage-ee 70
Taking a Three-Minute Energy Burst 71
More Ways to Relax...71

Chapter 5: Quieting Your Mind. 73
Where Do All These Thoughts Come From!? 74
    Sorting out your thoughts 75
    Thinking automatically 75
Turning Off Your Mind...76
    Stopping your unwanted thoughts..............................76
    Snapping out of it 78
Distracting Yourself 78
Using Your Imagination 79
Making Things Move 81
What, Me Worry?...82
    Scheduling your worries 82
    Blowing up your worries.......................................82
    Striking up the band (or better yet, the string quartet) 83
    Visiting the rain forest...84
    Using some common scents 84
Do Nothing: Meditation Is Good for You 86
    East comes West 86
    "What can meditation do for me, anyway?" 86
    But it's harder than it looks....................................87
    Preparing to meditate 87
    Meditative breathing 88
    Meditating with a mantra......................................90
    Finding time for mini-meditations 90
Hypnotize Yourself...91
    No, you won't be turned into a clucking chicken 91
    Surprise! You've already been hypnotized.....................92
    The power of a trance 92
    Inducing a light trance 92
    Going a little deeper 93
    Get me out of this trance 94
Want Some Feedback? Go the High-Tech Route....................95
    Hard-wired to your own body..................................95
    Biofeedback (without the wires) 96

Chapter 6: Cultivating Mindfulness. 97
Understanding Mindfulness 97
    Defining mindfulness 98
    Dispelling myths about mindfulness 99
    Figuring out whether mindfulness is right for you.............100

Recognizing Mindlessness...100
    Auto-pilot: The good, the bad, and the really bad.........101
    Mindless multi-tasking 102
    The dangers of mindless thinking.............................102
Understanding How Mindfulness Can Help Reduce Your Stress 104
Developing the Skills of Mindfulness 106
    Staying in the present..107
    Breathing more mindfully..107
    Revisiting your daily routines 108
    Learning how to detach 110
    Controlling your attention 111
Cultivating Mindful Acceptance..113
    Understanding acceptance 113
    Distinguishing acceptance from resignation..............114
    Non-acceptance and your stress 115

Chapter 7: Stress-Reducing Organizational Skills.............117
Figuring Out Why Your Life Is So Disorganized...................118
    Are you organizationally challenged? 118
    Identifying your personal disorganization 119
Clearing Away the Clutter..120
    Bust those clutter excuses 120
    Get yourself motivated...122
    Draw yourself a clutter roadmap...............................123
    Get your feet wet...123
    Stop kidding yourself...123
    Avoid discouragement 124
    Get down to the nitty-gritty 125
Organizing Your Space..128
Organizing Information 129
    Losing the paper trail 129
    Organizing the papers you do need to keep 131
    Organizing electronically...134
    Managing your email 135
Keeping Your Life Organized 136
    Being proactive 137
    Buying less..137

Chapter 8: Finding More Time 139
Determining Whether You Struggle with Time Management 140
Being Mindful of Your Time 140
    Knowing where your time goes...................................140
    Figuring out what you want more time for 142
    Knowing what you want to spend less time doing.......143
    Minding your time with cues and prompts 143
    Questioning your choices and changing behaviors.......144
Becoming a List Maker..145
    Starting with a master to-do list................................145
    Creating a will-do-today list.......................................146

Having a will-do-later list 147
Keeping some tips in mind as you make your lists 148
Minimizing your Distractions and Interruptions 150
Managing electronic interruptions 150
Losing the visitors 151
Lowering the volume 151
Limiting your breaks 152
Shifting your time 152
Turning it into a positive 152
Minimizing your TV time 152
Winning the waiting game 154
Getting around Psychological Roadblocks to Time Management 155
Getting over your desire to be perfect 155
Overcoming procrastination 155
Letting Go: Discovering the Joys of Delegating 158
The fine art of delegating 158
Delegating begins at home 159
Buying Time 159
Avoid paying top dollar 160
Strive for deliverance 160

Chapter 9: Eating, Exercising, and Getting Your Zzzs **161**
Stress-Effective Eating 161
Feeding your brain 162
Choosing low-stress foods 162
Stopping the stress-eating cycle 164
Eating mindfully 167
Mastering the art of anti-stress snacking 168
Eating out 169
Stress-Reducing Exercise and Activity 170
Calming your brain naturally 170
Thinking activity, not exercise 171
Doing the gym thing 173
Keeping yourself motivated 174
Getting a Good Night's Sleep 175
Knowing your sleep needs 176
Hitting the sheets earlier 176
Developing a sleep routine 177
Falling asleep 181

Part III: The Secrets of Stress-Effective Thinking .... **_185_**

**Chapter 10: Understanding How Your
Thinking Stresses You Out** **187**
Believe It or Not, Most of Your Stress Is Self-Created 187
Stress at 30,000 feet: Flight and fright 188
The presentation from hell 188

Remembering Your ABCs 189
    It's not exactly a new idea 190
    It's the thought that counts 191
Separating Thoughts from Feelings 192
Understanding Your Stress-Producing Thinking 193
    Figuring out whether your thinking is the problem 193
    Understanding your automatic thoughts 194
    Uncovering your hidden thoughts 194
Your Thinking Errors 195
    Catastrophizing and awfulizing 195
    Can't-stand-it-itis 196
    What-if-ing 197
    Overgeneralizing 198
    Mind reading and conclusion-jumping 199
    Comparativitis 199
    Personalizing 201
    Emotional reasoning 201
    Filtering 202
    Magnifying and minimizing 203
    Should-ing 203
    Self-rating 205
Using Your Coping Self-talk 207
    Talking like an air-traffic controller 208
    Putting it all together 208
    Taking time to make it work 210

Chapter 11: Stress-Resilient Values, Goals, and Attitudes 211
Recognizing the Value of Your Values 211
Clarifying Your Values and Goals 212
    The tombstone test 212
    Five-ish years to live 213
    The rating game 213
    Things I love to do 214
    Some other intriguing questions to ponder 215
Actualizing Your Values, Reaching Your Goals 215
    Staying on track 215
    Making the time 216
Expressing Gratitude 217
    Understanding how expressing gratitude
        reduces your stress 218
    Keeping a mental gratitude journal 218
    Remembering to actually express your gratitude 219
Cultivating Optimism 220
    Recognizing thinking errors that hinder optimism 220
    Arguing with yourself 221
    Constructing an optimistic future 222
Laughing Your Way to Stress Reduction 222
    He (or she) who laughs, lasts 223
    Some humorous suggestions 223
    Blow things up 224

Doing Something Good for Someone Else 224
    How helping helps 225
    How to get started 226
    How to offer random acts of kindness 226
Adding a Spiritual Dimension...227
    Understanding how faith helps you cope with stress.................227
    Appreciating the power of belief 228
Gathering a Little Wisdom...229

Part IV: Managing Your Stress in Real Life................... 231

Chapter 12: Overcoming Your Anger........................... 233

Figuring Out Just How Mad You Really Are 233
The Pros and Cons of Anger..234
    Looking at the positives of anger...234
    Examining the downside of anger...235
    Understanding when and why anger is appropriate....................237
Tempering Your Temper 237
    Keeping an anger log 237
    Checking your stress balance 238
Becoming Mindful of Your Anger 239
    Breathing mindfully 239
    Mindfully detaching 239
Modifying Your Mindset 240
    Thinking about your thinking...240
    Finding and fixing your thinking errors 241
    Expecting the expected..241
    Lengthening your fuse...242
    Using your coping self-talk 243
    To vent or not to vent? That is the question...............................244
    Rehearsing your anger 245
    Doing an emotional replay...246
    Becoming an actor...246
    Being discreet and choosing your moment.................................246
    Breathing your anger away..247
    Looking for the funny part...247

Chapter 13: Worrying Less 249

Do You Worry Too Much?..249
Don't Worry, Be Happy. Yeah, Right!...250
Identifying Your Worries 251
    Creating a worry list 251
    Spotting your hidden worries 252
Understanding Your Worries 253
    Comparing productive and unproductive worry.........................254
    Discovering why you worry unproductively...............................255

Controlling and Stopping Your Worrying..256
    Writing about your worries 256
    Scheduling your worries 257
    Having a place to worry 257
Thinking Straighter, Worrying Less 258
    Remember that feelings and thoughts aren't facts 258
    Stop feeding your worries...259
    Cultivate acceptance 259
Correcting Your Thinking Errors..260
    Minimizing your what-ifs 260
    Assessing the odds 260
    Realizing that Murphy's Law is wrong 261
    Cutting out your catastrophizing and awfulizing 261
    Getting perspective 262
    Watching out for conclusion-jumping...............................263
    Coping with uncertainty and lack of control...................263
    Watching out for self-rating...264
    Going to yourself for advice 264
    Becoming a problem solver (rather than a worrier).......265
    Using your coping self-talk 265
Escaping Your Worries 266
    Getting distracted 266
    Going for a walk..267
    Working up a sweat 267
    Talking about it 267
    Humoring yourself 268
    Relaxing your body and calming your mind 269
    Trying some positive imagery..269
    In a pinch, try this...270

Chapter 14: Reducing Interpersonal Stress....................271
Developing Stress-Reducing Communication 271
    Become a good listener...272
    It's your turn to talk..276
Discovering What It Means to Be Assertive 278
    How assertive are you?..278
    Not too hot, not too cold — just right...............................280
    Examples of assertive behavior 281
    What assertive behavior is not 281
Becoming More Assertive..282
    Observing assertive behavior 283
    Watching how you say things 283
    Saying "no" (oh, so nicely) 284
    Starting nice and working your way up to nasty 285
    Talking like a broken record..286
    Trying a little "fogging" 286
Coping with Difficult People...288
    Stay calm..288
    Focus on the issue 288
    Avoid kitchen-sinking...289

Don't be a labeler...290
Watch the "never" and "always" traps.................290
Hit above the belt 291
Stop personalizing 291
Curb your "should" statements 292
Have a dress rehearsal.....................................292
Lose the battle, win the war 293
Use the "stoplight" technique..........................293

Chapter 15: De-Stress at Work (And Still Keep Your Job) 295
Reading the Signs of Workplace Stress....................296
Knowing What's Triggering Your Work Stress 297
Making Positive Changes to Control Your Workplace Stress 298
Overcoming SNS (Sunday-night stress) 298
Starting your workday unstressed 299
Calming your daily commute 300
Minimizing your travel stress..........................301
De-stressing during your workday 302
Stretching and reaching for the sky 303
Creating a stress-resistant workspace.............305
Managing your work time 309
Nourishing your body (and spirit) 309
Taking Advantage of Company Perks 311
Gyms and health clubs....................................311
Flextime...312
Working from home 312
Employee assistance programs 312
Coming Home More Relaxed (And Staying That Way) 313

Chapter 16: Maintaining a Stress-Resilient Lifestyle 315
Making Stress Management a Habit 316
Making use of found moments 316
Using a "stress dot" 317
Remembering Your Ps (Prompts) and Cues 318
Making an appointment with yourself 319
Logging in once in a while...............................319
Becoming a freelance, unpaid, stress-management guru 320
Finding Your Oasis (Sand Optional) 320
Creating an inner sanctum...............................321
Taking a bath 321
Enjoying a walk in the park.............................321
Seeking sanctuary..322
Becoming a lobbyist 322
Losing yourself in the shelves.........................322
Accentuating the Positive(s) with Stress Buffers.....323
Connecting with Others...324
Family: The ties that bind 324
You need a Monica, a Rachel, or a Chandler.....324

Doing Something, Anything..325
    Joining the group..326
    Learning a thing or two...326
    Getting in the game...327
    Accomplishing something 328
    Becoming a volunteer..328
    Getting a pet 328
    Cultivating calm with gardening 329
    Getting in the kitchen..329
    Becoming a bookworm...329
    Remembering to enjoy the little things...........................330
    Getting out of the house 331
Regrouping and Getting a Grip 332
    Pre-schedule time away...332
    Build a getaway file..332
    Take a mini-vacation..333
Living Mindfully in the Present 334
Taking Your Fun Seriously 336

Part V: The Part of Tens 337

Chapter 17: Ten Habits of Highly Effective Stress Managers 339
Knowing How to Relax 339
Eating Right and Exercising Often 339
Getting Enough Sleep 340
Not Worrying about the Unimportant Stuff.......................................341
Not Getting Angry Often 341
Being Organized..341
Managing Time Efficiently 342
Having a Strong Support System 342
Living According to One's Values..342
Having a Good Sense of Humor 342

Chapter 18: Ten Events That Trigger Stress....................343
Losing a Loved One 343
Experiencing a Major Illness or Injury 344
Divorcing or Separating...344
Having Serious Financial Difficulties 344
Losing a Job...345
Getting Married...345
Moving to a New Place 345
Fighting with a Close Friend 346
Having a Child 346
Retiring...346

Index 347

Introduction

・・

*J*ust about everyone feels they have too much stress in their lives. Daily, I hear people complaining that stress is getting to them, robbing them of many of life's pleasures and depriving them of life's satisfactions. And that's not just from the people who walk into my office or show up at one of my stress-management workshops — stress seems to be everywhere. Just take a look at your local newsstand. You're bound to see more than a few cover stories on stress, warning you of its dangers and telling you what you can do about it. These days more and more people are signing up for stress-management workshops, taking yoga classes, and learning how to meditate, massage their bodies, and quiet their psyches.

You may think that modern advances in science and technology should have resulted in lower stress levels. Clearly, this hasn't happened — for anybody. Life has become more stressful, not less stressful. Your stressors may take the form of work pressures, financial worries, time constraints, or the demands that come with being part of a family. You may have more specific stress triggers — illness, unemployment, a new baby, or a new mortgage.

Whatever the source of your stress, having a guide would be helpful, right? Unfortunately, life doesn't come with an instruction booklet or a user's manual. You need to find your own help. Your stress *can* be managed. And in fact, much of your stress can be eliminated. You just need the right stress-reducing tools. In fact, you need an entire toolbox filled with a wide variety of stress-management techniques, strategies, and tactics. This book was written to give you these tools.

About This Book

Stress Management For Dummies, 2nd Edition, is your guide, helping you navigate the often-confusing array of stress-management options. It gives you the skills and expertise you need to effectively manage and minimize the stress in your life. Virtually every important aspect of stress management is covered in these pages. The book helps you understand where your stress comes from, how it affects you, and most importantly, what you can do about it. It shows you how to relax your body, quiet your mind, and let go of the tension that comes with too much stress. It shows you how you can control your anger, worry less, and create a lifestyle that is stress resistant.

In these pages, I have been careful to ensure that your stress-management program doesn't add to the stress in your life. I try to be practical and realistic, recognizing that you may not be able to meditate for 20 minutes twice a day and still keep your job. And, although I recognize that having a chauffeur, owning a fabulous house in the country, or having live-in help can lower your stress level, I also realize that this may not be an option for you (or for me, either!).

No one single idea or technique can magically relieve all your stress; nor does every technique or approach work equally well for everyone. You need to put together a package of ideas and methods that you can integrate into the various aspects of your life. It extends from caring about what goes into your mouth to thinking about the kind of chair you sit in, from monitoring how much sleep you get to knowing how to turn off your racing mind. Effective stress management really comes down to effective lifestyle management. That's why, in these pages, you can find a variety of stress-management approaches. You fill up your stress toolbox with the techniques in this book, and then you can take out the tool you need, when you need it.

If you can find someone — a friend, family member, or coworker — to whom you can teach your newly mastered skills, that's great. Most people learn best when they can teach someone else. If you can find someone to work with you on your stress-management program, even better. Having a stress buddy can help keep you interested and motivated. Most importantly, see your involvement with this book as an ongoing journey that will take some time — and some effort — but that is well worth the trip. Good luck!

Conventions Used in This Book

I use a few conventions in this book to help your reading go smoothly:

- ✔ *Italics* emphasize and highlight new words and terms that I define.
- ✔ **Boldfaced** text indicates keywords in bulleted lists and highlights the action parts of numbered steps.
- ✔ When I want to make a topic more easily understood, I break the essential points down into bulleted lists (like this one), so you can follow them easily without being confused by too many words.

What You're Not to Read

You don't have to read everything in this book. I have sprinkled in sidebars (the text in gray boxes), which offer extra information, such as interesting bits of trivia and examples that hopefully amuse and inform you. They are designed to spice up the book. If you're short of time, skip them and come back to them later when you have more time.

Foolish Assumptions

When I wrote this book, I made a few assumptions about who you, the reader, are:

- ✔ You want less stress in your life, and you're willing to devote a little of your valuable time to achieve this.

- ✔ You already know a lot about stress but welcome additional methods and strategies for coping with your stress.

- ✔ Your time is valuable and limited, and you want realistic and practical ways of reducing stress that can be easily integrated into your schedule and lifestyle.

- ✔ You're willing to try some ideas and approaches that are new to you and may require some openness and experimentation.

How This Book Is Organized

I've organized *Stress Management For Dummies,* 2nd Edition, into five parts. Each part covers a range of ideas and approaches that, when put together, give you a comprehensive understanding of what stress is and what you can do to manage, reduce, and even at times eliminate much of the stress in your life. Here's how the structure of this book breaks down:

Part I: Getting Started with Stress Management

I open the book by talking about what stress is and how it can affect you mentally, physically, and emotionally. I then discuss various techniques that you can use to get a rough measure of just how much stress you may be experiencing.

Part II: Mastering the Basics

What do I mean by "the basics"? This part presents common-sense ways for you to deal with stress. I show you how to treat the physical symptoms of stress, quiet your mind, and deal with day-to-day issues that may be causing stress: Maybe you aren't as organized as you'd like to be, or maybe your career is taking time away from your family, or maybe you're not eating right. I can help.

Part III: The Secrets of Stress-Effective Thinking

Think of this part as preventive medicine. It covers more advanced techniques that you can use to decrease the amount of stress in your life. If you make minor changes in the way you think when put in potentially stressful situations, you can actually reduce and perhaps eliminate stress.

Part IV: Managing Your Stress in Real Life

This part helps you develop day-to-day habits for home and work that will ultimately help you live a less stressful life. For example, the simple act of taking a break and doing a few stretches can really reduce the effects of stress at work. And has it occurred to you that if you do more fun things in life — hang out with friends or spend time on a hobby — you'll be better able to deal with stress?

Part V: The Part of Tens

This part presents some brief top-ten chapters. Find out the ten habits of effective stress managers and the ten most stressful life events.

Icons Used in This Book

This book has lots of little round pictures in the margins, calling your attention to various details in the text. Here's what these icons mean:

I use this icon to flag a particularly good idea that you should consider.

When presenting a concept that I feel you shouldn't forget, I use this icon.

When I need to give you a word of caution, I toss this icon your way.

This icon indicates that I'm about to present a specific technique for dealing with stress.

Throughout the book, I ask you to evaluate your situation — determine your stress level, examine how you react in given situations, and so on. When I give you one of these quizzes, I use this icon.

This icon flags anecdotes and trivia that you're likely to find interesting.

Where to Go from Here

Although it's possible to read this book sequentially, you don't have to do that. You can dip into any part that interests you. Most of the material stands alone and isn't dependent on the other chapters — with one exception. The chapters that show you how to relax your body and quiet your mind, Chapters 4 and 5, are particularly important, and they are central and pertinent to several other chapters. Try to read these chapters earlier on.

Don't try to master all of the material presented in one shot. Or even two shots. It takes time and practice to learn how to become comfortable with, and competent in, many of the exercises described. Don't rush yourself. After all, it took years to develop many of your stress-producing habits, so you can't expect to get rid of them in a flash. Every day, allow yourself at least some time to devote to some aspect of your stress-management program. It may only be a few minutes, but those minutes add up and can result in some impressive stress-management skills.

Part I

Getting Started with Stress Management

getting started
with
stress
management

web extras

In this part . . .

✔ Get a handle on your stress by finding out where stress comes from, how it affects you, and how certain kinds of stress can actually be good for you.

✔ Discover what, exactly, stress is and the function it was meant to serve. Identify symptoms that tell you when your stress level is getting out of control. Find out that understanding stress is as simple as ABC.

✔ Become familiar with stress-management tools, such as a stress gauge and stress journal, so that you can measure your stress, identify your triggers, and come up with effective ways to cope.

Chapter 1

Stressed Out? Welcome to the Club!

In This Chapter

▶ Figuring out why you feel more stressed

▶ Determining where your stress comes from

▶ Understanding how stress affects you

▶ Looking at the good kinds of stress

A re you feeling more tired lately than you used to? Is your fuse a little shorter than normal? Are you worrying more? Enjoying life less? If you feel more stress in your life these days, you aren't alone. Count yourself among the ranks of the overstressed. Most people feel that their lives have too much stress. Your stress may come from your job or lack thereof, your money worries, your personal life, or simply not having enough time to do everything you have to do — or want to do. You could use some help. Thankfully, you can eliminate or at least minimize much of the stress in your life and better manage the stress that remains. This chapter helps you get started.

Experiencing a Stress Epidemic?

You probably can't make it through a single day without seeing or hearing the word stress someplace. Just glance at any magazine stand and you'll find numerous cover stories all about stress. In most larger bookstores, an entire section is devoted to books on stress. TV and radio talk shows regularly feature stories documenting the negative effects of stress in our lives. Why all the fuss? Hasn't stress been around forever? Wasn't it stress that Adam felt when he was caught red-handed with little bits of apple stuck between his teeth? Is all of this just media hype, or are people really experiencing more stress today?

Less leisure time?

In her insightful book *The Overworked American: The Unexpected Decline of Leisure*, economist Juliet Schor points out that, in spite of all the new innovations and contraptions that could make our lives easier, we still need about the same amount of time to do what has to be done at home. In the 1910s, a full-time housewife spent about 52 hours a week on housework. Sixty years later, in the 1970s, the figure was about the same. Yes, some activities did become less time consuming. Food preparation fell almost 10 hours a week, but this was offset by an increase in the time spent shopping and taking care of the home and kids. Contrary to everyone's predicted expectations, we have less leisure time now than we did 50 years ago.

One good way of finding out how much stress people are experiencing is to ask them about the stress in their lives. Here are some findings from recent polls and surveys that did just that:

- A 2010 study published by the American Psychological Association found that 44 percent of Americans said that their stress levels had increased over the past five years.

- That same study reported that one in five American adults (22 percent) believe themselves to be in fair or poor health, and this group reports higher levels of stress than those in better health.

- A Harris Interactive survey of more than 1,550 Americans found that 46 percent reported that their stress level is higher than it was five years ago. Eighty percent said they experienced medium or high stress levels at work. Sixty percent said they experienced these same levels at home.

Our lives, it seems, have indeed become far more stressful. But why? The next section provides some reasons.

Understanding Where All This Stress Is Coming From

In his prophetic book *Future Shock* (originally published in 1984), Alvin Toffler observed that people experience more stress whenever they are subjected to a lot of change in a short span of time. If anything characterizes our lives these days, it's an excess of change. We're in a continual state of flux. We have less control over our lives, we live with more uncertainty, and we often feel threatened and, at times, overwhelmed. The following sections explain some of the more common sources of stress in our lives.

Struggling in a struggling economy

A 2010 study published by the American Psychological Association shows an America still recovering from the recession. Americans report that money (76 percent) and the economy (65 percent) are their most common sources of stress. A difficult and uncertain economy has become *the* major source of stress in our lives. The recession and its aftermath have resulted in prolonged financial and emotional distress for too many of us.

Money may or may not be the root of all evil, but worrying about it certainly is a major source of stress. Balancing your checkbook at the end of the month (if you bother) reminds you that living is expensive. You remember that your parents bought their house for a pittance and now realize that today you couldn't afford to buy that same house if you wanted to. The mortgage, college tuition, braces for the kids' teeth, camp, travel, taxes, savings for retirement — it all adds up. And so does the stress.

Getting frazzled at work

Having a job may mean avoiding the stress that comes with unemployment, but it certainly doesn't guarantee a stress-free existence. For many people, jobs and careers are the biggest source of stress. Concerns about job security, killer hours, long commutes, unrealistic deadlines, bosses from hell, office politics, toxic coworkers, and testy clients are just a few of the many job-related stresses people experience. Workloads are heavier today than they were in the past, leaving less and less time for family and the rest of your life.

A new lexicon of work-related stresses also exists: downsizing, organizational redeployment, forced early retirement. Whatever the word, the effect is the same: insecurity, uncertainty, and fear. People are experiencing more stress at work than ever before, as these findings illustrate:

- A 2012 workplace survey carried out by Harris Interactive for the American Psychological Association found that two in five employed adults (41 percent) typically feel stressed out during the workday.

- In that same study, fewer than six in ten (58 percent) reported that they had the resources to manage stress effectively.

- About two-thirds (62 percent) of Americans cite work as one of their main sources of stress.

- The overall cost of job stress at work is estimated at $300 billion.

✔ One in four workers has taken a "mental health" day off from work to relieve stress.

✔ About a quarter (26 percent) of workers say they are "often" or "very often" burned out by their work.

Feeling frazzled at home

After you leave work, you may start to realize that the rest of your life is not exactly stress-free. These days, life at home, our relationships, and the pressure of juggling everything else that has to be done only add to our stress level.

Life at home has become more pressured and demanding. True, we now have microwaves, robotic vacuums, and take-out menus, but the effort and stress involved seem to be growing rather than lessening. Meals have to be prepared, the house tidied, the clothing cleaned, the bills paid, the chores completed, the shopping done, the lawn and garden tended, the car maintained and repaired, the phone calls and e-mails returned, the homework supervised, and the kids chauffeured. And that's for starters. Did I mention the dog?

Acting like a woman, thinking like a man, and working like a dog

If you're a woman, you may experience even more stress on the job. Despite all the hoopla about women's rights and sexual equality, women still face added pressures and limitations in the workplace. Women are paid less and promoted less frequently than their male counterparts, even though they may be more qualified. If a woman has children, her career may be shunted onto the "Mommy Track," a glass ceiling that limits career advancement.

More subtle pressures come from the prevailing notions of the roles and behaviors expected from men and women. Men and women can act in similar ways that may advance their careers — competitive, aggressive, and assertive — but a double standard is common. When such behavior comes from a woman, people often view the behavior negatively as unfeminine and inappropriate. But when that same behavior comes from a man, people see him as strong and in control.

Sexual harassment for women on the job is no small source of stress. A woman may find herself in the no-win situation of either openly complaining or silently enduring the abuse. Both options can be highly stressful. Women who belong to a racial or ethnic minority may experience even more stress. Hiring and promotional practices may act in subtle and not-so-subtle discriminatory ways. Even where affirmative action policies are in place, women may experience the stress of feeling that others see any hiring or advancement as unfairly legislated rather than legitimately deserved.

"I need two more hours in the day!"

This plea is a commonly heard lament. The stress of not having enough time to do everything that has to be done is enormous. We overwork at home and at our jobs. The result? We just don't have enough time.

Ozzie and Harriet we ain't

Some of this stress comes from the ways in which families have changed over the years. In two-parent families, it's now common for both parents to work. One-parent families have even more stressors. These days, more women are the main earners in the home (almost 40 percent) or are bringing in essential income needed to maintain the family. Nearly half of all marriages end in divorce. The number of single-parent households is multiplying. Families tend be more fragmented, with relatives often living great distances away. Although in certain cases this situation can be stress-reducing (your annoying Aunt Agnes is moving to Dubuque?), more often it promotes a greater sense of disconnectedness and alienation.

A woman's work is never done

Forty years ago, one-third of all workers were women; now nearly half are. Add on the additional stress of being a mother with a family to manage at home, and you compound the level of stress. Women may find themselves in the not-so-unusual position of having to cope with the problems of aging and ailing parents in addition to the problems of their own children. Caught in this generational divide, this "stress sandwich" can be incredibly draining, both physically and emotionally. Although men give lip service to helping with the kids and the elderly (and they do, in fact, help more than their fathers or grandfathers did), woman are still the ones who most often take primary responsibility for these care-giving roles.

A 2009 study reported in *Time* magazine found that 55 percent of women strongly agree that in households where both partners have jobs, women take on more responsibilities for the home and family that their male partners do. The men in the study saw it differently: Only 28 percent agreed. Sixty-nine percent of women say that they are primarily responsible for taking care of their children; only 13 percent of men say this of themselves. As an old adage reminds us, "Father works from sun to sun, but Mother's work is never done."

Piling on new stresses with technology

People's lives have become stressful in ways they never would have imagined even a decade ago. Whoever said there is nothing new under the sun probably never Googled the name of a restaurant or texted a friend. Changes in technology have brought with them new pressures and new demands —

in short, new sources of stress. For example, one study of more than 1,300 people found that those who regularly used their cell phones or portable devices for communication experienced an increase in psychological distress and a decrease in family satisfaction, compared with those who used these devices less often. Imagine this implausible scenario:

You've been in a coma for the last 15 years or so. One day, out of the blue, you wake up and take the bus home from the hospital. You quickly notice that life has changed. Technology rules. On the bus you notice that everyone is pushing buttons on small plastic devices. You ask the person next to you what's going on, and he looks at you strangely and explains what a smartphone is, what downloading means, and what e-mail does. You reach your home and discover that your old television and computer have become relics. Everything is digital. Everything is portable. People are magically "downloading" movies and television shows on their telephones. Your cassette player is a joke, not to mention your record player. Just as quickly, you realize that you have no idea how to operate any of these digital tools. You have no idea what the words Skype, Netflix, Kindle, GPS, Facebook, Twitter, YouTube, podcast, iPad, and eBay even mean. All this technology is beginning to drive you a bit crazy. Your next-door neighbor, who was never in a coma and yet is just as stressed as you are, is also trying to keep up with all this technological change.

Dealing with daily hassles (the little things add up)

When you think of stress, you usually think of the major stresses you may face: death, divorce, financial ruin, or a serious illness. And then of course there are those so-called moderate stresses: losing your wallet, denting the car, or catching a cold. Finally, you face the even smaller stresses: the mini-stresses and micro-stresses. These stresses are what are known as hassles.

Here is just a sample of the kinds of hassles you face every day (a complete list would be endless):

- Noisy traffic
- Loud neighbors
- Rude salesclerks
- Crowds
- Long waits for telephone customer-service representatives

- Deliveries promised "sometime between 9 and 5"
- Computers that crash
- Airport delays
- Cell phones that go off in theaters and restaurants

Yes, I realize these things are relatively small. But the small things can add up. You can deal with one, maybe two, or even three of these at once. But when the number begins to rise, so does your stress level. When you reach a high enough level of stress, you overreact to the next hassle that comes along. And that results in even more stress. Alas, life is loaded with hassle. The funny part is, people usually deal fairly well with the bigger problems. Life's major stresses — the deaths, illnesses, divorces, and financial setbacks — somehow trigger hidden resources within us. We rise to each demand, summoning up some unrecognized inner strength, and we somehow manage to cope. What gets to us are the little things. It's the small stuff — the little annoyances, petty frustrations, and minor irritations — that ultimately lead to a continuing sense of stress.

Looking at the Signs and Symptoms of Stress

The signs and symptoms of stress range from the benign to the dramatic — from simply feeling tired at the end of the day to having a heart attack. The more serious stress-related problems come with intense and prolonged periods of stress. These disorders and diseases I save for later in this chapter. Here are some of the more benign, commonly experienced stress signs and symptoms. Many will be all too familiar to you.

Physical signs of stress:

- Tiredness, fatigue, lethargy
- Heart palpitations; racing pulse; rapid, shallow breathing
- Muscle tension and aches
- Shakiness, tremors, tics, twitches
- Heartburn, indigestion, diarrhea, constipation
- Nervousness
- Dry mouth and throat

✔ Excessive sweating, clammy hands, cold hands and/or feet

✔ Rashes, hives, itching

✔ Nail-biting, fidgeting, hair-twirling, hair-pulling

✔ Frequent urination

✔ Lowered libido

✔ Overeating, loss of appetite

✔ Sleep difficulties

✔ Increased use of alcohol and/or drugs and medications

Psychological signs of stress:

✔ Irritability, impatience, anger, hostility

✔ Worry, anxiety, panic

✔ Moodiness, sadness, feeling upset

✔ Intrusive and/or racing thoughts

✔ Memory lapses, difficulties in concentrating, indecision

✔ Frequent absences from work, lowered productivity

✔ Feeling overwhelmed

✔ Loss of sense of humor

That's just for starters. Prolonged and/or intense stress can have more serious effects: It can make you sick.

Understanding How Stress Can Make You Sick

Researchers estimate that 75 to 90 percent of all visits to primary-care physicians are for complaints and conditions that are, in some way, stress-related. About 50 percent of those surveyed said that stress was affecting their health. Every week, 112 million people take some form of medication for stress-related symptoms. This statistic isn't surprising given the wide-ranging physiological changes that accompany a stress response. Just about every bodily system or body part is affected by stress. Stress can exacerbate the symptoms of a wide variety of other disorders and illnesses, as well. Stress is linked to the five leading causes of death: heart disease, cancer, lung disease, accidents, and suicide. The following sections illustrate some of the more important ways stress can negatively affect your health and well being.

All of the symptoms, illnesses, and conditions I mention in this section can result from a number of medical conditions, not just stress. And for many of the disorders and diseases mentioned, stress may not be the direct cause of the condition, but stress may make these conditions worse. If you're concerned about one or more of these symptoms, be sure to consult your physician. He or she is the best person to give you advice and guidance.

Understanding how stress can be a pain in the neck (and other places)

Your muscles are a prime target for stress. When you're under stress, your muscles contract and become tense. This muscle tension can affect your nerves, blood vessels, organs, skin, and bones. Chronically tense muscles can result in a variety of conditions and disorders, including muscle spasms, cramping, facial or jaw pain, bruxism (grinding your teeth), tremors, and shakiness. Many forms of headache, chest pain, and back pain are among the more common conditions that result from stress-induced muscle tension.

Taking stress to heart

Stress can play a role in circulatory diseases such as coronary heart disease, sudden cardiac death, and strokes. This fact is not surprising because stress can increase your blood pressure, constrict your blood vessels, raise your cholesterol level, trigger arrhythmias, and speed up the rate at which your blood clots. We know that psychosocial stress induces a physiological inflammatory response in blood vessels. When vessel walls are damaged, inflammatory cells come into the vessel walls. Among other things, they release chemicals that may cause further damage. If the stress is chronic, the result can be chronic inflammation. A growing number of studies show that individuals with higher amounts of psychosocial stress and depression display elevated C-reactive protein and IL-6 levels, both markers of inflammation. Many researchers believe that stress, inflammation and heart disease are all linked. Stress is now considered a major risk factor in heart disease, right up there with smoking, being overweight, and not exercising. All of this becomes very important when you consider that heart disease kills more men over the age of 50 and more women over the age of 65 than any other disease.

A broken heart?

A study reported by the Mayo Clinic in 2010 found that extreme or sudden stress that may accompany a relationship breakup or the death of a loved one can lead to "Broken Heart Syndrome" (BHS), or stress cardiomyopathy (severe heart muscle weakness). The study notes that this condition happens rapidly, and usually in women. In Japan, BHS is called "octopus trap cardiomyopathy" because the left ventricle balloons out in a peculiar shape.

Hitting below the belt

Ever notice how your stress seems to finds its way to your stomach? Your gastrointestinal system can be a ready target for much of the stress in your life. Stress can affect the secretion of acid in your stomach and can speed up or slow down the process of peristalsis (the rhythmic contraction of the muscles in your intestines). Constipation, diarrhea, gas, bloating, and weight loss all can be stress-related. Stress can contribute to gastroesophageal reflux disease and can also play a role in exacerbating irritable bowel syndrome, colitis, and Crohn's disease.

Speaking of your belt, it's important to recognize that people under stress usually experience changes in their weight. Stress can affect you in two very different ways. When you're highly stressed, you may find yourself eating less. You may even find yourself losing weight. This "stress diet" isn't the best way to lose weight, and if the stress is prolonged it can result in lower overall health. For many others, though, stress, especially moderate stress, can result in overeating. In effect, you're "feeding your emotions." The intent, often unconscious, is to feel better — to distract yourself from the emotional distress. The trouble is that "good feeling" lasts for about 12 seconds before you need another fix. And that means putting another notch on your belt. But it's not just your caloric intake. When you're stressed, your body releases a hormone called cortisol, which causes fat to accumulate around your abdomen and also enlarges individual fat cells, leading to what researchers term "diseased" fat.

Compromising your immune system

In the last decade or so, growing evidence has supported the theory that stress affects your immune system. In fact, researchers have even coined a name for this new field of study: psychoneuroimmunology. Quite a mouthful! Scientists who choose to go into this field study the relationships between moods, emotional states, hormonal levels, and changes in the nervous system and immune system. Without drowning you in detail, stress — particularly chronic stress — can compromise your immune system, rendering it less effective in resisting bacteria and viruses. Research has shown that stress may play a role in exacerbating a variety of immune system disorders such as HIV, AIDS, herpes, cancer metastasis, viral infection, rheumatoid arthritis, and certain allergies, as well as other auto-immune conditions. Some recent studies appear to confirm this.

The cold facts: Connecting stress and the sniffles

In that wonderful musical comedy *Guys and Dolls*, a lovelorn Adelaide laments that when your life is filled with stress, "a person can develop a cold." It looks like she just may be right. Research conducted by Dr. Sheldon Cohen, a psychologist at Carnegie Mellon University, has concluded that stress really does lower your resistance to colds. Cohen and his associates found that the higher a person's stress score, the more likely he was to come down with a cold when exposed to a cold virus.

Chronic stress, lasting a month or more, was the most likely to result in catching a cold. Experiencing severe stress for more than a month but less than six months doubled a person's risk of coming down with a cold, compared with those who were experiencing only shorter-term stress. Stress lasting more than two years nearly quadrupled the risk. The study also found that being unemployed or underemployed, or having interpersonal difficulties with family or friends, had the greatest effect. The exact mechanism whereby stress weakens immune functioning is still unclear. Tissues, anyone?

STRESS TIDBIT

What about stress and ulcers?

Once considered the poster disease for stress, ulcers have lost much of their stress-related status in recent years. Stress is no longer considered the primary cause of ulcers. It now appears that a bacterium called Helicobacter pylori, or H. pylori for short, is the culprit.

However, the final word on the relationship between stress and ulcers has yet to be written. More recent thinking has begun to question whether stress plays some role after all. We know that stress can affect secretions in the stomach that may exacerbate ulcers. We also know that a majority of those who do carry the H. pylori bacterium do not develop an ulcer, and many who do not carry the bacterium still develop ulcers. And of course, there is that body of research that has linked stress to ulcers. For example, the bombing of London during World War II and the earthquake in Kobe, Japan, both precipitated outbreaks of ulcer disease. Stay tuned.

Stress can be taxing

A number of studies have shown that when you're under stress, your cholesterol level goes up. In one now-classic study, researchers looked at the stress levels of accountants before and after the month of April, a notoriously busy time for tax accountants. They also looked at cholesterol levels in corporate accountants, who had stressful deadlines in both April and January. The researchers found that for both groups, cholesterol levels rose significantly before the April deadline and fell after the deadline. They observed a second rise in cholesterol levels for the corporate accountants as their January deadline approached. Again, after the deadline passed, blood lipid levels fell back to normal.

"Not tonight, dear. I have a (stress) headache."

A headache is just one of the many ways stress can interfere with your sex life. For both men and women, stress can reduce and even eliminate the pleasure of physical intimacy. Stress can affect sexual performance and rob you of your libido. When you're feeling stress, feeling sexy may not be at the top of your to-do list. Disturbed sexual performance for men may appear in the form of premature ejaculation, delayed ejaculation, and erectile dysfunction. For women the most common effects of stress are a lowered level of sexual interest and difficulty in achieving orgasm. The irony is that sex can be a way of relieving stress. In fact, for some people, sexual activity increases when they feel stressed.

Stressing Out Your Family

Being stressed is a little like having a cold. Others can catch it. When you're stressed, your moods change, your behavior changes, and you trigger a downward spiral of negative interactions. You may find yourself more angry, more upset, and more worried. You're not the same you.

Your relationships

In a recent survey, 21 percent of those responding said that stress was negatively affecting their friendships. Nineteen percent said that stress was hurting their marriages. When you're distressed — anxious, upset, worried — your happiness level tanks. Your fuse gets shorter, and you become more irritable. People under stress can withdraw emotionally and communicate less. Friends and family may not understand what's going on and in turn become stressed. The cycle can escalate, leading to even more distress.

Your kids

Most parents don't think their stress affects their children. They're wrong. Just ask the kids. Ninety-one percent of children say they know when their parents are stressed. How do they know? They can see the worrying, yelling, complaining, and arguing. And they in turn become stressed. Children who see their parents stressing out tend to become stressed themselves.

A large survey completed in 2010 found that only 14 percent of children say that their parents' stress doesn't bother them. When children see their parents stressed or worried, they can also feel sad, worried, and frustrated. And it's not just their emotions that are affected. That same study found that nearly one-third reported physical health symptoms that tend to be stress-related. Thirty-eight percent reported trouble falling asleep at night. One-third experienced headaches, and almost one-third reported having an upset stomach in the past month. Chronic stress can also impair children's developmental growth by lowering the production of growth hormone from the pituitary gland. Traumatic, stressful experiences in childhood can cause damage to developing bodies and brains that lasts into adulthood.

Stress and infertility

Even before you have kids, stress can make it hard for you to become pregnant. Stress may account for 30 percent of all infertility problems. Stress changes your body's neurochemistry, which can affect the maturation and release of the human egg. Stress can also cause the fallopian tubes and uterus to spasm, which can impair implantation. In men, stress can alter the sperm count and cause erectile dysfunction.

Stress Can Be Good?

Not all the news about stress is bad. As Hans Selye, the pioneer researcher in the field of stress, said, "Stress is the spice of life." He termed the good kind of stress *eustress*, as opposed to distress, or the nasty kind of stress. (The "eu" part of eustress comes from the Greek, meaning "good.") Stress can be a positive force in your life. Watching a close playoff game, taking a ride at an amusement park, solving an interesting problem, falling in love — all can be stressful. Yet these are the kinds of stresses that add to the enjoyment and satisfaction of our lives. We want more of this kind of stress, not less.

And even many of the less pleasant uncertainties and surprises of life can be a source of challenge and even excitement and interest. That nervousness you're experiencing about that presentation you're making tomorrow can actually improve your performance. The right amount of stress can motivate you, focus you, and get you to perform at your peak. Change and the pressures of modern life don't necessarily create the bad kind of stress. Rather, how you view the potential stresses in your life and how you cope with them make all the difference.

The good news is that it's easier than you think to reduce and manage your stress. This book explains *how* to do just that. Each chapter gives you tools and techniques to move you closer to becoming your own stress therapist.

"But I thrive on stress"

"I'm at my best when I'm under pressure — a tight deadline, a major crisis. That's when I feel most alive, most vital." A surprising number of people claim to thrive on stress. They like to be challenged, to have their abilities stretched and tested. For them this is a good kind of stress that can be satisfying and rewarding. Many people who claim to thrive on stress are workaholics. They get stressed when they have nothing to do. Lying on a beach, sitting in the park — now that's stressful for them!

Interestingly enough, some research suggests that part of the addictive quality that some people feel about stress may be more than just psychological. It may be that people can become hooked on the adrenaline secretions that occur during a stress response. Like other addictions, this adrenaline boost may be experienced by some people as pleasurable. This could explain that feeling of being "truly alive" that some people feel when they are super-stressed. Most of the rest of us, however, could live quite nicely without this boost, thank you very much.

Chapter 2

Stress Explained (In Surprisingly Few Pages)

In This Chapter

▶ Understanding stress

▶ Looking at a model of stress

▶ Finding the right balance

*Y*ou've heard the word stress a thousand times. But if you're pressed to explain the concept, you may find yourself a little stuck. Intuitively, you know what stress is, but explaining it isn't easy. This chapter helps you answer the question, "What exactly is stress?" The next time you find yourself at a dinner party and someone asks, "Does anyone here know what stress is?" you can grin knowingly, raise your hand, and proceed to dazzle and delight your tablemates.

So What Is Stress Anyhow?

Defining stress isn't easy. Professionals who've spent most of their lives studying stress still have trouble defining the term. As one stress researcher quipped, "Defining stress is like nailing Jell-O to a tree. It's hard to do!" Despite efforts during the last half century to assign a specific meaning to the term, no satisfactory definition exists. Defining stress is much like defining happiness. Everyone knows what it is, but no one can agree on a single definition.

"Oops, pardon my English!"

An Austrian-born endocrinologist named Hans Selye actually came up with the word "stress" to describe a physiological and emotional response. In the 1930s, Selye came upon the stress response while working with animals in his laboratory at McGill University in Montreal. Selye went on to publish widely in the area of stress and is today considered the "Father of Stress." The word comes from the Latin *stringere*, "to draw tight." Before Selye coined the term, "stress" didn't have any of the meanings we associate with it today. Selye later admitted that he may have misnamed what he was studying. He borrowed the term from the fields of physics and engineering, where the concepts of stress and strain were in common use. English was not his mother tongue, and he later realized that the word strain would have been more appropriate. Too late. The term stuck.

"Sorry, but I really need a definition"

Perhaps you always began your high-school English essays with a dictionary definition ("Webster defines tragedy as . . ."), and you still have to start with a definition. Okay, here's the scientific definition:

> Stress describes a condition where an environmental demand exceeds the natural regulatory capacity of an organism.

Put in simpler terms, stress is what you experience when you believe you can't cope effectively with a threatening situation. If you see an event or situation as only mildly challenging, you probably feel only a little stress; however, if you perceive a situation or event as threatening or overwhelming, you probably feel a lot of stress. So, having to wait for a bus when you have all the time in the world triggers little stress. Waiting for that same bus when you're late for a plane that will take off without you triggers much more stress.

The other definition of stress

You may prefer the more tongue-in-cheek definition, commonly seen in business offices, usually taped to a wall in the employee washroom:

"Stress is created when your mind overrides the body's basic desire to choke the living daylights out of some idiot who desperately deserves it."

Stick with the first definition.

This difference between the demands of the situation and your perception of how well you can cope with that situation is what determines how much stress you feel.

Stress causes stress?

Part of the problem with defining stress is the confusing way the word is used. We use the word stress to refer to the thing or circumstance out there that stresses us (stress = the bus that never comes, the deadline, the traffic jam, the sudden noise, and so on). We then use the same word to describe the physical and emotional discomfort we feel about that situation (stress = anxious, headachy, irritated, and so on). So we end up feeling stress about stress! This can be confusing. In this book I try to use "stressor" or "stress trigger" when referring to a potentially stressful situation or event, and "stress" for your emotional and physical responses. But because the term is used so loosely, I won't be terribly consistent either. My advice? Don't worry about it. This chapter helps you understand what stress is all about, even if you can't spout an exact definition.

How This Whole Stress Thing Got Started

Believe it or not, you have stress in your life for a good reason. To understand why stress can be a useful, adaptive response, you need to take a trip back in time.

Imagining you're a cave person

Picture this: You've gone back in time to a period thousands of years ago when men and women lived in caves. You're roaming the jungle dressed in a loincloth and carrying a club. Your day, so far, has been routine. Nothing more than the usual cave politics and the ongoing problems with the in-laws. Nothing you can't handle. Suddenly, on your stroll, you spot a tiger. This is not your ordinary tiger; it's a saber-toothed one. You experience something called the *fight-or-flight* response. This response is aptly named because, just then, you have to make a choice: You can stay and do battle (that's the fight part), or you can run like the wind (the flight part, and probably the smarter option here). Your body, armed with this automatic stress response, prepares you to do either. You are ready for anything. You are wired.

Stress can convict you

One of your body's responses to a threatening situation is a dry mouth. In ancient China, this phenomenon was used as a lie-detector test. Interrogators filled suspects' mouths with cooked rice and then asked them questions. They assumed that a guilty suspect would be under such a high level of stress that his throat would be too dry for him to swallow and talk. Got milk?

Surviving the modern jungle

You've probably noticed that you don't live in a cave. And your chances of running into a saber-toothed tiger are slim, especially because they're extinct. Yet this incredibly important, life-preserving stress reaction is still hard-wired into your system. And once in a while, it can still be highly adaptive. If you're picnicking on a railroad track and see a train barreling toward you, an aggressive stress response is nice to have. You want to get out of there quickly.

In today's society, you're required to deal with few life-threatening stressors — at least on a normal day. Unfortunately, your body's fight-or-flight response is activated by a whole range of stressful events and situations that aren't going to do you in. The physical dangers have been replaced by social and psychological stress triggers, which aren't worthy of a full fight-or-flight stress response. But your body doesn't know this, and it reacts the way it did when your ancestors were facing real danger.

Imagine the following modern-day scenario: You're standing in an auditorium in front of several hundred seated people. You're about to give a presentation that is important to your career. You suddenly realize that you've left several pages of your prepared material at home on your nightstand. As it dawns on you that this isn't just a bad dream you'll laugh about later, you start to notice some physical and emotional changes. Your hands are becoming cold and clammy. Your heart is beating faster, and you're breathing harder. Your throat is dry. Your muscles are tensing, and you notice a slight tremor as you hopelessly look for the missing pages. Your stomach feels a little queasy, and you notice an emotion that you would definitely label as anxiety. You recognize that you're experiencing a stress reaction. You now also recognize that you're experiencing the same fight-or-flight response that your caveman ancestors experienced. The difference is, you probably won't die up there at that podium, even though it feels like you will.

In the modern jungle, giving that presentation, being stuck in traffic, confronting a disgruntled client, facing an angry spouse, or trying to meet some unrealistic deadline is what stresses you. These far-less-threatening stressors trigger that same intense stress response. It's overkill. Your body is not just reacting; it's overreacting. And that's definitely not good.

Understanding the Signs of Stress

An important part of managing your stress is knowing what your stress looks like. Your stress responses can take different forms: bodily changes, emotional changes, and behavioral changes. This section gives you a clearer picture of what these changes look like. Although they look very different, they are all possible responses you may have when confronted with a stressful situation.

Your body reacts

When you're in fight-or-flight mode, your physiological system goes into high gear. Often your body tells you first that you're experiencing stress. You may notice that you're breathing more quickly than you normally do and that your hands feel cool and more than a little moist. But that's just for starters.

If you could see what's happening below the surface, you'd also notice some other changes. Your *sympathetic nervous system*, one of the two branches of your *autonomic nervous system*, is producing changes in your body. Your *hypothalamus*, a small portion of your brain located above the brain stem, stimulates your *pituitary*, a small gland near the base of your brain. It releases a hormone into the bloodstream called *adrenocorticotropic hormone* (ACTH). When that hormone reaches your adrenal glands, they in turn produce extra *adrenalin* (also known as epinephrine) along with other hormones called *glucocorticoids*. (Cortisol is one.)

This biochemical domino effect causes an array of other remarkable changes in your body. Figure 2-1 shows a diagram to help you see what's going on.

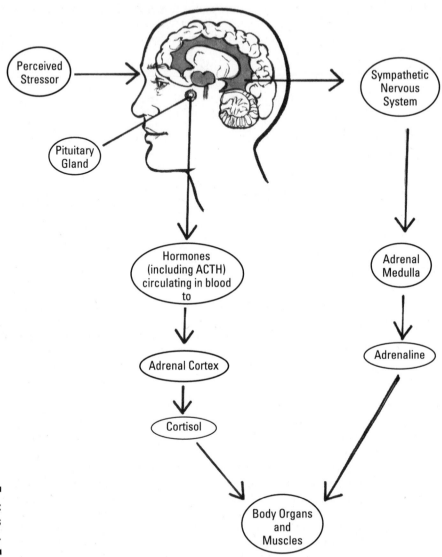

Perceived Stressor

Sympathetic Nervous System

Pituitary Gland

Hormones (including ACTH) circulating in blood to

Adrenal Medulla

Adrenal Cortex

Adrenaline

Cortisol

Body Organs and Muscles

Figure 2-1:
How stress affects you.

Illustration by Pam Tanzey

More specifically, here are some highlights:

- ✔ Your heart rate speeds up, and your blood pressure rises. (More blood is pumped to your muscles and lungs.)

- ✔ You breathe more rapidly, and your nostrils flare, causing an increased supply of air.

- ✔ Your digestion slows. (Who's got time to eat?)

✔ Your blood is directed away from your skin and internal organs and shunted to your brain and skeletal muscles. Your muscles tense. You feel stronger. You are ready for action.

✔ Your blood clots more quickly, ready to repair any damage to your arteries.

✔ Your pupils dilate, so you see better.

✔ Your liver converts glycogen into glucose, which teams up with free fatty acids to supply you with fuel and some quick energy. (You'll probably need it.)

In short, when you're experiencing stress, your entire body undergoes a dramatic series of physiological changes that readies you for a life-threatening emergency. Clearly, stress has adaptive survival potential. Stress, way back when, was nature's way of keeping you alive.

Your feelings and behavior change

Your body isn't the only thing that responds to a stressor. You also react to a stressor with feelings and emotions. A partial list of emotional symptoms includes feeling anxious, upset, angry, sad, guilty, frustrated, hopeless, afraid, or overwhelmed. Your emotional reactions may be minor ("I'm a wee bit annoyed" or "I'm a bit concerned") or major ("I'm furious!" or "I'm very anxious!").

Together your physiological responses and emotional reactions can activate changes in your behavior. These changes help you "fight" or help you "flee." Fight or flight may not be an appropriate response to a non-life-threatening situation such as misplacing your keys or failing your driving test. The right amount of anxiety can motivate adaptive behavior, such as doing your best and working toward important goals. However, too much anxiety, too much anger, or too much of some other emotional trigger can cause you to over-react or under-react. Annoyance can become anger, and concern can turn into anxiety. Excessive emotion can result in inappropriate responses. You may act too angrily, quarrel, and later regret what you said or did. If you're feeling anxious or fearful, you may go in the other direction. You may withdraw, avoid, and give up too quickly.

What makes stress such a problem — both physiologically and emotionally — is that your stress can be continuous and ongoing. Modern life demands much of us, and keeping up with these demands means lots of stress. A stressor here and there, now and then — that you can handle. If you're stressed out only once in a while, stress isn't really a concern. Your body and mind react, but you soon recover and return to a more relaxed state. But too often we experience a near-continuous stream of stressors. We don't get enough recovery time. Figure 2-2 helps you understand what this looks like.

It's like driving a car with your foot on the brake

Triggering this fight-or-flight response repeatedly can wear you down. The stress response was designed to work best in short bursts — hit and then run, or maybe just run — not the prolonged and chronic stress that you deal with on a routine basis.

I remember, as a child, riding in our car with my mother at the wheel. She had an overly cautious habit of driving with her right foot on the gas pedal and her left foot on the brake. We always had an incredibly jerky ride, and I'm certain the car had more than its share of brake adjustments. She wore them down. Stress has a similar wear-and-tear effect on you. Too much stress, day in and day out, exacts a price.

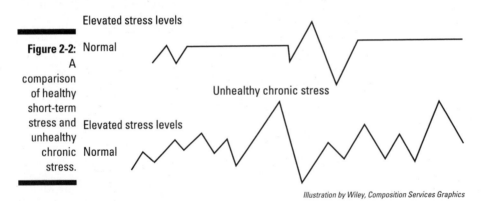

Figure 2-2: A comparison of healthy short-term stress and unhealthy chronic stress.

Illustration by Wiley, Composition Services Graphics

Understanding Stress Is as Simple as ABC

One of the best ways to understand stress is to look at a model of emotional distress elaborated by psychologist Albert Ellis. He calls his model the ABC model, and it's as simple as it sounds:

$A \rightarrow B \rightarrow C$ where

✔ A is the Activating event or triggering situation. It's the "stressor."

✔ B is your Beliefs, thoughts, or perceptions about A.

✔ C is the emotional, physical, and behavioral Consequence or "stress" that results from holding these beliefs.

In other words,

A potentially stressful situation → your perceptions → your stress (or lack of stress).

Real-life examples make this model more understandable. Following are two situations that may seem familiar.

Consider one of the more common sources of stress in our lives: the fear of being late. You're in a taxi headed for the airport, where you'll board a plane for Philadelphia to interview for a job. Traffic is heavy, and you didn't expect that. Your palms are sweaty, and your breathing is rapid and shallow. You're feeling anxious. You are stressed out!

Using the ABC model of stress, the sequence looks something like this:

A → B → C

Late for the plane → "I'm never going to make it, and I won't get this job!" → Anxiety and panic with sweaty palms and rapid, shallow breathing

Or consider this scenario: You're trying to get your two kids off to school in the morning. Your husband, who is normally terrific at helping, is on his way to Philadelphia for a job interview. He normally drops off the older child at school while you take your younger daughter to day care. You have a job, too, and today you're expected to show up for an important 9 o'clock meeting. The plan was for the three of you to leave earlier than usual so you would have time to drop them both off. But this morning your daughter woke up crying and feeling sick. You're caught off guard. You don't have a plan B and certainly not a plan C. You have to scramble to figure out whom to call and what to do. You feel anxious and panicky. You're more irritable. Your breathing is off. You're feeling very stressed.

With the ABC model, your stress looks something like this:

Important meeting this morning and daughter is not feeling well → "OMG! What do I do? I can't skip this meeting!" → Anxiety and panic

It all adds up: Laura's lament

Consider a typical day in Laura's life. Her alarm goes off, but she pushes the snooze button one time too many and has to hurry to get ready for work. She races to the train and sees that she has just missed it. She is late for work. Things at the office have become problematic. Because of layoffs, her workload is far heavier than it used to be. Her boss, who has never been a prince, is now even less understanding and supportive. The truth is, she hates her job but has no idea what she would do if she quit. And she can't quit, because she needs to pay the rent for her shoe-box apartment. But that's not all. Her two-year relationship with her boyfriend is rocky. They're fighting more often. She worries about her mother, who fell last month, is still in pain, and needs more attention and time. And time is what Laura has too little of. She feels overwhelmed.

What magnifies your stress is that the stressors in your life are cumulative. You may be able to juggle two balls. But juggling three balls, four balls, or five balls? Multiple stressors create a synergy that makes the resulting stress much greater than the sum of its parts. You can easily start feeling overwhelmed.

Managing Stress: A Three-Pronged Approach

This three-pronged model of dealing with stress provides you with a useful tool to help you understand the many ways you can manage and control your stress. You have three major choices, outlined in the following sections.

1. Managing your stressors

The events that trigger your stress can range from the trivial to the dramatic. They can be very minor — a hassle such as a broken shoelace, a crowded subway, or the world's slowest check-out line. They can be more important — losing your wallet, hearing sharp words from your boss, or getting a bad haircut a week before your wedding. The list of more serious stressors can be even more dramatic — a divorce, a serious illness, the loss of a job, or the loss of a loved one. The number of potential stressors is endless.

Changing your "A" means altering, minimizing, or eliminating your potential stressors. Following are some examples of what this may look like:

Potential Stressor	*Modified Stressor*
A crowded commute	Leaving home earlier or later
Constant lateness	Learning time-management skills
Conflict with relatives	Spending less time with them
Anger about your golf game	Taking some golf lessons
A cluttered home	Becoming better organized
Dissatisfaction with your job	Looking for another job
High credit-card bills	Spending less
Missed deadlines	Starting projects sooner
Angst about the subway	Taking the bus

I can hear you saying, "Give me a break! What planet does this guy live on? I *can't* quit my job! I *have* to see my annoying relatives!" And in many cases you're right. Often you can't change the world or even what goes on in your own house. You want to change what other people think or do? Good luck! But you *can* sometimes minimize or even eliminate a potential stressor. This ability is strengthened if you have the relevant skills. In Chapters 7 and 8, I discuss how you can develop better problem-solving and time-management skills and become more organized. Changing your world isn't always possible, but when it is, it's often the fastest route to stress relief.

2. Changing your thoughts

Even if you can't significantly change the situations and events that are triggering your stress, you *can* change the way you perceive them. What happens at "B" — your beliefs, thoughts, perceptions, and interpretations — is critical in determining how much stress you feel. Whenever you perceive a situation or event as overwhelming or beyond your control, or whenever you think you can't cope, you experience stress. You may find that much, if not most, of your stress is self-induced, and you can learn to see things differently. So, if you're waiting in a long line, perhaps you're thinking, "I just can't stand this! I hate waiting! Why can't they figure out a better way of doing this? I hate lines! I hate lines! I hate lines!" Chances are, you're creating more than a little stress for yourself. On the other hand, if you're thinking, "Perfect! Now I have time to read these fascinating articles on alien babies and celebrity cellulite in the *National Tattler*," you're feeling much less stress. Your thinking plays a larger role than you may believe in creating your stress.

3. Managing your stress responses

Even if you can't eliminate a potential stressor and can't change the way you view that situation, you can still manage your stress by mastering other skills. You can change the way you respond to stress. You can learn how to relax your body and quiet your mind. In Chapters 4 and 5, I show you how to reverse the stress response — how to turn off your stress and recover a sense of calm.

Tuning Your Strings: Finding the Right Balance

Stress is part of life. No one makes it through life totally stress free, and you wouldn't want to. You certainly want the good stress, and you even want some of the stress that comes with dealing with life's challenges and disappointments. But too much (or prolonged) stress can become a negative force, and it can rob you of much of life's joy. Too little stress means you're missing out, taking too few risks, and playing it too safe. Finding the right amount of stress is like finding the right tension in a violin string. Too much tension and the string can break; too little tension and there is no music.

You want to hear the music, without breaking the strings.

Chapter 3

Getting Started: Gathering Your Tools

. . . .

In This Chapter

▶ Measuring your stress

▶ Keeping tabs on your stressors

▶ Staying out of your own way

. . . .

As that Chinese proverb says, "A journey of a thousand miles must begin with a single step." You've taken that initial step by reading this book. So far, so good. But taking that first step isn't very helpful if it's in the wrong direction. On any long trip, you want to have a pretty good idea of where you're going and to make sure you have the right equipment to get you there. The same wisdom holds true as you begin your journey on the road to becoming your own stress manager. You want to begin with the proper gear — an accurate road map, a good compass, and the right attitudes (and maybe a light lunch).

This chapter gives you the important tools you need to become aware of your stress and to understand where stress comes from and what it looks like. I help you measure your stress and identify your stress triggers. I also show you how to create a stress journal, which helps you pinpoint more specifically when and where you're stressed. These insights become important as you add tools and strategies to your repertoire to help you manage, reduce, and even eliminate much of your stress.

How Stressed Are You? Finding Ways to Measure Your Stress Level

Certainly, one of the first steps in mastering your stress is knowing just how stressed you are. But measuring stress is a trickier business than you may think. Part of the difficulty stems from the multifaceted nature of stress. That is, stress is both a stimulus and a response; it's what's on your plate and how you react to what's on your plate. Unfortunately, your doctor can't just hook you up to a machine and measure your stress level as easily as she does your blood pressure or heart rate, even though stress can manifest itself as various biochemical and physiological changes in your body. So how exactly do you measure your stress level? The following sections show you some relatively easy ways to identify and quantify just how stressed you are.

Starting with a simple gut check

Oddly enough, one of the best ways to measure your stress is asking yourself this simple question:

> "How much stress am I currently feeling?"

In an age of high-tech, computer-driven, digitally monitored gadgets and gear, this lowest-of-low tech gauge may seem like a joke. Yet it really is an incredibly useful way of assessing your stress level. This subjective measure of your stress has some advantages. One, it measures those aspects of your stress — anxiety, anger, muscle tension, or whatever — that you feel truly reflect your stress. Two, it's sensitive to the ways in which your stress level can change from day to day and even from moment to moment.

 If you don't trust your own judgment, ask someone who knows you well to tell you how stressed you seem. Your spouse, sibling, and best friend may have a better handle on your distress level than you think. They see sides of you that you may miss.

Using a stress gauge

To help you put a number on your stress level (and to give this approach the appearance of technological sophistication), I suggest you use a simple ten-point scale (shown in Figure 3-1) that permits you to calibrate your level of stress in a more quantitative way.

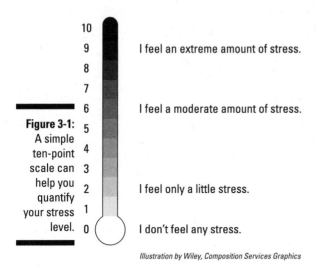

Figure 3-1:
A simple ten-point scale can help you quantify your stress level.

10
9   I feel an extreme amount of stress.
8
7
6   I feel a moderate amount of stress.
5
4
3
2   I feel only a little stress.
1
0   I don't feel any stress.

Illustration by Wiley, Composition Services Graphics

So right now, you may say to yourself, "I'm feeling a little five-ish." This morning when you were stuck in major traffic, you probably would've described your stress level as a seven.

You can get the hang of using this scale quickly. It is a handy tool for you to have as you master many of the stress-management tools presented in this book.

Measuring your stress in other ways

In order to get a more complete picture of your overall stress, a more objective measure of your stress level may be useful. Sometimes you experience stress but aren't aware of it. That's when a questionnaire may be appropriate. What follows are two such measures that provide you with valid and reliable measures of your stress level.

If you aren't in a test-taking mood right now, you can skip this section and come back to it later. But don't skip it entirely. These measures are useful in helping you understand your stress better. Also, if you retake these scales from time to time, your scores can tell you how well you're doing as you master the various stress-management techniques and strategies in this book.

The stress-symptom scale

This index gives you a measure of your stress level by looking at the number and the severity of your stress-related symptoms and behaviors. To use this measure, simply rate the frequency with which you've experienced each of the listed items during the last two weeks. Use this helpful rating scale:

✔ 0 = Never

✔ 1 = Sometimes

✔ 2 = Often

✔ 3 = Very often

Fatigue or tiredness   _____

Pounding heart   _____

Rapid pulse   _____

Increased perspiration   _____

Rapid breathing   _____

Aching neck or shoulders   _____

Low back pain   _____

Gritted teeth or clenched jaw   _____

Hives or skin rash   _____

Headaches   _____

Cold hands or feet   _____

Tightness in chest   _____

Nausea   _____

Diarrhea or constipation   _____

Stomach discomfort   _____

Nail biting   _____

Twitches or tics   _____

Difficulty swallowing or dry mouth   _____

Colds or flu   _____

Lack of energy   _____

Overeating   _____

Feelings of helplessness or hopelessness   _____

Excessive drinking   _____

Excessive smoking   _____

Excessive spending   _____

Excessive drug or medication use   _____

Upset feeling   _____

Feelings of nervousness or anxiety   _____

Increased irritability   _____

Worrisome thoughts	_____
Impatience	_____
Feelings of depression	_____
Loss of sexual interest	_____
Feelings of anger	_____
Sleep difficulties	_____
Forgetfulness	_____
Racing or intrusive thoughts	_____
Restless feelings	_____
Difficulty concentrating	_____
Periods of crying	_____
Frequent absences from work	_____
Your total stress-symptom score	_____

You compare your scores on the stress-symptom survey with the scores of others who complete this scale. No, I'm not saying you have to flag down passersby and make them take the test so you have scores to compare; you can use the handy chart in Table 3-1 instead. The higher your score, the more stress symptoms you're reporting. A higher frequency and/or intensity of stress-related symptoms and behaviors is generally associated with higher levels of stress.

Table 3-1	Determining Your Stress Rating
Your Score	*Your Comparative Rating*
0–19	Lower than average
20–39	Average
40–49	Moderately higher than average
50 and above	Much higher than average

Many of the symptoms and behaviors in this list can result from factors other than stress. Many medical conditions and disorders can have the same symptoms as those seen under conditions of stress. If any of your symptoms persist and/or are worrisome, be sure to speak with a medical professional. Your health-care provider is in the best position to tell you what your symptoms mean and what you should do about them.

The stressor-identification scale

This scale helps you not only assess the amount of stress you're experiencing now but also identify where that stress is coming from. Items in the scale include major life changes, important issues, and worries and concerns that you may be experiencing now. Use this simple scale to help you quantify how much stress the listed categories give you:

- ✔ N = No stress
- ✔ S = Some stress
- ✔ M = Moderate stress
- ✔ G = Great stress

Conflicts or concerns about your marriage or relationship	_____
Concerns or worries about your children	_____
Concerns or worries about your parents	_____
Pressures from other family members/in-laws	_____
Death of a loved one	_____
Health problems or worries	_____
Financial worries	_____
Concerns related to work/career	_____
Long or difficult commute to work	_____
Change in where you're living or will live	_____
Concerns with current residence or neighborhood	_____
Household responsibilities	_____
Home improvements or repairs	_____
Balancing demands of work and family	_____
Relationships with friends	_____
Limited personal time	_____
Concerns with social life	_____
Concerns with your appearance	_____
Issues with your personal traits or habits	_____
Boredom	_____
Feelings of loneliness	_____
Feelings about growing old	_____

Note that this scale isn't designed to provide you with a quantitative measure of your overall stress level. Rather, it's a tool that helps you pinpoint specific stresses in your life and assess the impact each may be having on your life at the present time. It's an index of what's on your plate.

Monitoring Your Stress with a Stress Journal

Hopefully, using the measurement tools in the preceding sections gives you a better picture of just how much stress you're currently experiencing. The next tool you need is one that both shows you what's triggering your stress right now and measures your ongoing stress level: a *stress journal.*

A stress journal or stress log is one of the more useful items you can carry in your tool belt. To effectively manage your stress, you need to become aware of when you're feeling stressed and be able to identify the sources of that stress. A stress journal can help you do just that by showing you very specifically when you experience stress and pinpointing the situations or circumstances that trigger those stresses. Your journal acts as a cue or prompt, reminding you that you should take some action and use one or more of the stress-management tools you've mastered. By keeping a longer-term record of your daily stress, you're in the best position to formulate a comprehensive stress-management program that can integrate various stress-reducing strategies and tactics.

Maintaining a stress journal as you read various parts of this book helps you focus your efforts and acts as a reminder that your stress needs tending to. Even after you complete your stress-management program, you should still monitor your stress on an ongoing (but perhaps less frequent) basis.

 Make your journal small and compact enough that you can carry it with you. I find that using a small notebook works well. Your journal's form and format are less important than the fact that you use it on a regular basis. If you're a high-tech kind of person, you can work your stress journal into your laptop, smartphone, or tablet. You can find apps that make your record-keeping easier.

Knowing how to record your stress

Here's what someone's stress log may look like on a Wednesday morning:

Day: Wednesday, November 6, 2013		
Time	*My Stress Trigger (Importance Level)*	*My Stress (Stress Level)*
7:45 a.m.	Couldn't find my keys (2)	Annoyed, upset (4)
9:30 a.m.	Subway stalled for ten minutes (1)	Annoyed (3)
11:30 a.m.	Mail came; big credit-card bill (6	Upset, worried (8)
12:30 p.m.	Given a deadline for project (4)	Worried, anxious (8)

The following sections walk you through the four steps you need to make your journal as useful as possible, with each day on a separate page.

Step 1: Write down what's stressing you

In the "My Stress Trigger" column, write down exactly what is triggering your stress. It may be an event, a situation, an encounter, or a problem. Be sure to also note the (approximate) time in the "Time" column.

Be brief in your trigger descriptions. You don't need to relive the event; you just want to record that it happened. For example:

> *"I was so annoyed because I thought I had left my keys on the hall table. They weren't there, and I had no idea where they were! What a pain! This is the third time this month this has happened. I need a brain transplant!"*

becomes

> *"Couldn't find my keys!"*

Or consider this potentially stressful trigger:

> *"I was so upset when I got that flat tire on my way to the bowling alley. This was our big night. We were in contention. We could win the team title. That is, if Mable shows up. She's the real star."*

becomes

> *"Flat tire on way to bowling!"*

Similarly,

> *"OMG, my mortgage payment is overdue! Heck, where am I going to come up with the money?"*

becomes

> *"Need mortgage money!"*

Step 2: Rate the relative importance of the stressor

Next to your stressor description, rate the relative importance of that stressor on a ten-point scale like this one in Figure 3-2.

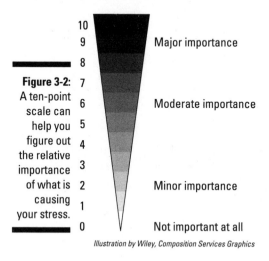

Figure 3-2:
A ten-point scale can help you figure out the relative importance of what is causing your stress.

Illustration by Wiley, Composition Services Graphics

To help you get the feel of the scale, think of major life stressors that could happen or have happened to you — the death of a loved one, a major financial loss, a life-threatening illness, the loss of your job, chronic pain, and so on. These major, life-altering events are your eights, nines, and tens.

More moderate stressors may include breaking your leg, losing your wallet, having your car break down on the highway, and so on. Big deals, but not catastrophes. These are your fours, fives, sixes, and sevens.

Your ones, twos, and threes are the everyday hassles: being late for a movie, getting caught in the rain with no umbrella, encountering a rude clerk, and so on.

Be careful here. You aren't rating how stressed you were about these events and situations; you're just rating their objective importance as a life stressor. So even if you go absolutely ballistic and sulk for days when your favorite team loses a game, the trigger "losing a game" is still only a one or two in life. (Okay, if it's a play-off game, maybe a three.)

Step 3: Write down what your stress looked like and rate your distress level

In the "My Stress" column, describe what your stress response looked like. Look at your emotional responses — worried, anxious, upset, fearful, angry, and so on.

Now rate the level of your distress about the stress trigger. Use a ten-point scale like the one in Figure 3-3.

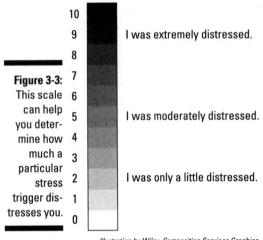

Illustration by Wiley, Composition Services Graphics

Figure 3-3: This scale can help you determine how much a particular stress trigger distresses you.

10

9   I was extremely distressed.

8

7

6

5   I was moderately distressed.

4

3

2   I was only a little distressed.

1

0

Knowing when to record your stress

Now that you have the format down, you need to use it.

What I don't want to do is add more stress to your already-stressful life. Make keeping your journal easy so that you're more likely to keep it up. Keep in mind that you don't have to record every single stressor in your day. A few of the more important and/or recurring ones will do.

Note when you're feeling stressed by becoming aware of negative emotional changes. Anxiety, worry, shame, upset, fear, and anger are usually a tip-off that you're feeling stressed.

You don't have to record your stressors at the exact time they occur. However, the sooner you make the entry, the more likely it will be that you recall what occurred and how stressed you were about that occurrence. Making the entry later in your day is still better than not making an entry at all.

Facing Roadblocks

If you recall your last attempt at losing a few pounds or getting rid of all the clutter in your house, you may recognize that good intentions don't always guarantee success. Almost always, you encounter one or two roadblocks. But being aware of potential obstacles in your path and figuring out ways of avoiding them makes reaching your goal more likely.

Here are some of the more commonly experienced roadblocks (whether your goal is managing stress, cutting clutter, or whatever) and some ways to help you avoid them:

- ✔ I don't have time.
- ✔ I'm too busy.
- ✔ I have too much stuff to learn.
- ✔ It's too much work.
- ✔ It's not my cup of tea.
- ✔ I tried it once and it didn't work.

Each of these excuses contains at least a grain of truth. But each of them can act as a roadblock, slowing or stopping you from getting the most out of your stress management efforts. In the following sections, I give you some ideas and suggestions to help you get around these potential obstacles.

Take it a step at a time

Learning any new skill takes time. The trick is not to tackle everything at once but rather to spread your learning out over time. Start slowly; don't overwhelm yourself. Set aside 15 or 20 minutes in your day and practice one of the methods or techniques in this book. It may be on your way to work in the morning, during a coffee break, on your lunch hour, or after work when you come home.

Give it a try

A few of the approaches in this book may feel a tad foreign and not immediately comfortable. Yet, with a little getting used to, these techniques may be the very ones you routinely use later on. You may not think, for example, that the breathing exercises are your thing, but you may be pleasantly surprised to find them wonderfully calming and relaxing. Many years ago, when I first began exploring various stress-management methods, I felt lukewarm about meditation as a relaxation tool. Now I swear by it. Hey, you never know. Keep an open mind. Give everything at least one good try.

Accept your different strokes

Although being open-minded about relaxation techniques is important, you ultimately need to put together a package of tools that reflects your personality and lifestyle. No two people are exactly alike. One size rarely fits all. For one person, the picture of ideal relaxation may be lying on a beach in the Caribbean with a page-turner in one hand and a piña colada in the other. For someone else, this scenario may trigger some an eye-rolling "Do I have to?" His or her idea of a relaxing vacation may be visiting every museum that's open. The general rule is, if you aren't comfortable with a technique or strategy, you're less likely to make it a part of your life. If meditation doesn't do anything for you, that's fine; move on to something that does.

Practice to make perfect

Most of the methods and techniques presented in these pages require some practice before you can master them. Even though you can pick them up pretty quickly at an intellectual level, you need to spend some time repeating them to truly reap their benefits. Don't give up too easily. Learning to ride a bike, drive a car, and play tennis all take time. Why should discovering how to manage the stress in your life be worth less time and effort?

Find a quiet place

You need a place to do all this practicing. Hopefully, you can find one that's relatively quiet and relaxing, at least for a short period of time. Given the realities of your life, your quiet place may have to be a setting that is far from ideal. Your office — when the door is shut — may work for you. You can also try your bedroom at home, or your car when you're stopped in traffic or commuting to work.

Link up

Listening to audio instructions can be a marvelous way to learn and practice many of the relaxation and stress-reducing exercises presented in this book.

Go to www.dummies.com/extras/stressmanagement to access a free guided relaxation that you can download to your computer or mobile device.

Get a stress buddy

Doing something by yourself can be hard. Losing weight, going to the gym, and stopping smoking are all easier when you do them with a friend. The same holds true for stress management. See if you can interest a friend in joining you. Your stress buddy can gently prod you to practice and put your new skills into daily use.

Don't expect overnight results

You've spent years creating your stress-producing styles and patterns. Fortunately, changing these patterns takes a lot less time, but it still takes some time. You need to change your behaviors and thinking, not to mention modify your lifestyle and work style. You get there step by step. See yourself as being part of a program that looks at your daily encounters and experiences as opportunities for growth and change.

Part II
Mastering the Basics

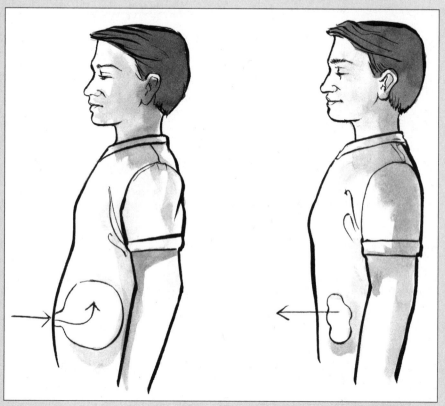

Illustration by Pam Tanzey

web extras

Feeling tense? Head to www.dummies.com/extras/stressmanagement and follow along with a guided muscle relaxation session.

In this part . . .

- ✔ It's no secret that too much stress can cause your muscles to become tense. Find out how to relax your muscles and let go of this tension.

- ✔ Get tips for quieting your mind, so that you can prevent stress and worries from taking over your life and interrupting your sleep.

- ✔ Discover the art of mindfulness and figure out how to mindfully reduce your stress.

- ✔ Mess causes stress. Find out how to get organized so that you can clear the clutter from your life and stay in control.

- ✔ Find out how to manage your time to get the most out of your day and have time for the things you really want to do.

- ✔ You're not your best self when you're tired, hungry, or feeling blah. Develop a stress-resistant lifestyle by eating properly, exercising, and getting enough sleep.

Chapter 4

Relaxing Your Body

. . . .

In This Chapter

▶ Understanding the effects of tension

▶ Recognizing your tension

▶ Breathing properly

▶ Using suggestion to relax

▶ Stretching and massaging

. . . .

*W*hen we hear the word relaxation, we tend to think of activities that take our minds off the stresses in our lives: watching some TV, curling up with a good book, playing a round of golf, taking a nap — anything that might take us out of our world of worry, fear, and concern. In this chapter, though, learning to relax means something different. It means acquiring specific relaxation skills that can help you reduce bodily tension in a direct and systematic way. Rather than simply distract you or providing you with some temporary pleasure, these approaches focus more directly on releasing muscle tension.

This chapter describes strategies and techniques that can help you let go of tension and relax your body. Chapter 5 shows you how to relax your mind. Together, these tools provide you with an important set of stress-management skills.

Stress Can Be a Pain in the Neck (And That's Just for Starters)

The following is a short — and only partial — list of some of the effects tension has on your body. Unfortunately, many of these symptoms are all too familiar.

Your mind-body connection

Your mind and body are far more interconnected than you might think. Separating the two isn't easy. When your mind tells you "you're worried" or "you're feeling anxious" or "you're afraid," your body hears this, as well. In turn, your body can become anxious and fearful. Your emotional distress (in your mind) is converted to physical distress (in your body). So, if you're worried, your body may become more tense and jittery, and you may start breathing faster. This process can also work the other way around. If your body is stressed, say from that fourth cup of coffee or a too-strenuous workout at the gym, your mind can interpret those physical states as stress, and you can become agitated or worried. That's why relaxing your body reduces not only bodily tension but also mental distress.

- ✔ Neck pain
- ✔ Headaches
- ✔ Stomach cramps
- ✔ Lower-back pain
- ✔ Clenched, painful jaw
- ✔ Teeth grinding
- ✔ Sore shoulders
- ✔ Muscle spasms
- ✔ Tremors or twitches

And that's just on the outside. Inside your body, other tension-related changes are happening. Here is a sampling of what else is quietly going on in your body when you feel tense:

- ✔ Your blood pressure goes up.
- ✔ Your stomach secretes more acid.
- ✔ Your cholesterol goes up.
- ✔ Your blood clots more quickly.

All in all, knowing how to prevent and eliminate bodily tension seems like a pretty healthy idea.

Funny, I don't feel tense

The fact is, you may not know when your body is tense. You get so used to being tense that you usually don't notice that you're feeling tense. Muscle tension creeps up on you. Slowly and often imperceptibly, your muscles tighten and, voila, the tension sets in. You don't feel the tension until you get a headache or feel the soreness in your neck and shoulders. The trick is to become aware of bodily tension before it builds up and does its damage. Tuning in to your body takes a bit of practice. The next section gives you a simple awareness technique that helps you recognize your tension before it becomes a bigger problem.

Invasion of the body scan

One of the best ways to recognize bodily tension is to use this simple one-minute scanning exercise.

Find a place where you can sit or lie down comfortably and be undisturbed for a moment or two (see Figure 4-1). Scan your body for any muscle tension. Start with the top of your head and work your way down to your toes. Ask yourself:

Figure 4-1:
A good position for body scanning.

Illustration by Pam Tanzey

✔ Am I furrowing my brow?

✔ Am I knitting my eyebrows?

✔ Am I clenching my jaw?

✔ Am I pursing my lips?

✔ Am I hunching my shoulders?

✔ Am I feeling tension in my arms?

> ✔ Am I feeling tightness in my thigh and calf muscles?
>
> ✔ Am I curling my toes?
>
> ✔ Do I notice any discomfort anywhere else in my body?

With a little practice, you can scan your body in less than a minute, finding your tension quickly. Once you have the hang of it, try the body scan while sitting at a desk or standing up. See if you can do a body scan three or four times a day. It's a great way of becoming aware of your stress.

When you find your stress, of course, you want to do something about it. The following sections give you some options.

Breathing Away Your Tension

Breathing properly is one of the simplest and best ways to drain your tension and relieve your stress. Simply by changing your breathing patterns, you can rapidly induce a state of greater relaxation. If you control the way you breathe, you have a powerful tool in reducing bodily tension. Just as important, you have a tool that helps prevent your body from becoming tense in the first place. This section shows you what you can do to incorporate a variety of stress-effective breathing techniques into your life.

Looking under the hood

Breathing provides your body with oxygen and removes waste products — primarily carbon dioxide — from your blood. Your lungs carry out this gas exchange. Lungs, however, don't have their own muscles for breathing. Your diaphragm is the major muscle necessary for proper breathing. The diaphragm is a dome-shaped muscle that separates your chest cavity from your abdominal cavity and acts as a flexible floor for your lungs.

When you inhale, your diaphragm flattens downward, creating more space in the chest cavity and permitting the lungs to fill. You can see your stomach rising. When you exhale, your diaphragm returns to its dome shape. Diaphragmatic breathing, also called abdominal breathing, provides the most efficient way of exchanging oxygen and carbon dioxide.

Your diaphragm works automatically, but you can override the process, especially when you're under stress. And that's where problems can arise. Too often you neglect to use your diaphragm when you breathe, and you interfere with the proper exchange of gases in your system, which can result in greater tension, more fatigue, and more stress.

Your breath is fine. It's your breathing that's bad.

"Bad breathing" can take a number of forms. You may be a chest and shoulder breather, bringing air into your lungs by expanding your chest cavity and raising your shoulders. This description certainly fits if you have more than a touch of vanity and opt for never sticking out your tummy when you breathe. You also may be a breath holder, stopping your breathing entirely when you're distracted or lost in thought. Both are inefficient, stress-producing forms of breathing. And when you're under stress, your breathing patterns deteriorate even more. To make things worse, once your breathing goes awry, you feel even more stressed. Quite a nasty cycle.

"Why change now? I've been breathing for years."

You probably take your breathing for granted. And why not? You've been breathing for most of your life; you'd think by now you would have figured out how to do it right. No such luck. When you're feeling stressed, your breathing becomes faster and shallower. When you breathe this way, your body reacts:

- ✔ Less oxygen reaches your bloodstream.
- ✔ Your blood vessels constrict.
- ✔ Less oxygen reaches your brain.
- ✔ Your heart rate and your blood pressure go up.
- ✔ You feel light-headed, shaky, and tenser.

Our primitive ancestors knew how to breathe. They didn't have to deal with the IRS, stacks of unpaid bills, or the Boss from Hell. These days only opera singers, stage actors, musicians who play wind instruments, and a couple of dozen moonlighting yoga instructors actually breathe effectively. The rest of us mess it up.

However, for a period of your life, you did get the whole breathing thing right. As a baby lying in your crib, you breathed serenely. Your little belly rose and fell in the most relaxed way. But then you grew up and blew it. Thankfully, all is not lost. You can re-teach yourself to breathe properly.

You probably think of breathing as a way of getting air into your lungs. However, in times past breathing was elevated to a more important status. Many religious groups and sects believed that a calming breath replenished the soul as well as soothed the body. In fact, the word *ruach* in Hebrew and the word *pneuma* in Greek have double meanings, connoting both breath and spirit. If you remember your Bible, the book of Genesis says that when God created Adam, he "breathed into his nostrils the breath of life, and man became a living soul."

Evaluating your breathing

You may be one of the few people who actually breathe properly. But before you skip this section, read a little further. To find out whether the way you breathe is stress-reducing, take this simple test.

1. **Lie on your back.**

2. **Put your right hand on your belly and your left hand on your chest, as shown in Figure 4-2.**

   Try to become aware of the way you breathe. Check to see whether your breathing is smooth, slow, and regular. If you're breathing properly, the hand on your belly rises and falls rhythmically as you inhale and exhale. The hand on your chest should move very little, and if that hand does rise, it should follow the rise in your belly.

Figure 4-2:
Evaluating your breathing.

Illustration by Pam Tanzey

Cutting yourself some slack

I commonly find that people who want to adopt new patterns of breathing have a fervent desire to get it perfectly right. They frequently get so lost in body parts or lung mechanics that they wind up more stressed out than they were before they started. Don't let this happen to you. And remember that there's no one exactly right way to breathe all the time. Give yourself lots of room to experiment with your breathing. And don't overdo it. If you've been breathing inefficiently for all these years, changing gears may take some time. Above all, you're not taking a test. Don't grade yourself on how deeply you can breathe or how flat you can make your diaphragm. Remember, the goal is to reduce your stress, not add to it.

Changing the way you breathe, changing the way you feel

Sometimes, all it takes to make you feel better is one simple change. Changing the way you breathe can make all the difference in how you feel. The following exercises present various ways to alter your breathing. Try them and discover whether all you need is one simple change.

Breathing 101: Breathing for starters

Here is one of the best and simplest ways of introducing yourself to stress-effective breathing.

1. **Either lying or sitting comfortably, put one hand on your belly and the other hand on your chest.**

2. **Inhale through your nose, making sure that the hand on your belly rises and the hand on your chest moves hardly at all.**

3. **As you inhale slowly, count silently to three.**

4. **As you exhale through your parted lips slowly, count silently to four, feeling the hand on your belly falling gently.**

   Pause slightly before your next breath. Continue to breathe like this until you feel completely relaxed.

Moving on to something more advanced: Taking a complete breath

Taking complete breaths (or doing Zen breathing, as it's often called) helps you breathe more deeply and more efficiently and helps you maximize your lung capacity.

1. **Lie comfortably on a bed, in a reclining chair, or on a rug.**

   Keep your knees slightly apart and slightly bent. Close your eyes if you like. You may feel more comfortable placing a pillow under the small of your back to help relieve the pressure.

2. **Put one hand on your abdomen near your belly button and the other hand on your chest so that you follow the motion of your breathing.**

   Try to relax. Let go of any tension you may feel in your body.

3. **Begin by slowly inhaling through your nose, first filling the lower part of your lungs, then the middle part of your chest, and then the upper part of your chest.**

   As you inhale, feel your diaphragm pushing down, gently extending your abdomen, making room for the newly inhaled air. Notice the hand on your abdomen rise slightly. The hand on your chest should move very little, and when it does, it should follow your abdomen. Don't use your shoulders to help you breathe.

4. **Exhale slowly through your parted lips, emptying your lungs from top to bottom.**

   Make a whooshing sound as the air passes through your lips, and notice the hand on your abdomen fall.

5. **Pause slightly and take in another breath, repeating this cycle.**

   Continue breathing this way for ten minutes or so — certainly until you feel more relaxed and peaceful. Practice this technique daily if you can. Try this exercise while sitting and then while standing.

With a little practice, this form of breathing comes more naturally and automatically. With some time and some practice, you may begin to breathe this way much more of the time. Stick with it.

Trying some "belly-button balloon" breathing

A simpler way of breathing more deeply and more evenly is to work with a visual image, in this case a balloon. Here's what you do:

1. **Imagine that a small balloon — about the size of a grapefruit — is replacing your stomach, just under your belly button, as shown in Figure 4-3.**

2. **As you inhale through your nose, imagine that you're actually inhaling through your belly button, inflating this once-empty balloon.**

   This balloon is small, so don't overinflate it. As the balloon gets larger, notice how your belly rises.

3. **Exhale slowly through your nose or mouth, again imagining that the air is leaving through your belly button.**

   Your balloon is now slowly and easily returning to its deflated state.

4. **Pause slightly before the next breath in and then repeat, gently and smoothly inflating your balloon to a comfortable size.**

   Repeat this exercise, as often as you can, whenever you can.

 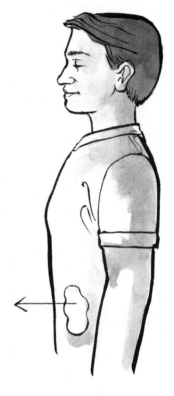

Figure 4-3:
Balloon
breathing.

Illustration by Pam Tanzey

Standing up straight

Your mother was right! When you're under stress, you have a tendency to hunch over, making your posture lousy and your breathing impaired. You then breathe less deeply, denying your system the proper supply of oxygen you need. As a result, your muscles get tense. When you stand or sit straight, you reverse this process. You needn't stand like a West Point cadet to correct bad posture. Overdoing it probably produces as much tension as you felt before. Just keep your shoulders from slouching forward. If you're unsure about what your posture looks like, ask your mother or a good friend.

Emergency breathing: How to breathe in the trenches

Breathing properly is no big deal when you're lying on your bed or vegging out in front of the TV. But what's your breathing like when you're caught in gridlock, when you're facing down a deadline, or when the stock market drops 20 percent? You're now in crisis mode. You need another form of breathing. Here's what to do:

1. **Inhale slowly through your nostrils, taking in a very deep diaphragmatic breath, filling your lungs and filling your cheeks.**

2. **Hold that breath for about six seconds.**

3. **Exhale slowly through your slightly parted lips, releasing all the air in your lungs.**

   Pause at the end of this exhalation. Now take a few "normal" breaths.

   Repeat Steps 1 through 3 two or three times and then return to what you were doing. This form of deep breathing should put you in a more relaxed state.

The yawn that refreshes

Yawning is usually associated with boredom. Business meetings you think will run well into the next millennium or painful telephone solicitors explaining (in detail) the virtues of their long-distance plan may trigger more than a few yawning gasps. However, your yawn may signal something more than boredom.

Yawning is another way Mother Nature tells you that your body is under stress. In fact, yawning helps relieve stress. When you yawn, more air — and therefore more oxygen — enters your lungs, revitalizing your bloodstream. Releasing that plaintive sound that comes with yawning is also tension reducing. Unfortunately, people have become a little over-socialized, making for wimpy yawns. You need to recapture this lost art.

The next time you feel a yawn coming on, go with it. Open your mouth widely and inhale more fully than you normally might. Take that breath all the way down to your belly. Exhale fully through your mouth, completely emptying your lungs. What a feeling! Enjoy it. So what if your friends don't call you anymore?

Tensing Your Way to Relaxation

After you master the art of breathing (see the exercises in the preceding section), you're ready to discover another way of relaxing your body. One of the better relaxation techniques derives from a method called progressive relaxation or deep-muscle relaxation. This method is based on the notion that you're not aware of what your muscles feel like when they're tensed. By purposely tensing your muscles, you're able to recognize what tension feels like and identify which muscles are creating that tension. This technique is highly effective and has proved to be a valuable tool for quickly reducing muscle tension and promoting relaxation.

Exploring how progressive relaxation works

You begin progressive relaxation by tensing a specific muscle or group of muscles (your arms, legs, shoulders, and so on). You notice the way the tension feels. You hold that tension for about ten seconds and then let it go, replacing that tension with something much more pleasant — relaxation. By the time you tense and relax most of your major muscle groups, you feel relaxed, at peace, and much less stressed. The following general guidelines set the stage for muscle-group-specific relaxation techniques later in this chapter.

1. **Lie down or sit, as comfortably as you can, and close your eyes.**

   Find a quiet, dimly lit place that gives you some privacy, at least for a while.

2. **Tense the muscles of a particular body part.**

   To practice, start by tensing your right hand and arm. Begin by simply making a fist. As you clench your fist, notice the tension and strain in your hand and forearm. Without releasing that tension, bend your right arm and flex your bicep, making a muscle the way you might to impress the kids in the schoolyard.

   Don't strain yourself in any of these muscle-tensing maneuvers; don't overdo it. When you tense a muscle group, don't tense as hard as you can. Tense to about 75 percent of what you can do. If you feel pain or soreness, ease up on the tension, and if you still hurt, defer your practice till another time.

3. **Hold the tension in the body part for about seven seconds.**

4. **Let go of the tension quickly, letting the muscles go limp.**

   Notice the difference in the way your hand and arm feel. Notice the difference between the sensations of tension and those of relaxation. Let these feelings of relaxation deepen for about 30 seconds.

5. **Repeat Steps 1 through 4, using the same muscle group.**

6. **Move to another muscle group.**

   Simply repeat Steps 1 through 4, substituting a different muscle group each time. Continue with your left hand and arm and then work your way through the major muscle groups listed in the following section.

You don't have to remember all the various instructions and muscle groups. Head to www.dummies.com/extras/stressmanagement and listen to a guided progressive muscle relaxation.

Relaxing your face and head

Wrinkle your forehead (creating all those lines that everybody hates) by raising your eyebrows as high as you can. Hold this tension for about five seconds and then let go, releasing all of the tension in your forehead. Just let your forehead muscles become smooth. Notice the difference between the feelings of tension you felt and the more pleasant feelings of relaxation.

Now clench your jaw by biting down on your back teeth. At the same time, force a smile. Hold this uncomfortable position for about five seconds and then relax your jaw, letting your mouth fall slightly ajar.

Finally, purse your lips, pushing them together firmly. Hold that tension for a bit and then relax, letting your lips open slightly. Notice how relaxed your face and head feel. Enjoy this sensation and let this feeling deepen by letting go of any remaining sources of tension around your mouth and lips.

Relaxing your neck and shoulders

Bend your head forward as though you're going to touch your chest with your chin (you probably will). Feel the tension in the muscles of your neck. Hold that tension. Now tilt your head slightly, first to one side and then to another. Notice the tension at the side of your neck as you do so. Tilt your head back as if you're trying to touch your upper back. But don't force it or overdo it, stopping if you notice any pain and discomfort. Now relax, letting your head return to a more comfortable, natural position. Enjoy the relaxation for a moment or so.

Now scrunch up your shoulders as though you're trying to reach your ears. Hold it, feel the tension (again for about five seconds), and let your shoulders fall to a comfortable, relaxed position. Notice the feelings of relaxation that are spreading through your shoulders and neck.

Relaxing your back

Arch your back, being careful not to overdo it. Hold that tension for several seconds and then let your back and shoulders return to a more comfortable, relaxed position.

Relaxing your legs and feet

Either sitting or lying down, raise your right foot so that you feel some tension in your thigh and buttock. At the same time, push your heel out and point your toes toward your head, as shown in Figure 4-4. Hold this tension, notice what it feels like, and then let go, letting your leg fall to the bed or floor, releasing any remaining tension. Let that relaxation deepen for a while. Repeat this sequence with your other leg and foot.

Figure 4-4:
Relaxing your feet and legs.

Illustration by Pam Tanzey

Relaxing your buttocks

Tense the muscles of your buttocks, noticing what that feels like. Hold that tension for several seconds. Slowly release that muscle tension, letting go, letting the muscles in your buttocks gently release. Notice those feelings of relaxation and let them deepen even further.

Relaxing your stomach

Take in a deep breath and hold that breath, tensing the muscles in your stomach. Imagine that you're preparing yourself for a punch in the stomach. Hold that tension. And relax, letting go of the tension.

After you finish this sequence, let your body sink into an even deeper state of relaxation. Let go more and more. Mentally go over the sensations you're feeling in your arms, face, neck, shoulders, back, stomach, and legs. Feel your body becoming looser and more relaxed. Savor the feeling.

Scrunching up like a pretzel

When pressed for time, you can do a quickie version of the progressive relaxation exercise that I talk about in the preceding section. Simply, this technique compresses all the muscle-tensing and relaxing sequences into one. Think of it as one gigantic scrunch.

In order to do this, you have to master the gradual version first. The success of this rapid form of relaxation depends on your ability to create and release muscle tension quickly, skills you master by slowly working through all of the muscle groups individually. Here's what to do:

Sit or lie comfortably in a room that is quiet and relatively free of distractions. Now, tense all of the muscle groups listed below, simultaneously:

- Clench both fists, bend both arms and tense your biceps. At the same time,
- Lift both legs until you notice a moderate degree of tension and discomfort, and
- Tense the muscles in your buttocks and hold that tension, and
- Scrunch up your face, closing your eyes, furrowing your brow, clenching your jaws, and pursing your lips, and
- Bring your shoulders as close as you can to your ears, while you
- Tense your stomach muscles.

Hold this "total scrunch" for about five seconds and then release, letting go of any and all tension. Let your legs fall to the floor or bed and let your arms fall to your sides. Let the rest of your body return to a relaxed position. Repeat this sequence at various points throughout your day.

Mind over Body: Using the Power of Suggestion

Another important approach to bodily relaxation is called autogenic training, or AT for short. The word *autogenic* means self-generation or self-regulation. This method attempts to regulate your *autonomic nervous functions* and more specifically your *parasympathetic nervous system* (your heart rate, blood pressure, and breathing, among others) rather than relaxing your muscles. With autogenic training, you use your mind to regulate your body's internal stress levels.

AT relies on the power of suggestion to induce physiological changes. These suggestions are mental images that your subconscious picks up and transmits to your body. Just thinking about certain changes in your body produces those kinds of changes. As a result, you experience deep feelings of relaxation. AT may sound mysterious, but it isn't. After you master this technique, AT is a highly effective way of putting yourself in a more relaxed state. The method I describe here is a more abbreviated form than the one originally devised. However, it's better suited to a busy lifestyle. Here's what you do:

1. **Get comfy.**

   Find a suitably quiet, not-too-hot, and not-too-cold place. You can sit or lie down, but make sure your body is well supported and as comfortable as possible. Try to breathe slowly and smoothly.

2. **Concentrate passively.**

   For this approach to be effective, you need to adopt a receptive, casual attitude of passive concentration. You want to be alert, not falling asleep but not asking your mind to work too hard. You can't force yourself to relax. Just let it happen. Be aware of your body and your mind, but don't actively analyze everything or worry about how you're doing. Should a distracting thought come your way, notice it and then let it go. If the relaxation doesn't come at first, don't worry. It comes with more practice.

3. **Allow various body parts to begin feeling warm and heavy.**

Although autogenic training utilizes many suggestions and images, the two most effective images are warmth and heaviness. Start by focusing on your right arm. Now slowly and softly say to yourself:

I am calm . . . I am at peace . . . My right arm is warm . . . and heavy . . . My right arm is warm . . . and heavy . . . My right arm is warm . . . and heavy . . . I can feel the warmth and heaviness flowing into my right arm. . . . I can feel my right arm becoming warmer . . . and heavier . . . I can feel my right arm becoming warmer . . . and heavier . . . I can feel my right arm becoming warmer . . . and heavier . . . I am at peace . . . I am calm . . . I am at peace . . . I am calm.

Take the time to become aware of the feelings in your arm and hand. Notice that your arm is becoming warmer and heavier. Don't rush this process. Enjoy the changes your body is now beginning to experience.

4. **After you complete the phrases, remain silent and calm for about 30 seconds, letting the relaxation deepen; then focus on your left arm.**

   Repeat the same phrases again, this time substituting left arm for right arm. (Hopefully by now you've memorized these phrases and can close your eyes and not worry about a script.)

5. **Move to other parts of your body.**

   Focus on other areas, repeating the same phrases but substituting other parts of your body. Here is the complete sequence: right arm, left arm, both arms, right leg, left leg, both legs, neck and shoulders, chest and abdomen, and finally your entire body.

   Completing the entire sequence shouldn't take you more than a half hour or so. If you can fit in two or three autogenic sessions a day, all the better. You may need some time to master this technique, but the results are well worth the effort.

TIP

Use your imagination? You're getting warmer!

With autogenic training, you may find that using the "warm and heavy" suggestions and images isn't effective for you. You may need a different image to release the tension in your body. Here are alternate suggestive images that I have found can induce feelings of warmth and heaviness.

✔ **Heat me up:** Imagine that the body part in question (arm, leg, and so on) is wrapped in a heating pad. Slowly but surely the heat permeates your body, relaxing your muscles more and more.

✔ **Get in hot water:** Imagine that you're immersing your arm or leg in soothing warm water.

✔ **Sunny side up:** Mentally direct a sun lamp to a particular part of your anatomy.

✔ **Heavy metal:** Visualize weights attached to your arm, leg, and so on.

✔ **Get the lead in:** Imagine that your limb is filled with lead.

Stretching Away Your Stress

Stretching is one of the ways your body naturally discharges excess bodily tension. You may notice that you automatically feel the need to stretch after waking up in the morning or just before retiring at night. But a good stretch can drain away much of your body's tension at other times, too. You may be desk-bound or otherwise required to sit for long periods of time during the day, causing your muscles to tense and tighten. Consider adopting one or more basic stretches and taking a stretch break at various points throughout the day. Cats do, dogs do, why not you?

Following are two tension-relieving stretches that I find to be wonderful ways of draining off a lot of excess tension. They are simple and shouldn't evoke much comment or ridicule from friends or coworkers.

✔ **The Twist.** This stretch is great for your upper body. Sitting or standing, put both your hands behind the back of your head, locking your fingers together. Move your elbows toward each other until you feel some moderate tension. Now twist your body slightly, first to the right for a few seconds and then slowly to the left. When you finish, let your arms fall to your sides.

✔ **The Leg-lift.** This stretch is good for your lower body. Sitting in your chair, raise both your legs until you feel a comfortable level of tightness in them. Maintaining that tension, flex and point your toes toward your head. Hold that tension for about ten seconds and then let your legs fall to the floor. If doing this with both legs together is a wee bit uncomfortable, try it one leg at a time.

Stretch slowly and don't overdo it. You're trying to relax your muscles, not punish them.

"All this relaxing is making me tense!"

Believe it or not, you may find that practicing relaxation can be stressful, at least at first.

Changing your breathing patterns, tensing and relaxing muscles, and exploring autogenic exercises can result in some strange side effects. You may notice some tingling or a feeling of restlessness and, paradoxically, an increase in tension. This is not unusual, and, although it's distracting, don't take this as a sign that you're doing something wrong. As you become more familiar with how your body feels when it's in a highly relaxed state, these sensations disappear.

Massage? Ah, There's the Rub!

Massage and other touch and pressure therapies are among the most popular ways of relieving muscle tension. These days you can get a massage almost as easily as you can get your hair cut. In the past, the idea of a massage usually conjured up an image of a liniment rubdown in a sweaty gym or pampered caresses in a swanky health spa. No more. Massage and related treatment have come of age.

The range and popularity of touch and pressure disciplines and therapies have grown enormously in recent years. A partial list of available methods and techniques include:

- Swedish massage
- Reflexology
- Shiatsu
- Chiropractic
- Acupressure

All of these methods have their origins in early medicine and healing. Many claim spiritual as well as physical changes. Rather than go into each of these disciplines separately, I'm going to discuss several of the simpler stress-relieving approaches from the above list that I find to be particularly useful and easy to grasp.

You have several choices when it comes to massage. You can spend some bucks and get a professional to give you a massage. Or you can find someone who will give you a massage for free. Or you can give yourself a massage. I'm going to start with the last option, which is often the cheapest and doesn't require friends.

Massaging yourself

You can go two ways: high-tech or low-tech.

The high-tech route usually requires a wall socket or lots of batteries. Many specialty stores stock massage paraphernalia. My favorite is a mega-buck relaxation chair that transports you to relaxation heaven with the flick of a switch. On the less expensive side, a handheld vibrator massages those tight and tired muscles, leaving you much more relaxed. Alternately, you can forego the batteries and the cash by letting your fingers do the work. Fingers are cheaper, easier to control, and readily available. Following are three simple ways to rub away your stress.

For your hands

Hold your left palm in front of you, fingers together. The fleshy spot between your thumb and index finger is a key acupressure point that should spread a sensation of relaxation when massaged. Using your right thumb, massage this spot in a circular motion for a slow count of 15. Switch hands and repeat.

For stress-related fatigue, pinch just below the first joint of your pinkie with the thumb and index finger of the opposite hand. (Pressure should be firm but not painful.) Increase the pressure slightly. Make small circular movements in a counterclockwise direction while maintaining pressure. Continue for 20 seconds. Release. Wait for ten seconds and repeat up to five times.

For your feet

Try this sole-soothing exercise. Take off your socks and shoes and sit comfortably with one leg crossed over the other. (The sole of your foot should be almost facing you.) With both hands, grasp the arches of your foot and apply pressure, especially with your thumbs. Now kneading (like you would bread dough, using your thumbs and fingers) every part of your foot, work your way from your heel right up to your toes. Give each of your toes a squeeze. Now massage the other foot in a similar way.

If crossing your legs is more stressful than it used to be, go to the kitchen and get your rolling pin. Sit in a chair and position the rolling pin next to your foot. Gently roll your bare foot back and forth slowly for two minutes or so. Then try it with the other foot. Now wash the pin.

If you don't own a rolling pin, work with a tennis ball. Put it under the arch of your bare foot, put some pressure on that foot, and move the ball backward and forward.

Keep this rhythm going for about two minutes, and then switch to your other foot.

For your neck and shoulders

Stress most often finds its way to your neck and shoulders. To dissipate that tension, take your left hand and firmly massage your right shoulder and the right side of your neck. Start with some gentle circular motions, rubbing the muscle with your index and pointer fingers. Then finish with a firmer massage, squeezing the shoulder and neck muscles between your thumb and other fingers. Now switch to the other side.

For your face

Start by placing both of your hands on your face with the tips of your fingers resting on your forehead and the heels of your palms resting just under your cheeks. Gently pull down the skin on your forehead with the tips of your fingers while pushing up the area under your palms. Rhythmically repeat this movement, contracting and releasing your fingers and palms.

You can also try pulling on your ears in different directions. My editor swears by it.

Becoming the massage-er or massage-ee

Having someone else give you a massage certainly has its advantages. When someone else does all the work, you can completely let go: Sit or lie back and totally relax. And another person can reach places on your body that you could never reach. You can, of course, visit a massage therapist; you can also ask a friend to give you a massage. Of course, you may have to reciprocate. But even giving someone else a massage can relieve some of your tension. Here are some general hints and guidelines to get you started:

- ✔ Use some massage oil or body lotion to add a relaxing aroma and smooth the massage process. (Warm the oil to room temperature so as not to shock your or your partner's system.)
- ✔ Lower the lights to provide a soothing, relaxing atmosphere. Calming music also adds a nice touch.
- ✔ Focus your massage on the lower back, neck, and shoulders — places stress tends to reside and cause the most discomfort.
- ✔ Start by applying pressure lightly until the massage-ee is relaxed. Then increase the pressure, using your palms to knead the muscles.
- ✔ Finish up with a lighter massage, and let your partner linger for a while after the massage to extend the sense of relaxation.
- ✔ Don't overdo it. A good massage shouldn't have the massage-ee writhing in pain. A bad massage can cause more stress than it attempts to relieve.

My own favorite way of relaxing my muscles

I'm not a bath kind of guy. I'm a shower guy. One of my more relaxing, soul-soothing experiences is luxuriating in a very hot shower with the faucet turned on full force and the spray massaging my body. My muscles go limp, my pulse slows, and I'm transfixed. A key to all this physiological bliss is the right showerhead. I prefer either the old, large, flat, showerheads with dozens of holes or the newer models that enable you to manually dial the spray, pressure, and even pulse. I just stand there until I look like a prune.

Taking a Three-Minute Energy Burst

Any concentrated expenditure of energy produces more stress by tensing your muscles, speeding your heart rate, and quickening your breathing. However, after you stop expending energy, you find that your muscles relax and your heart rate and breathing slow down to a level that is lower than when you started. This energy boost can come from walking briskly, running for a short distance, doing jumping jacks, jumping rope, doing sit-ups or push-ups, running up steps — anything that gets your body going.

✔ **Become a shaker.** Shaking off tension is fun. You can do this exercise either sitting or standing. Begin by holding your arms loosely in front of you and shaking your hands at the wrists. Now let your arms and shoulders join in the fun. Continue for a short while and taper off slowly, letting your arms fall comfortably to your sides. Now lift one leg and start shaking it. Then shift to the other leg. (If you're sitting, you can do both legs at the same time.) When you finish, notice the tingling sensations in your body and, more importantly, the feelings of relaxation. Admittedly, it looks a little strange, but it works.

✔ **Soak up your stress.** Think of your bathroom as a mini health spa and your bathtub as a pool of relaxation. Besides, not only do you emerge relaxed and de-stressed, but you're also clean. Here's the recipe for that relaxing soak:

- A spare half hour
- A tub of hot, soapy water
- Soothing scents, such as lavender Epsom salts
- Soft lighting
- Relaxing music
- A phone that is turned off or at least silenced

More Ways to Relax

A few relaxation techniques from off the beaten path:

✔ **Throw in the towel.** Barbers used to give their customers shaves along with haircuts. In those days, you felt marvelous as your barber carefully placed moist, hot towels on your face. These days, stylists only cut hair. And unless you fly first class to Europe or dine in an upscale Japanese restaurant, you're unlikely to experience the joy of a hot towel on your face — unless, of course, you put it there yourself. Simply take one or two washcloths and immerse them in hot water. Squeeze out the excess water, lie back, close your eyes, and put them on your face. Ah, nirvana.

And what if you don't have a towel or hot water? Use your hands. Rub them together till they feel warm. Place each hand on a side of your face. No, the feeling isn't quite as good as a moist, hot towel, but it can still help you relax.

✔ **Jump into a hot tub.** If you have a hot tub, great, but keep in mind that many bathtubs have the same benefits. Don't take my word for it. Just read this promo from one hot-tub manufacturer:

"When you slip into the hot massaging waters, your muscles will relax, and your mind will clear."

Maybe so.

✔ **Go East; try some yoga.** Why reinvent the wheel when some marvelous relaxation approaches have been around for many years? Yoga has been practiced for 5,000 years. Yoga looks at health and well-being from a broad, holistic perspective that sees the mind and body as dynamically interconnected. This ancient Eastern tradition combines physical and postural exercises with meditation practices, breathing techniques, and mindfulness that can help you relax your body and calm your mind. Most people who have tried yoga swear by it. Find a good teacher and give it a try. (Ask friends about yoga classes in your community.)

You might want to take a look at *Yoga For Dummies*, 2nd Edition, by Georg Feuerstein and Larry Payne (Wiley). While you're at it, consider other Eastern practices such as T'ai Chi (*T'ai Chi For Dummies*, by Therese Iknoian [Wiley]).

✔ **Relax in the bedroom.** Sex can be a marvelous way of unwinding and letting go of physical tension. Including some form of mutual massage in your love-making can increase the relaxation benefits.

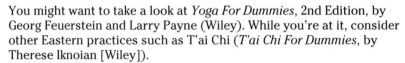

Have a drink?

Dare I suggest that you use an alcoholic beverage as an agent of relaxation?

Yes and no.

For some time now, research literature has been supportive of the value of moderate drinking (that is, no more than one or two alcoholic drinks per day). At this level of intake, alcohol has been found to raise levels of HDL (the good cholesterol) and lessen the risk of heart disease. However, the risks from excessive drinking far outweigh these benefits. For many, drinking can be a slippery slope, with the cure becoming the disease.

The bottom line: Don't put alcohol at the top of your stress-reduction list. If you have successfully integrated a drink or the occasional use of a pill into your life, fine. But always remember, you can reduce your stress in better ways.

Chapter 5

Quieting Your Mind

In This Chapter

▶ Stopping unwanted thoughts

▶ Using imagery to relax

▶ Investigating meditation

▶ Hypnotizing yourself

*Y*our mind is constantly working. Sometimes it races, sometimes it slows, but it rarely stops. Even when you're sleeping, the wheels are turning. You may be worrying about work, your relationships, your finances, or simply how you're going to juggle the hundred and one things on your plate. Whatever the source of your worry or distress, you clearly aren't going to relax until you stop — or at least slow — this mental mayhem.

Consider Matt's stressful night: Matt is in bed at 11:30, ready and determined to go to sleep. But he well knows that isn't going to happen. His thinking is just starting to rev up. He's worried about his job and what he'll do if that rumored layoff comes through. His credit cards, although not maxed out, are getting there. His relationship with Jenna is losing some steam. Maybe they should take a break for a while. He thinks about yesterday, when his friend Mark told him he wasn't being a good friend and wasn't spending enough time with him. Doesn't Mark understand how busy he is? He remembers his bad decision to buy this apartment. "Don't really love it. Costing me a fortune! Not worth it! How can I sell it in this market?"

Matt's worries are real. But if he continues to ruminate and obsess, he won't fall asleep until next week. It's not only the nights when his thinking starts to spin. The days are just as bad. He wishes he didn't have these problems, but it seems his mind races like this even when the problems change. He desperately wants his brain to shut off or at least slow down. Why do all his worries and anxieties keep spiraling in his mind? "Where," he asks, "is the off switch?"

Five signs that your mind is stressed

Below are some of the more common signs that indicate that your mind is working overtime. See how many of the following describe you.

✔ Your mind seems to be racing.

✔ You find controlling your thoughts difficult.

✔ You're worried, irritable, or upset.

✔ You're preoccupied more often and find concentrating more difficult.

✔ You find it difficult to fall asleep or fall back asleep once awake.

To be completely relaxed, you need to not only relax your body but also calm your mind. Chapter 4 shows you how to relax your body and let go of physical tension. This chapter details how to quiet your mind. For many people, and you may be one of them, stress takes the form of psychological distress, and you find that your mind is filled with distressing thoughts that prevent you from feeling at ease.

Where Do All These Thoughts Come From!?

The ability to think may represent one of the stellar achievements of scaling that evolutionary ladder. Your cat or dog probably doesn't wake at 3 a.m. worrying about how he's going to come up with that next mortgage payment. What goes on in your head comes from many different sources. A brief list would include:

✔ **Your DNA:** You are, in fact, born with a certain temperament and personality traits that may predispose you to think, feel, and react in more stressful ways.

✔ **Your family:** No surprises here. Mom and Dad play an important role, especially in your younger years, in determining who you are and how you think. Were they critical? Supportive? Were they an active part of your life, or were they absent?

✔ **Your life experiences:** Positive experiences and negative experiences — your joys, traumas, successes, failures, educational experiences, relationships, religious beliefs — all determine, to varying degrees, how you see yourself and your world.

Your thoughts can take a variety of forms. Much of your thinking can be positive, adaptive, and even fun. You plan for your future, you prudently construct a budget, you replay your daughter's performance in the school play, and so on. Unfortunately, too much of your thinking works against you, creating unnecessary stress. If you can identify your negative thoughts you are better able to manage them and, if need be, change them.

Sorting out your thoughts

Here is but a sampling of what this negative, not-so-adaptive thinking consists of:

- ✔ **Perfectionism:** Insisting that you (and possibly others) be perfect; setting unrealistically high standards for yourself and others.

- ✔ **Self-downing:** Putting yourself down when you fail, are rejected, or don't have those traits or abilities you think are important for your happiness.

- ✔ **Catastrophizing and awfulizing:** Exaggerating the importance and potential consequences of negative events.

- ✔ **Fear of disapproval:** Believing that being disapproved of says too much about your identity and value.

- ✔ **Fear of failure:** Seeing failure as a global negative rating of your worth.

- ✔ **Fear of uncertainty:** The inability to cope with the unknown and unpredictable.

Although the positive, "good" kind of thinking may keep you up at night, that's not usually the way it works. Most often it's your negative thinking that does you in, triggering unnecessary stress.

Thinking automatically

Much of your thinking, both good and bad, comes to you automatically, without your awareness or permission. And this is part of the problem. These automatic thoughts can run the show. Often this takes the form of ruminating, also known as over-worrying. Your thoughts race, shifting from one worry, regret, or failure to another. As you'll see in Chapter 6 and later in Chapters 10 and 11, becoming aware of your thought processes and identifying the negative, distorting aspects of your thinking becomes an important tool to help you change such thinking.

Turning Off Your Mind

If only you had a switch on the side of your head that, with a quick flick, could simply stop the ruminating, the worry, the anxiety, the hurt, the anger — all of the distressing thoughts and feelings that flood your mind. Clearly you don't have an on-off switch to control your thoughts. However you do have more control over your thinking and feeling than you may imagine. You can become more aware of what you're thinking and decide how much attention and importance you should give to these thoughts and feelings. Your goal is to see your mind, if not always as a friend, at least as a part of you that you can control, manage, and calm.

Simply saying to yourself, "I will absolutely *not* think about this stuff anymore!" rarely works. Suppressing unwanted thoughts by willing them away is tough to do. Remember when a friend challenged you: "Don't think about pink elephants"? Barely are the words out of your friend's mouth when a herd of pinkish elephants fills your mind. The harder you try to will yourself *not* to think of something, the more likely it is that you in fact *will* think of that something.

The following sections offer some effective techniques that have been shown to help you escape persistent negative thoughts. I start with a technique that focuses on specific unwanted thoughts and progress to other ways of coping with more generalized forms of emotional distress.

Stopping your unwanted thoughts

Sometimes an unwanted thought or worry grabs you and won't let go. Perhaps you have an upsetting worry that continually intrudes into your thinking and keeps you from enjoying a pleasant evening with friends. Or maybe you're trying to fall asleep, and the thoughts racing around in your head make sleeping impossible. You recognize that there's nothing you can do about your worry and that your worrying is only making things worse. You'd be better off if you could somehow stop thinking about this. But how?

That's where a technique called *thought stopping* can be useful. It's an effective way of keeping repetitive worries and upsets temporarily out of your mind, and it's also effective in weakening those thoughts, making it less likely that they'll return. Concentrating on two things at the same time is hard. So if your mind is flooded with distressing thoughts, change course. Find something else, a "wanted" thought you actually enjoy thinking about.

Here's how to get this technique to work for you:

1. Write down your unwanted thoughts.

On a piece of paper, write down three or four thoughts that repeatedly trigger distress. It could be an upsetting memory (your embarrassment when you said something dumb at a meeting), a future fear (an upcoming dental visit), or an imagined anxiety (a plane crash).

2. Think of some pleasant replacement thoughts.

Write down three or four pleasant, happy thoughts you may have, such as taking a great vacation, achieving a long-term goal, skiing down a mountain, shopping — any pleasant experience, past or future. Keep these pleasant thoughts in your memory so you can easily bring them into consciousness.

3. Focus on an unwanted thought.

Find a place where you'll be undisturbed for about 20 minutes. Sitting or lying comfortably, take some deep breaths and relax your body as much as you can. Close your eyes and select one of your unwanted thoughts. (Don't choose your most distressing thought at the beginning. You'll get to the tougher ones later.) Get into your distressing thought using all your senses — what it looks like, feels like, and so on. Hold onto that unwanted thought for a bit.

4. Yell "stop!"

Now (and this may sound a bit strange) yell out the word "stop." *At the same time,* picture a red-and-white hexagonal stop sign — you know, the kind you see on the street corner. Make your sign large and vivid.

5. Replace that thought.

Replace that unwanted thought with one of your pleasant thoughts. Mentally shift your attention to that positive image and feeling. Immerse yourself in this replacement thought, strengthening it with visual images, sounds, and maybe even smells and tastes (Thanksgiving dinner?).

6. Repeat this process.

Do this again with the same unwanted thought. Then try it with another unwanted thought. If your pleasant replacement thought loses some of its potency, use one of your others. After you get better at this, stop yelling "stop" and only yell the word in your head. You're now ready to put this into practice in real life.

The image of the sign and the vocal or silent "stop" will disrupt your thought sequence and temporarily put the unwanted thought out of your mind. Be warned, however: It probably will return, and you may have to repeat this sequence again. And again. If your stress-producing thought or image is strong, it may take many repetitions of this technique to weaken or eliminate it. Stick with it.

Snapping out of it

A variation of the thought-stopping technique that has proved useful for many people is to use a rubber band to help interrupt a distressing thought. Simply take an ordinary rubber band and put it around your wrist. Now, whenever you notice an intrusive or unwanted thought crowding your thinking, pull the elastic and let it snap your wrist. This shouldn't be painful — just a sharp reminder that you want this distressing thought to go. Use your mental stop sign and remember to replace your unwanted thought with something more pleasant.

One way of enhancing this "stop" technique is to combine it with a breathing technique. It works like this. Instead of replacing your unwanted thought with a pleasant one, focus instead on your breathing. Take some slow, deep breaths and begin counting your exhaled breaths, forward from one to ten and then backward from ten to one. Repeat this process every time you encounter those unwanted, distressing thoughts.

Distracting Yourself

Often your thinking heads south and your worries and fears escalate when you have too much free, unfocused time. You may find something to worry about no matter what's going on in your life. It seems that as soon as one stressful situation is resolved, you find something else to be distressed about. Perhaps the simplest way to calm your mind is to distract yourself by focusing on some other thought, interest, activity, that holds and redirects your attention. This idea may sound obvious, but you'd be surprised how often people overlook this option. Psychologists know that concentrating on two things at the same time is very hard. Therefore, if your mind is flooded with distressing thoughts, change course. Find something else to think about. Just like the "pink elephant" challenge I mentioned earlier in this chapter, you can eliminate a negative image by replacing it with another — say "white polar bears." Every time a worrisome, undesired image or thought presents itself, distract yourself with some other, more positive thought or activity. Here are some suggested thought and involvements to consider:

- ✔ Recall something in your life you're grateful for.
- ✔ Remember something good that happened to you.
- ✔ Think of something you're looking forward to.
- ✔ Go to the gym.
- ✔ Read a book, newspaper, or magazine.

✔ Watch some television.

✔ Go to a movie.

✔ Talk to a friend.

✔ Work or play on your computer.

✔ Play a sport.

✔ Immerse yourself in some project or hobby.

✔ Listen to some favorite music.

✔ Work in the garden.

Jumping into any of these thoughts or activities doesn't mean that you're eliminating or changing your stressful situation (more direct approaches in other chapters will help you do just that), but it can pull you out of your ruminations, worries, and upsets until you come up with a longer-term strategy.

Like everything else in life, you can overdo distraction. Vegging, zoning out, or losing yourself in some pleasurable activity can be relaxing and provide some balance to other parts of your stressful life. Too much distraction, however, may not be better. Spending hours watching TV, playing a computer game, or browsing online may be distracting, but you may be missing out on other more rewarding experiences. Go for balance.

Using Your Imagination

One of the best ways to calm your mind and stop those unwanted, persistent worries is to use your imagination. If you can replace that stress-producing thought or image with one that is relaxing, chances are you'll feel much better. Here's how:

1. **Find a place where you won't be disturbed for a few minutes and get comfortable, either sitting in a favorite chair or lying down.**

2. **Think of an image — a place, a scene, or a memory — that relaxes you.**

   Figure 5-1 shows an example.

   Use all of your senses to bring that imagined scene to life. Ask yourself: What do I see? What can I hear? What can I smell? What can I feel?

3. **Let yourself become completely immersed in your image, allowing it to relax you completely.**

Figure 5-1:
Isn't this
relaxing?

Illustration by Pam Tanzey

"Sounds good," you say, "but what is my relaxing image?" Try taking one of these mental vacations (airfare included):

✔ **The Caribbean package:** Imagine that you're on the beach of a Caribbean isle. The weather is perfect. Lying on the cool sand, you feel the warm breeze caress your body. You hear the lapping of the ocean waves on the shore and the tropical birds chirping in the palms. You're slowly sipping a piña colada. You can smell your coconut-scented suntan lotion. You feel wonderful. You're relaxed. Your mind is totally at peace.

✔ **The pool package:** You're lying in a large inflatable raft, floating blissfully in a beautiful swimming pool. The day is perfect. The sky is a deep blue, and the sun is warming your relaxed body. You feel the gentle rocking of the raft in the water. You hear the soothing voice of the waiter announcing a buffet lunch in half an hour. You're content. You could lie here forever (at least until they serve that buffet).

✔ **The winter wonderland package:** Picture yourself in a small cabin in Vermont. (If your tastes lean to the more extravagant, switch the scene to Aspen or Gstaad — the cost is the same no matter where you go.) You're snowed in, but that's fine because you don't have to be anywhere and no one needs to contact you. Also, you're not alone — a favorite person is with you, and you're both lying in front of a crackling fire. Soft music is playing in the background. You're sipping hot toddies, mulled wine, or champagne.

> ✔ **A pleasing memory:** Picture a memory, possibly from your childhood or from a more recent time, that you find particularly happy and satisfying. It could be a vacation long ago, a birthday party you loved, or time spent frolicking with a childhood pet.

None of these examples do it for you? Then come up with your own personal relaxation image. You might try one of these:

> ✔ Soaking in a hot, soapy bath . . . soft music . . . candlelight . . .
>
> ✔ Walking in a quiet forest . . . birds chirping . . . leaves rustling . . .
>
> ✔ Lying under a tree in the park . . . warm breezes . . . more chirping . . .
>
> ✔ In your most comfortable chair . . . reading a great book . . . no chirping . . .

 What you see and hear usually dominates your imagination. But don't forget your senses of touch, taste, and smell. By adding these sensual dimensions, you can enrich your images and make them more involving. Feel the sand between your toes; smell the freshly brewed coffee; taste the salt in the air.

Making Things Move

Your image need not be a static scene. It can change and move. You may, for example:

> ✔ Imagine a sports event that you enjoy. It could be a baseball game that you attended. Or make one up. Mentally follow the plays as you work your way through the innings. Not a baseball fan? Try imagining a tennis match.
>
> ✔ Try replaying favorite movies in your mind, visualizing different scenes and filling in bits of dialogue. Scenic movies work wonderfully.
>
> ✔ Remember the details of a trip you've taken and retrace your journey from place to place.

This guided imagery, as it's called, can help keep you focused and interested in your image and ensure that unwanted, intrusive thoughts stay out of the picture.

What, Me Worry?

Worrying is one of the major ways your mind stays revved and keeps you stressed. You may find yourself worrying during the day or at three in the morning when you'd rather be sleeping. You may worry about a relationship or how you're going to come up with the money to pay for all the things you charged this month. Whatever your worry, it may be keeping your mind running a mile a minute. Turning off these worries warrants a whole chapter by itself — Chapter 12. It provides you with a number of effective techniques and strategies that can help you reduce and control those distressing worries. However, here are two simple strategies that should give you some stress relief and reduce your level of worrying.

Scheduling your worries

Sometimes your worries cry out for a solution. You can't leave them be. Distraction or evasion may provide some temporary relief, but they aren't the answer. These may be real problems or issues that need to be resolved: How are you going to get a better job? How can you help your child be happier at school? How do you tell your significant other that you want to break up? Trying to resolve these stressors in the moment may not be a good idea for at least two reasons:

- It's 3 a.m. and you need your sleep.
- You're too stressed, and your thinking is muddled and distorted.

One solution is to schedule a time when you can problem solve and figure out what to do. It may be "tomorrow morning at breakfast" or "this weekend when I'm at the gym." Rita, for example, is ruminating endlessly but getting nowhere, trying to figure out how to tell her manager that she's bored with what she's doing and wants a change. She schedules a morning meeting with herself at a coffee shop. At the "meeting," she puts down on paper some thoughts about what she wants to say. She rehearses how she will present her ideas. Her thinking is clearer, more focused, and less emotional than it would have been at 3 a.m. or at the end of another long, frustrating day at work.

Blowing up your worries

Sometimes humor can help you diffuse a worry. It can help you gain perspective and look at your worry at a distance. For example, suppose you're worried that you may say something dumb at a meeting. "OMG," you're thinking, "this is awful!" You ruminate, over-worry, and cause yourself more grief than is appropriate.

Instead, try blowing up the consequences:

"OMG, they'll be laughing at me forever! I'll be the office joke! Posters of me will be plastered in the kitchen. Every year they'll set aside a special day memorializing my gaff!"

I don't think so.

Striking up the band (or better yet, the string quartet)

As playwright William Congreve observed, music has charms to soothe the savage breast. He was right, though he could have added the savage leg, arm, jaw, and others parts of the human anatomy. Music therapists know that listening to music can result in significant physiological changes in your body: Your heart rate drops, your breathing slows, and your blood pressure lowers. But not all music does the trick. Some music can upset you, making you more stressed. (Think of that Metallica groupie living upstairs.) Other music may delight you but still not have a calming effect.

Go for Baroque

Following is a short list of field-tested composers and compositions (Baroque and otherwise) that should slow your pulse.

- ✔ **Bach:** The slower second movements are particularly appropriate for relaxation. "Air on the G String" is a real calmer.
- ✔ **Handel:** *Water Music.*
- ✔ **Chopin:** *Nocturnes.*
- ✔ **Schubert:** *Symphony No. 8 in B Minor.*
- ✔ **Pachelbel:** *Canon.*
- ✔ **Albinoni:** *Adagio in G Minor.*
- ✔ **Mozart:** *Piano Concerto No. 21.*
- ✔ **Beethoven:** *Symphony No. 6*, also known as the *Pastoral Symphony.*
- ✔ **Elgar:** *Salut d'Amour.*

Not a fan of the classics?

Of course, relaxing music need not all be classical. Bach and Mozart probably aren't as effective as Charles Mingus if you're a jazz fan. Other forms of music can be incredibly soothing. Many of the New Age recordings work nicely.

No one piece of music works for everyone. Experiment. Find what relaxes you. Listen in your car while commuting, in bed before going to sleep, and in your favorite chair in your favorite room. Headphones and a personal music player allow you to take your music — and a state of relaxation — wherever you go.

Visiting the rain forest

Some years ago, I was vacationing by the ocean, and as I was lolling by the water, I was transfixed by the soothing sounds of the waves rhythmically caressing the shore. Gee, I thought, wouldn't it be nice if I could have this sound lull me to sleep in my home in the city? Well, I can, and so can you.

These days, electronic sound machines can reproduce virtually any sound you can imagine. These machines cost dramatically less than they did just a few years ago and are also available as apps on your laptop or smartphone. So if, like me, you like the sounds of waves, no sweat. Or how about a tropical rain forest? Perhaps you like to be soothed by the sound of rain on a roof, a gurgling brook, or a beating heart. Your choice.

Using some common scents

Your ears aren't the only road to mental relaxation. Your nose can work, as well. People have been using scents to relieve stress and tension for centuries. An aroma can elicit feelings of calm and serenity. In fact, a school of therapy called *aromatherapy,* a complementary and alternative treatment to medicine, is devoted to using your sense of smell as a vehicle for emotional change.

Studies carried out by Alan Hirsch, M.D., neurological director of the Smell and Taste Treatment and Research Foundation in Chicago, suggest that there is a connection between smell and mood: Your mood may have a biological basis.

Dr. Hirsch found that the part of the brain that registers smell may be biologically linked to the part of the brain that registers emotion. Certainly, the right scent can relax you and put you in a better mood. Here are some easy-to-find, soul-satisfying smells you may want to consider:

- A bowl of green apples on your table
- Suntan lotion
- Vanilla extract
- Freshly baked just-about-anything

    ✔ Soaps, hand creams, bath oils, perfumes, and aftershave

    ✔ Freshly brewed coffee

Light up

Candles can be a wonderful addition to your repertoire of stress-reducing devices. A burning candle connotes romance, warmth, peace, and a sense of tranquility. The flickering of the flame can be hypnotic. Burning scented candles only adds to the effect. Which scent to use depends upon what you find most pleasant and appealing. Vanilla and floral fragrances tend to be most relaxing. Often these aromas recall pleasant memories of childhood. And just think of the money you can save on your electric bill.

Mix your own aroma cocktail

If you have no time to bake bread or perk coffee, try concocting your own stress-reducing aroma by using commercially available oils. "Essential oils" and "natural oils" tend to produce better therapeutic benefits, but synthetic oils are less costly. You can buy these pleasing fragrances from a number of shops or mail-order places. You can find essential oils in gourmet shops or at craft stores at a price far less than in a more upscale boutique or spa. If you're in a do-it-yourself mood, you can find books at your local library that show you how to derive essential oils from flowers. Some of the more common oils used to induce a relaxed, calm state are lavender, rose, jasmine, chamomile, orange blossom, vanilla, bergamot, geranium, and sandalwood. Often, you can combine oils to produce a new, relaxing aroma.

Some oils can be inhaled directly, while others are better when added to your bath. Certain oils can be applied directly to your body, but some oils act as irritants for some people. Certain oils should be avoided during pregnancy. It's best to get some knowledgeable advice before you begin experimenting. You can consult *Aromatherapy For Dummies*, by Kathi Keville (Wiley). In addition, the National Association for Holistic Aromatherapy in Raleigh, North Carolina, can help you with questions about which oils to use and how to use them, and how to find a professional aromatherapist in your area.

The scent of a memory

A scent can trigger early memories. There appears to be some link in our brains between memory and smell. The trick, of course, is to find the smell that triggers a pleasant, relaxing memory. One of my very favorite smells is the one that comes from a dryer vent when clothes are drying, because I spent many happy hours in my aunt's laundry as a child. For most people, that smell just means work. Freshly mown grass tends to recall my days as a child playing in front of the house. Try to harness this phenomenon by discovering scents that trigger happy memories for you.

Do Nothing: Meditation Is Good for You

Of all the ways to relax, probably the one that evokes the most suspicion is meditation. When you think of meditation, chances are you conjure up images of bearded gents in saffron robes sitting in the lotus position. You feel that this wouldn't go over well at the office. It's not surprising that you may be a wee bit leery about jumping in and joining the movement. Yet, it's likely that you have *already* meditated. You may not have been aware that you were doing so, but at those times when your mind becomes calm, uncluttered, and focused, and you're not processing your day or thinking about a million things — you're doing something that closely resembles meditating.

The sections that follow present meditation as an important stress-reducing tool that fits nicely in your stress toolbox.

East comes West

People in the East — especially those who subscribe to certain religious or philosophical beliefs — have been practicing meditation for literally thousands of years. These practitioners use meditation as a means to search for and find inner peace, enlightenment, and harmony with the universe.

Meditation has not received such ready acceptance in the western world, however. Westerners have tended to view meditation as foreign and remote, and sometimes as religious zealotry. In the '60s, when the Maharishi — a then-popular guru — came along, westerners began to associate meditation with a somewhat wild fringe group of society.

Researchers have been aware of the positive effects of meditation for some time now. Herbert Benson, M.D., of the Benson-Henry Institute for Mind-Body Medicine at Massachusetts General Hospital, was one of the first to adapt and introduce meditation to broader western audiences. Since then, the principles and practice of meditation have enjoyed widespread acceptance and enthusiasm in the West.

"What can meditation do for me, anyway?"

The benefits of meditation are wide and varied. You'll notice many of those benefits immediately, but others are less obvious, affecting you in more subtle ways. Most importantly, meditation can help you relax your mind and body and turn off your inner thoughts. Meditating can help you feel less stressed; your body will be less tense, and your mind will be calmer. With some practice, after meditating you should feel rested, renewed, and recharged. Meditation allows you to develop greater control over your thoughts, worries, and anxieties. It's a skill that, once mastered, can serve you well throughout your life.

But it's harder than it looks

Meditating for a short period of time (like a minute) is pretty do-able. The challenge is being able to meditate for longer periods of time. Westerners in particular have some built-in resistance to meditating. You may share some of the following traits:

✔ **Westerners like to be busy:** You probably like to be active and do things, rather than be passive and let things happen to you. Lengthy periods of immobility tend to elicit feelings of boredom and restlessness.

✔ **Westerners need scorecards:** You may feel a need to evaluate yourself on how well you're doing. If, after a brief period of practice, you find that you're doing well, you may rate yourself — and your performance — accordingly. One of the keys to meditation is not rating yourself — good or bad.

None of this should discourage you or deter you from practicing your meditative skills. No, you won't become an accomplished meditator in 12 minutes. However, you may be surprised at how quickly you begin to see positive results. I repeat: Stick with it. The results are well worth it.

Preparing to meditate

This section presents a step-by-step guide to preparing for meditation. Remember that there are many ways of meditating. These suggestions help you prepare for different types of meditation, especially the exercises featured in this chapter.

1. **Find a quiet place where you won't be disturbed for a while.**

   No telephone, no beeper, no TV — nothing.

2. **Find a comfortable sitting position, like the one shown in Figure 5-2.**

   Contorting yourself into some yogi-like, snake-charmer squat (albeit impressive) may not be the best way to start meditating. Remember that you're going to remain in one position for fifteen to twenty minutes.

Figure 5-2:
Sitting in
a relaxed,
comfortable
position.

Illustration by Pam Tanzey

3. **Focus on a sound, word, sensation, image, object, or thought.**

4. **Maintain your focus and adopt a passive, accepting attitude.**

   When you're focusing in meditation, intrusive thoughts or images may enter your mind and distract you. When those thoughts occur, notice them, accept the fact that they're there, and then let them go: No getting upset, no annoyance, no self-rebuke.

Try not to get hung up on the timing. Meditate for about fifteen or twenty minutes. If you want to meditate longer, fine. If you find you're becoming uncomfortable, you can stop and try it again another time. Remember, this is a non-pressured, non-ego-involved exercise.

After you have everything in place, you're ready to begin meditating. Although you have many forms of meditation to choose from, the most common ones are breath-counting meditation and meditation with a mantra. The following sections deal with each type.

Meditative breathing

Breath-counting meditation builds on the controlled breathing techniques and exercises that I discuss in the previous chapter. (For more information on getting your lungs in shape for meditating, check out Chapter 4.) Breath-counting meditation is one of the most basic and commonly used forms of meditation. Here's what to do:

1. **Sit comfortably.**

   You can position yourself on the floor or in a chair. Keep your back straight and your head up. Dress comfortably, as well — no tight shoes, belt, necktie, underpants, bra, or anything else that constricts you.

2. **Close your eyes and scan for tension.**

   Scan your body for any tension by using the one-minute body-scan technique I describe in Chapter 4, and then let go of any tension that you find.

3. **Begin to breathe in a relaxed way.**

   Relax by taking some abdominal breaths (breathing using your diaphragm). Breathe slowly and deeply through your nose.

   To help you breathe in a relaxing manner, imagine a small balloon just under your belly button. As you inhale through your nostrils, imagine that balloon gently inflating; as you exhale through your nostrils, imagine the balloon slowly deflating.

4. **Focus on your breathing.**

   Your breathing now becomes the object of your focus. When you inhale, count this breath as "one."

   The next time you inhale is two, and so forth until you reach ten. Then you start again at one. Count silently to yourself, and if you lose count, simply start back at one. If you lose count, don't worry — the number is merely something to focus on. There's no right or wrong number here.

5. **If you find a distracting thought or image intruding, let it go and return to your count.**

   Continue this exercise for about 20 minutes, and — if you can — do this exercise twice a day.

Psst, looking for a good mantra?

The word mantra comes from Sanskrit: "man" means "to think," and "tra" means "to free." Often mantras take the form of one or two syllables, such as *om*, meaning "I am," or *soham*, meaning "I am that." Many teachers of meditation believe that your mantra should have personal meaning.

In *The Relaxation Response*, cardiologist and researcher Herbert Benson says that a personal mantra isn't necessary for successful meditation. In his teaching of meditative relaxation, Dr. Benson suggests using the word "one" as a mantra. That word has very little meaning for most of us and is therefore not terribly distracting. Your mantra can also be a soothing word, such as "peace," "love," or "calm." Whatever you come up with, choose a word or sound that has a relaxing feel for you.

If you want some additional information on mantras, and on meditation in general, take a look at *Meditation For Dummies,* 2nd Edition, by Stephan Bodian and Dean Ornish (Wiley).

Probably the most common complaint among beginning meditators is that their minds keep wandering off, especially at the beginning of a meditation. Even on those days when you face no major pressure or pending deadline, your mind can still come up with a million and one things to think about. That's normal. Expect it, and don't beat yourself up when it happens. Don't make this exercise into a test of your ability to concentrate. Getting good at focusing without undue distractions may take some time. Hang in there.

Meditating with a mantra

Probably the best known and most popular form of meditation is meditation using a mantra. A mantra is a sound or word that you repeat; it can help you focus your mind and avoid distractions. After you select your mantra (see the sidebar, "Psst, looking for a mantra?"), you're ready to put it to use:

1. **Sit quietly, either in a chair or on the floor as you did for the breathing meditation detailed in the preceding section.**

   Eliminate any distractions. Close your eyes and relax as much as you can.

2. **Start with some deep breathing and try to clear your mind of the day's hassle and worry.**

   Remember not to breathe with your chest alone. Breathe until you notice that you feel much more relaxed. (About a dozen breaths should do it.)

3. **Do a body scan to see where any residual tension may be hiding.**

4. **Focus on your breathing and begin to repeat your mantra to yourself, either repeating it silently or chanting it softly.**

   As you say your mantra, see the word in your head. Repeat your mantra over and over. Find a timing and rhythm that is comfortable for you. As before, if you find your concentration slipping, simply become aware of that fact and gently guide your mind back to your mantra.

   Do this exercise for about 20 minutes or so and try to squeeze in as many meditative sessions as you can in your week.

Finding time for mini-meditations

Someone once asked a meditation teacher, "How long should I meditate?" "For about 20 minutes," the wise man answered, quickly adding, "but five minutes of meditation you do is better than 20 minutes of meditation you plan on doing, but don't."

I recognize that you may not have 20 minutes twice a day to peacefully meditate in some quiet corner. And even if you have the time, you may find that your boss — who is not nearly as enlightened as you are — frowns on your meditative sessions. Fortunately, you can practice "abbreviated" forms of meditation — they can be as long or as short as the time you have available. You can "mini-meditate" when you find a few extra minutes, for example, during the following listed opportunities. (I don't advise meditating in your car, unless you're the passenger.)

✓ Sitting in traffic (if you're the passenger)

✓ Waiting for your doctor or dentist to see you

✓ Standing (for what seems like forever) in line

✓ Sitting in a boring meeting (where you don't have to present anything, and won't be asked questions)

✓ Riding the bus, subway, or taxicab

Hypnotize Yourself

When you think of hypnosis, two images probably come to mind. The first is from a B-grade movie where you see a Svengali-like doctor — usually deranged — dangling a pocket watch in the face of some innocent victim. The second is of a hypnotist on a stage with a dozen or so audience volunteers who are either dancing with brooms or clucking like chickens. Fortunately, neither image is accurate.

Actually, hypnosis is less mysterious and far more mundane than you may think. Hypnosis is totally safe, but, more importantly, it can be an effective way of helping you relax and cope with stress.

No, you won't be turned into a clucking chicken

Probably no other psychological technique for stress reduction is as misunderstood as hypnosis. Some things you need to know:

✓ You aren't asleep.

✓ You aren't unconscious.

✓ You won't lose control or be under someone's spell.

✓ You won't do anything that you don't want to do.

Hypnosis is simply a deeply focused state that makes you more acutely aware of suggestions and allows you to be more receptive to those suggestions.

Some people are more susceptible to hypnotic suggestion. For hypnosis to be as effective for you as possible, try to adopt a receptive, non-critical attitude. Don't fight the process. Just go with it. If you remain totally skeptical and resistant, not much is going to happen. Have an open mind.

Surprise! You've already been hypnotized

You may not realize it, but chances are you've been in a hypnotic trance many times before. We slip in and out of hypnotic states all the time. Remember those times when you were driving on the highway and it scarily dawned on you that you hadn't been paying attention to the road or your driving for the last five minutes? Or remember those times when you left the movie theater and realized that your attention was so glued to the screen that you had no idea who was sitting next to you or what was going on around you? Or when you were daydreaming, or just lost in thought? In each case, you were in a hypnotic trance.

The power of a trance

When you're in a trance, you're in a different mental state. You're still awake and in control, but your attention becomes narrow and incredibly focused. In this state, you're more receptive to any suggestions you may give yourself, or that a hypnotherapist may offer. You basically give yourself a shortcut to your subconscious. These suggestions can take many forms: cigarettes taste lousy, I'm growing taller day by day, I'm getting smarter, whatever. (Clearly some suggestions are more realistic than others.)

Some trances are deeper than others. In a light trance, you feel more relaxed and are able to respond to simple suggestions. In a heavier trance, you can choose not to respond to pain and even to forget what occurred during hypnosis. In what follows, my aim is to induce a light trance, which is all you need to achieve a peaceful state of deep relaxation.

Inducing a light trance

You can induce a hypnotic trance in many ways (even the dangling watch can work). Here is one of the simpler induction techniques I've found to be useful in reducing tension and stress.

1. **Find a comfortable position in a quiet, dimly lit room where you won't be interrupted.**

    Relax as much as possible. If you want, take off your shoes and loosen any tight clothing.

2. **Focus on an object across the room.**

    The object can be anything — a smudge on the wall, the corner of a picture, it really doesn't matter. Just choose an object that is above your normal line of sight so that you have to strain your eyeballs a bit looking up to see your spot.

3. **As you look at your spot, silently say to yourself,**

    > "My eyelids are becoming heavier and heavier."

    > "My eyelids feel as if heavy weights are pulling them down."

    > "Soon they will be so heavy they will close."

    Repeat these sentences to yourself about every 30 seconds.

4. **Focus on your eyelids.**

    Soon you'll notice that, indeed, your eyelids are beginning to feel heavier. Feel this heaviness deepen with time. Don't fight these sensations, just let them happen. Let your eyes close when you feel they want to close themselves.

5. **As your eyes begin to close, say to yourself, "Relax and let go."**

6. **When your eyes close, take in a deep breath through your nostrils and hold that breath for about ten seconds.**

7. **Slowly exhale through your slightly parted lips, making a "swooshing" sound.**

    At the same time, let your jaw drop and feel a wave of warmth and heaviness spread from the top of your head, down your body, all the way to your toes. Continue to breathe slowly and smoothly. As you exhale, silently say the word "calm," or some other relaxing word, to yourself. As you breathe, let the feelings of relaxation deepen for another few moments.

Going a little deeper

After you induce a light trance, you're ready to move into a deeper state of hypnosis.

1. **Take a deep breath and hold it for about ten seconds.**

Exhale slowly through your lips while saying the word "deeper" to yourself. Continue this process for several breaths more, saying the word "deeper" to yourself with every exhalation.

2. **Imagine that you're stepping onto a descending escalator, a long, slow escalator that will take you into a state of deeper relaxation.**

   As you begin your descent, silently say to yourself,

   "I am sinking slowly into a deeper state of relaxation."

3. **As you descend, count backward on each exhalation, from ten to one.**

   When you reach the bottom of the escalator, imagine that you're stepping off this escalator and onto a second descending escalator. As you imagine your descent, deepen your trance with each breath, again counting backward from ten to one.

4. **Continue to deepen your trance until you feel you have reached a comfortable level of relaxation.**

   You may need only one escalator ride, or you may need several. With practice, a deeper trance will come more easily and more quickly.

Get me out of this trance

Alright, you're now in a trance. You're feeling quite relaxed, and your mind is totally at peace. You can choose to remain in this relaxed state and simply enjoy the benefits of relaxation and calm. You can also give yourself a suggestion that can extend this relaxation beyond the trance state. Here's what to do:

Simply count slowly backward from five to one. Say to yourself beforehand,

"When I reach one, my eyes will open, and I will feel totally awake and refreshed."

As you count, notice your eyes beginning to flutter and partially open as you approach one.

These suggestions should help you overcome one or more of the possible roadblocks that may arise as you practice self-hypnosis:

✔ **Give yourself enough time to reach a trance state:** This process may take 15, 20, or even 25 minutes.

✔ **Don't ask yourself, "Am I hypnotized yet?":** This performance pressure only sets the process back. Don't force it or demand it; let it happen.

✔ **As you move into a trance, use the breathing and muscle-relaxation skills that I discuss in Chapter 4.** These techniques speed the hypnosis process and help you attain a greater level of relaxation.

For more information, consult a certified hypnotherapist who can show you how to use self-hypnosis to achieve benefits other than relaxation. Hypnosis has been shown to be effective in helping individuals overcome insomnia, smoking, overeating, and a variety of other problems and disorders.

Want Some Feedback? Go the High-Tech Route

Biofeedback is a fancy term that means letting you know (the feedback part) what your body is up to (the bio part). Of course, biofeedback is nothing new. Getting the results of a blood test, having your blood pressure taken, or getting an EKG at your doctor's office are all examples of medical biofeedback. However, these days, the term biofeedback is usually used for the electronic devices that measure your stress level or, more technically, your levels of physiological arousal.

Hard-wired to your own body

In the clinic or doctor's office, biofeedback is a wonderful tool that can tell you a lot about your stress and, more importantly, help you learn ways of reducing that stress. Depending on the biofeedback device used, it may measure your heart rate, body temperature, blood pressure, skin conductivity (sweating), levels of stomach acid, muscle tension, and even brain activity (see Figure 5-3). Each of these can be controlled to some extent, and working with biofeedback can be useful in controlling each of these functions.

Biofeedback is no substitute for learning the tools and techniques presented in these chapters. It can, however, help you use them more effectively. You may want to consult a certified biofeedback therapist who can work with you, showing you how biofeedback can help you relax and reduce your levels of mental and physical stress.

Many companies now make inexpensive home biofeedback trainers that you can purchase and use by themselves or hooked up to your computer. Again, a certified biofeedback therapist can tell you whom to contact.

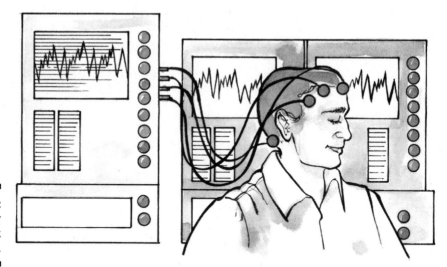

Illustration by Pam Tanzey

Figure 5-3:
Wired up for
biofeedback
readings.

Biofeedback (without the wires)

But what if you can't afford the time or money to use biofeedback equipment? Not to worry. You can come up with your own biofeedback tools. For example:

- ✔ **A watch with a second hand.** By taking your own pulse (on your neck or even your index finger), you get a measure of your heart rate, which varies according to your level of relaxation.

  Also, by counting the number of breaths you make in a fixed period of time, you have a measure of your rate of respiration. This should decrease as you become more relaxed.

- ✔ **A thermometer.** Holding the bulb of a thermometer between your fingers can give you a measure of your skin temperature. Relaxing your body should raise your skin temperature.

- ✔ **A stethoscope.** By counting heartbeats, you have a measure of your stress level. Lowering your stress should result in a lowered heart rate.

- ✔ **A pressure cuff.** These days, a home blood-pressure monitoring device isn't all that expensive. Lowering your stress and tension levels should result in lower blood-pressure readings.

- ✔ **A mirror.** The way you look can be a pretty good indicator of just how stressed you are. Furrowed brows, a clenched jaw, bags under your eyes — all can be signs of stress. Take a look!

Chapter 6

Cultivating Mindfulness

In This Chapter

▶ Understanding mindfulness

▶ Becoming more mindful in daily life

▶ Using mindfulness to reduce your stress

▶ Cultivating mindful acceptance

*W*e tend to think of stress management as a relatively new idea. Recall that the word "stress" has only lately come into our language. While people have always been stressed, most approaches to managing stress are fairly recent. But not all. Mindfulness is both a very old and a very new approach to managing your stress. The "old" part reminds us that people have been using mindful approaches for as long as they've had the ability to be aware of their thoughts and feelings. The "new" part reflects the growing integration of mindfulness with current models of emotional distress.

A wide and growing body of evidence supports mindfulness training as an effective way of managing stress. In the past decade, more and more professionals have come to see the value of a mindful approach to stress reduction, helping people reduce their levels of anxiety, worry, and upset. Mindfulness, in fact, has become an important, if not essential, element in any stress-management program.

This chapter helps you understand what being mindful really means and shows you how it can play an important role in helping you manage your stress.

Understanding Mindfulness

The origins of mindfulness can be traced back to Hindu and Buddhist writings. The word itself is a translation of the ancient East Indian word *sati,* meaning "awareness," and Buddha considered it to be an important factor on the path to enlightenment. The concept of awareness remains an important part of our understanding of how a mindful approach to life can help us manage our stress.

In this section, I provide you with a basic explanation of what mindfulness is and then discuss what mindfulness isn't.

Defining mindfulness

Mindfulness isn't the easiest concept to grasp or define. In part this reflects its long connection with Buddhism and other early spiritual traditions, as well as its association with the practice of meditation. Mindfulness can mean different things to different people.

Simply put, mindfulness is about being fully aware in the present moment. Being mindful means attending to your immediate experience; detaching from your thoughts and feelings; viewing them with a sense of openness, curiosity, and compassion; and accepting them without judgment.

The following components are necessary to become more mindful:

- **Maintaining awareness:** This means you're able to step out of your usual routines, worries, and fears and be conscious of what's happening in your life. You become an impartial observer both to your inner world — your thoughts, feelings, and bodily sensations — and to what's happening in the outside world.

- **Paying attention:** Attention involves focused awareness. To be mindful, it's important that you pay attention. Mastering mindfulness means training yourself to sustain your focus on whatever becomes the object of your attention.

- **Remembering:** You have to remember to be mindful — to control your awareness and attention. In fact, the word "remember" comes from the Latin *re* meaning "again" and *memorari* meaning "be mindful of."

- **Being in the moment:** Being in the present is an important concept in practicing mindfulness. You need to be aware of specific aspects of your world just as it is right now.

- **Being non-judgmental:** Our minds are hard-wired to make judgments. We make judgments all the time, both consciously and unconsciously. It certainly worked for humans in their cave days, when not making a judgment could result in becoming the entrée for a hungry stalker. But letting go of judgments frees you from your history, your expectations, and your distorted thinking. Rather than looking at your world with judgmental constructs, such as good-bad, right-wrong, like-dislike, and so on, you can begin looking at your world more openly and with more acceptance.

- ✔ **Being non-reactive:** Reacting implies an immediacy of response that most often reflects pre-existing judgments, historical patterns, and emotional biases. Reactions are usually automatic. *Responding*, however, is a more deliberate and controlled action. It gives you more options.

- ✔ **Practicing compassion:** When you practice compassion, not only are your mental processes changed but you also become more caring. Freed from negative judgments and biases, you can let go of your critical self, and you become kinder, gentler, and warmer.

Much of your stress comes from a lack of awareness. Your mind is constantly processing thoughts, feelings, sensations, and behaviors that have happened in the past or may happen in the future. You can easily get overwhelmed by all the activity and become a prisoner of your worries, fears, angers, and upsets. While much of this processing is conscious, much of your thinking and feeling is automatic. If you can step back and gain more awareness of what your mind is doing, you can cope with your stress more effectively. Mindfulness is a valuable way of doing just that.

Dispelling myths about mindfulness

- ✔ **Mindfulness is hard to learn:** Actually, cultivating mindfulness is like acquiring many of the other abilities you have learned, such as driving, operating your computer, learning a second language, or playing an instrument. It takes some time, effort, and practice. In the same way, time, effort, and practice are needed to make mindfulness an effective tool in your stress-management arsenal.

- ✔ **It's just a New Age fad:** In fact, an impressive and growing body of research supports mindfulness as an important approach to stress management.

- ✔ **Mindfulness is just about relaxation:** Mindfulness *can* result in a relaxed state, but that isn't its main goal.

- ✔ **Mindfulness is the same as meditation:** While you can meditate mindfully, a major objective of mindfulness is being in the world and coping with others less stressfully.

- ✔ **Mindfulness is just distraction:** Not really. True, you may be distracted by some of the mindfulness training exercises, but that definitely isn't the goal. In fact, mindfulness gives you the ability to step back from your stressor but attend to it and experience your stress in a different way.

- ✔ **Mindfulness is just positive thinking:** Mindfulness is more about giving up any kind of evaluative thinking, positive or negative.

- ✔ **It's like a religion or cult:** Nope. Mindfulness can be practiced without any connection to a religious group or sect, or any body of beliefs.

Figuring out whether mindfulness is right for you

You may be thinking, "I don't know. This mindfulness stuff is a little too New Age for me. I'm not a sit-in-a-corner, cross-my-legs-and-stare-at-my-navel kinda person. I'm sure it works wonders for many people, but it's not my style. I get bored pretty quickly. Maybe I'm less spiritual or not evolved enough, but it all sounds a little cultish to me. I'm not sure I have the patience to do the exercises you're going to want me to do. What if I just skip all this?"

If you're thinking that, you're not alone. Many years ago, when I began exploring ways of reducing stress, I too was wary of the more meditative approaches that seemed to be anchored in early religious or philosophical teachings. They seemed a bit alien and mystical. But, as I eventually learned, a better way to look at mindfulness is to view it as a tool that can help you focus your attention and awareness — and eventually free you from being an unwilling victim of your negative and automatic thinking. Mindfulness gives you options. It isn't just meditation. It's a highly practical stress-reducing tool that can be integrated into other parts of a more complete stress-management program.

Yes, I will ask you to try some simple meditative exercises. I'll ask you to sit in a chair and focus on your breathing, and I'll ask you to eat something mindfully. These and other such exercises are valuable ways of training yourself to turn off the worries and concerns filling your mind. But mindfulness is much more than this. So, no, you don't need to light up some incense, join a cult, or become more religious. You just need to put aside your misconceptions and give this approach a real try.

Recognizing Mindlessness

The polar opposite of mindfulness, *mindlessness* is a state of mind where you are largely unaware of what you're thinking, feeling, and doing. It's like being on a plane running on auto-pilot mode. The plane flies automatically, and for the most part the system works well, until the plane runs into trouble. The problem is the "running into trouble" part. When people run on auto-pilot, they create lots of opportunities for that trouble to take the form of excessive stress.

Auto-pilot: The good, the bad, and the really bad

Many times in your day, you'll find that you too are running on auto-pilot. Recall those times when you were driving on the highway and realized that you hadn't been paying the slightest bit of attention to the road or your driving but had instead been daydreaming about something else. Or all those mornings when you got dressed, washed up, and left your bedroom, paying almost no attention to what you were doing. (One day I showed up at my office wearing unmatched shoes.) You and I were running on auto-pilot. When you're in auto-pilot mode, you're at the mercy of unfocused attention, often subconscious, which takes your thoughts, feelings, and actions where they want to go, but not necessarily where you want them to go. You're not mindful; you're mindless.

The good

Not all auto-pilot behavior is bad. Imagine your day if you couldn't remember how to do even the most routine tasks. Suppose you needed an instruction manual to guide you through your day. Getting dressed in the morning, preparing breakfast, figuring out how to get to work, driving your car — every routine would demand your full awareness and attention. *"Put your socks on before your shoes." "Push down on the gas pedal on your right and use the brake to the left if you have to stop."* It would be exhausting! Mindlessness, it appears, has its place in our lives. That's the good part.

The bad

But here's the bad part about running on auto-pilot. You can wind up spending most of your life on auto-pilot, missing out on wonderful aspects of life that make it so much more meaningful. I'm reminded of those many car trips with our kids and our constant unheeded nagging, such as "Wow, look at the color of those leaves!" or "Just look at that sunset!" Too much auto-pilot can restrict your experiences and your appreciation of the world around you. Your life can feel boring and routine. You get short-changed.

The really bad

Here's the really bad part. When you're on auto-pilot, your thoughts, feelings, and behaviors can become distorted and stress-producing. In auto-pilot mode, much of your inner experience can take the form of ruminating, over-thinking, exaggerating, fearfully anticipating, feeling anxious and upset, overreacting, and avoiding — to mention but a few of the stress-producing traps you can fall into. Stress thrives in a mindless environment.

Mindless multi-tasking

Multi-tasking may seem like an efficient way to get a lot accomplished. After all, you can write that history paper, text a friend, listen to music, and check out your favorite social-media site all at the same time. So, you may ask, what's the problem? There are downsides. The person who drives on the highway and simultaneously figures out how to end his current relationship may be using his time incredibly efficiently, but he may not be attending to what is happening on the road. His attention is stretched far too thin, and when this happens he is running on auto-pilot. Multi-tasking increases your stress levels. You have too many balls in the air, with insufficient attention paid to any one ball.

The negative consequences abound. Your performance may suffer, and you may retain information poorly. People close to you may feel hurt and neglected, and you may feel overwhelmed. What might first seem like the perfect antidote to inefficiency may, in the final analysis, contribute to more inefficiency.

The dangers of mindless thinking

Our minds are a thought factory. Always busy, always active. Not only do we think all the time, we have feelings, and we act and react all the time. And though we have all these internal experiences, we often aren't consciously aware of them. They're just there. We can get locked into our automatic thoughts.

The relationship between our thoughts, feelings, and actions is a close one. To put it most simply, we feel the way we think. Feelings of stress are no exception. If we think in distorted, unrealistic ways, we wind up feeling much more stressed than we have to. Whenever we are in auto-pilot mode — unaware of what we are thinking, feeling, or doing — we are at the mercy of those automatic experiences. And often, that's not good. The following sections explain why.

Your thoughts are not facts

Generally, it's a good idea to listen to yourself. One of the advantages of being higher on the evolutionary scale is having the ability to think. Our thoughts allow us to make plans, solve problems, make decisions, and figure out how much to tip the waiter. Sometimes, though, it's not a good idea to listen to yourself. Your thoughts can create unnecessary worry, anguish, upset, anger, resentment, guilt, and depression, to mention but a few distressing emotions.

Sometimes you give your thoughts and feelings too much power. A thought comes to mind, and you feel compelled to listen to that thought and automatically assume the thought is a valid one. You believe that your thoughts tell you the truth. Well, sometimes yes and sometimes no. As I discuss in Chapter 10, a good deal of your stress-producing thinking is not an accurate reflection of the world. Thinking can be irrational, overly emotional, and at times distorted. Some examples:

"I'm a loser!"

"I can't stand being in traffic!"

"I'll never meet anybody!"

"Nobody likes me!"

"People should treat me fairly!"

"People are just out for themselves!"

While there may be a grain of truth in some of these statements, they are, for the most part, distortions or biased perceptions. (Chapter 10 makes all of this a lot more clear.)

Your feelings aren't facts, either

Many times when you feel a certain way, you believe "If I'm feeling this way (such as angry, upset, or anxious), I should listen to these emotions, believe what these feelings are telling me, and act on them." So when Lucy's friend shows up late for lunch, Lucy is angry and lets her friend know that she is angry — in no uncertain terms and in a very loud voice. The friend has an understandable reason for being late, but Lucy still feels quite angry. Her feelings of anger tell her that her feelings are the right feelings to have. She assumes that her feelings accurately reflect the appropriateness of her emotional response. She tunes into her feelings, believes them, and acts upon them.

Feelings come and go. So do the bodily sensations that can come with feelings. We can be in a bad mood, be angry, feel down, and still realize that at some point these feelings will pass. In some ways, it's easier to accept our emotions as transient but not always trustworthy. We may not be able to escape the grip of the emotion, but often the wiser observer within us says, "Don't trust this feeling!" If we let our thoughts and feelings take over, they can define us. They can lock us into a worldview that is narrow and restricted. Bodily sensations can have the same effect. Tightness in the chest, rapid breathing, heart palpitations, lumps in the throat, and other bodily sensations can be mistaken as valid reflections of the importance and validity of the situations and events we encounter.

Beautiful mindfulness

Several years ago I saw a movie called *A Beautiful Mind*, which is based on a real-life story of a man diagnosed with paranoid schizophrenia. The story describes the agonizing consequences of his delusional episodes on himself and his family. I found it especially interesting to watch his growing awareness that his disturbing hallucinations were just that — hallucinations. He came to realize that he was seeing things that, well, weren't there. He was able to step back and reject his perceptions as truth. He was, to a large extent, freed from the power of his misperceptions, and he could respond to them in more adaptive ways. In short, he became more mindful.

Your "fused" thinking

Whenever you believe that your thoughts and feelings are "the truth," you give them an enormous amount of power. You can get stuck in your world of thoughts and feelings and have trouble getting out. You can become *fused* with your thoughts and feelings. You have no psychological distance. You are too close to your inner experiences, and you let them run the show. Because you're on auto-pilot, you're not aware of what you're thinking or feeling. You truly believe that all of your thinking and feeling is sensible and should be listened to. The following example gives you a taste of what fused thinking feels like.

Imagine you're in a theater watching a movie. The movie starts out pretty well, with lots of action, good acting, and an interesting plot. You're glued to the screen. The guy next to you could be carving a pumpkin, but you wouldn't notice. You and the movie are fused. After about an hour, you realize that the story has run out of gas. The love affair between the two main characters just doesn't work for you. And ten shots with a six-shooter? Give me a break! You mentally step back, and rather than being fused with the movie, you're now thinking *about* the movie. You've shifted your attention. You're aware of the movie as something "out there." You've detached, and you're a step closer to becoming more mindful.

Understanding How Mindfulness Can Help Reduce Your Stress

Our world can be a source of contentment, happiness, and even, at times, joy. Alas, this same world can be uncertain, unpredictable, and distressing. Our world seems to be in turmoil: political upheaval, terrorism, climate change, the economy, personal relationships, our finances, our health . . . I could go on. Your life has no shortage of stressors. You need a tool that helps you slow down your thoughts, feelings, and reactions to this stressful world. In other words, you need a pause button. That's where mindfulness comes in. The following are some ways that mindfulness can help you manage your stress.

- ✔ **Creating calm and relaxation:** Relaxing your body and quieting your mind aren't the primary goals of mindfulness, but they can be a welcome and valuable by-product. Mindful meditation can help you escape your stressful thoughts and feelings by learning to attend to a breath, an image, or a relaxing thought. In Chapter 5, I discuss how mindful meditation can help you calm your mind. By focusing on your breathing, a sensation, or an object, you can create your own quieter place, undisturbed by the fears, worries, and distractions that punctuate your day. If you're interested in exploring the benefits of mindful meditation as a relaxation tool, take a look at Chapter 5.

- ✔ **Living in the present:** Mindfulness can give you an appreciation of the richness that life has to offer by teaching you to notice the fullness of your experience. It shows you how to live more fully in the present. Too often, you have one foot in the past and the other in the future, and as a result you miss out on the present. You lose any appreciation of what's happening to you right now. You get lost in rumination, worry, and fear. Your thoughts, feelings, and actions become automatic, reactive, and distressing, and your life becomes less authentic and less meaningful. But mindfulness can pull you out of auto-pilot and give you greater awareness of and appreciation for the life you want to live.

- ✔ **Coping with stressors:** Mindfulness can function in more direct ways, giving you an important tool to cope with specific stressors and stress reactions. Becoming mindful can help you detach from your stressful world and observe it without judgment, criticism, or resistance. You can learn to step back and view your thoughts, emotions, and behaviors as by-products of an overactive and, at times, distorting mind. This gives you coping options: You can become aware of these thoughts, feelings, and behaviors without fighting them or feeding them, and, if you choose, you can more calmly and effectively explore avenues of change.

It really works

Research shows that mindfulness can result in a significant reduction in stress levels. Dr. Jon Kabat-Zinn, at the Center for Mindfulness in Medicine, Health Care, and Society, in Worcester, Massachusetts, followed a group of more than 6,000 patients presenting a variety of stress-related conditions and disorders. He found that when patients followed an eight-week program of mindfulness training, their stress-related symptoms decreased and their conditions improved. Kabat-Zinn also found that following the mindfulness program helped people reduce their anxiety levels and lessen the severity of depressive episodes. More importantly, these changes were maintained on follow-up visits.

The more specific uses and benefits of mindfulness are described more fully later in the chapter. For now, here's a simple exercise that will take only a moment or two and will give you a sense of what mindfulness is like. Read the following instructions and then close the book and do the exercise:

1. **Stop whatever else you're doing, take a deep breath, and try to become more relaxed.**

2. **Now, take this book in both of your hands.**

   Try to become aware of the book as if it's the first time you've ever seen a book. Become curious, wanting to know more about this thing called a book. Holding it in your hands, gently focus all of your attention on the book.

3. **Focus on the weight of the book in your hands.**

   Does it feel light or heavy?

4. **Notice the texture of the paper by rubbing your fingers over a page.**

   Does it feel totally smooth, or can you feel some roughness?

5. **Without reading the text, pay attention to the print — the types of fonts used, the size of the print, and the word patterns.**

6. **Look at the cover of the book and notice the different colors and designs.**

   Notice the way light is reflected on the cover. Now feel the cover of the book. Running your fingers over the cover, notice its glossy smoothness.

This exercise seems so simple that you may miss what's happening. What you discover is that you're attending to something in a way you normally wouldn't. Hopefully you were able to slow yourself down and take your time as you became an observer, noticing, without any judgments, a very small piece of your experience. There was no analysis, no over-thinking, just observation. Your awareness was focused; you were in the moment. This ability allows you to detach from your world of automatic thinking, feeling, and behaving. This detachment puts you in an accepting, non-judgmental frame of mind, where you choose to simply be. You can use this frame of mind as a base for exploring better ways of coping with your stress.

Developing the Skills of Mindfulness

As with mastering any worthwhile skill, you sometimes have to practice. The word "practice" can have multiple meanings. In one way, it means putting to use or applying, as in "He practices what he preaches." Another meaning suggests repeating a skill or behavior until you get good at it, as in "He practices the piano." Mindfulness can be practiced in both ways. In the following sections, I encourage you to work with more structured exercises geared to help you practice and eventually master the skills of mindfulness. It does take some effort, but the results will be well worth it.

Staying in the present

I'm sure you've heard slogans like "Stay in the present!" or "Be here now!" And for good reason. The reality is that all you really have is the present. Running on auto-pilot robs you of your present experience. You fail to appreciate the meaningful details that make up the fabric of your life. Your automatic behaviors can hijack the present, leaving you unaware of what's happening right now. You miss life! Your thoughts and emotions can also become automatic. Too much of our mental and emotional life is spent reflexively, looking backward, rehashing the past, lamenting, and regretting things we said or did (or failed to say or do). And if we aren't looking backward, we're worrying about or planning for what the future will bring. In contrast, mindfulness invites you to live your life as it unfolds, in the present.

Breathing more mindfully

This simple breathing exercise can help you stay focused on the present.

1. **Find a place where you will be relatively undisturbed for a few minutes.**

   Set a timer for a length of time that realistically fits your schedule. A few minutes should work fine.

2. **Sit comfortably in a chair or on a cushion.**

3. **Begin paying attention to your breathing.**

   Notice where you feel your breath. Is it higher in your chest or lower in your belly? Do you inhale and exhale through your nose or mouth?

4. **Focusing on your breathing, begin counting upward from one to ten and then backward from ten to one.**

   If your attention wanders, you lose count, you over-count, or you find your thoughts taking you to another place, gently bring your attention back to the breathing and counting. Simply start again at one.

So, how did you do? Were you able to detach and get some separation from your thoughts and feelings? It's not easy. Our minds are busy generating thoughts — all kind of thoughts all the time. Our thoughts and feelings grab us and pull us in. Too often our minds get locked into our worries, opinions, judgments, and concerns. We need some psychological distance.

Picturing a day at the beach

Not long ago I came across an issue of *New Yorker* magazine with a cover illustration depicting a family — a mom, dad, and two kids, posing for a picture on the beach while on their vacation in Hawaii. The resulting photograph showed all four of them glued to their digital devices. No one looked up. They were oblivious, completely unaware of being photographed or of anything else around them — the bright blue sky, the swaying palm trees, the turquoise ocean. For me, this captured the essence of what it means not to be living in the present.

Don't worry if you had to restart several times. Don't judge your performance. Cut yourself some slack. The goal is *not* to do this exercise perfectly but rather to become aware of how you can control your attention and focus, stay in the present, and recognize how easily your thoughts can pull you off track.

Exercises like this one can help you be more in the present. They can free you from the pull of everyday concerns and worries. The goal isn't primarily to relax you or quiet your mind, though this is often a benefit. The goal of this and similar exercises is to train you to become aware of what you're attending to and to become better able to shift that attention — and eventually to be more aware in the present moment.

Revisiting your daily routines

Your daily life provides many built-in, informal opportunities to practice this shifting of attention, of becoming more aware of what is happening right now. Consider the simple act of eating.

Eat something!

In the past I've generally been a mindless eater. I ate too quickly, mostly unaware of how and what I was eating. Often I watched television or read a newspaper while I ate. Many of us are like that. Yes, we're somewhat aware of the taste and the short-lasting effect of feeling good, but the experience is remarkably quick. Eating has become automatic.

This exercise is a simple way to demonstrate what it means to become more mindful in daily life. This takes only about five minutes. It involves eating a piece of food mindfully. Usually the food of choice has been a raisin. But you may not have a raisin in your cupboard. It doesn't matter. Simply find food — a bowl of cereal, a grape, an apple, an orange segment, anything. Here's what to do:

1. **Find a place where you won't be disturbed or distracted for a short while.**

2. **Let's say you've decided to work with an orange segment. Hold the segment in your fingers. Pretend this is the first time you've ever seen a piece of orange.**

3. **Focus on the segment and pay attention to what it looks like — its texture, its shape, the lines, the colors, and the way the light reflects on its surface. Does it feel hard or soft? Rough or smooth?**

4. **Smell the section. Sweet? Citrusy?**

5. **Very slowly put the orange segment in your mouth.**

   Don't chew or swallow just yet. Notice what it feels like in your mouth. Is your mouth watering?

6. **Bite down, noticing what the sensation feels like.**

   Soft? Hard? How does it move around your mouth? Notice the taste you experience.

7. **Begin to chew, noticing how the consistency changes as you chew.**

   Chew for a short while and then swallow, noticing the sensations in your throat and what it feels like as the bits of orange move from your mouth, down your throat, and into your stomach.

8. **Step back and take a moment to reflect on the process.**

Go beyond fruit

Here are some other built-in opportunities to introduce more mindfulness into your life. In each case, decide to pay attention to this routine behavior in a curious, exploratory way, as if this is the first time you're doing this. Bring as many of your five senses to bear as possible. Ask yourself, "What do I see, hear, feel, smell, and taste?"

Brushing your teeth

Taking a bath or shower

Getting dressed

Washing dishes

Eating a meal

Cleaning the house

Sitting on a train

Driving your car

Working out in a gym

Walking down the street

Or any other automatic behavior you can think of.

Learning how to detach

Detaching from your stress means you're able to step away from that situation, event, memory, or worry — whatever form your stress takes at that particular time. Stepping away may sound easy, but often it's not. Our thoughts and feelings are compelling. Like a spider's web, they can entrap us in an ever-spiraling web of rumination, worry, and upset. The pull of your stress-producing thinking is incredibly strong, and once it has you in its grip, escaping is not easy. That's why detaching yourself from your thoughts and feelings becomes so important.

Creating awareness

The first step is becoming aware of what you want to detach from. The goal is to be able to detach from a stressful situation before it has you in its grip. Learning to detach from non-stressful triggers is much easier and therefore a better place to start. Start by asking yourself this simple question: What am I paying attention to right now?

By posing this question, you create an awareness of exactly what is holding your attention. The following is a simple exercise that can help you develop greater awareness of how and to what you're paying attention.

1. **Every time you check the time on your watch, computer, or cell phone, use this as a cue to pause briefly, take a deep breath, hold it for a bit, and slowly exhale.**

2. **Now ask yourself: What am I thinking about right now? What am I feeling? What am I doing?**

Crack a smile?

Detaching from a stressor or stress reaction can be hard. One tool that can help you transition from an emotional state to a more mindful state is to smile. "Wait a minute," you say, "when I'm waiting in traffic or worried about my finances, you want me to smile? Get real!" Yes, I recognize that this will be a phony smile — forced and artificial. Do it anyway. It can help you gain objectivity and psychological distance. It distracts you momentarily, and the changes in facial muscle tension can alter your mood. Smiling gives you important seconds to regroup, gain some objectivity, and become more aware. Try it!

This simple response can refocus your attention. With practice, you won't need a cue to be able to create this awareness on your own.

Creating distance

Here is another exercise that will help you get some psychological and emotional distance from a potential stressor.

1. **Suppose you feel an itch on your arm.**

   Your natural response is to scratch it. Suppose, however, that rather than immediately reacting to the itch by scratching, you simply become aware of the sensation of itching and choose not to do anything about it.

2. **Imagine that you're able to step away from the sensation.**

   The scientist in you takes over, and you become a neutral observer. In a mindful way, you're able to describe what the sensation of itching feels like (perhaps irritating, frustrating, or annoying).

3. **If you can mentally step back a little further, you can suspend any judgment about the itch ("This is driving me crazy! I hate this!").**

   You can also withhold your assessment of your ability to cope with the itch ("I can't stand it! I just have to scratch!").

4. **You can view the itch with a certain curiosity.**

   Now you have distance. You're not a prisoner of the itch.

A major aim of mindfulness is to become aware of your thoughts, feelings, and sensations *without reacting to them*. This sentence, on first reading, may seem a bit puzzling. We're so accustomed to responding to our thoughts and feelings that it's second nature to do so. But as you recognized while doing the itch exercise, you do have a choice.

Controlling your attention

If awareness is the first step in becoming more mindful, learning how to control and direct your attention is the next step. This next exercise will help you figure out how to shift your attention.

I like this exercise because it gives you the experience of focusing your attention on one part of your inner and outer world and then switching attention, moving to some other aspect of your world. Here's what to do:

The first part:

1. **Find a place where you can sit comfortably without being disturbed for about five minutes.**

   The place doesn't have to be totally quiet. In fact, some ambient sounds make this exercise work even better.

2. **Close your eyes and begin directing your attention to your breathing.**

   You don't have to change the way you breathe, just focus your attention on what is happening in your body when you breathe.

3. **Notice the way the cool air feels when you inhale through your nostrils.**

4. **Notice how the stream of air goes to the back of your throat and into your lungs.**

5. **Notice how your diaphragm rises as you inhale and falls when you exhale.**

6. **Notice how much warmer the air is leaving your body.**

7. **Be aware of any other aspects of your breathing.**

   Is your body making any sounds as you breathe?

8. **Notice that your breathing slows as you keep focusing on your breathing.**

   If your thoughts wander, simply notice that they have wandered and return your attention to your breathing. Keep this up for about two minutes.

The second part:

1. **Let your attention shift to your stomach.**

   Pay attention to how it feels. Full? Empty? Do you notice any movement? Any sounds? Notice how your stomach moves in and out with your breathing. See if you can maintain this focus for another minute or so.

2. **Shift your attention to the way your body feels in the chair.**

   Notice the sensations it creates in your body.

3. **Shift to noticing any sounds you hear outside of your body.**

4. **Try shifting the focus of your attention back and forth between inner-body sensations and external sounds.**

   A funny taste in your mouth? A breeze on your face?

This exercise hones your ability to maintain your attention and become more sensitive to subtle changes and variations in your experience. It also, and more importantly, shows you that you aren't locked into these feelings and experiences but can remain apart from them. They don't define you or limit you. They are not you.

Cultivating Mindful Acceptance

Many of the ideas, suggestions, and directions in this book are designed to help you cope with stress in highly immediate, responsive ways. In various chapters I discuss how you can modify your environment, change how you think, and master more effective behavioral skills. The emphasis here is on *doing, fixing,* and *changing.*

While many of your stressors *can* be changed, fixed, or even eliminated, many times this isn't possible. Sadly but realistically, your life will always be punctuated by major stressors. They may take the form of the death of a loved one, a major illness, a divorce, or a serious injury, to mention but a few of life's major blows. Change may not be easy or even possible. In such cases, your first step becomes *acceptance.* Whenever you can't change or fix a stressful situation, your most effective stress-management strategy may be acceptance. But the value of acceptance extends beyond coping with life's major stressors. Effectively coping with *any* stressor, big or small, starts with acceptance.

Understanding acceptance

Acceptance, put most succinctly, means:

✔ Recognizing and expecting that your life will be punctuated by pain, sorrow, loss, discomfort, and disappointment.

✔ Acknowledging and tolerating that distress without denying it, fighting it, judging it, or immediately trying to change it.

✔ Looking at your reality and accepting it *the way it is*, not demanding that it be the way you want it to be.

When you accept an unpleasant or unwanted experience, be it a situation, an event, a feeling, or a thought, you acknowledge that *it is*. You may not like it or want it, but it's there. Your smartphone is on the bottom of the lake. You have to wait for the plane to take off. You didn't get the job. Accept it! Acceptance is not always easy. Our instincts tell us to fight it, change it, fix it, or get rid of it. And sometimes you can. But a more effective way of coping is first learning to accept what is. Without acceptance, you're in a constant battle with the stressors around you. Sometimes it's best not to fight. Sometimes it's best to accept.

Distinguishing acceptance from resignation

Probably the most common and immediate response I get to the preceding advice is disbelief:

> "Are you suggesting that I accept everything that happens to me without working to change it? Should I be passive all the time and just accept whatever I get, every bad situation, every frustration? What about all this stuff about being assertive and proactive?"

Acceptance doesn't mean you're resigned to a situation or circumstance without the possibility of changing it. In fact, it can mean just the opposite. Acceptance and change are not mutually exclusive. When you accept yourself and your world in a mindful way, you're in the best position to examine the situation and explore more effective alternatives in a calmer, less distorted manner. Acceptance can slow or even stop your unrealistic resistance. It centers you and allows you to move on, solve problems, and, if possible, change things. The following are some examples that illustrate how acceptance and change can coexist.

Judy's dream house

Jeff and Judy want to buy a new house, and every weekend they go with their realtor to look at potential places to live. It's slim pickings. They see nothing of interest until one Saturday morning when they see "it." Their perfect house. It has it all. Wasting no time, they offer the asking price, sit back, and wait nervously. Alas, someone else has submitted a much higher offer, which the seller has accepted. The house is gone, but the distress is only starting, more so for Jeff. He thinks:

> "We should've been more on top of this!"

> "The owner should've come back to us for a counter bid!"

> "We'll never find another house like this one!"

> "I'll never be truly happy living someplace else!"

For Jeff, anger, upset, and more than a little depression follow for many weeks after. He can't accept the loss. He's uselessly fighting it and struggling to change a situation that can't be changed. The house is gone.

Judy is more accepting. She is saddened by the loss but looks at it as spilled milk. Yes, it's painful, but it needs to be put into the past. She's eager to keep looking and hopeful that even though that particular house is off the market, she and Jeff can find something they'll be happy with. Jeff is immobilized with upset, but Judy is realistically optimistic that something will work out.

In bad shape

Diane is, if the truth be told, out of shape. She's heavier than she wants to be. She isn't pleased with what she sees in the mirror. Is she happy with this situation? No. Is she determined to change it? Yes. She comes up with a game plan to eat differently and hit the health club. Diane is able to accept the reality that she isn't where she wants to be physically without putting herself down. She acknowledges her problem and accepts it but is determined to change.

The accident

Evan loses his leg in a bad car accident. Understandably, this is a life-changing event. His life will never be the same. Fairly quickly, though, Evan is able to accept the loss. He's able to get past the "why me?" stage and the limitations and look at his situation with acceptance. Life has dealt him a misfortune, and he will cope. And he does. He accepts his new reality. Rather than focusing on what happened he focuses on what he can do to regain a greater degree of normalcy in his life. He is determined to work hard in physical and rehabilitation therapy and master new ways of doing many of the things he used to do.

Non-acceptance and your stress

Sometimes the best way to understand acceptance is to understand what non-acceptance looks like. Consider some of these examples:

One weekend, Amanda goes to her friend's summer house on a lake. As she's texting in the motor boat, her hand slips, and the phone falls overboard into the lake. It's a deep lake. Understandably, she's upset, but she is overly upset and continues to be so for many days afterward. She beats herself up and just can't believe it happened.

Josh goes to the movie theater, buys his ticket, and enters the theater, only to discover after much searching that the only available seats are in the first three rows. He takes a seat but remains annoyed for most of the movie, grumbling, "This is the worst seat ever! I just hate this!"

Katy, who hates waiting, is on her way to Pittsburgh but finds herself waiting on the tarmac for the plane to get permission to take off. The pilot announces that it will be another half hour. She is seething. When the plane later lands safely in Pittsburgh, she's still feeling furious.

Leslie interviews for a job she wants, does well, and is told that the choice is between her and one other candidate. She gets the call that the other person got the job. She is upset and resentful, thinking that life is unfair, that she will never get a good job, and that she is pretty much a loser. Two weeks later she is still holding onto these same feelings.

Alas, the universe (and others in it) don't always comply with what we want, and things don't always work out the way we'd like them to. Frustration and disappointment, unpleasantness and discomfort, rejection and disapproval will always be part of your life. You'll never get everything you want in life. If you fight this reality, you magnify your stress — you experience more stress, and that stress lasts longer. If Amanda could accept that her phone is gone, she could figure out her next move. If Josh could accept that sitting in a bad seat isn't so terrible, he could still enjoy the movie. If Katy could accept that planes often fail to take off on time, she would be less stressed. If Leslie could accept that she didn't get the job, she too would be feeling less stressed. They would all be in a better position to explore positive alternatives and find more effective ways of coping with their stress.

Chapter 7

Stress-Reducing Organizational Skills

In This Chapter

▶ Understanding your disorganization

▶ Clearing away clutter

▶ Motivating yourself

▶ Organizing electronically

▶ Staying organized

*I*f you've ever felt like screaming or maybe tearing out some hair when at the last minute you can't find your keys or that paper napkin on which you wrote important information, you're probably sympathetic to the notion that disorganization can trigger a whole lot of stress.

Sure, a little bit of disorder doesn't rival developing a serious illness, getting fired, or having your house burn down. Yet being disorganized can fuel a long list of frustrations, delays, lost time, and missed opportunities — all accompanied by varying levels of anger and irritation.

Who needs it? Your stress level is already high enough. This chapter shows you how to get organized. It gives you the tools you need to overcome the disarray, chaos, and confusion in your life.

Figuring Out Why Your Life Is So Disorganized

Okay, so your life is not a model of order and organization. Being disorganized is nothing to be ashamed of. In fact, it's totally understandable. Our days are crammed with too much to do, with too little time to do it. Our possessions threaten to drown us.

In this section, I help you get to the bottom of your organizational challenges so that you can take action.

Are you organizationally challenged?

Your first step in coming up with effective organizational strategies is recognizing that you may be truly disorganized. Take this unofficial "test" and see whether becoming better organized is an area you need to work on.

Read each of the following statements and see to what extent each statement describes you. Use the following ratings to help you better gauge how disorganized you are:

3 = Very much like me

2 = Somewhat like me

1 = A little like me

0 = Not at all like me

- ✔ Your home is filled with far too much stuff.
- ✔ Your closets, drawers, and cabinets are disorganized.
- ✔ You're frequently late for your appointments.
- ✔ You're a big procrastinator.
- ✔ You find that you spend lots of time looking for things you've misplaced.
- ✔ You're often late paying your bills.
- ✔ Your friends and family tell you that you have a problem with clutter.
- ✔ You feel stressed out by all the stuff in your home.
- ✔ Your computer files are generally disorganized.
- ✔ You rarely use lists to help you get organized.

✔ You buy duplicates of things you already own because you can't find the originals.

✔ Your desk or workspace is disorganized.

✔ You feel you don't have enough time to get organized.

You probably answered with twos or threes for at least a few of these quiz items. However, if you identify strongly with many or most of these statements, poor organizational skills may be playing an important role in creating excessive stress in your life.

More important than determining a global organizational score is identifying your specific areas and patterns of disorganization. The following categories help you do this.

Identifying your personal disorganization

Getting better organized means being aware of the areas in which you could use some help. Disorganization can be broken down to more discrete subgroups. See which ones best describe your own forms of disorganization.

✔ **You don't manage your time well.** If your time-management skills are wobbly, you find that you often run late, miss deadlines, work inefficiently, procrastinate, plan poorly, and feel overwhelmed by not having enough time. Too many things don't get done. Time management is such an important stress-reducing skill that it warrants its own chapter — the next chapter, in fact.

✔ **You're surrounded by clutter.** You own far too many things, and those things are way out of control. Your flat surfaces are invitations to put stuff on, preferably in piles. You have great difficulty getting rid of your stuff. It could be clothes, books, papers, out-of-date electronics, or broken just-about-anything. You feel like you're drowning in your stuff, and you're not terribly optimistic that the situation is going to change.

✔ **Your home is in constant disarray.** Your storage spaces are randomly organized. Cabinets and closets are a mish-mash of organization. Finding anything is a hit-and-miss affair. You make poor use of containers, storage bags, shelves, and drawers. You rarely use labels.

✔ **You lack a good system for keeping track of bills and other important information.** Your personal records, bills, passport, mortgage paperwork, and important files are somewhere, but you aren't sure just where. You have no filing system. You don't use your computer, tablet, or smartphone to help you organize your life.

If you struggle with any or all of these areas, the following sections provide specific guidance for getting your life (and your stuff) in order.

Clearing Away the Clutter

If you lived in a place with infinite space, had a live-in maid, and were independently wealthy, you could consider your clutter a charming quirk, an amusing oversight. But I suspect that your clutter has become a pain and threatens to stress you out even more. De-cluttering can seem overwhelming. It's only a matter of time before you feel like you're lost in your clutter. You need help. You're ready to start. But where? The following sections walk you through the de-cluttering process.

Bust those clutter excuses

If you're going to war with clutter, it's important to know exactly what the enemy looks like. Here are ten reasons why people hang onto stuff. At times, giving up your prized possessions is harder than pulling teeth. When pressed, you may vigorously defend your decision to hold onto some small thing. All the following excuses contain at least a sliver of truth. And all guarantee that after your funeral, your relatives will hold the world's biggest garage sale. See if you can recognize some of your favorite clutter excuses.

- **"Someday I'll need it."** This clutter excuse can be compelling. After all, you *might* need it someday. This is where your "what-if-ing" comes into play. The odds of your actually needing this are probably very small. That unread article or outdated computer cord will most likely never be reused. Do a cost-benefit analysis and ask yourself: "Aren't I better off just getting rid of this stuff rather than keeping it on the very unlikely chance that I *may* use it?"

- **"It was a present for my ninth birthday."** This is your sentimental clutter. Anything that reminds you of your past or has sentimental value can be tough to let go. This category of clutter can include every piece of artwork you or your child brought home from school. It can include every playbill from every play you have seen and every picture that was ever taken of you. Create a scrapbook of selected items, letting the rest go. Better yet, scan into your computer all the items you want to save and keep only a select few original items. If you don't have a scanner, take pictures. Who says you can't have your cake and eat it too?

- **"Somebody will want to buy this."** Good luck with this one! If I'm wrong and this treasure has eager buyers, list it on eBay or find another way to sell it. But make the decision: "I will put this up for sale now, or I will give it away, or I will chuck it."

- **"I'm sure I'll find the matching one."** Usually this excuse is for orphaned socks or gloves. If you haven't found the matching item in three months, let it go. Besides, everybody knows that washing machines eat socks.

✔ **"Yes, it's broken, but it can be fixed."** Fix it, give it away, or throw it out. These days it will probably cost you more to fix something electronic than to replace it, but if you feel it can be reasonably repaired, commit to locating a repair service this week.

✔ **"If I just lose 30 pounds, I'll fit into this."** I certainly hope you *will* lose that weight (I know you can do it!), but for many people this is a difficult task. Why not keep a few items of clothing that you absolutely love and donate all the rest? After you've shed those pounds, you can reward yourself with some serious shopping for smart new togs.

✔ **"My kids will want to give it to their kids."** My experience with my kids is that they rarely relish getting old stuff from us. Ask them if they would like these objects. If they say yes, ask them to take possession of them now. If your kids are very young, don't hold your breath.

✔ **"I got it on sale."** This is your bargain clutter. It's hard to resist a good deal. Half-price sale? No problem! Buy one get one free? Let's do it! Shopping at the big-box stores can be a trap. When you see something on sale, it becomes hard to resist. And if you buy it, it's hard to get rid of because it was a bargain. What you want to avoid is *impulse* buying. If you're seduced by a "bargain," whether you see it online, in print, or in a store, stop and ask yourself some pertinent questions:

- "Do I really need this?"

- "Would I ever buy this if it weren't on sale?"

- "Do I have a place to put this?"

If possible, give yourself time to reflect on whether you really think this is a smart purchase. Most sales give you some wiggle room to think before you buy. If the idea still seems right the next day, and you're still determined to buy it, go ahead. If you're in a store and it's now or never, do your other shopping first, and then ask yourself the three questions above. If the answer is "no" to any of these, take a pass. Even if you regret not making the purchase later on, you'll almost always have a second chance to buy it at a bargain price. And if you're still paralyzed with indecision, get another opinion from someone who knows you well.

✔ **"It will be a collector's item one day."** If you've ever watched those *Antiques Roadshow* programs on PBS, you know that one man's garbage can be another man's treasure. Alas, the truth is, one man's garbage is usually another man's clutter. Get an objective appraisal from a trusted, neutral source. If the item is worth something, sell it now.

✔ **"I plan on reading this."** This is the excuse that keeps you from ever throwing out a book you haven't read or that newspaper, magazine, or article you hope to read one day but probably never will. If you haven't read it by a reasonable time, you probably won't. Give your books to the school or library rummage sale. Your shelves will thank you. If an article is important to you, scan it and put it in an organized digital file.

How your clutter stresses you out

Your biggest clutter-related stress may be how to get from your bed to the bathroom without injuring yourself on the boxes of stuff in your path. But clutter can also induce other sources of stress. Here is the list:

✔ Mess creates stress. A cluttered environment creates a stressful mindset.

✔ It takes time to find things.

✔ You may not find these things.

✔ Clutter can be expensive if you miss a bill payment because it's lost under a pile.

✔ Your living space can feel claustrophobic.

✔ Clutter can affect your social life because when your home is cluttered, you may be reluctant to have people over.

Get yourself motivated

Sometimes good intentions alone just don't cut it. You may find that you need a kick in the pants or some other form of external motivation to get you to clean up. Here are some field-tested ideas that can keep you on track:

✔ **Schedule it.** When you schedule things, you have a better chance of getting them done. People generally show up for dentist and doctor appointments, business meetings, and other engagements that they purposefully schedule. The same tactic can work when it comes to getting things done around the house. Commit to a definite time and write down the "appointment" in your calendar, daily planner, or whatever you use to keep track of your life.

✔ **Work with shame.** My wife and I discovered long ago that our home is at its neatest about three minutes before a bunch of invited guests ring our doorbell. We're motivated and determined to make sure that others don't see how disorganized our place can be. You can do the same. Set a date and invite over some new friends whose approval you desperately want or need. Take this time to make some real organizational changes. It works like a charm for us.

✔ **Find your clutter threshold.** Frankly, I don't mind a little clutter in my life. For me, those minimalist, absolutely-nothing-out-of-place living spaces are scary. I require a touch of clutter to make me feel emotionally comfortable. Yet anything more than just a little bit of clutter begins to stress me out. Other folks are totally clutter averse. For them, any clutter is too much. You have to find your own clutter threshold, below which you get twitchy and above which you feel stressed. Then work hard to keep your clutter level under that threshold.

Draw yourself a clutter roadmap

Rather than seeing all the clutter in your life-space as one massive pile, see it as a succession of tasks that you can chip away step by step. One way to decide where to start, and where to go after you start, is to create a clutter roadmap. Begin by choosing a number of areas of your life-space that desperately need organizing. These areas may be geographical (a specific room in your home, the yard, or the garage) or topical (your clothing, magazines, or toys). Then come up with a sequence of areas that you want to work on. After you deal with one bit of clutter on your list, move on to the second and then on to the next, and so on. Think of your map as a kind of sequential "to do" list. It takes you where you want to go.

A clutter roadmap gives you the feeling that you know where you're going — and also a pretty good idea of how far you've moved toward your final goal. For many people faced with overwhelming clutter, having this game plan creates a feeling of being in control, which can reduce much of the anxiety often associated with de-cluttering. Be sure to make each piece on your map relatively small and doable. Also start by choosing areas of your life-space that will give you a great deal of personal satisfaction after they're organized.

Get your feet wet

One of my favorite bits of self-help advice is that Nike slogan, "Just do it!" However, my experience as a psychologist has taught me that "just doing it" for most people is probably not going to do it. My sweatshirt would read a bit more realistically, saying, "Just get started!" Deep down, you realize that you'll be better off if you get rid of much of that unneeded stuff. So jump in.

Have you ever noticed that after you start something, the momentum of doing that thing keeps you going? This is especially true when you're de-cluttering. After you get yourself in de-cluttering mode, go with it. Don't stop just because you finish a small section. Keep going. Build on your success. You may be surprised at how much you can get done when you're into it.

Stop kidding yourself

It's easy to fool yourself. That's because some small part of you really does believe that you'll clean out the basement, put those old clothes in boxes and give them to a thrift shop, and throw out those magazines that you've been hanging onto forever.

The reality is that unless you take your clutter seriously, it will continue to spread. If you're going to successfully de-clutter, you need to convince yourself that the quality of your life will improve measurably after you unload much, if not most, of those collected objects. It will also feel so nice when you find that long-lost birth certificate and all the mates to those single socks lying in your bedroom drawer.

Simplifying your life-space takes grit. Your attitude as you approach the task should be, "I'm sick and tired of this, and I'm not going to take it anymore!" You may find this approach a bit too merciless, but be clear: You're dealing with a powerful force. Give no ground. Take no prisoners. Ask yourself the following questions to help increase your de-cluttering grit:

- ✔ Do I really want to spend the next 20 years living with this item?
- ✔ If my place were on fire and I could save only half of what I own, would I save this particular item?
- ✔ Would the quality of my life be seriously diminished if I didn't own this item?
- ✔ Can someone else use this more than I can?

In 90 percent of the cases, the answers to these four questions are no, no, no, and yes.

Avoid discouragement

A mistake that many people make when de-cluttering is thinking that they can finish their de-cluttering in one short Saturday afternoon. They get discouraged when they realize just how much stuff they have and how much de-cluttering they still have to do.

Face it: It took you years to amass all your wonderful possessions, so it's prudent to assume that reversing the process may take you some time. However, when you figure out how much time you can save by not having to look for misplaced items, you quickly realize that you'll be way ahead of the game after you finish. Accomplishing most anything in life that is worthwhile takes effort and persistence. Mastering golf or tennis, learning to ski, or figuring out how to get the most out of your computer don't happen overnight. Stick with it.

Are you a hoarder?

You've probably heard the term "hoarder" on reality TV shows and talk shows. The most iconic hoarders are the Collyer brothers, Homer and Langley, who lived in New York. Both were eventually found dead in the Harlem brownstone where they had lived, surrounded by more than 140 tons of items they had amassed over several decades. You're not a hoarder just because you like to collect things and have too many possessions. It's not considered hoarding even if you have trouble getting rid of your stuff. Hoarding refers to a more severe form of cluttering. For some people, the degree of clutter becomes dysfunctional and life-limiting. Their clutter is so excessive that it becomes a central disabling force in their lives. Here are some warning signs:

✔ The amount of clutter is so excessive that your living space is severely compromised. You can't use your living space in the way it was intended or the way you would like.

✔ Your clutter causes you significant stress and upset, overwhelms you, and affects your relationships.

✔ Your clutter makes it difficult for you to navigate your living space.

✔ The degree of clutter threatens your health and well-being.

✔ You've been told by many others that you could use professional help. And they are not kidding.

If several of these criteria describe you, you may want to seek additional help. Professional groups and organizations can provide assistance and direction. Therapists who have some expertise with hoarding, as well as expertise with anxiety, depression, obsessive-compulsive disorders, addictions, phobias, and so on, are also a good source of help.

Get down to the nitty-gritty

Okay, you've psyched yourself up for some serious de-cluttering. When you get into the trenches, try using the following clutter-busting techniques:

✔ **Pick any number from one to two.** When considering what to do with an item of clutter, remember that you have two basic options: Keep it or lose it. If you decide to keep it, you must figure out what to do with it. If you choose to lose it, you can chuck it or give it away. Clearly, the biggest obstacle to getting rid of anything is having to make this choice.

✔ **Take a second look.** It's never too late to get rid of some of the stuff you decide to keep. Go back over your keeper pile and take a second look. Organizing even a small pile of things takes a lot of time. And although storage and filing play an important role in managing all the possessions that clutter your life, simply getting rid of stuff often makes more sense.

✔ **Use the Triage Method of Clutter Control.** One approach I find useful in making difficult keep it/pitch it decisions is something I call the Triage Method of Clutter Control. First, I create three categories: Definitely Keep, Definitely Get Rid Of, and I'm Not Sure. Then I throw out or give away everything in the last two categories. The upside of unloading much more of your clutter far outweighs the downside of making a mistake. Don't look back.

✔ **Get a clutter buddy.** I've noticed that whenever I decide it's time to de-clutter, I come up with marvelous ideas for organizing my wife's side of the room. I have even better ideas when it comes to our children's rooms. I've also noticed that my wife is equally creative in disposing of the stuff on my side of the room. You're probably less sentimental, less ambivalent, and more determined when dealing with other people's clutter rather than your own. Make this concept work for you. Ask your mate or a friend to help you de-clutter. Listen to that person, and do what he or she tells you.

✔ **Get some emotional support.** De-cluttering can be a lonely and emotionally taxing job. You may need someone more emotionally supportive than your clutter buddy. This should be someone you feel comfortable talking with — a family member, a good friend, a colleague you trust, or perhaps a therapist. This support can keep you going when the going gets tough and you start to feel discouraged.

✔ **Play the dating game.** If you can't bring yourself to throw something out, put it in a box and put a date on the box that is exactly a year away. Don't list what's in the box — just the date. If the future date comes and goes without your needing anything in the box, take a quick look inside. If nothing critically important catches your eye, chuck it without a second look. Don't look back. If you *do* need an item from the box, find a better place to keep it.

✔ **Use the three-month rule.** I tend to keep old magazines around the house far too long with the noble intention of reading them. But after a certain point, I rarely do. Take a look at the dates on your magazines, and if they are older than three months for monthly publications or three weeks for weekly ones, chuck 'em.

✔ **Find a clutter recipient.** Getting rid of stuff is much easier when you know that it won't end up in the trash but rather in the hands of somebody who wants it and can use it. In fact, your rejects may be someone else's cup of tea. Clothing, sports equipment, books, and furniture are often welcomed by others. Give your relatives and friends first crack at your treasures (but give them a definite time limit to come, look, and take). The Salvation Army, Goodwill Industries, thrift shops, and charity drives will be delighted (usually) to take the stuff that your family and friends turn down. You can even get a tax deduction for donating to charitable organizations.

✔ **Consider consignment.** Sometimes it's hard to give an object away because you really do believe it's worth something. And you may be right. Putting it up for consignment may just do the trick.

✔ **If it doesn't work, toss it.** Look around your home for a broken toaster, blender, vacuum cleaner, radio, or clock — any small appliance that hasn't worked for a long while. Once you find one, ask yourself whether you truly need it. If you decide to fix it, fix it. If not, replace or discard it. These days you may find that replacing the item is cheaper than having it repaired. However, chances are good that if you haven't needed it in the last year, you probably don't need it at all.

✔ **Whatever you do, don't leave the broken item in your home.** Throw it out or, better yet, give it to a charitable organization that will repair it and give it to someone who will use it. I often put a little note on the item explaining what's wrong with it and then leave it at the side of our building. When I come back to check in about an hour or so, the piece is usually gone.

✔ **Handle things only once.** You may be in the habit of putting some things aside and saying you'll figure out later what to do with them. This just adds to the problem. Deal with it right in the moment. File it! Pay it! Delete it! Chuck it! Deal with it only once!

✔ **Invest in doors and drawers.** If you absolutely must keep something, hide it. Unless the object in question is something you're very fond of or somehow adds to the visual aesthetic of your decor, keep it out of sight. Store things in cabinets, closets, bureau drawers, or file cabinets — any-place that contributes to a sense of visual order. But remember that the space things occupy behind doors is still space that you could use for something else.

Whole stores are now dedicated exclusively to storage furniture and containers. Their catalogs are great fun to look through, but remember not to make them a new part of your clutter.

✔ **Take a sample.** I'm not sure at what point my wife and I realized we couldn't keep absolutely every piece of artwork, craft project, or report card that our children brought home. I think it was when every major appliance in the kitchen was covered in crayon drawings. Then my wife came up with a brilliant idea: She brought home a large folder and began taking samples of the masterpieces we were especially fond of. This "art" folder is neatly stored in a back closet. The smaller master-pieces and mementos we scan and electronically file. When our children become famous "artistes," we'll cash in. You can do the same.

✔ **Take a picture.** Often, items in your "I'm Not Sure" pile have sentimen-tal value but are too big to keep around. You want the memories, but not necessarily the object. Take its picture. Pictures (especially the digital variety) take up far less space and still can bring a warm smile to your face. I remember a rather large stuffed animal that our children had when they were smaller. There came a time when it had to go, but sentiment was holding us back. We decided to take its picture and give the teddy bear to a thrift shop. This compromise worked well. The photograph on our computer collects far less dust. You may also want to include someone in the picture. Looking at your daughter squeezing Cuddles is a lot more satisfying than just looking at Cuddles by herself.

Organizing Your Space

Being organized is about more than just being neat and tidy. It also means having items and information in places where you can reliably find them, use them, and then put them back where they came from. Part of your problem may be that you don't know how to organize and store your things. Here are some guidelines and suggestions:

- **Start big.** Rather than organize your stuff item by item, start with a more ambitious agenda. First pick an area you want to organize. Let's say it's your medicine cabinet. Take out everything and put it on the bathroom counter. Have a trash can handy. Give the cabinet a wipe and you're ready to go. Now group the cold medicines together and put them on a shelf. If you come across items that you never use or that are out of date, throw them into the trash can. Move on to another category. Put the stuff you use most in the most convenient locations. Label the items that are hard to spot or aren't clearly marked. When you've finished with the medicine cabinet, you can move on to your refrigerator, clothes closet, shoes . . . Remember, not everything has to be saved.

- **Use containers.** Yes, I *am* advocating that you go out and buy more stuff! *But not just yet.* First figure out which containers you need. Jars, hooks, plastic boxes, plastic bags, and even baskets can find their places in your reorganization planning. Your first step is determining what you want to store. Food containers should most often be clear with lids. Objects like crayons, small toys, and blocks all do well in see-through containers, as well. To save space, go with square containers rather than round ones. Stackability is also a plus because it takes advantage of vertical space. Containers make cleaning up a lot easier by giving you definite places to return the things you use.

- **Label it.** Whatever container you use, it helps to label the contents. For opaque containers and boxes, labeling becomes a must. On plastic bags, a permanent marker does the trick. An inexpensive labeler also proves useful when you can't write on a container.

- **Categorize.** While it's true that if you stick all your books into a book-case it will look orderly, it may not be the best organizational strategy. Come up with some basic categories without overdoing it. Start with fiction/nonfiction and add one or two more sub-categories. Similarly, in the kitchen, rather than having all your spices thrown together, use a simple A-F, G-N, and so on. Grouping can help you navigate. Labeled spice racks could do the trick, as well. Just keep them where you can see them.

- **Group.** Rather than having your electronic gadgets all over the house, create a drawer or shelf just for these alone. Have a container for the small stuff that might otherwise get lost. Put all your sports equipment into a bin labeled for each particular sport. Again, smaller sports items (balls, pucks, and tees) could go in a box or container within the bin. In your medicine cabinet, group your medicines, soaps, and razors in separate sections or on different shelves.

✔ **Prioritize usage.** Some things you use frequently, others much less. In your refrigerator, keep the most-used items near the front and on the most accessible shelf. The same with clothing. Socks, underwear, and favorite shirts and pants should be where you can easily reach them. Put the once-in-a-blue-moon stuff in the back. Better yet, give it away.

✔ **Put it back!** If you use it, put it back where you found it. Don't let all that organizational effort go to waste.

Organizing Information

Organizing the "stuff" in your life is only part of the problem. You may not know if you have paprika in the back of that kitchen cabinet, but do you know where your birth certificate, mortgage or lease paperwork, and college transcripts are, not to mention that fabulous chicken recipe you cut out of last month's magazine? To make things even more complicated, more and more information now comes to you electronically. You can be swamped by your emails, tweets, attachments, and more. Here are some suggestions to help you manage this information overload.

Losing the paper trail

When computers first began appearing, we were told that we would be living in a paperless world. We're not there quite yet. In fact, our use of paper has doubled in the last ten years. Those who have made the study of clutter their life's work say that paper is the real enemy. Your paper clutter can include everything from a toaster warranty to your last electric bill to the endless stream of circulars, catalogs, junk mail, instruction manuals, and other paper items that pass through your hands every day. Here's how to start organizing that proliferation of paper.

To merge or to purge? That is the question.

The two secrets to managing the paper in your life are fairly simple. In fact, they are amazingly similar to the two options you have when considering what to do with your non-paper clutter. You can either throw out the paper if you don't need it or find an effective way to organize it if you do need it.

This approach to paper sounds pretty easy, but the problem lies in actually doing the throwing out and organizing. Sorting through all that paper takes time and effort, and who knows — you might really need that coupon for a ten-gallon jar of spaghetti sauce, or you might actually read that article on skiing in the Himalayas. Yeah, right! You need help.

Your snail mail: Cut 'em off at the pass

Finding a birthday card or letter from a friend in your mailbox is fun. Finding bills and junk mail? Not so much. Your mailbox can be an insidious force, feeding you an unstoppable river of solicitations, announcements, catalogs, and bills. You can slowly drown in this incoming sea of paper. The trick is to catch it early, before it has a chance to collect. Following are some tips for keeping your mail from becoming a huge problem:

- **Junk junk mail.** Keep a wastepaper basket near your front door. Throw out junk mail immediately. Do not open it. Do not be intrigued. Realize that no matter how much mail you receive telling you that you've probably won a million dollars, the chances of it actually happening are infinitesimal.

- **Get yourself off mailing lists.** I remember subscribing to something and, when I received it, noticing that they had spelled my name wrong. Then I noticed that I was getting tons of other unwanted stuff in the mail with the same wrong name. Being on one list quickly put me on many others. Get yourself taken off mailing lists. The Internet can make this task relatively easy. The World Privacy Forum research group offers a how-to list titled "Top 10 Opt Outs" (`www.worldprivacyforum.org/topten optout.html`), which gives you a number of suggestions for cutting down on unwanted mail.

- **Curb your catalog habit.** Leafing through a catalog and mentally shopping can be fun. And if you have an absolute favorite, keep it. But cancel the others. Virtually every catalog you receive in the mail can be viewed online. Peruse the Web and save the paper. Catalogchoice.org, a service of TrustedID, and dmachoice.org, created by the Direct Marketing Association, allow you to opt out of a particular company's catalogs. Both are free.

- **Go electronic.** Ask that bills, credit-card statements, bank statements, investment information, catalogs, and magazines — just about anything, really — be sent to your computer, tablet, or smartphone. If possible, create a separate and secure email address for your important documents so they don't get lost in your email shuffle. Remember, you can pay many of your bills online without using a single sheet of paper. (You'll save money on stamps, too.)

Organizing the papers you do need to keep

I suspect that the notion of having a method of organizing the paper in your life doesn't come as an earth-shatteringly new idea. Yet I wager that you still don't have one, or if you do, you use it inefficiently.

Coming up with a system of organization takes thought and planning. And making use of it requires time and effort. In the short run, letting papers pile up is a lot easier. But in the long run, doing so can turn into a major headache. Taking the time and effort to develop a systematic way of organizing your papers can result in a lot less stress and hassle. Try the following as you create your filing system:

Start simple

Come up with a filing system that's relatively easy to use. You don't want your filing system to be more stressful than the stress it's supposed to alleviate. You may not need a formal filing cabinet at home, but if you have the room, and if you have a lot of paper to file, it may not be a bad idea. Alternatively, you can work with desk drawers that hold files, or even plastic or cardboard filing boxes.

Be colorful — with your files and folders, that is

Files and folders of different colors, or tabs and labels of different colors, can not only turn your filing system into a work of art but also make it easier to find different subjects and interests. Make your files easy to recognize so you can identify the contents. Put those files you need most often in a place that is easy to access.

Keep important papers where you know how to access them

Keep your original documents in a safe place, but make sure you can easily get hold of them when you need them. And back them up! Keep a digital copy that is easily findable. Lest you forget, here are some of the more important documents to keep track of:

- Automobile registration, title, and insurance documents
- Bank-account information
- Birth certificates
- Citizenship papers
- Credit-card numbers
- Bank-account numbers
- Deeds, leases, and contracts
- Mortgage documents
- Important receipts

- ✔ Instruction manuals
- ✔ Insurance policies
- ✔ Loan agreements
- ✔ Marriage license
- ✔ Divorce decrees
- ✔ Estate-planning documents and wills
- ✔ Adoption papers
- ✔ Medical records
- ✔ Passports
- ✔ Power of attorney
- ✔ Health proxies

- ✔ IDs and passwords
- ✔ PIN numbers
- ✔ School transcripts
- ✔ Service contracts
- ✔ Tax returns
- ✔ Warranties
- ✔ Back-ups of important computer files
- ✔ Photographs, letters, and other personal papers
- ✔ Anything else you don't want to lose

Some of these categories will warrant their own separate files. Some, like your important account and PIN numbers, can be combined. For the more important documents, you may want to keep the originals in a fireproof safe or safe-deposit box and keep copies in your files. Storing them on your computer may be a better option and certainly a good back-up option. Storing them in the "cloud" makes it easier to access this information from any computer. If you choose to store information virtually, it's important that you consider the possible risk that others may obtain access to your files and documents.

Safeguarding your digital documents

It's more likely that someone will steal files and information from your computer than from your bottom dresser drawer. Although you may not care much if someone hacks into your computer and steals your Aunt Agnes's prized recipe for brisket, you probably will be much more distressed if someone steals your Social Security number, passport information, or personal IDs and passwords. Here are some steps to help you store your digital information more safely:

- ✔ **Go to the cloud.** Find a cloud storage company that is well-regarded and has a solid reputation and clear security policies. This may take some research on your part, but the result is well worth the effort.

- ✔ **Get encrypted.** Find out if your data and documents will be encrypted when stored in the cloud. With no encryption, anyone may be able to get access to your files. You want to ensure that files you don't want others to read are protected and accessible only by you.

✔ **Pick a strong password.** Whether your personal documents are stored on your computer and/or in cloud storage, it's vital that you have a password that protects you. In general, the longer the password, the better. It's best to use seven or eight characters with at least two being numeric. Also try to include punctuation characters and mix in upper and lower-case letters.

✔ **Stay away from "Whiskers."** Don't use personal information as your password. Don't use the names of any family members or pets. Don't use your telephone number, anybody's birth date, any part of your Social Security number, your driver's license number, or any of the above spelled backwards.

✔ **Have more than one.** Don't have just a single password for everything. If someone cracks that password, he or she has easy access to everything you've got.

✔ **Store your passwords.** After you come up with these hack-resistant passwords, you need a place to put them. These days password-management systems will store your passwords and other login info either on your computer on in the cloud. You can create a setup whereby your multiple passwords can be accessed only with the use of a master password. This master password is a lengthy, brilliantly conceived winner. (Some apps will do this for you.) If you want to go lower tech, and your computer is in your home, jot down your password and keep it in a safe place.

✔ **Have a magic number.** As an added safeguard, create a PIN, a personal number (three or four digits) that is never written down, stays stored only in your head, and is memorable. Your new password is a combination of what you have written down or stored on your computer or in the cloud *plus* your PIN. I use the number of the house where we lived when I was five. Even if your written-down passwords are discovered, you have another layer of protection.

My way of remembering my password

A great password you can't remember may not be the best password. One way of remembering your password is to come up with a phrase or expression that is easy to recall. It can be a favorite song lyric, a line from a poem, or a catchy slogan — anything you can easily recall. One of my former passwords comes from an old song I like and remember: "Do you know the way to San Jose?" I created the password by linking together the first letter of each word — Dyktwtsj? — and replaced the "to" with 2, ending up with "Dyktw2sj?" You can be even more creative. Just don't be so creative that you can't remember how you came up with your masterpiece.

Never put all your papers in one basket

I like very much (and actually use) an approach described by organizational expert Stephanie Culp. She suggests that you have four baskets for your paper (in addition to the extremely important wastepaper basket):

- ✔ **A "To Do" basket.** The wire see-through kind works best.
- ✔ **A "To Pay" basket.** Again, wire works best here.
- ✔ **A "To File" basket.** Use a larger wicker basket.
- ✔ **A "To Read" basket.** Try an even larger wicker basket with handles.

Culp recommends that you stack your "To Do" basket on top of your "To Pay" basket on your desk. Keep the "To File" basket under your desk, out of the way of your more immediate paper needs. You can keep the "To Read" basket in a different part of your home — such as your bedroom or study (or bathroom!) — so that you can catch up on your reading whenever the opportunity arises.

Make filing a habit

Find a time during the week to empty your "To File" basket and file those needed papers away. This task really shouldn't take long; 15 or 20 minutes should do it.

Fine-tune later

At a later date, take a look at what's in your files. Usually, you find that a file is either underused or bulging. If you find that you have only one or two things in a file folder, find or create a file that's broader in scope. Alternatively, if you find that a folder is overflowing with contributions, create subcategories, either by topic or by dates.

Organizing electronically

When it comes to getting organized, your computer can be your best friend. It may not help you with your shirts or sports equipment, but it can be invaluable with records, papers, pictures, and other forms of information. An organized electronic filing system is the key to effective electronic organization. Without it you can find yourself spending lots of time trying to locate a document, article, or file you know you have — somewhere. If this sounds very much like finding your misplaced phone charger, you're absolutely right. The good news is that filing electronically uses the same principles as manual filing.

Decide what you want to keep electronically

Your first step is asking yourself what you want to store on your computer. Some of the more common choices include photos, recipes, music and video files, personal documents, movies, tax information, letters of recommendation, college transcripts, books, contacts, restaurant information, children's art, report cards, and so on. As you can see, the list of categories could be endless. Pick the ones that make sense for you.

Create folders

Your computer already has wonderful organizational tools built in. It starts you off with the more common organizational folders or categories. You'll probably need to create additional folders that are relevant to your needs. "My recipes" or "my taxes" are good examples. Create these categories or folders as concisely as you can, but make it clear what is in each folder.

Think hierarchically

Create sub-folders that fine-tune the information you have in the primary folder. For example, a folder for recipes can have sub-folders for desserts, soups, entrees, and so on. Similarly, a "travel" folder may have sub-folders for specific countries. Your "tax" folder may include individual years.

Watch out for too many levels. Going deeper than a few sub-folders may cause confusion down the road. Come up with a digital organizing system that's relatively easy to use. You don't want your filing system to be more stressful than the stress it's supposed to alleviate.

Scan, scan, scan

A scanner can be an important tool in helping you become better organized. I know, I know, I've been telling you over and over again to get *rid* of stuff, not buy new stuff. A scanner, however, can make your paper-filled life a lot easier. You can scan all of your important papers, articles, documents, receipts, children's artwork, report cards, business cards, and recipes into your computer, where they can be organized and shared with others without taking up any physical space. Just be sure to keep important originals in a safe place.

Back it up!

You may think your computer will never let you down. But it can, and at some point it will. You've heard this many times before: Always back up your important files on discs, flash drives, or external hard drives. Better safe than sorry. If you prefer (or are perpetually forgetful) some online backup services automatically create backup files for you.

Managing your email

Your email can be a source of delight or major stress depending on how many messages you get, whom they come from, and what the senders want from you. Not only do you have to read most email, but sometimes you even need to respond. You can easily feel overwhelmed. The following are some simple strategies to help you manage your inbox.

Check your email, but don't overdo it

Most people fall into one of two groups: They either under-check or over-check their email. Checking your email too infrequently can get you into trouble. When people send you an email, they expect that you will respond in a reasonable time frame. That time frame is usually mere hours, not days. Delaying responses to personal emails can trigger the ire of family and friends. The damage of tardy responses in work-related situations can be more serious. But you can also go too far in the other direction. Constantly looking at your email can resemble an addiction, becoming somewhat compulsive. It can disrupt the flow of your day and become an unwelcome source of distraction.

Find some set times when it's convenient for you to check your email. It could be in the morning with your coffee, before lunch, and toward the end of the day. This will ensure that your inbox doesn't overflow and that you respond to important emails in a timely manner. A good time to check your email is after you've completed some other chore or piece of work. You're ready for a break, and looking at your email gives you breathing space.

Be efficient

Reading your email can become a black hole that sucks up your time and attention. Minutes can turn into hours. Unless you have that free time or you just really enjoy the process of email correspondence, keep your time per email short and to the point. Remember that bit of sage advice: "Only handle your mail once." The same principle holds for email. If you read it, answer it right away as briefly as is necessary.

Have more than one email address

One effective way of organizing your email is to have a second email address. This will ensure that email regarding specific parts of your life can be separated. For example, we rent out our house upstate for several weeks a year. Any email regarding this rental is directed to a different email address. It works for us.

Keeping Your Life Organized

Say you manage to reverse eons of disarray and disorganization and now, having applied much grit and determination, you have a clean slate. Rather than waiting for the disorganization to return, you can do a number of things to maintain the order and harmony that you've achieved.

Being proactive

Following is a list of tips to help you keep your life organized:

- **Do it now.** Rather than postpone clearing up clutter, do it as soon as you create it.

- **Do it every day.** Try to spend 15 to 30 minutes at the end of the day putting things away so that you can start tomorrow in a (relatively) organized place.

- **Become aware.** Every time you come across an item or piece of paper, ask yourself two questions:

    - How long have I had this?

    - Do I really need this?

- **Build it in.** I go to my gym because it is in my schedule (every Monday, Wednesday, and Friday in the morning). I don't have to make a decision. You can do the same for getting organized. Create patterns. I clean up the yard in the spring. We do the shopping on Saturday. We clean the house on Wednesdays. (Okay, Emlyn cleans our house on Wednesdays.) Create a routine that frees you from having to make decisions. You do it automatically. You do it because your calendar says so.

- **Delegate.** You may not have to do all of this alone. Don't be bashful about getting others (your partner, your kids, your guests) to pitch in with the program.

Buying less

One of the reasons your life becomes more stressful is that you probably have too many "things." Fewer possessions mean a less complicated life. You can really live happily without many of the things you buy. So before you pull out your wallet at the cash register or pick up the phone or computer mouse to order something, ask yourself the following questions:

- Do I really need this item?

- Would the quality of my life be seriously compromised if I passed this up?

- How many of these do I already have?

If you're like most people, I suspect that your answers to these questions are no, no, and enough.

Shop but don't buy

I love to shop, but I've gotten pretty good at not buying the items I see in shops or catalogs. I find that the vicarious satisfaction of shopping is usually enough, and actually buying and owning the item is not that critical. Indulge your desire to shop; curb your impulse to buy.

Here are some other buying suggestions that you may want to consider:

- ✔ Don't buy stuff just because it's on sale. It's not a good deal if you don't use it.
- ✔ Don't buy in bulk unless you're sure that you'll use all of it.
- ✔ Don't buy anything without considering where you're going to put it.

Chapter 8

Finding More Time

· ·

In This Chapter

▶ Identifying your time-management challenges

▶ Making time for yourself

▶ Getting more done in less time

▶ Overcoming procrastination

· ·

*H*ave you noticed how quickly your days fill up? You often find yourself hurried, harried, and rushing to do all that you feel has to be done. Putting out fires, dealing with last-minute crises, and taking care of unending details leave little spare time for anything else. Add to that a busy job, a family, and at least a few other obligations, and you notice that your stress level is escalating. And something else is happening: You have less and less time to spend on the things that you really enjoy and that bring you satisfaction. Fortunately, managing your time more effectively is something you can master.

This chapter gives you direction and strategies to help you manage your time more efficiently and effectively, and reduce your time-related stress.

For even more information on this topic, try *Successful Time Management For Dummies,* by Dirk Zeller (Wiley*).*

Effective time management is really all about managing your priorities. The trick is figuring out what those priorities are and making time for them to happen. Remember those wise words of Bertrand Russell: "The time you enjoy wasting is not wasted time."

Determining Whether You Struggle with Time Management

Maybe you don't experience time-related stress. Let's find out. Take a look at the following list and check off those items that seem to describe you:

✔ I don't have enough time for myself, my family, or my friends.

✔ I waste too much time.

✔ I'm constantly rushing.

✔ I don't have enough time to do the things I really enjoy.

✔ I frequently miss deadlines or am late for appointments.

✔ I spend almost no time planning my day.

✔ I almost never work with some kind of prioritized to-do list.

✔ I have difficulty saying no to others when they make demands on my time.

✔ I rarely delegate tasks and responsibilities.

✔ I procrastinate too often.

Checking off only one or two items on this list suggests that your time-management skills require only a tune-up. Checking off more than four of them suggests that your time-management skills may be in need of a major overhaul.

Being Mindful of Your Time

An important step in changing the way you manage your time is becoming aware of how you use your time. Without awareness, your time management can become a victim of your time-wasting patterns. As I discuss in Chapter 6, much of your life is lived on auto-pilot. You repeat the same patterns of thinking and behavior, failing to step away and consider how you're using your time. The price you pay ranges from the minor (lateness, procrastination, missed deadlines) to the more dramatic (missed opportunities and life experiences).

In this section, I show you how to be more mindful about time management to get the results you want.

Knowing where your time goes

For a short period of time, perhaps a day or two, keep a simple time log. A sheet of paper will do or, if you're more comfortable with your electronic device, use that. At convenient times during your day, enter what you did, or are doing, in the appropriate time slots. Don't become compulsive about this; you don't have to make it exact to the minute. However, be sure to record your electronic time usage — those times when you checked your e-mail, made or received a phone call, texted or IM-ed, visited social-networking sites, or surfed the Net. A sampling of a day or two should supply enough data to give you a rough picture of how you use — or misuse — your time. Use this simple rating code:

1 = Great use of my time

2 = Okay use of my time

3 = So-so use of my time

W = Waste of my time

Also add some comments that reflect how you feel about the way you used that time.

Table 8-1 gives you a sample of what one day may look like.

Table 8-1	Time Log for Monday		
Time Spent	*Activity*	*Rating*	*Comments*
7–7:20	Overslept	W	I didn't need it
7:20–7:45	Got ready for work	1	
7:45–8:05	Ate breakfast	1	
8:10–8:45	Commuted to work	1	
9–9:20	Read/answered e-mail	2	Ten minutes would do it
9:20–9:40	Returned phone calls	2, but W	Could have been a lot shorter
10–10:45	Did productive work	1	
10:45–11	Took a coffee break	2	
11–12	Sat through a meeting	3	Unnecessary meeting
12–12:30	Read/answered e-mail	2	
12:45–2	Lunch	1, but W	Too long
2:15–3:00	Did productive work (paying bills)	1	Good use of my time
3–3:45	Read/answered e-mail	2	Could have done it another time
3:45–4:00	Fiddled on computer	W	Dumb!
4–4:30	Did productive work	2	

(continued)

Table 8-1 *(continued)*

Time Spent	Activity	Rating	Comments
4:30–5	Paid bills	2	Do at home?
5–5:30	Made phone calls	3	
5:45–6:20	Commuted home	1	Listen to news and music
6:30–6:50	Talked with spouse	1	Don't do it enough!
6:50–7:15	Read newspaper	2	
7:15–8	Ate dinner	1	Over too quickly
8–9	Watched TV	2	Love this program!
9–10	Watched TV	W	Not worth watching
10–10:30	Watched news	2	
10:30–11	Read in bed	2	

Figuring out what you want more time for

As an exercise, grab a sheet of paper and jot down activities that you would like to spend more time doing. This exercise helps you get in touch with those activities that you value and derive satisfaction from.

The following is a sample of general items you may want to consider. (You can, of course, add others.)

- Spending time with your family and friends
- Advancing your job or career
- Pursuing a hobby or interest
- Reading
- Exercising
- Nurturing your soul
- Volunteering for community activities
- Traveling
- Sleeping

Knowing what you want to spend less time doing

Knowing what you want to spend more time doing is only half the battle. Knowing what you *don't* want to spend time doing is just as important. Here are some things I wish I spent less time doing. Make a list of your own.

- ✔ Working late at night and on weekends
- ✔ Doing office paperwork
- ✔ Attending events I don't enjoy
- ✔ Cleaning the house
- ✔ Doing laundry
- ✔ Spending time with people I don't enjoy
- ✔ Surfing the Web
- ✔ Watching so much television

Your goal is to fill your life with more of the things you *want* to do — things that bring more meaning and joy to your life. This means knowing how to minimize time spent doing the things you *have* to do.

Minding your time with cues and prompts

One good way of becoming mindful of your time is to use naturally occurring cues and prompts as signals to stop for a moment, take a breath, and consider how you're using your time. A prompt or cue can take various forms. It can be as simple as turning on your computer or beginning a new task. These basic behaviors prompt you to mentally step away from what you're doing and take a more careful look at what you have done and what you will do.

You can also introduce cues or prompts that are not naturally occurring. Stick a small paper dot on your watch face or use that photograph of your last family vacation as reminders to become more mindful of what you're doing or not doing.

Here are some other possible cues and prompts that could act as reminders:

- ✔ Hanging up after a phone call
- ✔ Feeling the urge to check your e-mail
- ✔ Leaving your office or cubicle
- ✔ Sending the kids off to school

- ✔ Finishing a task
- ✔ Taking a bathroom break
- ✔ Ending a meal
- ✔ Checking the time
- ✔ Turning on the TV
- ✔ Thinking of visiting your favorite social-media site

So, instead of automatically checking your e-mail every ten minutes or turning on the TV every time you're bored, use the behaviors as your cues to stop what you're about to do, step back mentally, take a breath or two, and gain some emotional distance. When you have that distance and awareness, ask yourself some pertinent questions that can help you evaluate how you're about to use your time.

Questioning your choices and changing behaviors

One great way of creating awareness is to have some questions ready to ask yourself. These can free you from the grip of auto-pilot and set a more productive course. Here are a few to help you get started:

- ✔ "Am I making the best use of my time right now?"
- ✔ "Am I procrastinating and avoiding doing something more important?"
- ✔ "Could I be doing what I'm doing in a more efficient way?"
- ✔ "Could I delegate or share this task with someone else?"
- ✔ "Do I really need to check my e-mail so frequently?"
- ✔ "Do I really need to be on the Internet right now?"
- ✔ "Should I really be watching TV right now?"

Rather than answer these questions with a simple yes or no, expand your answer to include additional material that either strengthens your rationale for doing what you plan to do or provides you with strong counter-arguments motivating you to spend your time doing something else. For example, your internal dialogue might sound something like this:

> "Okay, I'm about to pick up the TV remote. Is there something on now that I really want to watch? Not really. I'm a little bored and am avoiding doing stuff that I really should be doing. Watching TV is fine, but not right now. What could I be doing now that could be more important, more satisfying, or even more fun? What about hitting the gym or finishing that article? Watch TV later when there's something good on, and use it as a reward for doing other things first."

By introducing this "wise voice," you create a strong ally that can defend or revise how you spend your time. This makes it more difficult to be seduced by your avoidant automatic behavior. This awareness and self-talk makes it more likely that your use of time will be productive and worthwhile.

Becoming a List Maker

Making lists might seem so obvious and sooo last century, yet lists can be one of your better time-management tools. I suggest that you work with three lists:

- **A master to-do list.** This list is your source list, detailing all the tasks and involvements that you want to accomplish. This is your primary list.
- **A will-do-today list.** This list details how you want to spend your time *today*.
- **A will-do-later list.** This list enables you to schedule tasks in the *coming days or weeks*.

All these lists work together, providing you with a comprehensive time-management plan.

Starting with a master to-do list

You want to start with a master to-do list. Simply create a list of things you want to do or have to do either now or in the near future. Try to rank these items in order of importance, putting the more important ones first.

To help you rate the importance of the things on which you spend your time, try using this simple rating system:

1 = High priority (highly valued or important to me)

2 = Medium priority

3 = Low priority (not especially important to me)

D = Difficult or time-consuming

E = Easy or enjoyable

Q = Quick! Could do this in less than five minutes

Here is a sample of my current master to-do list:

To Do	*Priority/Rating*
See my patients	1
Call plumber re: water heater	1
Pay estimated taxes	1

(continued)

To Do	*Priority/Rating*
Pay phone bill	1-Q
Look into refinancing mortgage	1-D
Finish Chapter 8	1-D
Buy two books	2-E
Clean bedroom	2
Paint Katy's room	2
Get to the gym	2
Call Aunt Rose	2-E
Get a haircut	2
Do billing paperwork	2
Pick up printing paper	1-Q
Get plane tickets for trip	2
Pick up meds	2
Download photos	2-E
Download new music	3-E
Pick up lunch food	2-E

Review and update your list daily, adding items and tasks as they come up and removing tasks when they are completed or become irrelevant.

Creating a will-do-today list

When you have your master to-do list in hand, you're ready to create your more specific will-do-today list. Actually, this looks more like a daily planner than a usual list. It schedules how you want to spend your time *today*. This can be created the night before or first thing in the morning. You'll need a day planner, either paper or electronic. Both will work well.

Working from your master list, schedule your day. Enter the activities and tasks, work and personal, that you'd like to accomplish today. Table 8-2 shows a sample of what one of my "planned" days looks like.

Table 8-2	Will Do Today: Tuesday, January 5	
Time	*Task*	*Outcome*
7:30	Create my daily to-do list; check e-mail	✓
8	See patient A	✓
8:45	Make calls; send e-mail	✓
9	See patient B	✓
9:45	Make calls; send e-mail	✓

Time	Task	Outcome
11	See patient C (cancelled but paid estimated taxes instead)	
12	See patient D	✓
12:45	Eat lunch	✓
1	See patient E	✓
1:45	Make calls (Aunt Rose); check e-mail	✓
2	Do insurance billing (needs more time)	
2:45	Pay phone bill	✓
3	Go to the gym	✓
4	See patient F	✓
4:45	Buy plane tickets (try again tomorrow)	
5	See patient G	✓
5:45	Return phone calls	✓
6	See patient H	✓
7	Work on chapter at home	✓
8	Work on chapter at home	✓
8:30	Have dinner; watch news	✓
9	Have dinner; watch news	✓
9:30	Watch TV	✓
10	Read in bed	✓
11	Sleep	✓

Okay, I realize my days are pretty repetitive. Your days, I'm quite sure, are more varied, and more problematic in terms of time management.

Having a will-do-later list

As you look at your master to-do list and daily will-do-today list, you may decide that some items would be best done a day or two (or five) later. You need an extension of your will-do-today list where you can enter tasks to be done later on. Enter those tasks into your weekly or monthly planner. These may be tasks that can't be done until an earlier part is finished or until you obtain some additional information. It may be that the person you need to deal with won't be in the office until later in the week. It may simply be that you don't get around to it. Whatever the reason, keeping a longer-term list gives you more flexibility and comprehensiveness.

Keeping some tips in mind as you make your lists

Here are some suggestions and ideas to keep in mind as you put your daily lists together. Remember, not every idea works equally well for everybody. Give each suggestion some thought and give it a fair try. Ultimately you'll put together your own unique time-management ideas that best match your style and personality.

- ✔ **Don't overdo it.** Don't make your to-do list so long that it becomes unwieldy. Watch the number of tasks you stick on that list.

- ✔ **Don't schedule the "guaranteed to happen" stuff.** Don't include tasks you know for certain you'll be doing. On my daily list, for example, I don't include activities that will automatically be done, such as commuting to and from work and eating dinner. (I actually end up with a very short list.) These tasks happen without my prompting and don't require any special motivation or pre-planning. These are usually not time wasters for me. Again, come up with a daily plan that works best for you.

- ✔ **Do the important tasks first.** Starting a new year, a new week, or even a new day often fills us with resolve. We begin our days with a higher level of motivation and determination. It probably makes sense to schedule the tougher, less desirable tasks first thing in your day. Pick a more difficult high-priority task first. Commit to staying with that task long enough to finish it or make a significant amount of progress.

- ✔ **Be flexible with priorities.** When you write down your daily tasks, don't feel compelled to fill your day with all Level 1 items (the most difficult tasks). They *are* important and should have a place on your daily calendar. But don't be compulsive. Plan your day knowing yourself and what will work best for you. For some, doing a challenging, difficult task first thing makes sense; for others, later in the day might work better. You can mix it up a bit, juggling the difficult tasks with the easier ones.

- ✔ **Identify your best work times.** You may be a morning person. You may be a night owl. The hours right after lunch may be your least-effective working hours. Try to match your more-difficult, higher-priority tasks with your more-productive working times. Save easier tasks for times when you feel less motivated.

- ✔ **Don't over-commit.** Recognize that you may be less efficient than you expect to be. Be realistic. Be reasonable. If you do it all and have time to do more, that's great.

- ✔ **Break bigger tasks into smaller pieces**. If you're intimidated by the time it may take to do a major or complex task, break it up into smaller pieces and focus on one piece. It's hard to start a task that seems overwhelming. Create smaller chunks. For example:

- Clean up the house → Clean the kitchen

- Write the chapter → Write the outline

- Pay all the bills → Pay the high-priority bills

✔ **Schedule breaks.** Recognize that a break between tasks can give you a breather and even act as a reward for your impressive effort. These few minutes can be used to catch up on e-mail, make some social calls, text a friend — whatever. You can also take a quick walk, do some stretches, or do one of the many relaxation exercises I describe in Chapter 4.

✔ **Do the "quickies" quickly.** During breaks or other down times, you may be able to knock off some easy tasks fairly quickly. Just do it. Anything that you've given a "Q" ranking (meaning it can be done in less than five minutes), do right away. Get it off your list.

✔ **Group similar tasks together.** Save yourself a great deal of time by doing similar tasks at the same time. Grouping tasks is much more efficient and much less stressful. You can, for example:

- *Pay all your bills at the same time.* Designate a time to go through the bills, write the checks, address the envelopes, and mail them.

- *Combine your errands.* Rather than running to the store for every little item, group errands together. Keep a "Things We Need or Will Need Soon" list in a handy place and refer to your list before you dash out for that single item. An even simpler way to do this is to photocopy a master list with the common items you usually need to replace and stick it on the fridge. Check off a needed item when you notice that you're running low. When you've checked off a bunch of items on the list, head to the store.

✔ **Indicate outcome.** When something is completed, either cross it off your list or make a "done" comment in your outcome column. If you don't get around to starting or finishing something, make a note about when you plan to complete the task.

✔ **Update your master list.** What you don't accomplish by the end of the day should be reassessed the next day. It stays on your master list until it's done or you deem it unimportant.

✔ **Use the 80/20 rule.** Apply the Pareto principle, also known as the 80/20 rule, to your time-management analysis. Simply put, it states: Of the things you have to do, doing 20 percent of the most-valued tasks will provide you with 80 percent of the satisfaction you may have gotten by doing them all. In other words, skipping your lower-priority items doesn't really cost you a whole lot in the long run. Don't get fixated on those less-valued, less-productive activities. Ask yourself, "Would it really be so awful if I didn't do this task?"

Go low or high tech?

You can create your to-do list on paper or electronically, working with your smartphone, tablet, or computer. Going digital, if that's your preferred medium, can add a little fun to the otherwise mundane business of scheduling your time. And we know that we tend to use those tools that are the most fun to work with. Good time-management software and apps, such as Outlook, Google Calendar, and Lotus Notes, can make your time-management monitoring easier. On the other hand, you may prefer going the low-tech route, using a pencil and paper or small notebook (nothing to be ashamed of here). In any case, just make it easy to access your lists wherever you may be.

Minimizing your Distractions and Interruptions

It's not only the "too much to do in too little time" that creates stress; it's also how your time is wasted by others or yourself. Much of your time can be consumed by small interruptions or distractions that take you away from what you're doing and thereby lengthen the time spent on the task at hand. Your distractions and interruptions may take the form of obsessively checking your e-mail while in the middle of doing something else or being sidetracked by a spouse or roommate who has "just one quick question." Here are some suggestions to help you avoid wasted time.

Managing electronic interruptions

✔ Whenever you can, "bundle." Make phone calls and e-mails in batches. Rather than interrupting your schedule to make or return noncritical phone calls or send e-mails, wait until you have several items and do them all at once.

✔ Just because you receive a phone call, text, e-mail, or IM doesn't mean you have to respond to it at that moment (unless your job requires that you do!). Let things go to voicemail. Turn off the pop-up notification that alerts you to every new digital message. When you take a break or finish a task, *then* check your digital messages.

✔ Respond to your messages during low-productivity times. If answering your electronic messages is critical to what you're doing, put it on your to-do list. Build it in.

✔ When you do check your digital messages, realize that you don't have to respond to everything. Filter out the more important messages and let the less urgent stuff go until you have more time.

✔ Whenever possible (and appropriate), use e-mail or texting rather than the telephone. It's far more efficient and gives you more control over your time. (On the other hand, use the phone when you care about the person on the other end!)

Losing the visitors

Other people can be pesky. These "others" may be family members, room-mates, co-workers, or others who like to pop their heads into your space and chat whenever they get a chance. (To be fair, you may be the problem, dis-tracting others while robbing yourself of productive time.) Some ideas:

✔ **Be polite but firm** and tell your visitors that "this really isn't a good time to talk. I absolutely have to finish this task. But I'll get back to you."

✔ **Hide.** If you can find a room or space that is off the beaten track and where you can do some solid work, give it a try. Sometimes a restaurant or coffee shop can work.

✔ **Look unavailable.** If you have a door, keep it closed. If you have an empty chair, put something on it. It can be books, files, clothing — any-thing that may dissuade a would-be sitter.

✔ **Try some headphones.** People tend to steer away from people with headphones on. Remember, you don't need to be listening to anything on your headphones. Just having them on should do the trick.

✔ **Talk to your recurring interrupter.** Tell the person about your problem with distractions. The person may not realize that he or she is part of your problem.

Lowering the volume

Noise can be a subtle or not-so-subtle source of distraction. It may be a loud co-worker or street noise. Shutting your door can help, but it may not be an option. Some other suggestions:

✔ **Consider noise-canceling headphones.** Use them with or without some relaxing music. Quality ear-buds can have a similar effect without your looking so anti-social.

✔ **Get a white-noise machine,** which can mask a variety of distracting sounds (traffic in the street, the upstairs neighbors). You can download white-noise files and have them repeat on a playback loop.

✔ **Leave.** If a task or project demands a high level of attentiveness, find a quieter place to work. Sometimes a conference room at work goes mostly unused. At home it may be another room, or possibly space in the base-ment or attic. Sometimes less obvious places can work. On fine days, try the park or a quiet section of a lobby in a nearby hotel. Be creative.

Limiting your breaks

Taking a break can be a sensible and necessary part of your day. It can give you the opportunity to re-group, refresh, and start your next task with a clearer head. The problem is taking too many breaks, or taking them at the wrong times. Some suggestions:

- ✔ **Schedule your breaks to follow the completion of a task.** This can be your reward for finishing.

- ✔ **Do something that is relaxing or even fun.** It can be browsing the Internet, shopping online, or playing a digital game. Of course, it can also be listening to music, watching a video, or reading an article or a few pages of your current book.

- ✔ **Limit the time you take for a break.** The most common trap is socializing with others for far too long. After you've mingled for a bit, take your coffee with you back to your space.

Shifting your time

A more radical solution is to re-arrange the times you need to concentrate and think so as to avoid interruptions and distractions for at least part of your day. Can you get up earlier and start your day (either at home or at the office) sooner, before the distractions appear? Doing some work after the kids are in bed may be more productive than sitting at the dining-room table on a Saturday afternoon. Your office may be much quieter after most of your co-workers have left. Just consider it.

Turning it into a positive

Whenever possible, turn your interruptions into something positive. Use those interruptions as cues to step back, do some relaxing breathing, and refocus your thoughts and direction. This brief breather can be a useful reminder, making you more aware of what you were doing and what you should be doing.

Minimizing your TV time

As one of my children once commented, "Have you ever noticed how much longer the days are when you don't watch TV?" Although some television is terrific, a lot of it is not terrific. It's clear, at least to me, that people waste too much time watching television. I'm convinced that the quality of our lives would be greatly enriched if we watched less television.

TV reduction tactics include the following:

- ✔ **Use your DVR.** Almost never watch a television program when it's originally broadcast. Record the programs you like and watch them in a block, at a time you choose. You may feel left out at the water cooler, but your time management will be amazingly better.

- ✔ **Try to cut back drastically on the time you spend watching TV.** Never just randomly channel surf, sticking with the least-objectionable program. Even if you pre-record shows, watch only those shows that you *really* want to watch. Try to keep your TV time down to less than two hours per night.

- ✔ **Make one evening a week a no-TV night.** Instead of watching television, do something else. Read a book. Go to the gym. Make soup. Make love. Go to bed earlier. You can always watch that show at a later time.

- ✔ **Avoid DVR pileup.** When you've collected more recorded programs than you could possibly watch in one day of dedicated TV viewing, start winnowing. Begin deleting rather than adding to your growing collection. Use the one-month rule. If you haven't watched it within a month, delete it.

A few less obvious time-management tips

If you still have some room in your time-management toolbox, here are some additional tips to help you manage your time more effectively and efficiently.

- ✔ **Buy some things in bulk.** You can save time (and often money) by buying many of your more frequently needed items at the same time. Many items around the house and office have to be replaced regularly. Buying office supplies, toilet paper, canned goods, paper towels, pet food, and so on in larger quantities can make sense, if you have enough room to store all your bulk purchases. But be careful! Ask yourself how many months will pass before you use up that mega-gallon jar of spaghetti sauce.

- ✔ **Cook ahead.** Preparing meals can be incredibly time-consuming. Whenever possible, prepare enough food so that you have several meals available. You can cook soups, stews, casseroles, and sauces in larger quantities so that you can freeze additional meals. A dismal day on the weekend is the perfect time to cook up a storm. Just make sure to clearly label those plastic containers.

- ✔ **Work the Web.** These days you can do almost anything on the Web. Shopping online can be a great way to save time, and many companies offer free shipping. If you're not happy with your purchase, most companies let you ship the item right back. The downside? It's all too easy to find things that you really can live without. The Internet can speed up your banking and help you place reservations for hotels, restaurants, planes, trains, and just about anything else. You can also buy anything from books to automobiles and often save a lot of money, as well as time.

Winning the waiting game

You may find that much of your time is lost while waiting. It may be waiting 45 minutes for the doctor to see you; waiting for the cable guy to come for his promised 9:30 a.m. appointment (good luck with that!); waiting for your bus, subway, plane, or train to show up or depart; or waiting for that meeting to get started.

The trick to beating the waiting game is to *expect* that at various times you'll find yourself having to wait — and then to put that waiting time to good use. Have some form of involvement, task, or activity easily available. This time-filling activity doesn't have to be actual work, though it can be, but it should be something you pre-plan to do when you find yourself having to wait.

I assume that most folks these days own some form of digital device, and many automatically listen to music or play a video game. Here are some less obvious ways of putting that wait time to better use:

- ✔ **Read.** Have a book, newspaper, magazine, or digital counterpart with you at most times. Fun reading, work-related reading, whatever.

- ✔ **Learn.** Podcasts are a welcome way to pass the time. For the last year I've been trying to learn Spanish via a series of podcasts. While pedaling on the elliptical or heading home from work on the subway, I master the skill of declining irregular verbs. My favorite radio shows are usually available in podcast form, too.

- ✔ **Play.** Do the crossword puzzle, challenge yourself to Sudoku, or, yes, even play a computer game.

- ✔ **Breathe.** Take this time to do some relaxation and meditation. Focus on your breathing, introduce some relaxing imagery, and turn your waiting time into a mini-vacation.

- ✔ **E-mail.** Work on your laptop, tablet, or smartphone to read and answer your e-mail. You can also make phone calls, as long as you don't annoy your neighbors.

- ✔ **Work.** Do actual work, whether it's that pesky little task your boss assigned or personal tasks like balancing your checkbook.

- ✔ **Update.** Update your to-do list and daily calendar.

- ✔ **Sync.** You probably own more than one digital device. By syncing your computer with your phone and tablet, you can create a continuous link with your electronic life.

Getting around Psychological Roadblocks to Time Management

You probably recognize that simply knowing the tricks of time management doesn't guarantee that you'll put them into practice. You're human! Your emotional and psychological dynamics come into play and can act as barriers that slow or even halt your good time-management intentions. Identifying those self-defeating patterns becomes just as necessary to effectively managing your time as is your to-do list. This section covers two of the more common time-wasting patterns. See which ones fit you and what you can do to overcome them.

Getting over your desire to be perfect

The old adage "Anything worth doing is worth doing well" is misguided. There's nothing wrong with wanting to do something well, even very well. But when your standards are too high, and you aim for perfection, you will feel stress. Perfection is overrated. Being perfect for any longer than three minutes is hard. Whenever you strive for perfection, you fall into one of two time-wasting and stress-producing traps:

✔ You spend more time on the task or activity than is warranted.

✔ You avoid doing the task altogether for fear that you won't do it well enough.

Strive for "pretty darn good" instead of "perfect." And, sometimes, let yourself strive for "just okay."

Overcoming procrastination

Procrastination may be one of the main time robbers and ultimate stress producers in your life. I have yet to see more than a handful of people who don't lose time by procrastinating. By avoiding the kinds of activities that are important and valued, you wind up spending a lot of time doing activities that are less valued and less satisfying. Procrastinating on writing that letter to a loved one, updating your resume, or making that phone call to a friend almost always leads to regret.

You probably procrastinate for one of four major reasons:

✔ **Discomfort dodging.** Life often involves doing things that involve some degree of effort and discomfort. When you're experiencing low discomfort tolerance (LDT), you begin looking for ways to avoid doing that discomforting task.

✔ **Fear of failure.** You're afraid that you may not be able to do the avoided task as well as you'd like. Fear of failure and feeling bad about yourself make it less likely that you'll do what you ought to be doing. You see failure as a reflection of your self-worth and believe that if you fail, you are a failure. You figure, mistakenly, that maybe if you avoid the task or situation, you won't have to deal with failure. Not a great game plan for life.

✔ **Fear of disapproval.** As is the case with fear of failure, you're afraid that somebody will be displeased with your performance and disapprove of you. You over-value other people's opinions and equate that approval or disapproval with your self-worth. Misguidedly, you avoid doing what you ought to be doing to spare yourself the bad feelings you create when you think you will be disapproved.

✔ **Anger or resentment.** You feel that you shouldn't have to do the task or activity, and you're angry at having to do it. You feel that the world, or some of the people in it, are not treating you fairly. You resent having to do that task or face that situation because of that anger and resentment.

Any or all of the preceding reasons can stop you in your tracks. If one or more of these dynamics describes you, head to Chapter 10 to find out how you can turn around this "procrastinatory" thinking.

Bite the bullet

If you find that dislike and discomfort are steering you away from doing what you should be doing, see if you can challenge your assumptions. Ask yourself, "Why must I always do the things I like and want to do?" The answer, of course, is that you don't have to avoid difficulty and discomfort. Just do it! Then ask yourself a second question: "Wouldn't I be better off putting up with some discomfort and getting it out of the way?" The answer: Absolutely!

Commit to a chunk of time

My son introduced me to this approach. He sets the timer app on his computer to, say, 30 minutes. (Somebody once estimated that 25 to 30 minutes is the optimal attention period for maximum performance.) He commits to working on a project or task for those 30 minutes without stopping, without being distracted. When the alarm beeps, he can stop and take a brief five-minute break. Or, if he feels like he's on a roll, he can continue working on the task.

Motivate yourself

Sometimes your level of internal motivation doesn't get you where you need to go. You need external motivation. You can either reward yourself for doing something or penalize yourself for not doing it.

Try the reward approach first. Create your own motivational ladder by coming up with a list of rewards that can motivate you to get the job done. Then rank them in order of their importance to you. For example:

✔ Treat yourself to a mini-vacation.

✔ Buy yourself something big that you've been dying to get but have been denying yourself.

✔ Treat yourself to a great meal or a dessert.

✔ Go to the movies, see a play, or do something fun.

✔ Buy yourself a small present.

However, being nice, even to yourself, doesn't always cut it. You may respond better to the threat of pain and suffering than to a positive reward. If pain is your thing, try creating a penalty for not completing a task:

✔ Deny yourself a favorite pleasure for a day (TV, a movie, a dessert, going out, and so on).

✔ Deny yourself a favorite pleasure for a week.

✔ Send a donation to a political candidate you dislike.

✔ Send cash anonymously to a person you know and dislike. (Make it one week's salary and I personally guarantee success.)

Use the smallest reward or penalty that gets the job done. If that doesn't work, move up to the next reward or penalty on your motivational ladder. Be creative.

To make sure that you do enforce a penalty, tell a friend about your plan and ask him or her to make sure that you follow through. I find that this approach improves your chances of successfully breaking through procrastination. If money is involved, put it in an envelope, address it, put a stamp on it, and give it to a friend, telling him or her to mail it if you don't come through on your end of the deal.

Go public

Make a public commitment. Tell a good friend about a task that you want to get done and tell him or her when you will complete it. Better yet, tell a bunch of people, perhaps in your next tweet or status update. Be sure to remind that friend or friends to ask you if you have done what you said you would.

Become more selective and assertive

After you identify those activities and tasks that have a lower priority in your life, discover ways to reduce or even eliminate them. For example, social engagements can easily eat up a good deal of your time. You probably attend many engagements out of a sense of obligation or habit. But you don't have to attend absolutely every party or dinner you're invited to. Nor do you have to attend every meeting posted by your church, temple, school, or any other organization you're affiliated with. Go to those events that you truly want to attend, but be selective and assertive. Give yourself permission to say no to many other invitations. You won't end up being hated by others or ostracized from the community.

Letting Go: Discovering the Joys of Delegating

Remember that old slogan, "If you want something done right, do it yourself"? Yes, it holds some truth. However, by doing it all yourself, you quickly discover that your stress level shoots skyward. Delegating tasks and responsibilities can save you time and spare you a great deal of stress.

You may have a problem delegating for several reasons. Here are some of the more common ones:

- ✔ You believe that no one else is competent enough to do the task.
- ✔ You believe that no one else really understands the problem the way you do.
- ✔ You believe that no one else is motivated quite the way you are.
- ✔ You don't trust anyone else to be able to manage the responsibilities.

All these reasons can hold some truth. But in many cases, these reasons aren't accurate at all. The reality is that other people can be taught. You may be pleasantly surprised by the level of work others can bring to a task or responsibility.

Even if you're right, and others don't do the job as well as you do, you're probably still better off delegating than taking on everything yourself and feeling incredibly stressed.

The fine art of delegating

You may be from the "Do this, and have it on my desk by tomorrow morning!" school of delegating. Here are some tips to help you delegate more effectively:

- ✔ **Find the right person.** Make sure that your delegatees have the knowledge and skills to do the tasks asked of them. And if you can't find a person who has the knowledge and skills, consider investing the time in training someone. In the longer run, you'll be ahead of the game.
- ✔ **Package your request for help in positive terms.** Tell the person why you selected him or her. Offer a genuine compliment reflecting that you recognize some ability or competence that makes that person right for the job.
- ✔ **Be appreciative of that person's time.** Recognize that you're aware that the person has his or her own work to do, but that you would really be grateful if he or she could help you with this task.
- ✔ **Don't micro-manage.** After you assign a task and carefully explain what needs to be done, let the person do it. Keep your hands off unless you clearly see that things are taking a wrong turn.

✔ **Reward the effort.** If the person does a good job, say so. And if he or she doesn't do it quite the way you would have but still put a lot of effort into the task, let him or her know that you appreciate the effort.

Delegating begins at home

You may associate the word delegating with working in an office and handing off a project to an associate or assistant. However, delegating tasks and duties at home is a major way to save a lot of time. Here are some suggestions:

✔ **Let one and all share in the fun.** Everyone in the family (assuming that he or she is old enough to walk and talk) can, and should, have a role in sharing household duties and responsibilities.

✔ **Start with a list.** Divvy up those less-desirable chores, such as washing dishes (or putting them in the dishwasher), doing laundry, cleaning up bedrooms, taking out the trash, and emptying the dishwasher.

✔ **Start small.** Don't overwhelm your family right off the bat. Give them one or two assignments and then add on as appropriate.

✔ **Don't feel guilty.** In the long run, your family will come to value the experience. (Recognize that it may be a very long run, however.)

Buying Time

You may subscribe to the old work ethic, "Never pay anyone to do something that you can readily do yourself." This is a mistake. Hiring someone to help you can give you more time for the things you want to do and, in the process, make your life simpler and less stressful.

Am I being casual about your finances? I don't think so. I realize that you may not have a lot of extra money in your pocket. However, gone are the days when only the rich hired other people to help them out. Sometimes hiring someone else is clearly wise.

Here are some questions to help you decide whether hiring someone else or paying for a service makes sense:

✔ What chores do I absolutely hate?

✔ Which chores constantly provoke a battle between me and my spouse or me and my roommate?

✔ What chores do I merely dislike doing?

✔ What chores do I not do very well?

✔ What chores do I not mind doing, but really aren't worth my time and effort?

Tasks that you may want someone else to do for you include cleaning, doing laundry, grocery shopping, painting, handling pet care, mowing the lawn, and so on.

Avoid paying top dollar

Getting someone else to do less-than-desirable chores need not cost you a bundle. You probably don't need an expensive professional. Lots of people who are "between opportunities" will be willing to do chores for you if you pay them. Go online. A number of Internet services can match you up with someone who is willing to help you out (for a fee, of course). Friends on social-networking sites can also be a source of referrals. Don't rule out non-digital sources — supermarket billboards, neighborhood circulars, or your local newspaper. (When you find someone, be sure to check his or her references.) And don't overlook high-school and college students. Schools often have an "employment-wanted" service, especially during the summer months. These students can be cheaper and surprisingly reliable.

Realistically assess your financial ability to hire someone to do a few or many of the items on your list. Remember, too, that the emotional relief and the extra time you gain are well worth the money in many cases. Spend the bucks.

Strive for deliverance

These days, many of the things you need can be delivered. If you live in a good-sized city, almost everything can be delivered. You can save time by dialing the right series of digits or clicking the right places on the Internet. In addition to take-out food, items that you can have delivered to your door include the following:

- Groceries
- Clean laundry
- DVDs
- Meats from the butcher
- Sweets from the bakery
- Liquor from the liquor store
- Books
- Actually, just about everything

Chapter 9

Eating, Exercising, and Getting Your Zzzs

In This Chapter

▶ Understanding how what you eat can affect your level of stress

▶ Exercising to reduce your stress

▶ Getting a good night's sleep

Remember when you were a young child and you got cranky when you were hungry or tired? Those were not your finest moments. Just ask your parents. Your ability to cope with frustration and disappointment was all but nonexistent.

Now that you've grown up, your stresses may be different, but your physical state still plays a major role in determining how stressed you become. What you eat, when you eat, your level of overall fitness, and the quality of your sleep all affect your ability to cope with stress.

This chapter shows you how you can develop a more stress-effective lifestyle — through diet, exercise, and sleep — which can, in turn, strengthen your body's ability to cope with potential stress and help you resist its negative effects. Simply put: Your body is a temple. Treat it nicely.

Stress-Effective Eating

If you're like most people, I suspect that your dietary habits are less than perfect. Your eating is probably a hit-and-miss affair — inconsistent, rushed, and tailored to meet your busy schedule.

I know your life is already stressed enough without having to worry about what goes into your mouth. However, what you eat — and how you eat it — can contribute significantly to your ability to cope with stress. Eating the wrong things or eating at the wrong times can add to your stress level. Not to worry. Help is here.

Feeding your brain

In recent years, a lot of attention has been paid to the relationship between food and mood — what you eat and how you feel. Researchers now have a better idea of how different foods affect your psychological states and how food can increase or decrease the stress in your life.

One of the major biochemical elements involved in your stress experience is something called *serotonin*. Serotonin is a naturally occurring chemical neurotransmitter in your brain. Changing serotonin levels can dramatically change the way you feel. Antidepressant medication like Prozac, Paxil, and Zoloft can alter the amount of serotonin in your brain, which can alter your mood and affect how you cope with a potential stress.

The foods you eat can also change the serotonin levels in your brain. Your diet is an important way of regulating your serotonin levels. Putting the right stuff on your plate means you have a better chance of giving your brain what it needs.

Choosing low-stress foods

The following are some specific food guidelines that can help you choose foods to lower your stress and help your body cope with stress:

- **Include some complex carbohydrates in every meal.** Complex carbohydrates, such as pasta, cereals, potatoes, and brown rice, can enhance your performance when under stress. Foods rich in carbohydrates can increase the levels of serotonin in the brain, making you feel better. Too many complex carbohydrates, however, are not the best thing for you. Remember: Moderation.

- **Reduce your intake of simple carbohydrates.** Sweetened, sugary foods — simple carbohydrates, like soda and candy — can make you feel better in the short run but worse in the long run.

- **Eat adequate amounts of protein.** This means eating more fish, chicken, and other lean meats. Foods high in protein enhance mental functioning and supply essential amino acids that can help repair damage to your body's cells. Should your dietary preferences take a vegetarian direction, look to beans, nuts, and seeds (garbanzo beans, pinto beans, soybeans, tofu, and lentils), dairy (yogurt and cottage cheese), eggs, and fruits and vegetables (avocados, broccoli, and spinach) to meet this source.

- **Eat your vegetables.** Beans, peppers, carrots, squash, and dark-green leafy veggies, whether cooked or raw, provide your body with the vitamins and nutrients it needs to resist the negative effects of stress.

✓ **Don't forget fruit.** Fruit can be a good source of vitamins and minerals that can help your body combat stress. Vitamins A, C, and E are antioxidants which have been shown to relieve stress. The B vitamins, thiamin (B1), riboflavin (B2), niacin (B3), pantothenic acid (B5), pyridoxine (B6), and biotin (B7), help your our body obtain energy from the food you eat.

✓ **Get plenty of potassium.** Milk (especially the low-fat variety), whole grains, wheat germ, and nuts all can provide your body with potassium, a mineral that can help your muscles relax. Bananas, a personal favorite, are also a good source of potassium.

Ten stress-relieving foods

Here's a more specific list of ten foods that are not only good for you but also can help lower your stress level:

✓ **Nuts:** Especially almonds, which have lots of magnesium, B2 (riboflavin), zinc, and vitamin E. Almonds can help regulate cortisol levels. But don't overdo it. Nuts can be caloric, but they're great as a snack.

✓ **Broccoli:** Your mother was right. Eat your broccoli. It contains lots of B vitamins and folic acid, and it's great as a side dish with fish or chicken. Spinach is good, too — lots of magnesium.

✓ **Fish:** Most varieties of fish contain the important B vitamins, B6 and B12. These can play a role in synthesizing serotonin, which can affect your moods. Tuna and salmon are loaded with omega-3 fatty acids that can play a role in regulating adrenaline.

✓ **Milk:** Again your mother was right. Milk contains vitamins B2 and B12, along with antioxidants that are often associated with reducing stress. It also contains tryptophan, which can increase the production of serotonin. Milk also has calcium, magnesium, and potassium, which are important stress-regulating elements. You don't have to drink your milk straight; pour it on some cereal instead. Go for the skim variety.

✓ **Bananas:** They're full of potassium. They're also a great snack when you need some fuel in your system, and they're a great addition to fortified cereal.

✓ **Blueberries:** These are filled with antioxidants and vitamin C, which help fight stress. Grab a handful when you need a healthy treat or sprinkle some on your morning (or evening) cereal.

✓ **Oranges:** Stress can reduce your levels of vitamin C, but oranges can replenish that vitamin, which boosts your immune system. Oranges also make a great snack.

✓ **Sweet potatoes:** Actually, they're not really potatoes — they're roots. They're also a great source of vitamin B6, vitamin A, and antioxidants such as beta-carotene.

✓ **Brown rice:** This is much better for you than the white variety. Brown rice has much more manganese and phosphorus than does white rice. It contains more iron and greater amounts of vitamins B3, B1, and B6, all known to have stress-reducing properties. Brown rice is richer in fiber, selenium, and antioxidants. It also has a great "nutty" flavor.

✓ **Avocados:** These are loaded with potassium and vitamin A. The taste and texture can be highly satisfying.

Stopping the stress-eating cycle

Are you an emotional eater? If so, you may eat whenever you're anxious, upset, nervous, or depressed. Although emotional eaters can still put it away when they're happy, delighted, non-anxious, and non-depressed (and yes, during those rare times when they're actually hungry), most emotional eaters eat when they feel they need to feed their stress.

When you feed your stress, a destructive cycle begins. You feel stressed, so your food choices are not always the best. For some reason of cruel fate, foods that tend to make you feel good are usually the foods that are not so good for your body. Research studies have shown that stressed emotional eaters eat sweeter, higher-fat foods and more energy-dense meals than unstressed and non-emotional eaters. Chocolate, ice cream, pizza, cake, donuts, and cookies may make you feel terrific — but, unfortunately, only for about 17 seconds. Then, of course, your stress returns (plus a ton of guilt), and you feel the need for another bout of eating. The cycle repeats itself.

The first step in breaking the cycle is becoming aware of exactly when you are distressed and identifying your feelings. When you feel the urge to open the refrigerator door, you need to realize that you're experiencing some form of discomfort. It may be hunger, but more likely it's stress.

Before you put any food in your mouth, stop and take stock of your emotional state. Ask yourself, "Am I really hungry or am I feeling emotionally distressed?" If it's truly hunger, eat. Otherwise label your feelings (for example, "I'm upset," "I'm nervous," or "I'm a wreck!"). One way of determining whether you're truly hungry or merely having an emotional desire to eat is to ask yourself another question: "Would healthy foods (a salad, low-fat yogurt, banana, or apple) appease my desire to eat?" If not (and you're thinking about fast food, chocolate, pizza, cake, or ice cream) your eating is probably not about satisfying basic hunger. It's about eating in response to stress. Simply breaking the stress-eating connection for even a moment can give you a different perspective and an increased level of motivation that can sustain you, until you find something a little more redeeming than filling your mouth.

The following are some other tips that you can use to improve your relationship with food when you're stressed.

Distract yourself

One of the best things you can do is involve yourself in some activity you enjoy that will take your mind off eating. Do something. Anything. Some eating substitutes that will keep you away from the kitchen include the following:

- ✔ **Get out of the house.** Often, simply changing your environment can rid you of the old eating cues. Go for a walk. Do an errand. Visit a friend.

- ✔ **Get some exercise.** Hit the stationary bike or treadmill, or simply do some floor exercises like sit-ups or even just stretching.

✔ **Read a good book.**

✔ **Watch an interesting television program.**

✔ **Cook something.** This may seem like asking for trouble, but often the process of cooking can serve as a substitute for eating. A hint: Don't make cookies or cakes. Try something like a soup or a casserole, something that is filling, takes time to prepare and cook, and isn't immediately ready to eat.

Substitute relaxation for food

Whenever you're about to open the refrigerator to calm your frayed nerves, consider substituting a relaxation break. Simple deep breathing, rapid relaxation, relaxation imagery, or any of the other marvelous techniques I describe in Chapters 4 and 5 can induce a feeling of emotional calm that can reduce your desire to eat. That's all you may need to ease you past a difficult moment.

Work with a stress cue

Sometimes a little reminding goes a long way. Create a stress-eating reminder that you can put on your fridge or on the cabinet where you keep delicious snacks. One of my patients came up with what I thought was a beaut: She put a not terribly attractive picture of herself in her heavier days in a small magnetic frame that she stuck on her refrigerator.

You may decide to be less brutal and opt for something more neutral. One friend has the question "Are you really hungry?" taped to her kitchen door. Even more innocuous is a simple little colored circle of paper you can affix at strategic places in your kitchen. It reminds you that you shouldn't open the door unless you're hungry. Only you know what it represents and why it's there.

Eat your breakfast

Again, your mother was right! Research shows that eating a nutritious (low-fat, high-carbohydrate) breakfast makes you more alert, more focused, and in a much better mood than if you have a high-fat, high-carbohydrate breakfast; have a moderate-fat, moderate-carbohydrate breakfast; or have no breakfast at all.

Skipping breakfast can lower your body's ability to cope with the stress that lies in wait for you later in the day. Starting the day on the right nutritional foot is important. When you wake up in the morning, as many as 11 or 12 hours have passed since you last ate. You need to refuel.

And don't forget lunch

Lunchtime tends to be one of the busier times of your day. With a lot to do, eating lunch may be low on your list of priorities, but don't skip it. Your body functions best when it gets fed regularly. Missing lunch can leave you feeling tense and edgy.

When you do have lunch, don't overdo it. A big lunch can leave you lethargic and dreaming of a mid-afternoon siesta, a practice frowned upon by many businesses.

Eat like a cow

Eating a big meal can result in your feeling lethargic soon after eating. To digest that heavy meal, your body needs a greater supply of blood. This blood has to come from other places in your body, like your brain, depriving it of some of the oxygen it needs to keep you alert. The solution? Graze like a cow.

Spread out your eating fairly evenly throughout the day. Avoid those huge meals that load you down with calories and leave you feeling ready for a nap. Instead consider smaller, lighter meals at your regular mealtime. Supplement them with healthy snacks. Have breakfast, a mid-morning snack, and then a light lunch, another snack later in the afternoon (a piece of fruit is good), and a moderate dinner. A snack later in the evening (try some air-popped popcorn) should avert any hunger pangs. It seems to work for cows, doesn't it?

Drink like a camel

Most people don't get enough liquids. Every day you lose water through your breath, perspiration, urine, and bowel movements. For your body to function properly, it's important that you replace this water loss by drinking beverages and eating foods that contain water. So how much should you drink? The oft-heard advice is, "Drink eight eight-ounce glasses of water a day." Although the "8 by 8" rule isn't supported by hard scientific evidence, it remains popular because it's easy to remember. The Institute of Medicine's estimate agrees with this determination (1.9 liters per day). You can re-write this rule as: "Drink at least eight eight-ounce glasses of fluid a day," because all fluids count toward the daily total.

The notion of drinking this amount of liquid is, for many of us, a joke. If you're like most people, you usually wait until you're thirsty before heading for the kitchen. Unfortunately, by then it's a little late. Your body needs the liquid before you feel that thirst. You may need to modify your liquid intake depending on your level of activity, the climate you live in, your health status, and whether you're pregnant or breast-feeding.

Load up earlier in the day

For most people, the simplest way to lose weight is to eat more in the first half of the day than they do in the last half. Then they have time to burn off many of those earlier calories. Recall that old bit of nutritional wisdom, "Eat like a king in the morning, a prince at noon, and a pauper at night."

Simply supplement

If you think you may not be getting enough of your needed vitamins and minerals, consider taking a daily multiple vitamin and mineral supplement. If your daily diet gives you all the nutritional good stuff you need, this may not be necessary. However, you may be one of the many whose diet is not nutritionally praiseworthy and could benefit from some supplemental help. Talk to your doctor first if you feel you're not getting enough nutrition and are thinking about taking supplements.

Eating mindfully

Mindful eating can not only help you become more aware of what you eat but also help you control what and how much you eat. Shamash Alidina, in his useful *Mindfulness For Dummies* (Wiley), suggests the following steps to help you master mindful eating.

1. **Remove distractions.**

   Turn off the TV. Get away from your computer. No book, newspaper, nothing. Just you and your meal.

2. **Do three minutes of mindful breathing**.

   Simply notice and focus on your breathing. (Chapter 6 offers tips for mindful breathing exercises.)

3. **Become aware of what you're eating.**

   Notice the colors and shapes of the food on your plate. Notice how it smells.

4. **Notice what your body is doing**.

   Salivating? Notice what your hunger feels like. Pay attention to your thinking. See your thoughts as thoughts rather than facts. Let any extraneous thoughts go.

5. **Slowly put a morsel of food into your mouth.** Be mindful of the taste, texture, and smell of the food. Chew slowly, noticing how the texture of the food changes.

   Don't swallow immediately. Chew fully.

6. **When you're ready, repeat with another mouthful.**

   Continue to eat mindfully, becoming aware of how your stomach feels. Are you feeling more full?

7. **Stop eating when you feel that you're full and don't need to eat more.**

   You may find that you're full a lot sooner than you might have felt previously.

8. **Do some additional mindful breathing.**

   If you still feel like eating more, remember that your desire to eat may reflect a thought ("I have to eat!") rather than a genuine hunger. You don't have to react to every urge. Let the urge slip by. Don't trust your emotional eating.

Try this approach once a day for a week or so and see if it changes the way you look at food and eating.

Mastering the art of anti-stress snacking

Feeling anxious, nervous, stressed out? Need a quick food fix? Snacking, when done right, is an art. Anyone can down a candy bar or a bag of chips and a soda. The real skill is coming up with a snack that not only doesn't add to your stress level but also helps you reduce the stress you already have. Here are some guidelines:

- ✔ **Avoid highly sugared treats.** They'll give you a boost in the short run but let you down in the long run. You'll crash.

- ✔ **Stick with snacks that have high-energy proteins and are high in complex carbohydrates.** They'll give you a longer-lasting sustained pick-me-up.

Here are some specific suggestions of quick bites and snacks that can boost your mood and help alleviate some of your stress:

- ✔ A piece of fruit — an orange, peach, apple, or banana. Just about any fruit is fine.

- ✔ A handful of mixed nuts.

- ✔ A bowl of whole-grain cereal with a sliced banana.

- ✔ A spinach salad.

- ✔ A bowl of fruit salad.

- ✔ A soft pretzel.

- ✔ A handful of blueberries.

- ✔ Air-popped popcorn.

- ✔ An English muffin. (Go easy on the butter or margarine. A little jelly is fine.)

- ✔ A container of high-protein Greek yogurt.

- ✔ A piece of dark chocolate (but just a piece!).

- ✔ A serving of sorbet.

Eating out

These days it seems as though more of us are eating out or bringing in already prepared foods. To be fair, more fast-food places have modified their menus to include healthier fare. Still, temptations can run high, and you're more than a little likely to fall into a nutritional pothole. Here are some fast-food guidelines:

- Go with turkey, chicken breast, or lean roast beef instead of salami, ham, and cheese.
- Avoid the chef's salad. It sounds terrifically healthy, but it isn't. The eggs, bacon, cheese, and dressing can turn it into a nutritionally bad idea.
- Tuna is great. But add a lot of mayo and it becomes a mistake.
- Have a hamburger instead of a cheeseburger.
- Never order a large-sized anything.
- Eat only half of your French fries or split a regular order of fries with someone.
- Have a slice of pizza without any meat toppings.
- Take the skin off your roasted chicken.
- Eat half of your meal and wrap up the rest to take home.

Curing "menu weakness"

Menu weakness is a condition you may encounter when you sit down in a restaurant and the server hands you a menu. All you can see are the alluring descriptions of food possibilities. Any healthful habit or nutritional resolve vanishes. You wind up ordering things you later regret. Usually, the wonderfully tasty items such as the French fries, the cheeseburger, or that incredible dessert are the ones that get you.

To cure this affliction, you need a strategy. The best thing you can do is be prepared. Before you enter a restaurant, decide what you'll order. By now, you probably have a pretty good idea what types of dishes are available on most menus (salads, fish, chicken, and so on). Or, you can look up the menu online ahead of time. When the server comes, tell him or her what you want without glancing at the menu. Yes, in the short run it's less satisfying, but you'll have fewer regrets later on.

Becoming salad bar savvy

I remember when salad bars first became popular. They really were "salad" bars. They contained mostly foods that were green, foods that are healthy and nutritious. That was the first week. Then the good-tasting stuff starting filling the trays, and there has been no going back. However, with some control over your tong-hand, you can again make the salad bar your body's friend.

Here's the secret to healthy salad-bar visits: Never eat anything in a heated bin. The hot items are the most toxic. True, tuna salad loaded with mayo will not win any nutritional awards, but compared to the food farther down the line, it can be considered a health food. By steering clear of anything reheated, you can avoid such nutritional disasters as sweet-and-sour chicken, greasy lo mein, ribs, fried rice, lasagna, and all the rest of the wonderfully tasting foods that beckon you from their aluminum trays.

Not going hog wild

At this point, you may feel that much of the joy and pleasure of eating has been taken from you. To some extent, yes. However, my philosophy about food has always been "Everything in moderation — *including moderation.*" You really don't have to give up anything entirely. You can still have a steak, pizza, ice cream, or anything else that captures your fancy. Just eat less of it. Bon appetit!

Stress-Reducing Exercise and Activity

You already know how beneficial exercise can be as a way of keeping your weight down, your body buff, and your heart ticking for many more years.

What you may not know is that exercise is one of the better ways of helping you cope with stress. Exercise and sustained activity — in whatever form — can decrease your blood pressure, lower your heart rate, and slow your breathing — all signs of reduced arousal and stress. Exercise is a natural and effective way of slowing and even reversing your body's fight-or-flight response. This section shows you how you can make exercise and activity your allies in winning the battle against stress.

Calming your brain naturally

When you exercise, you feel different; your mood changes for the better. This difference is not only a psychological response to the fact that you're doing something good for your body. It's physiological as well.

When you exercise, you produce endorphins (literally, natural morphine from within your body), which can produce feelings of well-being and calming relaxation. This positive feeling helps you cope more effectively with stress and its effects.

Thinking activity, not exercise

The word exercise has never been a favorite word for most people. It connotes too much work with too little fun, like taking out the garbage or making the bed. Exercise is something you endure and complete as quickly as possible. The word exercise is associated with sweating, stretching, straining, pulling, lifting, more sweating, and taking a long shower. At least the last part is fun.

You may think of exercise as something outside the range of your normal day-to-day activities. However, a better way of thinking about the goal of staying fit is to replace the word exercise with the term activity.

The word exchange is more than semantic. Any increase in your level of bodily activity — aerobically or non-aerobically — and any muscle-toning or stretching contributes positively to your state of physical well-being. And who ever said activity has to be in a gym, on a court, or with a dumbbell? Many people mistakenly believe that to exercise you must engage in rigorous sports, go to a health club, or find some other specialized facility. Not so.

After a hard day of work, the chances of your putting on a sweat suit and lifting weights or completing a 6K run are slim. The good news is, you don't have to. The trick is to find naturally existing outlets for activity that are readily available and easily integrated into your lifestyle and work style.

For example, I paid a health club big bucks to let me use a machine that simulates stair-climbing. I finished my encounter with the stairs feeling self-righteous and satisfied. Yet when I returned home after my workout, I resented climbing the four flights to where we lived. After several years it dawned on me that climbing my own stairs was not that different from climbing the stair machine. "Wow," I realized, "a free health tool right in my own home!"

Exercise, cleverly camouflaged as daily physical activity, is all around you. The hard part is knowing it when you see it.

Never jump abruptly into a new program of physical exercise. Your head may be ready for the change, but your body may need more time to get used to the idea. This strategy becomes all the more important if you've led a rather sedentary life in the past. Check with your doctor first for an official okay, and then begin slowly, gradually adding more time and effort to your workout.

The following are some simple ways you can introduce small bits of activity into your day:

- ✔ **Park your car a little farther from your office and walk the rest of the way.**
- ✔ **Use your TV time effectively.** While you're watching TV, do some sit-ups, jumping jacks, push-ups, or stretches.

✔ **Walk away from your stress.** As an exercise, walking has always had wimp status. But if done consistently and for a sustained period of time, it can be a terrific way of staying in shape. The nice thing about walking is that it can be pleasantly camouflaged as strolling or sight-seeing — both painless activities. And if you crank up the pace and distance a bit, you have a wonderfully simple form of aerobic exercise that can enhance your feeling of well-being, mentally and physically. Walking is a great way to clear your head and calm your mind.

And remember to take a mini walk or two during your day. Your walks can be as short as down the block to the corner store or a lap around your office or house.

✔ **Do something you like.** I was on the swim team in high school, but even though I was pretty good, I really disliked it. I dreaded the early-morning dips in that overly chlorinated pool, and as soon as I could, I dropped out. The moral here is, if you don't like the exercise or activity you're doing, the chances of sustaining it are small. Find something you really enjoy, like one of the following:

- A favorite sport. Golf, tennis, bowling, baseball, basketball, racquetball — whatever.

- A favorite activity. Horseback-riding, dancing, trampolining, swimming, ice-skating, or rope-jumping — or anything that gets your body moving.

- Gardening. Yes, if done for a sustained period, gardening can be considered a form of exercise.

- Bicycling. Find a place where you can bike safely and enjoyably. If you don't know where those places are, contact your local parks and recreation office. Or ask friends or people you see on bikes what they suggest.

- In-line skating. In-line skating is here to stay, because it's great exercise and one of the more painless ways of getting a physical workout. After you've figured out how to stop, no one will be able to hold you back. And be sure to wear the safety gear (a helmet, elbow pads, wrist pads, and knee pads). The stress of finding yourself in an ER should not be included in your already stressful day.

Be sure to wear a helmet and other protective gear when you're on your bike or on blades — even on short rides in your neighborhood. Accidents can happen anywhere.

✔ **Become a player.** One of the better ways of staying in shape is playing at something you like. Every big city has just about every conceivable kind of sports team, from Little League to pick-up games in the park on a Saturday or Sunday morning. You don't even have to be especially proficient at a sport to get on board. Check with your local YMCA or community center for teams that are forming, and ask at work if teams already exist. Go online to find a meet-up site that brings together like-minded weekend players for just about any activity.

✔ **Climb your way out of stress.** I have good news, and I have better news. The good news is, research done at Johns Hopkins University shows that, by climbing stairs for a mere six minutes a day, you can add up to two years to your life. The better news is, if you live in a big city, you encounter lots and lots of stairs every day. With land at a premium, most cities are designed with height, rather than width, in mind. Although some cities are more vertical than others, all have more than their share of opportunities to climb stairs.

And, if you don't live in a big city, you can find climbing opportunities in other places. Ask at your local high school to see whether you can climb the football stadium bleachers. Does your shopping mall have stairs? If so, become a mall walker! Opportunities for stair-climbing aren't limited to the big cities. Consider it a challenge to find stairs wherever you live.

Given a choice between a flight of stairs and an escalator or an elevator, you probably prefer the easier route. I'm not suggesting that you frenetically seek out exit doors to uncover hidden stairwells, but given a simple choice between stairs or no stairs, take the stairs.

Doing the gym thing

Maybe it's a case of misery loving company. Or maybe it's just more fun to do something with others around. Whatever the case, consider joining a gym or health club. After you enter the door of a health club or gym, you rarely leave without some kind of workout.

The biggest obstacle to joining a health club is the cost. You'll find that, like the airlines, each gym charges a different price to do exactly the same thing. You have to shop around for the best deal. Generally, a YMCA or community center, though less trendy, offers better bargains. Also, if you can arrange your schedule so that you can go at off-peak times, many gyms will give you a cheaper rate. Almost all health clubs offer some corporate discount, especially if your corporation is in the neighborhood. Some companies even subsidize your membership.

Try out a club before you join. Ask for a guest pass or two. Many clubs offer short-term trial memberships that allow you to try them out before signing on for a longer period of time.

Go electronic with your workouts

These days your DVD player, computer, tablet, smartphone, and gaming system can be valuable sources of workout material. The menu ranges from aerobics to Zumba. These videos and games can inject a fun and exciting quality into what normally would be a repetitive, uninspiring workout. Many are interactive, with motion-based sensors that literally put you in the picture. Some are incredibly intense, guaranteed to work up a sweat. Your options can include yoga, tai chi, volleyball, football, table tennis, salsa, and just about every classic form of exercise.

Finding those "hidden" health clubs

These days more places are available to work out than you may expect. More and more health clubs and gyms are scattered around in hotels, office buildings, and apartment buildings. No signs advertise their existence, but they are there. The equipment at a "hidden" health club may not be elaborate, but you probably don't need elaborate to get the job done.

To find these hidden treasures, you need to do a little detective work. Start with the newer apartment buildings and the bigger hotels in your area. Some of these places offer memberships to non-residents and guests at a reasonable cost. Ask at your place of employment if another company in the building where you work or in a neighboring building has any health facilities. You may be surprised by the number of companies that have installed workout equipment on their premises.

Sweating at home

Of course, you don't need to lay out money for a gym or health club if you purchase a piece or two of exercise equipment that you can use right in your own home. Alas, many pieces of home exercise equipment go badly underused. They become places to hang your clothes or serve as dust collectors.

However, don't let this deter you from converting an extra bedroom or study into a home fitness center. To make sure that your killer ab machine doesn't just collect dust, schedule time with yourself when you commit to working out. And stick to it. Turn on the TV when you exercise to help ease any discomfort. I like to do the crossword puzzle and read the paper when I'm on my stationary bike.

Keeping yourself motivated

Often, remaining motivated is no small matter. You start with the best of intentions but somehow run out of motivational steam fairly quickly. The following tips and suggestions should help you stay the course.

Get a workout buddy

A workout buddy or partner provides you with added incentive to make sure you get there. Working out can also be more fun if you go with someone whose company you enjoy. The time on the treadmill just whizzes by when you're lost in talk with the person next to you. As a bonus, many health clubs offer a membership discount if you bring in a friend.

Get your day off to an active start

Some exercise, especially aerobic exercise just after you get up in the morning, is a great way to get your juices going and get you prepared for any stress that may come your way later in the day. Aerobic activity introduces more oxygen into your body and makes you more alert and focused. If you make that activity a little more vigorous, your system will release those endorphins, which can produce a calming feeling of relaxation.

Remember that every little bit counts

You may have a mistaken idea that if you do something for only a small bit of time, it really isn't worth much. The reality is, if you do it consistently, it adds up. For example, a recent research study found that if you walk briskly for only ten minutes a day, three times a day, you get the same fitness and weight loss benefits as you would if you walked briskly for 30 minutes, once a day.

Do it; don't overdo it

Yes, you really can have too much of a good thing — even exercise. Anecdotal reports show that elite athletes complain of being more susceptible to colds and other maladies when they over-train, or merely train intensely. Recent studies further suggest that your immune system can be weakened by excessive, exhaustive exercise. So take a pass on that triathlon if you haven't run more than twenty feet in the last ten years.

Getting a Good Night's Sleep

The first thing you notice when you work with people under a lot of stress is how often they say, "I'm tired." For some, the stress of the day is what wears them out. But for most people, it's a matter of not getting enough sleep. And they are hardly alone.

The fact is, most people don't get enough quality sleep. Unfortunately, when you're tired, your emotional threshold is lowered. You're more vulnerable to all the other stresses around you. Stress breeds even more stress. Breaking the cycle and getting a good night's sleep becomes very important.

The secret to getting a good night's sleep is figuring out your sleep needs and what strategies work best for you. You need to experiment. Something that works for one person may not work for you. What follows are a number of techniques, ideas, and strategies that have been shown to be effective in helping people get a better night of sleep. Consider them all and put together your own personal sleep program.

Knowing your sleep needs

Your first step is knowing just how much sleep you need. Most Americans get between 60 and 90 minutes less a night than they should for optimal health and performance. Though most people need about seven or eight hours of sleep a night, 20 percent of Americans get less than six hours of sleep, and 50 percent get less than eight hours. And it doesn't look like the situation is going to improve anytime soon.

No fixed rule can tell you how much sleep you need. So take the following simple sleep quiz to see whether you're getting enough sleep at night. Answer true or false, depending on whether the following statements apply to you.

- ✔ I notice a major dip in my energy level early in the afternoon.
- ✔ I need an alarm clock to wake up in the morning.
- ✔ On the weekends, when I don't have to get up, I end up sleeping much later.
- ✔ I fall asleep very quickly at night (in less than 15 minutes).
- ✔ On most days, I feel tired and feel as though I could use a nap.

Answering "that's me" to any of the above suggests that you may want to re-evaluate how much sleep you're getting and how much sleep you truly need. Try experimenting by getting a bit more sleep at night and see if you notice any changes in your stress level.

Hitting the sheets earlier

I recognize that for many, getting to bed earlier is easy to suggest but much harder to do. Face it, staying up at night is when you do the things you need to do (doing laundry, cleaning, paying bills). Or, if you're lucky, late nights are when you do the things you want to do, whether that's vegging out in front of the TV or turning the pages of the latest bestseller. You may try to burn the candle at both ends — stay up late and get up early. Often, this strategy just doesn't work, and you're tired the next day. An important element in helping you get the sleep you need is realizing that you have to get to bed earlier. It's as simple as that.

If you determine that you are, in fact, not getting enough sleep at night, try getting to bed 20 minutes earlier and see if the quality of your day improves. To get to bed just a few minutes earlier, turn off the TV or computer at a more reasonable hour. If you must watch that *Seinfeld* rerun or catch *The Daily Show*, record it and watch it earlier the next evening.

Developing a sleep routine

The best sleep comes from having a regular sleep pattern. Your body's internal clock becomes stabilized with routine. This means getting to bed at the same time and getting up at the same time.

The following sections provide tips for putting together a successful sleep routine.

Getting a comfortable mattress

All mattresses are not created equal. You may be ready for an upgrade. Ask yourself when you last bought a mattress. Is it really comfortable? You may need a partner or friend to give you another opinion. You shouldn't wake up with a sore back, sore neck, or sore anything. Try out different mattress surfaces and firmnesses at a showroom to see what you may be missing.

Using the bed for sleep (and sex) only

Ideally, you want to establish a set of reminders and habits that promote an effective sleep routine. The relationship in your mind should be that lying down in bed means you're going to sleep.

That's the ideal. However, if you live in a small house or apartment, you may not have the luxury of keeping a whole room dedicated to just one or two activities. You may be one of the many who use the bedroom for just about everything. This is understandable, but unfortunately, it's less than ideal for the purposes of optimizing your sleep patterns.

Avoiding late heavy meals

A big dinner late at night may make you drowsy, but it may also interfere with your sleep. Avoid fatty and rich foods late at night. Otherwise, your digestive system will function on overdrive, and the quality of your sleep may be disrupted. And did I mention heartburn?

Watching how much you drink

Too much liquid in your system may result in too many night-time awakenings to go to the bathroom. Try to restrict your late-night liquid intake. And remember that caffeinated drinks can act as diuretics (in other words, more trips to the bathroom). If you enjoy a sip before bed, try a cup of the many wonderful de-caffeinated herbal teas available.

Exercise helps you sleep

Studies have shown that exercise during your day can improve your sleep at night. Not only is your body more tired, but you may experience an increase in body temperature as you exercise. This can be followed by a drop in body temperature a few hours later, which can make it easier for you to fall asleep and stay asleep. A study at Stanford University found that subjects who exercised regularly with moderately intense aerobic exercises for 30 to 40 minutes four times per week slept almost an hour longer than those who didn't exercise. These subjects were also able to cut the time it took to fall asleep by half. But while exercising is great, exercising too close to your bedtime can rev you up and keep you awake.

Creating a sleep ritual

If you can't make your bedroom a room devoted only to sleeping, you may find that creating a bedtime ritual is more realistic. At a certain hour, make the bedroom a place where you wind down and relax. This means no upsetting discussions, no work from the office, no bill-paying, no arguments with the kids, no unpleasant phone calls, or anything else that may trigger worry, anxiety, or upset. You can read, watch a relaxing TV show or movie, or whatever else it is that calms your body and quiets your mind. I would advise against watching your local news. Today's robbery, fire, or general mayhem isn't the last thing you want to hear about before your head hits the pillow.

Turning the noise down

You may have trouble sleeping soundly because of noise. This is especially the case if you live in a place where wailing car alarms or party-loving neighbors interrupt even the pleasantest of dreams. Worse yet, you may be a very light sleeper and vulnerable to a host of far less dramatic noises. Here are some suggestions:

- ✔ **Sound-proof it.** Even with the windows shut, a lot of sound still comes through. Consider installing double-pane windows. Heavy drapes or shutters can add to the sound-proofing. Carpets, rugs, wall hangings, pictures, bookcases, and book shelves all help absorb excess noise.

- ✔ **Mask it.** The secret of masking is finding a more tolerable noise and making it the one you hear. Most of us first experience masking in the summer, when the soothing hum of the air conditioner or whir of the fan drowns out just about everything else. A sound generator can also mask less pleasant sounds and calm you down. Inexpensive models, which are available at most discount and department stores, can reproduce a variety of soothing sounds: white noise, a waterfall, a rain forest, or the chirping of crickets in a meadow. Inexpensive smartphone apps can also provide a variety of soothing sounds. You can also download white-noise files onto your smartphone, MP3 player, or laptop and create a repeating audio loop.

✔ **Block it.** That Metallica groupie upstairs or a deafening sanitation truck outside may call for stronger measures. Sometimes earplugs are in order.

Turning the heat down

If your bedroom is too warm, it may affect your ability to get to sleep. Most people sleep better when the temperature is slightly cool (around 65 degrees). Also make sure that your bedroom gets enough ventilation.

Turning off the light

There has been many a time when wearing a sleep-mask has rescued me from the sleepless consequences of an overly-lit bedroom. Perhaps your source of unwanted light comes from your partner who chooses to read in bed long after you close your eyes. It may come from street lights on your block. Or it simply may be the (oh so early) onset of daylight. Not all sleep-masks are created equal. Get one that you find very comfortable and doesn't feel like someone has wrapped a tight elastic band around your head.

Watching the pills and the booze

The quality of your sleep is as important as the number of hours you sleep. A nightcap does little harm, but greater amounts of alcohol (even though they may help you fall asleep) can disturb the quality of your sleep and leave you waking up feeling tired. Sleeping pills have their place, and when used appropriately, they can be useful. However, routine use of medication for sleeping can quickly become psychologically addictive and actually impair sleep.

Looking out for hidden stimulants

Besides that cup of coffee or caffeinated soda that will probably keep you up until the middle of next week (coffee usually contains anywhere from 95 to 150 mg in an eight-ounce cup), other less-obvious sources of caffeine creep into your diet. Tea contains caffeine, but generally in much smaller amounts than coffee (about 15 to 40 mg in an eight-ounce cup). Chocolate contains caffeine, but only in small amounts (unless you eat a lot of chocolate!). The amount varies according to the type of chocolate, but it's generally in the range of five to ten mg per ounce of chocolate. Generally, the darker the chocolate, the more the caffeine.

Sleeping less can make you fat?

In a recent study, Harvard University researchers followed about 68,000 middle-aged women for more than 16 years and found that women who slept five hours or less per night weighed an average of 5.4 pounds more — and were 15 percent more likely to become obese — than women who got at least seven hours of sleep a night. Maybe being awake longer means more opportunities to eat. The weight gain may also be the result of possible changes in the hormones ghrelin and leptin, which regulate appetite. Related studies from the University of Chicago found that when volunteers were allowed to sleep less (five and a half hours per night), they ate an average of 221 more calories from snacks when compared with non-sleep-restricted controls. In just two weeks, that extra nighttime snacking can add a full pound of body weight.

Napping carefully

As one who was never able to nap successfully, I always envy those who can drift off for a quick snooze and return to their world refreshed and ready to go. Naps can be a wonderful tool. A short nap (try to keep it in the 15 to 20 minute range) can reinvigorate you and give you the energy to enjoy the rest of your day. Research has shown that naps may help you lower your stress. Taking longer naps may leave you feeling somewhat groggy. Blocking out light, perhaps with a sleep mask, can help you fall asleep faster. Naps are best taken between 1 and 3 p.m. Napping too late in your day can make it hard to fall asleep later that night.

However, if you aren't sleeping well at night, you may seriously consider abandoning your daytime nap. Four out of five people with insomnia find that they do better during the night if they don't nap during the day. Also watch out for after-dinner drowsiness. A heavy meal may result in your dozing on the couch or in your favorite chair in front of the TV. This unplanned nap can interfere with your nighttime sleep pattern. If you're feeling drowsy, get up and do something — call a friend, do something on your computer, or clean your closet.

Checking for medical problems

Your sleep problem may reflect the existence of some common medical condition. A variety of medical problems can result in sleep disturbances and chronic insomnia.

- **Heartburn.** Heartburn is a common source of sleep distress. Certain foods — such as heavy meals, rich foods, fatty foods, alcohol, and coffee — ingested later in the evening can cause or exacerbate heartburn.

✔ **Sleep apnea.** Sleep apnea is a sleep disorder that occurs when a person's breathing is interrupted during sleep. People with untreated sleep apnea stop breathing repeatedly during their sleep, sometimes hundreds of times. This can result in frequent awakenings and poor-quality sleep.

✔ **Diabetes.** Symptoms of this common, chronic condition can include night sweats, a frequent need to urinate, and possibly nerve damage in the legs that might produce involuntary movement or pain.

✔ **Arthritis.** Pain from arthritis can make it difficult for people to fall asleep. The need to change position can also interfere with sleep.

✔ **Muscle pain.** Conditions such as fibromyalgia may result in abnormal sleep patterns and poor quality of sleep. Leg cramps and restless leg syndrome can also disrupt sleep.

✔ **Breathing problems.** Conditions such as asthma can interfere with breathing and awaken the sleeper. Emphysema and bronchitis may make it more difficult to get to sleep because of coughing, shortness of breath, or excessive phlegm.

Falling asleep

At this point you've taken all the wonderful advice I give in the preceding sections. You have the right mattress, your bedroom is the right temperature, the noise level is low, the room is dark, you've eaten lighter meals before going to bed, you've skipped naps, and you've avoided alcohol and caffeine. You're convinced that nothing "medical" is going on. Still you find yourself hitting the sheets and staring at the ceiling wide awake. Or you may have another form of sleep disturbance. You may actually *fall* asleep pretty quickly but wake up in the middle of the night, unable to fall *back* asleep. In both cases you need some additional help.

Do you have delayed sleep-phase disorder?

Individuals with this disorder generally fall asleep a few hours after midnight and find it hard to wake up in the more usual morning hours. This condition differs from true insomnia because the *timing* of sleep is altered. Affected individuals are on a different cycle. A typical sleep schedule might be falling asleep around 4 a.m., sleeping soundly, and awakening well rested at noon (although this sounds suspiciously like the sleep habits of my "millennial" children). One way of determining whether you have delayed sleep-phase disorder or insomnia is to track your sleep on a longish vacation. Notice what time you go to bed and when you wake up on your own. If you sleep a full six to nine hours, you may have DSPD and not insomnia. Best to consult your doctor if you suspect you have this condition.

Relax your body, quiet your mind

When your body is relaxed, your mind slows. When your mind is calm, your body relaxes. Learning to relax physically and mentally is an important key to falling asleep. The good news is that in Chapters 4 and 5 I share some pretty good ideas for how to relax. You can select from a variety of approaches or put together your own personal relaxation package. Here's a brief summary:

Relaxed breathing. I can't recommend this strongly enough. It works on two levels. By focusing on your breathing, you can distract yourself from your mental stressors. The breathing itself induces a deeper state of physical relaxation that can get you closer to sleep. Simply focus on your breathing, noticing the air entering and leaving your nose and mouth. The breathing itself doesn't have to be complicated. Simply try to breathe more slowly and more deeply. Silently say the word "calm" to yourself each time you exhale. Don't force the breathing but rather let the breathing find its own rhythm.

Progressive muscle relaxation. Working your way up your body, from your toes to your head, tense and then relax each muscle group. After you've gone through one tense-relax cycle, focus on deepening the relaxation without the tensing phase.

Relaxation imagery. Visualize a place, situation, or experience that you find calming and peaceful. It can be a vacation, a room at home, the beach — anything you find relaxing. Get into that image, noticing the sights, sounds, and even smells. Let the image transport you.

Turn off your mind

Being tired means you're more likely to fall asleep. Alas, it doesn't ensure that you will. You may find that your mind is racing a mile a minute. You hope you'll fall asleep at least before next Friday. The problem is the level of mental arousal. This mental mayhem may take the form of mental distress. You may be worried, upset, angry, or otherwise distressed, guaranteeing that you'll be revved up and awake. But it may have nothing to do with distress. You may be happy or excited, replaying some event or success that genuinely delights you. Or you may be happily anticipating or planning some future positive event or experience. The result is the same. You can't fall asleep. Here are some additional tools and techniques to help you turn off your mind.

Don't try to fall asleep

This advice may sound curious given the goal of getting you to fall asleep. Yet one of the biggest obstacles in getting to sleep is the self-induced pressure that you have to get to sleep. Have you ever noticed that you fall asleep most quickly when you don't intend to go to sleep? Think about sitting in front of the TV or in the back of the classroom, or during that slow part of that talkie movie. When you're lying in bed thinking, "I just have to get to sleep! I'll be dead tired all day tomorrow! I'll never get past this sleeping problem!" you almost guarantee that falling asleep will elude you. This performance anxiety creates even more mental arousal and makes it harder for you to fall asleep. Your first step toward easier sleep is accepting that it may take longer than you would like to figure out what to do, and that sometimes you won't get enough sleep. Your catastrophizing and awfulizing only make things worse. If you can, replace that "I have to get to sleep — right now!" with "I'd like to be asleep, but if I'm not, I'm not." Therapists often use the technique of para-doxical intention to help people get to sleep by telling them to try not to fall asleep. The pressure lessens, and the chances of falling asleep increase. This may be too much of a stretch for you, but the principle still holds. Lower the pressure to be asleep.

Don't look at the time

Looking at your clock or watch in the middle of the night isn't going to help you fall asleep. You've probably noticed how quickly time flies when you can't fall asleep. You look at your clock, and it's 2 a.m. And what seems like only ten minutes later, you notice the clock says 3:15 a.m. The pressure to get to sleep increases. This won't help you.

Aim for relaxation

Your goal should be to get into the right "pre-sleep" mode. You have control over this part. What you don't have control over is the falling into sleep part. That happens on its own. Start by relaxing your body and slowing down your mind. Choose one or more of the preceding techniques or those I describe in Chapters 4 and 5. Your new goal, remember, is not being asleep, but rather being in a relaxed state that will allow your body to fall asleep on its own.

Refocus your mind

The next step is to shift your focus away from any worrying, planning, rumi-nation — anything that increases your level of cognitive or physiological arousal. Put more simply, you want your thoughts focused on more relaxing stuff. Shift your attention to pleasant or emotionally neutral content that takes the place of any negative, unwanted, or stimulating thinking. You may start with some image or memory that you find pleasing. The choice is a per-sonal one. For me it can be a favorite past vacation, seeing myself on a warm beach, with the coral blue ocean in the background and a pina colada in my hand. Come up with your own content. You may have to experiment a bit. If you're pulled away from these thoughts by intrusive worries, gently bring yourself back to your more neutral content. Again, your goal is not being asleep; it's being relaxed.

Does counting sheep help?

The notion of counting those wooly critters as a sleep-inducing remedy as they jump over that fence has been around forever. It probably has something to do with the counting system devised by shepherds in ancient Britain. But does it work? Researchers at Oxford University put it to a test. They split insomniacs into 23 groups and looked at how effectively different techniques for falling asleep worked. They found that the group instructed to count sheep took slightly longer to fall asleep than subjects who were given no instructions at all. When members of the sheep-counting group were instructed to imagine a relaxing scene, they fell asleep an average of 20 minutes sooner than they did on the sheep-counting nights. The scientists concluded that counting sheep can be too boring and can fail to hold your attention, letting those worries creep back in. I would add that your anxiety level is likely to rise sharply as you hit the 740th sheep, guaranteeing a long (sleepless) night.

Deal with specific, persistent worries

Sometimes a specific worry or set of concerns is so strong that it dominates your thinking. You may need other strategies. Try these:

- ✔ **Jot it down.** Keep a small pad and pencil near your bed. Jot down the worrisome problem or thought on a piece of paper and decide that you will work on the problem the next day. This strategy gives you some closure and allows you to leave that little bit of business alone.

- ✔ **Just stop it!** Try something called the Stop Technique. I describe this in detail in Chapter 5, but it's worth summarizing here. Whenever you catch yourself obsessing or worrying about something, visualize a large red-and-white hexagonal stop sign. At the same time, silently yell the word "stop" to yourself. What you'll find is that this temporarily interrupts your worrying. Then replace the worry with a welcome and pleasant thought or image. Keep repeating this process until you've sufficiently broken the worry cycle or fallen asleep. This technique takes a bit of practice, but it really works.

Part III

The Secrets of Stress-Effective Thinking

The ABCs of How Your Thinking Affects Your Stress — and How to Achieve a More Positive Outcome

A (The Situation or Event)	B (Your Thinking)	C (Your Stress)	Try This Instead
You're trapped in a slow-moving supermarket checkout line.	"I hate this! Why does this always happen to me?"	Angry, upset, and frustrated	You pick up a magazine with a story that intrigues you. Now you're pleased that the line is moving so slowly because you want to finish that article on celebrity cellulite.
You're facing an upcoming test at school.	"I'm stupid! I'll fail! I'll never get anywhere in life!"	Worried and nervous; tense	You remember that the upcoming test at school only counts for a small part of your final grade.
Your neighbor is playing his music too loudly.	"Why can't people be more considerate? I'll fix him!"	Angry and upset.	You decided it's a lovely evening for a walk anyway. Tomorrow, you can try to talk to your neighbor calmly.

If you're overwhelmed by life's pressures and your stress levels are getting seriously high, head to www.dummies.com/extras/stressmanagment to find guidance for talking yourself through a stressful situation.

In this part . . .

- ✔ Understand how your own thinking can cause stress every bit as much as environmental triggers.

- ✔ Discover ways to identify your stress-causing thoughts and turn them into stress-resistant thoughts instead.

- ✔ Define your personal goals and values and find out how to view the world in more stress-resistant ways. Add humor, optimism, gratitude, and a sense of community to your set of values and see how much less stressful everyday life can be.

Chapter 10

Understanding How Your Thinking Stresses You Out

In This Chapter

▶ Understanding how you create much of your stress

▶ Figuring out how to separate thoughts and feelings

▶ Recognizing and correcting your stress-producing thinking

*I*f someone corners you at a cocktail party and asks you where most of your stress comes from, chances are you'll tell them it's your job, family pressures, or not having enough time or money. You probably won't tell them that your own thinking is creating much of your stress.

Yet your thinking plays a larger role in producing stress than you may imagine. Fortunately, learning how to change your thinking is not all that difficult. This chapter shows you how your thinking creates excessive stress in your life. It shows you how you can identify your stress-producing thinking and offers step-by-step advice on how to turn that stress-producing thinking into stress-resistant thinking.

Believe It or Not, Most of Your Stress Is Self-Created

Feeling stressed is, and always has been, a two-part process. First you need something "out there" to trigger your stress, and then you need to perceive that trigger as stressful. Then you feel stressed. You empower these external events and situations by viewing them in certain ways. Look at something one way and you feel major stress; look at it another way and you feel less stress, maybe even no stress at all.

Your attitudes and beliefs about any potentially stressful situation or event determine how much stress you experience. By changing the way you look at a potentially stressful situation, you can change the way you emotionally react to that situation. This concept underlies a number of important approaches to psychotherapy and emotional change. A major tool in your stress-management toolbox is understanding how your thinking helps create your stress and knowing how to change that thinking.

Stress at 30,000 feet: Flight and fright

Consider this scenario: You're sitting on a plane high over the Atlantic, and you notice that the person sitting next to you is looking worried — very worried. She's breathing much too quickly and has just downed her third scotch.

She is thinking:

> *"Oh my gosh, I'm going to die! I know this plane is going down. We'll all be killed! That left engine sounds funny! Why is the seat-belt sign on? And why is that flight attendant asking me now what I want for lunch? This plane is in real trouble! Lord, just get me through this one and I promise . . ."*

She's experiencing lots of stress. You, however, are happily sitting in your seat, smiling contentedly. You're experiencing absolutely no stress.

You are thinking:

> *"This is the best! I just love flying. Nobody can reach me up here. I'll just relax with my Grisham novel and nurse this scotch. Ah, here comes lunch. This feels so good! I think I'll have the chicken."*

Same plane, same noise, same chicken, but a different way of thinking about what is happening and what might happen. You're not thinking the worst. She is. And that's why she's so stressed and you aren't.

The presentation from hell

Or consider this very different scenario: Your boss asks you to present ideas about increasing business and bringing in new clients. He's also asked a colleague in a different office to do the same. You're feeling incredibly stressed.

You are thinking:

> *"This is not good! I'm going to freeze! I'll look like an idiot! I'm going to screw up, and then what? I hate presentations! What am I going to do? I'm such a loser!"*

Your colleague, however, looks at it differently. She's feeling much less stress. *She* is thinking:

> *"I'm not crazy about doing this, but I'll get through it. I'll have to work late this week to organize my ideas, but it's doable. I know I'll be nervous at the beginning, but that will pass once I get into the material. It won't be fun, but it won't be a disaster. I think I can pull this off."*

If only the external situation caused stress, everyone would feel the same stress when placed in the same situation. Clearly, this is not the case. A group of people will exhibit a wide range of reactions when exposed to the same stress trigger. What's stressful for somebody else may be less stressful for you, or maybe not stressful at all. Depending on *how* you think about a situation or event, you create different feelings. You can create more stress than necessary, or less stress. In short, your thoughts have the power to determine the amount of stress you feel.

I'm not saying that by changing your thinking you'll never feel *any* stress. Feeling stress is an appropriate response to a variety of situations. The trick, or rather the skill, is to recognize when your stress is excessive and be able to identify and correct any thinking that is producing and maintaining it.

Remembering Your ABCs

In Chapter 2, I introduce an ABC model of stress that can help you understand the role your thinking plays in creating your stress. It's a simple yet highly useful way of analyzing your stress. It looks like this:

A → B → C

where

A is the Activating event or triggering situation. It's the stressor or stress trigger.

B are your Beliefs, thoughts, or perceptions about A.

C are the Consequences, or "stress," that result from holding these thoughts and beliefs.

In other words:

A potentially stressful situation → your thinking → your stress (or lack of stress!)

Table 10-1 gives you some further examples of the relationship between your A's, B's, and C's.

Table 10-1 The ABCs of How Your Thinking Affects Your Stress

A (The Situation or Event)	B (Your Thinking)	C (Your Stress)
You're trapped in a slow-moving supermarket checkout line.	"I hate this! Why does this always happen to me?"	Angry, upset, and frustrated
You're facing an upcoming test at school.	"I'm stupid! I'll fail! I'll never get anywhere in life!"	Worried and nervous; tense
Someone's poking you from behind in the elevator.	"That's rude! He should know better! I'll tell him off!"	Upset and annoyed
Your picky Aunt Agnes is coming to visit for a week.	"This is the worst! My week is a total waste!"	Upset and feeling blue
Your neighbor is playing his music too loudly.	"Why can't people be more considerate? I'll fix him!"	Angry and upset; homicidal?

It's not exactly a new idea

Whoever said there's nothing new under the sun probably never Skyped their mother or ordered Mexican food with their smartphone. But the notion that our thoughts can create our feelings has been around for quite a while. Consider these insights from the past:

> *"People are not disturbed by things, but by the views they take of them."*
>
> — Epictetus (55A.D.)

> *"People are about as happy as they make up their minds to be."*
>
> — Abraham Lincoln

> *"No one can make you feel inferior without your consent."*
>
> — Eleanor Roosevelt

It's the thought that counts

If by any chance it's you who is described in the previous situations, you may feel that your stress is a direct consequence of the stressful event or trigger. You may think that "the situation made me stressed." You could revise the ABC formula to read: A → C (no thinking involved). And that would be entirely understandable. However, the reality is, slow lines, difficult relatives, and loud music don't in themselves have the power to make you automatically feel stressed. (Yes, I realize I've never spent a week with your Aunt Agnes.) For a situation or circumstance to trigger stress, you have to perceive that situation as stressful. It's your B's that are producing your stress.

For each of the preceding examples, we would feel much less stress (and maybe no stress) if our thinking had somehow changed — if circumstances had changed our thinking and we looked at these stressors differently. Consider how your stress level might be very different:

1. You're still in that slow-moving supermarket line, but you pick up a magazine with a story that intrigues you. Now you're pleased that the line is moving so slowly because you want to finish that article on celebrity cellulite.

2. You remember that the upcoming test at school only counts for a small part of your final grade.

3. You turn around in the elevator and realize that the person behind you is blind and using a cane.

4. You're reliably informed that your Aunt Agnes has rewritten her will and made you the sole beneficiary to her rather large estate. "You're staying only *one* week, Aunt Agnes!?"

5. Noisy neighbor? Who cares? Just that morning, you signed the papers on a wonderful new place across town. Half the cost, twice the size. Knock yourself out, buddy!

I realize that your thinking in each of these scenarios had changed because circumstances or new information changed your perceptions of each potential stressor. I also realize that life only rarely rewards you with these bits of good fortune (and let's face it, your Aunt Agnes isn't that crazy about you, either.) My point is, you have the potential to *think* about a stressor differently if you can find a way of *looking* at that stressor differently. The same trigger viewed with a different mindset can result in different feelings. In my revised scenarios, the altered *circumstances* changed your thinking. But what if you could learn to change your thoughts — your perceptions and expectations — on your own, independent of the circumstances? You would feel differently. You would experience less stress. Fortunately, this is a skill you can master. Your first step is understanding the difference between your thoughts and your feelings.

Separating Thoughts from Feelings

It's important to recognize the difference between a *thought* and a *feeling*. Most of us confuse our thinking (our B's) with our feelings (our C's). For example, if I ask you how you feel about your best friend forgetting your birthday, you might say you feel that she was insensitive and uncaring. But that's really what you *think*. What you *feel* is upset, angry, and disappointed. This may seem like a minor distinction, but these differences are important in understanding your stress.

Here are some *thoughts* (your B's) you might have in the course of a day.

- ✔ No one likes me!
- ✔ I'm going to screw up!
- ✔ What if people see me freaking out?
- ✔ What if something bad happens to my kid?
- ✔ She should have remembered my birthday!
- ✔ I forgot my appointment!
- ✔ I'd really like some double-chocolate fudge-ripple ice cream.

Here are some *feelings* (your C's) you might experience during that same day.

- ✔ Happy
- ✔ Afraid
- ✔ Angry
- ✔ Anxious
- ✔ Worried
- ✔ Joyful
- ✔ Upset
- ✔ Sad
- ✔ Hopeful
- ✔ Depressed
- ✔ Guilty
- ✔ Hopeless
- ✔ Lonely
- ✔ Helpless
- ✔ Panicky

✔ Embarrassed

✔ Elated

✔ Regretful

✔ Resentful

✔ Loving

Separating your thoughts from your feelings (your B's from your C's) helps you identify those thoughts that are producing your stress. You're then in a good position to evaluate your thoughts and, if need be, change your way of thinking.

Changing the way you feel and your level of stress can be the result of a number of changes in your life. Your world can change — you finally get that better job, you meet the person of your dreams, or your doctor tells you everything is fine. Your needs can change — your monthly expenses are lower, you fall out of love with a person, or that promotion becomes less important than you once thought. Many of these changes can happen on their own. Having the ability to control how you look at yourself and your world gives you even greater control over how you feel and the amount of stress you experience. Using the ABC model, this means changing your B's. The rest of this chapter shows that your thinking is an important tool in changing your feelings and reducing your stress.

Understanding Your Stress-Producing Thinking

Most often we think of our thoughts as our friends. Thoughts can act as a helpful guide, directing our feelings and behavior. But not always. This section describes the kinds of thoughts, beliefs, and attitudes (your B's in the ABC model) that get you into trouble and create excessive stress.

Figuring out whether your thinking is the problem

Who knows, maybe your thinking is faultless. You may be one of the fortunate few who look at themselves and their world with a clear eye and a steady compass. You may be experiencing stress, but your negative thinking isn't the culprit. One useful way of assessing the role of distorted thinking in your life is to check your *stress balance*. Here's how you do that.

In Chapter 3, I show you how to rate the *relative importance* of your stressor on a ten-point scale and how to rate your *level of distress* triggered by that stressor on a similar ten-point scale. Taking a simple example from my morning, I got up and discovered that my car battery had died. (I had left the glove-compartment light on.) I rated my stress level (upset, annoyance, tension) as a seven. Next I rated the relative importance of the stress trigger (compared with life's more serious problems) and decided it merited a three rating. (It wasn't like being late for my own wedding.) Then I asked myself:

"Does the level of stress I'm feeling match the importance of the situation?"

I had a "seven" response to a "three" situation. I was "off balance." I was over-reacting. This problem didn't deserve this level of emotional investment. My thinking was creating more stress than was appropriate or necessary. My thinking needed some changing.

Give this technique a try with one or more of your stressors and stress reactions. See to what extent you're off balance and need to take a closer look at how you think.

Understanding your automatic thoughts

When you think about thinking, you generally conjure up an internal voice that warns you, "Don't forget to pick up milk at the supermarket" or "Get out of bed! You can't sleep all day." This internal voice guides you, helping you make plans and decisions. It helps you decide whether to choose the chicken or beef on your next flight. So, if I ask you, "What are you thinking," you can probably tell me.

But the reality is, much of your thinking is hidden. In fact, you may be unaware that there is *any* thinking going on. Much of your thinking is auto-matic and computer-quick. Your thoughts can become compressed and may appear in shorthand form. They may appear not as words but as images or feelings in your gut. You may be more aware of your feelings than your thoughts.

Uncovering your hidden thoughts

Consider this example. A friend criticizes you, and you feel upset and angry. Your A is the criticism and your C is your stress — the anger and upset. But where's the B, the thinking part? It's there, but it's automatic and hidden. Your automatic thinking can be incredibly strong and believable. When you notice these automatic (usually negative) thoughts, you believe they are reasonable and appropriate. But often they're not. They can be distortions of your reality and create a good deal of unneeded distress. Here are some questions you can ask yourself to help you uncover these hidden, automatic thoughts:

✔ What am I so stressed about this event or situation?

✔ What might I be saying to myself about what happened to create this anger (or any other stress emotion)?

✔ If a friend asked me why I was so stressed about this event or situation, what would I tell him?

This kind of inquiry can help bring to the surface thoughts that may otherwise go unrecognized. For example, referring back to that criticism from a friend, you can tell yourself:

"I am so upset and angry because my friend criticized me unfairly, and she shouldn't have!"

Uncovering these automatic thoughts and bringing them into awareness is an important step in changing your thoughts. In each case, your thinking may be sensible and rational, or it may be distorting and stress producing. To figure out which category your thinking falls into, you need to determine if your thinking contains any *thinking errors*. Here's what they look like.

Your Thinking Errors

The simplest and fastest way to minimize your stress-producing thinking is to start correcting your thinking errors. What follows are descriptions and illustrations of each of the major thinking errors that most people make. You can see how each error produces excessive stress. More importantly, you can figure out how to challenge and dispute this thinking, correcting your thinking errors and replacing them with more adaptive, less stress-producing thoughts and beliefs.

Catastrophizing and awfulizing

Having a low-stress day? Why not catastrophize and awfulize? This form of distortion guarantees that you'll experience at least some stress. Put simply, catastrophizing and awfulizing is making a mountain out of a molehill. With little effort, you can turn an everyday hassle into a major disaster. Here's how to become a better catastrophizer and awfulizer:

1. Find a commonly occurring situation or event with the potential to stress you out. How about this: You're put on hold while you wait for the "next available representative."

2. Now, exaggerate the importance and meaning of this situation. Say to yourself: "Oh my gosh, this is the worst thing that could happen to me! I can't believe it! This is terrible! This is awful!"

A pained look adds to the effect.

By escalating from a hassle to a catastrophe, you elevate your stress level. The reality is, unless you're getting married in 20 minutes, having to wait for that representative (or getting stuck in traffic or losing the remote for your TV), is just a small inconvenience, and you should view it as such. Even many of the bigger hassles can be emotionally exaggerated and blown out of proportion, creating more stress than is necessary.

Ask yourself these two questions to help reduce your catastrophizing and awfulizing:

✔ How important is this? Is it really a big deal?

✔ Will I remember this event in three years, three months, three weeks, or three days (or even three hours)?

By challenging your exaggerated thinking, you can begin to look at the situation differently. And as a consequence, you feel less stress.

Can't-stand-it-itis

Can't-stand-it-itis may sound like some rare neurological condition, but it's just another form of emotional distortion that increases your stress level. Unlike catastrophizing and awfulizing, where you exaggerate the importance of the situation or event, here you're exaggerating your inability to cope. Here's how this little number works:

1. Find some situation or circumstance that you don't like.

2. Then (and this is the important part) turn that "I don't like it" into an "I can't stand it!"

3. Now, say with conviction:

   "I *can't stand it* when I have to wait in long lines!"

   "I *hate it* when I'm caught in traffic!"

   "It *drives me crazy* when people are late!"

When you say and believe that you can't stand something, or that you hate, despise, or loath something, your emotional temperature rises, and you become more upset — more stressed — than you would if you merely disliked that same something.

Even when you don't like the hassles and frustrations you're confronted with, you don't have to explode with inflated rage: "I just hate traffic (or crowds, lines, or rude people)!" When you believe you can't stand something, you produce far more stress than is warranted by the situation. You make yourself upset, angry, and distraught. But when you recognize that some can't-stand-it-itis is contributing to your emotional stress, you can step back and challenge your thinking. Ask yourself:

- Can I really not *stand* it? Or do I actually mean I don't *like* it?
- Is my overreacting helping in any way? Or is it really making things worse?
- Couldn't I really stand it for a bit longer? And if someone were willing to fork over really big bucks, couldn't I stand it for even longer?

What-if-ing

If you're having a slow day, consider stressing yourself out about some of these things:

- What if there's a transit strike?
- What if my company downsizes?
- What if my waiter has a transmissible disease?
- What if there are terrorists on my plane?
- What if I'm kidnapped?
- What if the stock market crashes?
- What if I get hit by a car?
- What if rock musicians move in next door?
- What if my mail carrier is a serial killer?

When you what-if, you take a situation or event that *could* happen and make it into something that *probably will* happen. This way of thinking adds unnecessary stress to your life. Most often, what-if-ing is followed by some form of catastrophizing and awfulizing. For example: "What if the boss sees me at the movies on a day I call in sick?" (That's the what-if-ing part.) "He'll fire me, and I'll never get a job this good!" (That's the catastrophizing and awfulizing part.) Yes, it's possible. It's just not very likely.

Of course unpleasant things happen. Sometimes they even happen to you. But most of the things you worry about won't happen. To cut out your what-if-ing, ask yourself these thought-straightening questions:

✔ Realistically, what are the chances of this event happening?

✔ Am I over-worrying about this?

✔ When my life is nearing its end, will this be something I should have worried about?

Overgeneralizing

If you overgeneralize, you cause yourself to be more stressed than you have to be. Take a look at the following overgeneralizations and see whether you recognize yourself:

✔ "Nobody in this town knows how to drive!" (When someone cuts you off in traffic.)

✔ "I always have to do everything myself!" (When your request for someone to take out the trash goes unheeded.)

✔ "The country is run by idiots!" (When you disagree with one political position.)

✔ "You're always late!" (When your spouse shows up ten minutes late to meet you for dinner.)

✔ "I'm stupid!" (When you get one bad grade on a test.)

Though there may be some truth in these statements, they're all clearly overgeneralizations. When you overgeneralize, you create a distorted image of what is really happening and imagine a reality that invites excessive and inappropriate anger and frustration. You take a single instance of something you don't like and decide it's a trend.

To help you curb the tendency to overgeneralize, here are some useful ideas:

✔ Ask yourself whether you are seeing only one small part of a person's overall behavior and too quickly assuming that this sample characterizes that person as a whole.

✔ Try to think of individuals or situations that don't fit into your overgeneralization.

✔ Look out for language that reflects this all-or-nothing thinking — words like "always" and "never," "nobody" and "everybody." Examples are believing "people are never friendly" or "people always take advantage of you when they have the chance."

A kissing cousin to overgeneralizing is *black-and-white thinking* or *all-or-nothing thinking* — creating discrete categories like "good-bad," "right-wrong," and "smart-stupid." The reality is, the world and the people in it rarely fall into discrete, easily identified categories. Try to find the gray areas and spare yourself a lot of stress.

Mind reading and conclusion-jumping

You mind read and conclusion-jump whenever you believe that you know something to be true, even when it may not be true at all. Some examples of mind reading and conclusion-jumping make this clear:

- ✔ You don't receive an invitation to a friend's party and conclude that she hates your guts.

- ✔ You see a brown spot on the back of your hand and conclude it's a terminal disease.

- ✔ You do a complete personality evaluation on someone you just met, based largely on what she was wearing.

- ✔ You conclude that your husband is having an affair with someone at work when you see a picture of him sitting with a woman at a company function.

Sometimes you simply don't have enough information to come to a conclusion with any degree of certainty. But that may not stop you from trying. One way to determine whether you're mind reading or conclusion-jumping is to play the role of a prosecuting attorney. Simply ask yourself, "Do I really have enough evidence to support my beliefs? Would a jury of my peers return a guilty verdict?" If the answer is no, reconsider your case and hold off on coming to any premature conclusions and reactions. Who knows? You may be right. However, if you're like most people, you're also wrong much of the time.

Comparativitis

If you suffer from comparativitis, you negatively compare yourself to others, usually about a trait, possession, or ability, and you come out the loser. It's normal to make those comparisons. What's stressful is turning a comparison into a thought that makes you feel upset, angry, anxious, or depressed. You focus on the difference, "She's prettier than I am" or "He's more successful than me," which in fact may be the case. The distortion comes when you feel diminished and less worthy than that other person. Here's an incomplete list of things you can compare yourself to, if you really want to feel stressed.

- ✔ Other people's looks
- ✔ Other people's money

- Other people's success
- Other people's popularity
- Other people's jobs
- Other people's children
- Other people's spouses
- Other people's personalities
- Other people's fame
- Other people's houses
- Other people's intelligence
- Other people's clothes
- Other people's stuff

The toxic part of comparativitis is that you end up putting yourself down and feeling bad about who you are and what you have. You may feel diminished and have less self-worth. In addition, you may feel jealous and resentful of those who you feel are "winning" the comparison.

To correct this error, start by realizing that you can't escape the comparativitis trap. You can *always* find people who can beat you in a comparison. A better way of thinking is to accept yourself as you are and not rate yourself on your traits, abilities, or possessions. Remember, life is not a zero-sum game where the winner is the one who is smarter, more successful, richer, or better looking. You want your life to be happier, less stressed, and more meaningful. Convince yourself that not playing the comparativitis game is just fine, and that you're doing okay. Ask yourself:

- Do I believe that the people I'm comparing myself to are really happier?
- Do I really believe that people who are less successful, smart, or (you fill in the blank) are doomed to unhappiness?
- Aren't I buying into what society tells me is essential to be happy? Is society right?
- Doesn't my resentment and jealousy of others make me less happy?

You may "lose" in a comparison, but if you can like and accept yourself as you are, you win something much bigger.

Personalizing

You commit this error when you wrongly believe that *you* or *your behavior* are to blame for a criticism or negative outcome. Here are some examples:

- ✔ Assuming that you were fired because of your incompetence when in fact you were the victim of a more widespread economic layoff.
- ✔ Believing that if someone is angry at you, you must deserve that anger.
- ✔ Thinking that if someone dislikes you, it's because of something you did wrong.
- ✔ You're part of a larger group that has been criticized, but you assume you deserve a disproportionate amount of the criticism.

Of course, sometimes you *are* the guilty party. But this way of thinking becomes an error when you assume blame even though your behavior isn't the problem. It's also an error when you have only partial responsibility but accept *all* of the blame. Here are some things you may want to ask yourself or say to yourself to help you correct this form of distortion:

- ✔ When I take a step back and look at what happened from a distance, do I really think I'm the one who is totally at fault?
- ✔ If this episode happened in front of a jury of my peers who knew the whole story, would they blame me?
- ✔ Is this a pattern in my thinking? Do I too often feel shame or guilt for things I may not be responsible for?

Emotional reasoning

Making this error, you mistakenly believe that your feelings are an accurate barometer of the objective truth of a situation. You allow your feelings to interpret your external reality. For example:

- ✔ You feel anxious about doing something out of your comfort zone and believe that anxiety is correctly warning you not to do it.
- ✔ You feel depressed at some points in your relationship and conclude that the relationship should be ended.
- ✔ You feel angry at someone for criticizing you and believe that, because of those feelings, that person is bad and you should have nothing to do with him or her.

Now, I'm not suggesting that your feelings can't be a useful guide to interpreting your world. "Listening to your gut" has its place and can have value in making decisions. However, feeling (especially strong and short-lived feelings) can be misleading. Feelings aren't facts, and giving your feelings too much weight can lead to stressful decisions. Try asking yourself:

✔ Can I trust this feeling, or is this feeling temporary?

✔ Can I put these feeling into words, and do the words make sense to me?

✔ Might I feel differently about this situation in a week? A day? An hour?

✔ Other than these feelings, is there other evidence that supports my judgments or decisions?

Filtering

When you filter, you look at only a small part of the bigger picture, make some judgments about that smaller part, and mistakenly judge the much larger part based on this partial information. For example, at work your boss has been generally pleased with your work and your level of performance. You hand in a project, and he is generally positive but critical of your wording in one section. You go home feeling somewhat down and upset. You think he was unhappy with your efforts and was less than thrilled with you. You have filtered out the good feedback and focused only on the negative.

Or consider this example of filtering. You're dressed up and all ready to go to the party when you notice a small pimple on your face. You're upset and anxious. You feel everyone will notice. You think the evening is ruined. You consider not going out at all. You do go, and get lots of compliments on the way you look. You filter out these positives, believing people are just being polite and sparing your feelings by not commenting on your blemish.

In both cases, you mistakenly see only the negative. You filter out the positives. You conclude that your boss's criticism is far broader and more scathing then it really is. You believe the pimple overshadows any other positives about your appearance. Challenging this distorted, negative thinking, you may ask yourself:

✔ Am I working with a limited amount of information and not including other parts that might get me to look at this situation differently?

✔ Are my insecurities biasing the true reality of the situation?

✔ If a good friend were in my place and described the situation to me, would I feel so negative?

Probably not!

Magnifying and minimizing

You *magnify* whenever you escalate something smallish into something much larger. Making a small mistake becomes a big failure. A well-meaning suggestion becomes a hurtful criticism. A small physical discomfort becomes an exaggerated pain.

The companion thinking error to magnifying is *minimizing*. Committing this error, you go in the other direction. Someone compliments you on a skill or attribute, and you quickly minimize the intent. Someone tells you, "You really did that project incredibly well," and you feel anxious and discount that appraisal by saying, "I just got lucky." You minimize your strengths and assets.

To correct this error, dispute your negative thinking with some challenging questions:

✔ Maybe I'm exaggerating here just a wee bit! Is this as big a deal as I'm making it out to be?

✔ By looking at this situation this way, am I creating more stress than is appropriate?

✔ Why do I always feel uncomfortable with positive comments and compliments? Maybe I deserve them.

Should-ing

You make this error whenever you hear yourself saying, in a rigid, angry way, things like:

"People shouldn't be rude!"

"People shouldn't cut me off in traffic!"

"Life should be fair!"

What's that you say? There's nothing wrong with these statements? People *shouldn't* be rude, insensitive, and unfair? Here's the issue: It's okay to express preferences or give prescriptions for a better world. However, when your "shoulds" and "shouldn'ts" take the form of rigid demands — when they become "musts" and create inflexible expectations — you're going to be mighty upset when people don't follow your rules. When others (even you, for that matter) violate one of these unrealistic demands, you find yourself judging them and becoming indignant and angry. And you'll have lots to get stressed about, because people often won't conform to your idea of "correct living." Psychologist Albert Ellis has dubbed this way of thinking *musterbation* (with a U!).

The antidote? Stop should-ing. Give up the rigid demands and replace them with healthier, more flexible, preferences. Make your expectations more in tune with the way the world really works. Judge people's behavior, not their character. Try saying to yourself:

> "It would be better if I ate more healthfully and went to the gym."

> "I would really like it if people were nicer."

> "It certainly would be a better world if people were more considerate."

This is more than just switching words. You want to look at your "shoulds" and "have tos" not as demands, musts, and needs but as wants and preferences. Whenever you suspect you may be using an unrealistic "should" or "shouldn't," challenge this thinking and ask yourself the following two questions:

✔ Is my "should" really a disguised "must" or "have to"? Am I really making a demand in disguise?

✔ Why *must* other people act the way I want them to? (Answer yourself by saying, "They don't, and often won't.")

By changing your unrealistic demands — your "shoulds" and "musts" — to healthy preferences, you'll feel much better. And certainly less stressed. Part of what creates your "shoulds" and "musts" are your expectations. They play an important role in determining how stressed you feel in reacting to a potentially stressful situation. If your expectations are out of whack, you're likely to overreact. The brief tongue-in-cheek Reality Test that follows should give you a better sense of what I mean.

Take the Reality Test

Take this short quiz to see how realistic your expectations are. Simply answer Likely (L) or Unlikely (U) to each of these items:

1. You've been searching for a parking place for the last 45 minutes when you finally see a spot opening up. The guy in the car ahead of you also sees the spot and, in fact, is closer to it than you are. You tell him how difficult it's been for you to find a parking place. You expect he will say, "Why don't you take this spot? I have lots of extra time today." L or U

2. You're waiting for the department store to deliver your new bed. The delivery person said he would be there at 9 a.m. You're quite certain he'll be there by 9:15, tops. L or U

3. You arrive at your doctor's office ten minutes early for your 3 o'clock appointment. You expect that promptly at three a nurse will emerge and say, "Follow me, please. The doctor is ready to see you." L or U

4. Your two adolescent children have sworn they will be totally responsible for taking care of a dog if you get them one. You expect that they'll honor their promise, feed the dog, and take him out for twice-daily walks. L or U

If you answered Likely to any of these items, I wish you luck. Could any or all of the above expectations come about? Absolutely. However, the reality is, things often don't work out the way you'd like them to. Be realistic in what you expect.

Watch out for "exclamation mark" behavior

One way of finding out whether your expectation is realistic or unrealistic, and whether you are should-ing, is to look for exclamation-mark behavior. Some examples include saying any of the following when you're faced with a situation that angers or upsets you:

How can this be!

I don't understand this!

How could you do this!

I don't believe this!

This behavior is characterized by the tone of surprise and disbelief in your reaction. Accompanying such exclamations are tell-tale "I just can't believe this!" gestures. Common examples include:

- ✔ Excessive eye-rolling and eyebrow-lifting
- ✔ Excessive and loud sighing
- ✔ Head shaking with accompanying "tsk-tsks"
- ✔ Hands thrown into the air indicating total frustration

This behavior indicates the presence of unrealistic "shoulds" and "musts." Implicit in your disbelief is the more magical demand: "Other people should and must be more like me. I wouldn't act like that; therefore, neither should they." But they do.

Self-rating

Whenever you equate your entire self-worth with your traits, abilities, or performance, or whenever you feel the need for the approval of others, you're self-rating. In essence you're saying:

"If I'm not handsome, tall, smart, rich, and successful, I have less worth as a person."

"In order for me to feel good about myself and have self-esteem, I must be approved of by others."

This implies that you can only have positive self-esteem and feel good about yourself if:

✔ You've accomplished great things.

✔ You have marvelous traits.

✔ Other people approve of you or what you have done.

I can hear you asking, "What's the matter with that? Don't we all want the approval of others, want to do well, and want to have terrific traits?" Yes, we do. The problem arises when you feel you *need to* and *must* do well or must have success and the approval of others. The reality is, many times you don't do as well as you'd like, your performance is less than stellar, and you don't get approval from others. By making your worth contingent on any or all of the above, you lose your self-esteem and become vulnerable to unnecessary stress.

The close relative of self-rating is other-rating. The process is exactly the same. The difference is that you negatively rate *someone else.* So "I'm stupid" becomes "he's stupid," and so on. Just in case you're a wee bit short of ways to negatively self-rate or other-rate, here are some convenient labels to get you started:

"I'm . . . !" or "You're . . . !"

✔ An idiot!

✔ A loser!

✔ Pathetic!

✔ A failure!

✔ A fat pig!

✔ Useless!

✔ A fool!

✔ A jerk!

Frankly, giving up this self-rating tendency is not the easiest thing to do. It takes time and effort. To start, ask yourself the following questions:

✔ Do I really need to have others' approval to feel good about myself?

✔ Do I really have to be the best to feel good about myself?

✔ I don't expect other people to be perfect, so should I expect it from myself?

✔ Can I rate my total worth as an individual on the basis of one or two traits or abilities?

The answer to each of the above is, of course, "No." None of the above is truly necessary for you to be happy in life — or to feel good about yourself.

Using Your Coping Self-talk

Recognizing and understanding your thinking errors is an important step in replacing stress-producing thoughts with their stress-reducing counterparts. But to complete the change process, you need one more tool in your toolbox. This is your *coping self-talk*.

Your coping self-talk is an internal dialogue, a verbal back and forth you have inside your head when faced with a stressor. Let me give you a taste of what your coping self-talk might look like. Let's say you find yourself caught in a horrific traffic jam and realize you're becoming terribly stressed. You mentally step back, and rather than staying in auto-pilot, listening to your distorting, stress-producing voice, you gain some emotional distance and begin talking to yourself in a different way. You can say to yourself:

> *"What a hassle! Unfortunately, there's nothing I can do about it. If I'm late for the meeting, the world won't end. Don't go ballistic here. Stop catastrophizing and awfulizing! May this be the worst problem you face in life! Try some of that deep breathing you've been reading about . . . Hey, that feels pretty good. Put on that new CD and make the best of it. I'll certainly survive this.*

Your coping self-talk allows you to construct a comprehensive coping narrative that guides your thinking and responses, both for current stressors and future ones. This self-talk helps you in several different ways.

- ✔ It allows you to step back, get out of auto-pilot, and distance yourself from your automatic thoughts and any accompanying negative thinking, feelings, or behavior.

- ✔ It gives you the chance to "assess your balance" and determine whether your negative thinking is playing an important role in producing your stress.

- ✔ It gives you a chance to express your wiser, more therapeutic voice. This voice is that more rational, realistic side of you that is more mindful. It is more accepting and compassionate and less reactive and judgmental.

- ✔ It can help you discover your thinking errors or any other thought distortions you may be making. It's the voice that corrects your thinking errors by challenging and disputing their reasonableness.

- ✔ It can help integrate other stress-management techniques (relaxation, meditation, problem-solving, and so on) into a more comprehensive stress response.

- ✔ It can help you explore other ways of dealing with the stressor, giving you a wider variety of response options. It can suggest better ways of handling stressful situations and dealing with others.

Talking like an air-traffic controller

One way to use your coping self-talk is to think like an air-traffic controller. Consider this B-grade movie scenario:

The weather at the airport is foggy. Very foggy. You're the air-traffic controller in charge. You learn that a novice pilot is having trouble landing and is panicking. He badly needs your help. You begin to talk him down. You say:

> *"You're doing just fine, son. Hang in there . . . Take a deep, slow breath . . . Great! Now, remember what you learned in pilot school. Pull the throttle toward you. That's it. You can do this . . . Let her steady out. Begin your descent. Good. Take another deep breath. Don't panic. Hold her steady . . . you're almost down . . . You're doing great . . . You're on the ground. You made it!"*

You get the idea. Talk to yourself in a way that helps you cope better with the stressful or potentially stressful situation.

Putting it all together

These three examples demonstrate how your self-talk can become a powerful vehicle in helping you cope with a potentially stressful event or situation.

Your situation: "She never e-mailed me back!"

You're stressed out because you e-mailed a woman you met last week at a party, and she hasn't e-mailed you back. You find yourself quite upset and more than a little annoyed. Your negative self-talk sounds like this:

> *"There's something wrong with me! Girls don't like me! I'll never get a date! She should at least have the courtesy to get back to me! I hate when this happens!"*

Your coping self-talk

Here's how to talk yourself down from the negative self-talk:

> *"Stop mind reading and conclusion-jumping! You have no evidence to back up your assumption that she isn't interested. There can be a dozen reasons why she hasn't gotten back to you yet. You have no idea what she's thinking. Give her some more time. And even if she's not interested in you, it's not the end of the world. Stop catastrophizing and awfulizing! Not everyone you're interested in may be interested in you. Accept it without personalizing and putting yourself down. This doesn't mean that you're not okay. Remember, your worth isn't tied to her approval or disapproval. And don't overgeneralize. If this doesn't work, you'll find other people to date. Not everybody feels the same."*

Your situation: "The baby blues"

You're a newish parent, and your five-month-old son still hasn't gotten the hang of going to bed and staying asleep. It's your turn to be up with the baby. It's 3 a.m., and he's crying. Your negative and perhaps automatic self-talk sounds something like this:

> *"It's 3 in the morning! I'm still up! The baby is crying. I'm tired! I'm fried! I can't take any more of this! My day tomorrow is lost! I'll get absolutely nothing done! My nights on duty are always the worst! This isn't fair!"*

Your coping self-talk

Try telling yourself the following:

> *"Yes, you are indeed tired. But this is hardly a major tragedy. You're truly catastrophizing. The baby is great! Yes, he cries. That's what babies do. Don't make this into a bigger problem than it is. Watch your should-ing! Stop demanding fairness, especially in this case when fairness has nothing to do with it. Your spouse is more than fair about taking care of the baby. Put this into perspective. This is a "seven" response to a "three" problem. You may be tired tomorrow, but don't exaggerate and assume your whole day will be ruined. It may not be ideal, but you'll get through it fine. Calm yourself down. Believe it or not, this is a good problem to have in life. Try the bottle again. You can cope!"*

Your situation: "Locked out!"

You come home and discover that the door is locked and that you've left your key in your other pants (for the second time!). You are upset, frustrated, and angry at yourself. You're probably saying something to yourself that sounds like this:

> *"I'm an idiot! I've done it again! When will I learn! Why can't I catch a break! I hate when this happens! This always happens to me!*

Your coping self-talk

Try this:

> *"Calm down and take a breath . . . and take another. You don't have to catastrophize or awfulize. Don't make this into a bigger deal than it is. On a scale of one to ten, this is still only a two or three. Stay in balance. Just getting upset isn't going to help anything. Think. Who has another key? Nobody. Okay, Beth will be home in an hour. Give her a call and tell her what's happening. Go to the coffee shop, read the paper, and relax. You can handle this. I am handling this. Good for me. At times I may be a forgetful idiot, but at least I can cope with the consequences."*

Taking time to make it work

Changing thoughts and feelings can look deceptively simple. But it's not! Just because you've started using your coping self-talk and are saying the right words doesn't guarantee that it will immediately turn off your stress. The problem is, on an intellectual level you believe your coping self-talk, but your distorted, automatic, negative thinking can still be running the show. Part of you still strongly believes the automatic thinking you've been telling yourself for years. Your goal is to internalize your new thinking and truly come to believe it. This takes some time, some effort, and lots of practice. But you'll get there.

Chapter 11

Stress-Resilient Values, Goals, and Attitudes

· ·

In This Chapter

▶ Recognizing how your values and goals create stress

▶ Discovering what's important to you

▶ Finding your sense of humor

▶ Seeing the value in helping others

▶ Adding a spiritual dimension

· ·

*J*ust as your thinking plays an important role in creating (and relieving) your stress, your values, goals, and attitudes can increase or decrease the amount of stress in your life. This chapter helps you identify and clarify your personal values and goals and shows you how you can create more stress-resilient ways of looking at your world.

Recognizing the Value of Your Values

"What," you may ask, "have my values and attitudes got to do with the stress in my life?" The answer is, "Lots." Your personal values and your overall philosophy of life play a major role in determining your stress level. What you think is important and what you value act together in often subtle yet important ways to either protect you from stress or make your life more stressful. Rarely a day goes by without some decision, some opinion, or some action being determined, or at least shaped, by your values and attitudes. Your values in large part determine your goals, your needs, and your wants. And when you don't reach these goals, or fulfill these needs and wants, you feel stressed.

You may not even be aware of holding such values and attitudes. Yet you do. And either consciously or subconsciously they guide many of your more important decisions — everything from what you eat to how you vote, from what work you do to how you spend your time and money. Clarifying your values and attitudes is an important first step in moving toward developing a stress-resilient philosophy of life. The greater the congruence between your values and your goals, and between your decisions and actions, the lower your stress level. Think of your values and attitudes as your roadmap in life. The better the map, the smaller the chance that you may make a wrong turn.

At various points in life, you realize that some of your values and goals are not providing you with the kind of happiness and satisfaction you want. Many of your core values may not be the values you truly believe in. They may be values you inherited from others, without much thought on your part. These values can come from your parents, your peers, your religion, your teachers, television and the movies, the corporation or organization you work for, or the community you live in. Such values can match your own values. However, in some cases, they may not reflect what is truly meaningful or important to you at this point in your life. Yes, you're climbing the ladder, but it may be the wrong ladder. What may have seemed worthwhile and important at one stage of your life may not seem as important later on. Your values and goals change, and reevaluating and reconsidering your values from time to time is important.

Clarifying Your Values and Goals

In this section, I provide you with several exercises designed to help you discover and clarify what values and goals are important to you. These exercises aren't about passing or failing or being right or wrong, so just be honest. Does this mean some values are less stress-resilient than others? Absolutely. But you alone can determine which of your values and goals you should hold onto, and which of your values and goals you need to revamp or even throw out altogether.

The tombstone test

Contemplating your own demise may seem like an overly dramatic way of getting in touch with your core values and central goals, but it can be remarkably effective. The following exercise was designed to give you the ultimate perspective. Take a pen or pencil, and a piece of paper (or your keyboard), and answer the following question:

When I'm gone, what would I like my tombstone to say about me?
(Assume you have a very large tombstone.)

Include in your tombstone description the answers to the following, more specific questions:

- How would I like people to remember me?
- What would I like to have accomplished in life?

This exercise should help you step back and look at the bigger picture. It forces you to consider what exactly you value as worthwhile and important. This approach worked for Ebenezer Scrooge. Give it a try.

Five-ish years to live

This section gives you another upbeat exercise. In this one, you aren't dead yet, but you will be shortly. You've been told that you have at least five years left, but not much more. You're reassured that you will experience no pain, and you can carry on a totally normal life until your death. This exercise differs from the preceding "tombstone test," in that it looks less at the "big" picture and asks that you re-consider and re-evaluate your present day-to-day involvements and concerns.

Ponder the following question:

> **If you had just five more years to live, would you spend the time you have left any differently than the way you are spending it now?**

If yes, what would you do that is different? Would you stay at your job? Would you live where you're living? Would you finally call your mother? And so on . . .

The rating game

One of the simplest ways of uncovering your values and goals is to rate a list of the most common ones. Use this simple ten-point rating system, where ten means "extremely important to me" and zero means "not at all important." You're not ranking the items in order from least to most important. You're just considering each item individually and rating it on a scale of one to ten. Take a stab at it:

____ Achieving financial success

____ Being seen as smart

____ Being powerful

_____ Being a leader

_____ Winning at most things

_____ Helping others

_____ Being seen as physically attractive

_____ Being admired

_____ Being seen as honest

_____ Spending time with family

_____ Spending time with friends

_____ Achieving fame

_____ Being respected

_____ Being loved

_____ Having a strong spiritual foundation

The purpose of this exercise is to get you to re-assess specific goals and involvements in terms of their value and importance for you. After you rate these values and goals, take a moment to consider which items you rated a seven or greater. Elaborate on what that value or goal means to you. For example, does "financial success" mean having millions of dollars, or does it mean having enough money so that you don't have to worry about paying your bills? A sentence or two should do it. Hopefully, completing this exercise will help you discover something about what is important to you, and perhaps identify some aspects of your life that you may want to change.

Things I love to do

This exercise is a lot easier. I'd like you to simply list 15 things you really enjoy doing. I'm not talking about bettering the world; I'm talking about things you really like to do. It can be anything — traveling, playing a favorite sport, reading pot-boilers, learning, gardening, sleeping, watching TV, or whatever else you really like to spend your time doing. Sometimes just putting these activities down on paper can trigger a realization that you're missing out. Then ask yourself:

"Why am I not doing more of these things?"

If you love playing golf or you'd like to spend more time traveling, ask yourself why you're not spending more time on these kinds of activities. Later sections in this chapter can help you figure out how to find the time to build in the activities you love into your busy life.

Some other intriguing questions to ponder

If your brain isn't completely drained by now, here are several questions that you can ask yourself to get to know your values and goals a little better. If you'd rather not ponder these questions now, jot down the questions and pull one out next time you find yourself waiting in a long line or sitting on a plane or train.

- ✔ If I could come back in another lifetime as someone else, who would it be? Why?
- ✔ If I had oodles of money, what would I do with it?
- ✔ If I could make only three phone calls before I had to leave this world, who would I call? What would I say?
- ✔ And the old job-interview favorite: Where do I want to be in one year? In five years?

Actualizing Your Values, Reaching Your Goals

Having identified your values, you may realize that you've been paying lip service to them without following through. People have a tremendous ability to hold a set of values they feel are meaningful, yet in their day-to-day lives they can sometimes fail to recognize the importance of those values. Thus, you may value the notion of spending time with your family yet find yourself, for whatever reason, actually spending very little time interacting with family members, even when you have the chance. The way to avoid this trap is to become more conscious of how exactly you do spend your time, money, and energy.

Staying on track

This exercise will help you organize much of the material culled from the preceding exercises and also enable you to assess the extent to which you're actualizing and achieving those goals and values you feel are highly important to you. The following sections take you through this process.

Step 1: Ranking your primary values and goals

From what you discovered about yourself by doing all the preceding exercises, come up with a ranked list of your top ten values. These values can include more abstract ones (such as honesty and integrity) and more specific goals (spend more time with family, get more involved with the community, and so on).

Step 2: Evaluating your progress

In a second column, rate the extent to which you feel you have achieved or actualized those values and goals listed in the first column. Again, use a simple ten-point scale, where ten indicates "completely" and zero indicates "not at all."

To help you think of specific goals and values, here are some categories to get you started: Job/Career, Family, Friends, Health, Money, Hobbies, Interests, Travel, and Spirituality.

My important values and goals	My success at actualizing these values or reaching these goals
_____	_____
_____	_____
_____	_____
_____	_____
_____	_____
_____	_____
_____	_____
_____	_____
_____	_____
_____	_____

Making the time

Actualizing your values and reaching your goals require time. And because you're incredibly busy already, finding time for the more important things in your life may take some planning. You need to schedule your priorities, rather than merely prioritizing your schedule. In other words, start out by determining which activities are more important in your life, and then make the time to do them.

To help you identify those activities, here's a starter list for you to begin with. For each of the items below, indicate the extent to which each is a priority and exactly how, when, and where you can find or create the time for that priority.

I would like to spend more time . . .	*How, when, and where can I do this?*
With my kids	_____
With my spouse	_____
With friends	_____
On my job or career	_____
On a hobby or interest	_____
Playing sports	_____
Reading	_____
Keeping in shape	_____
Nurturing my soul	_____
Doing community activities	_____
Traveling	_____
(Add any others you may have)	
_____	_____
_____	_____
_____	_____

Expressing Gratitude

Psychologist Robert Emmons defines gratitude as "a felt sense of wonder, thankfulness, and appreciation for life."

I also like the definition developed by another psychologist, Sonja Lyubomirsky, who defines the process of gratitude as "a focus on the present moment, on appreciating your life as it is today and what has made it so."

Gratitude can mean different things to different people. In its simplest form, it can be saying thank you for a gift or service. For you it may mean feeling thankful when you dodge a bullet or get over something bad that happens to you. The word may take on a religious meaning, thanking a higher power for bestowing goodness and "counting your blessings." For others it can mean feeling grateful when others are less well off than they are. (This may take a less commendable form when a person "compares downward," identifying others who have less money, less success, less attractiveness, or less intelligence and feeling grateful to be better off.)

Understanding how expressing gratitude reduces your stress

Research has shown that people who feel gratitude are happier, report more life satisfaction, and report less stress. Grateful people are less likely to be depressed, anxious, lonely, and neurotic. But it also appears that grateful people don't live in a world of denial. They don't ignore the negative parts of their lives.

The connection between gratitude and stress may not be immediately obvious. After all, why should I feel less distressed when I feel grateful for something? Here's how it works:

- ✔ **Gratitude allows you to detach from a stressful period and savor a positive memory or experience.** This positive focus can create a positive sense of well-being. This can distract you from your worries and upsets. Remember that it's hard to think of two things at the same time. Feeling gratitude probably means you're feeling less stress.

- ✔ **You can feel better about yourself.** When you express gratitude, you recognize that people care about you and have done a lot for you. This can enhance your positive sense of self, reducing levels of negative, self-downing thinking.

- ✔ **When the gratitude is aimed at others, you feel better about yourself because you're recognizing and emotionally giving to others.** Giving to others more often than not makes you feel better about who you are.

- ✔ **Gratitude pulls you out of your negative mindset.** Much of your stressful thinking is automatic. By focusing solely on your negative experiences, you can spiral downward. By expressing gratitude, you give your thinking a more positive target. You feel better; you feel less stress.

- ✔ **Gratitude puts things into perspective.** Gratitude provides you with a sense of balance that can help you avert feelings of hopelessness and despair that can play a major role in creating stress.

- ✔ **Expressing gratitude to others can create and enhance relationships.** You feel better about yourself, and others in turn feel better about you.

- ✔ **The bonus is that you may get a thankful response of gratitude from the person to whom you express gratitude.** Most often that can make your day and lower your stress.

Keeping a mental gratitude journal

Intuitively you know you should feel and express gratitude, but you may put it into practice less often than you think. You may look at exercise in the same way: You know you should do more of it, but you just don't. Sometimes you need to be reminded and encouraged. Keeping a journal makes it more likely that you'll be aware of the importance of gratitude and express gratitude more frequently. Here's what to do:

Find a time when you have a few moments to yourself and think about four or five things in your life right now for which you are thankful. This could be on the train on your way to work, on a coffee break at your desk, or at any quiet moment when you can step back and reflect. Here are some things you might be grateful for:

- ✔ Your health
- ✔ Your friends
- ✔ Your children
- ✔ Your relationship
- ✔ Your skills and talents
- ✔ Your home
- ✔ Your job
- ✔ Your life itself

Add to this list and come up with additional aspects of your life for which you can feel grateful.

For some people, carrying out this exercise daily may work best; for others, once a week may be enough. If you're a good journal-keeper, you may want to jot down these objects of gratitude. Either way, try to make this exercise a regular part of your day or week.

Remembering to actually express your gratitude

Acknowledging those parts of your life for which you should be grateful is important; expressing gratitude to others is the other part.

Too often we feel gratitude but fail to express it. Our hearts are in the right place, but we don't communicate our gratitude to the other person. This communication can take the form of a simple thank you or a more elaborate expression of gratitude. It can be in response to a specific behavior or a larger pattern of behavior on the other person's part. It can be something that happened recently or something that goes way back. It can be someone you know personally or someone you only know of. It can be a close connection, such as a family member, or someone more remote, such as a mail carrier, an author, or your child's teacher.

These days, you have plenty of options for delivering your message. The vehicle for your gratitude could be a face-to-face meeting, a phone call, an e-mail, an instant message, a text message, or perhaps even a letter. Don't wait for next Thanksgiving.

Cultivating Optimism

Much of our stress comes from looking at the future with either anxiety or hopelessness. We fear the uncertainty of the future, often believing that the worst will happen. We depress ourselves about the future, believing that nothing good will come of it. But our lives can be far less stressful if we look forward with more optimistic and hopeful attitudes. Being optimistic is not simply believing that everything in your life will turn out wonderfully. Being optimistic means believing that your important life goals can somehow be accomplished and that you can find ways to make those goals happen.

Recognizing thinking errors that hinder optimism

A first step in cultivating optimism is recognizing the distorting attitudes that undermine how you view your future. If you look closely, you realize that you may be experiencing some of the common thinking errors I define in Chapter 10. Here are some examples of these cognitive distortions, which might reflect your own pessimistic and hopeless thinking:

- ✔ **Overgeneralization:** Thinking in terms of "all or nothing," always and never, and black-and-white opposites such as good and bad, right and wrong. For example:
  - "Everybody thinks I'm stupid!"
  - "People never change!"
  - "Everybody is always only out for themselves!"
- ✔ **Conclusion jumping:** Taking one small bit of current evidence and wrongly predicting negative future outcomes. For example:
  - "Because I failed this test, no college is going to admit me."
  - "Because he didn't say hello to me yesterday, I have to assume he doesn't like me."
  - "Because she wasn't interested in me, I'll never be in a relationship."

✔ **Self-rating:** Taking one of your traits, abilities, or performances, and/or other people's disapproval, and equating that with your self-worth. For example:

- "My boss criticized my handling of the project. I'm incompetent!"
- "I failed that test. I'm stupid!"
- "I let her down! I'm really a bad person."

✔ **Catastrophizing and awfulizing:** Predicting that the worst will happen in the future. For example:

- "I know this headache means I have cancer!"
- "I know I'll screw up this interview!"
- "I know I'll grow old alone with no one to be with me!"

Arguing with yourself

As you can see, these thinking errors can create a rather pessimistic and hopeless view of the future, and with that bleak picture comes much unnecessary stress. Chapter 10 shows you in detail how to identify these distortions and dispute the thinking behind them. Here are some useful challenges and quick questions to ask yourself:

✔ "Am I over-reacting here?"

✔ "Do I have any real evidence that my predictions will come true?"

✔ "Haven't I been wrong in the past about what I thought would happen?"

✔ "Because something happened once or twice, does that mean it will always happen?"

✔ "How can I tie my entire self-worth to one bit of failure or disapproval?"

✔ "What advice would I give someone else who was thinking the way I am?"

✔ "Most of the bad things I'm imagining probably won't happen."

✔ "Accept uncertainty! There are lots of things in life you can't control."

✔ "Don't assume the worst!"

✔ "Thoughts aren't facts! You don't always have to trust them."

✔ "I can come up with a new game plan to change things. Let me look at this differently."

Constructing an optimistic future

You probably have many stories you tell yourself about your life that give it meaning and shape the way you think, feel, and act. Three such stories concern your past, present, and future.

- ✔ **Your history** — the story of where you came from and how you got to be who you are today.
- ✔ **Your present life** — a description of where you are right now in life.
- ✔ **Your future** — what your life will look like in the future.

These stories play an incredibly important role in determining how you look at yourself and the direction your life will take. Particularly important is the story of where your life will be in the future.

Try this exercise: Take a piece of paper (or use your tablet or computer) and construct a realistically positive picture of where you want to be in five or even ten years. Be specific, describing your goals, dreams, and aspirations. Include your relationship goals (marriage? children?), career goals, and any other important goals. Don't censor yourself, but be realistic. Allow your thoughts to go in optimistic directions. Repeat this exercise on a regular basis, updating your goals and wish list.

Research has shown that writing this way on a regular basis can make you think more optimistically. This is more than just positive thinking ("If I think about it, it will happen"). The writing and thinking help you escape the barriers of negative, limiting thought. Writing down your goals certainly makes you feel happier and shows you that you have a choice in the way you view your world. It suggests more options and helps you identify unrealistic goals and potential roadblocks. The more you practice optimistic thinking, the more internalized these thoughts become. And when you really believe them, they become more possible.

Laughing Your Way to Stress Reduction

If you take life (and yourself) too seriously, you can just about guarantee that your stress level will be higher than it has to be. Life is filled with hassle, inconvenience, and a myriad of other nuisances that can either drive you crazy or bring a smile to your face. And even the more serious problems that may come your way often contain a trace of humor. Humor gives you the ability to defuse much of the potential stress and pressure all around you. A sharp sense of the absurd combined with a dash of whimsy can make your life far less stressful.

He (or she) who laughs, lasts

Humor is a more serious stress-reducer than you may think. Here are some of the ways it can lower your stress level:

- ✔ **It relaxes your body.** The physical act of laughing can result in an overall lowering of your physiological stress level. After rising briefly while you're laughing, your blood pressure drops and your heart rate slows. The brain may also release endorphins, which can induce a more calming physical state.

- ✔ **It can enhance your immunity.** Researchers are beginning to discover that humor may have even more important health-enhancing effects. Laughter reduces your body's production of stress hormones while increasing production of disease-resisting T-cells and the chemical interferon, all of which can result in a stronger immune system.

- ✔ **It gives you perspective.** Humor creates distance and objectivity. If you can find some way to see a potentially stressful situation in a humorous way, you reduce the stress potential of that experience.

- ✔ **It can get you to take yourself less seriously.** Much of your stress comes from giving too much importance to how you see yourself or how others see you. If you can learn how to laugh at yourself, you rob other people — and circumstances themselves — of their ability to trigger your stress.

Some humorous suggestions

Very few of us would admit to not having a good sense of humor. Yet too often, we lose the ability to laugh (or at least smile) at the nonsense and lunacy of life all around us. You don't have to be a standup comic or dazzle the group with side-splitting one-liners to make humor work for you. Here are some ways you can make humor one of your stress-reducing tools.

- ✔ **Reframe the situation.** Dr. Joel Goodman, director of the HUMOR Project in Saratoga Springs, New York, suggests that if you're having trouble finding humor in a potentially stressful situation, try to see that situation through someone else's eyes. Try to imagine how a friend with a particularly offbeat sense of humor may see it. Or ask yourself how not finding a parking spot or losing your wallet may have been handled on an episode of *Seinfeld*.

✔ **Be around others who make you laugh.** The humor of other people can be contagious. Not only can their laughter and humor lower your stress level, but you can begin to talk about your own stresses in more comical ways.

✔ **Tickle your fancy.** Try to find and collect bits of humor that you can use to induce a smile or a laugh. It can be that picture of you with that ridiculous look on your face. Stick it up on your bathroom mirror. Or it may be a humorous quip or cartoon that makes you chuckle. Put that on the fridge or stick it on your desk at work. Whenever I'm stressed by the need to clean up the house, I recall that marvelous Joan Rivers quip: "I hate housework! You make the beds, you do the dishes — and six months later you have to start all over again."

Anything that can evoke a smile can change your mood for the better.

Blow things up

Exaggeration is a great way of diffusing a potentially stressful situation, robbing it of much of its impact. One form of exaggeration uses the Blow-up Technique. Here's how it works. Suppose you're angry because your neighbor has the TV sound turned up too loud. Let your imagination take it from there. Now imagine that he has turned it up full blast. Not only that, but he has turned every radio he owns up to ear-splitting levels. You notice that you hear live music and realize a high-school band is practicing in his living room. The walls are now shaking. You get a phone call from your cousin half a mile away, asking what's going on. The police and fire department start arriving . . . and then you smile.

Exaggeration and distortion can help you put things into clearer perspective. Try it.

Doing Something Good for Someone Else

Doing something for another person can act as a stress buffer, enhancing your stress resilience. Most often, you get back just as much, if not more, than you give. And this can be achieved without drastic commitments on your part. You don't have to become a Mother Teresa or have homeless families come and live with you. Small, simple acts of generosity and kindness can go a long way.

How helping helps

The rewards of helping others may not have to wait until the hereafter. Here's how doing community service can be good for your stress level:

✔ **It gives you a sense of purpose.** At least some of your stress may come from a feeling of uncertainty about the nature of your existence and a search for some meaning and purpose in your life. Helping others can add to a sense of doing something worthwhile with your life and making a genuine contribution to others. You feel better when you help.

✔ **It connects you.** Almost all acts of community service (short of writing an anonymous check) bring you into contact with someone else. It can be the person or group you're helping, an agency or service, a board, a committee, or a fellow volunteer or caregiver. The act of helping adds to your social support system and increases your sense of connectedness to the world around you.

✔ **It keeps you busy.** Helping others in your community, in whatever form, is an involvement that channels your time and energy. It can distract you from your cares and worries and focus your attention in a rewarding and certainly less-stressful direction.

✔ **It increases your sense of self-worth.** When you help others, you feel good about yourself. Your self-esteem is enhanced; you feel valued. Because so much of your stress is related to a feeling of a lack of self-worth, doing something for others becomes a truly valuable way of changing the way you see yourself.

You'll live longer

Some research now suggests that the benefits of altruism may not be only psychological. In one study, researcher Allan Luks, founder of the Center for Nonprofit Leadership at Fordham University, found that volunteers who had some of the more commonly reported stress symptoms — headache, arthritis pain, and back pain — reported a reduction of these symptoms after volunteering. The pain, it would seem, was masked by the positive involvement of the volunteers.

In a second study, Phyllis Moen, Ph.D., then at Cornell University in Ithaca, New York, looked at the effects of volunteering on women's physical health and longevity. She found that women who devoted time and effort to a volunteer organization lived longer than those who didn't. They were less likely to be depressed, and they felt more satisfaction with the quality of their lives. In a related study, conducted at the University of Michigan on men who volunteered their time and effort at least once a week, researchers found that the death rate for these individuals was about half that of those who didn't volunteer. Maybe it really is better to give than to receive?

How to get started

Often the biggest obstacle to volunteering is figuring out what to do and where to go. Most communities have one or more umbrella organizations or volunteer clearinghouses that are aware of all the volunteering opportunities in your area. To find it, contact any major volunteer group. They will know where to send you.

Here are some ideas of ways to volunteer:

- Become a Big Brother or Big Sister.
- Volunteer to help out at a local homeless shelter.
- Help out at a library.
- Help at a local museum (serve as a tour guide or help with fundraising).
- Improve a neighborhood garden, park, or sidewalk.
- Coach kids in a team sport.
- Deliver food to the homebound or the elderly.
- Become a tutor in the public school system.
- Help administer a favorite charity.
- Help out at the ASPCA or Humane Society.
- Help organize a blood drive.
- Be part of a hotline.
- Teach literacy for adults.
- Become part of an ESL (English as a second language) program.
- Help with fundraising at a public radio or television station.
- Work at a nursing home or senior-citizen center.
- Be a helper at a nonprofit daycare center.

How to offer random acts of kindness

Remember, you can be altruistic in ways that don't involve a regular time commitment or membership in an organization. You can "freelance." Dozens of opportunities exist for you to help someone or do something positive for another person. Random acts of kindness — a kind word, a small deed, a courtesy — all work to produce positive and satisfying feelings within you, and within the people with whom you interact.

The power of the Word

Dr. Herbert Benson, a pioneer in the field of faith, relaxation, and stress reduction, has studied the role of prayer and its effects on stress. Benson found that by having individuals include words or sentences with religious meaning in their program of meditative relaxation, the levels of relaxation they attained were significantly higher than in those who didn't include religious content. The content could be as simple as a word or phrase taken from a traditional prayer (the Lord's Prayer, for example) or a word from a spiritual text (such as *shalom*, meaning "peace," or *echad*, meaning "one").

Adding a Spiritual Dimension

Having a belief in something greater than your immediate experience can be a powerful force in helping you create inner peace and cope with the stress in your life. We live in a universe that is both mystifying and, at times, overwhelming. We attempt to give meaning and purpose to our all-too-brief lives. Faith in something bigger, something cosmic, can help us come to grips with the unknown and perhaps unknowable. No one right way exists for finding a sense of spiritual connectedness. For many, this belief may take the form of a belief in God and involvement in a traditional religious system of beliefs. However, your spirituality may take a different form. It may be a belief in a more global, more vaguely articulated higher power or higher purpose. Or it may take the form of a belief in such values as the human spirit, the human community, or nature.

Understanding how faith helps you cope with stress

Whatever form your spiritual beliefs take, growing evidence shows that faith can be a powerful stress buffer, enhancing your ability to cope with life's more serious stresses. Faith can help you cope with illness, and it may even help you live longer. The reasons why faith helps are both direct and indirect:

- ✔ **Faith can provide meaning and purpose.** Having a deeply felt belief system can help you cope with many of the perplexing and distressing questions that surround the meaning of existence. Why are you here? What is the meaning and purpose of life? What happens when you die?

✔ **Faith can strengthen stress-effective values.** Virtually all religions promote the values of love and kindness and condemn stress-producing feelings such as anger, hostility, and aggression.

✔ **Faith can provide hope and acceptance.** It encourages a sense of optimism and hopefulness that things will work out for the best. Faith also helps you accept what doesn't work out and what you can't control.

✔ **Faith unites you with others.** It can create a sense of community that often brings people together in a mutually supportive way. Having others to be with and share with can lower your stress. Belonging to a religious organization can put you into contact with others in the wider community who are less fortunate in some way, which allows you to play a helping role.

✔ **Faith can calm you.** It often involves prayer and contemplation, which, like meditation and other forms of bodily relaxation described in other chapters, can result in a range of physical changes that reduce stress.

Appreciating the power of belief

A number of studies now document the importance of faith in strengthening one's coping ability. Just take a look at these:

✔ A recent National Institute of Mental Health study, for example, found that people who consider religious beliefs to be a central element in their lives experience lower amounts of depression than does a control group.

✔ In another study, researchers in Evans County, Georgia, looked at the stress-reducing effects of regular churchgoers when compared with non-churchgoers. They found that blood pressure measurements were significantly lower for the committed churchgoers. In a different study, in Washington County, Maryland, researchers found that those who attend church on a routine basis are much less likely to die of heart attacks than are infrequent churchgoers. (Researchers made sure the results had nothing to do with smoking, drinking, and other variables that may have clouded the results.)

✔ In a study conducted in Israel, researchers compared the health of secular and orthodox Israelis and found that the less-religious or non-religious group had a risk of heart attack that was four times higher than their religious counterparts. Also, the non-religious group had higher levels of cholesterol than did the more religious group.

Helping hints

In his book *The Healing Power of Doing Good*, Allan Luks offers some guidelines about which volunteering experiences are the most stress-effective. Here are some of his suggestions:

✔ Find situations that bring you directly into contact with others who need the help. Stuffing envelopes is okay, but you'll find greater satisfaction in a hands-on situation.

✔ Find an area of helping where you feel empathy for those with whom you're working.

✔ Find an involvement that can utilize a skill or ability you have.

✔ Don't over-commit yourself. You're better off starting small and adding on.

✔ Exert yourself to reach out. Stretch yourself in some way.

Gathering a Little Wisdom

A storehouse of collected wisdom can insulate you from many of life's stresses. If your collection is a little thin, you can begin collecting the wisdom of others. Kindergarten wisdom, Chicken Soup stories, sayings, affirmations, insights, parables, and maxims can help you cope with a potentially stressful situation. Stick them on your refrigerator or bathroom mirror. Here are some of my favorites to start you off:

"When you get there, there isn't any there there."

— Gertrude Stein

"If I had my life to live over, I'd try to make more mistakes next time. I would relax, I would limber up. I would be sillier than I have been this trip. I know of very few things I would take seriously. I would be less hygienic. I would take more chances. I would take more trips. I would climb more mountains, swim more rivers, and watch more sunsets. I would eat more ice cream. I would have more actual troubles and fewer imaginary ones."

— John Killinger

"I am an old man and have known a great many troubles — but most of them never happened."

— Mark Twain

"No one on their deathbed ever wished they had spent more time at the office."

— Anonymous

"It's not the large things that send a man to the madhouse. Death he's ready for, or murder, incest, roguery, fire, flood . . . no, it's the continuing series of small tragedies that send a man to the madhouse . . . not the death of his love, but a shoelace that snaps with no time left."

— Charles Bukowski

"Live each day as if it was your last, because someday you're going to be right."

— Anonymous

"Life is what happens to you while you're busy making other plans."

— John Lennon

"Rule Number 1: Don't sweat the small stuff. Rule Number 2: It's all small stuff."

— Richard Carlson

"The true value of a person is to be measured by the objects he pursues."

— Anonymous

"If you never want to make a mistake, do nothing, say nothing, be nothing."

— Anonymous

"Other people are not in this world to live up to your expectations."

— Fritz Perls

"For every minute you are angry, you lose sixty seconds of happiness."

— Ralph Waldo Emerson

Part IV
Managing Your Stress in Real Life

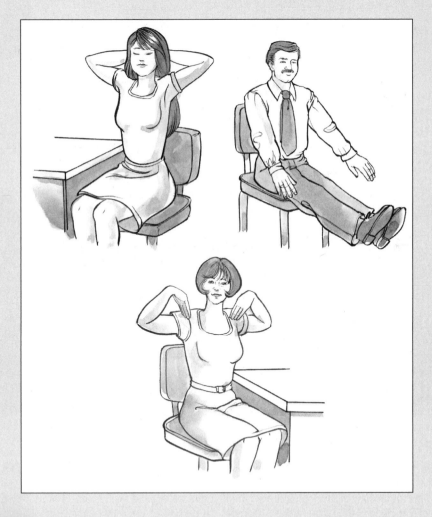

Head to www.dummies.com/extras/stressmanagement for a free article that looks at why some jobs seem to take their toll on people more than others.

In this part . . .

- Everyone gets angry sometimes, but if you find that you're becoming angry all the time, you need to get a grip because too much anger causes stress and harms your physical well-being. Find out how to reduce and control your anger to keep it from getting the best of you.

- Although worrying can be good when it motivates you to take action, *excessive* worry can be debilitating. Manage your stress by discovering how to control your worrying.

- Some people just rub you the wrong way. Find ways to interact with demanding, rude, or annoying people without letting your stress levels rise.

- Whether you're dealing with a lack of job security, too many responsibilities, office politics, or simply an uncomfortable office environment, workplace stress is all too common. Discover ways to de-stress at work to remain a happy and, therefore, productive employee.

- Figure out how to make stress management a part of your daily routine. Balance stress-reduction techniques with positive experiences that make you more stress resilient.

Chapter 12

Overcoming Your Anger

· ·

In This Chapter

▶ Understanding your anger

▶ Figuring out how anger affects your well-being

▶ Controlling your anger

· ·

*A*re you angry because someone cut you off in traffic or kept you waiting for what seemed like an eternity? Are you angry because that clumsy guest spilled red wine on your sofa, or because your printer refuses to print? Everyone feels anger sometimes. Unfortunately, too many people — and you may be one of them — experience too much anger too much of the time. Anger is not only terribly stressful, but it can also be harmful to your physical well-being and destructive to your relationships. Fortunately, ways of reducing your anger and limiting its consequences do exist. This chapter shows you how to control your anger — instead of letting your anger control you.

Figuring Out Just How Mad You Really Are

Does a big part of your stress come from your anger? Do you get just a little angry, or does your anger get out of control? The first step in reducing your anger is knowing how angry you are. In this section, I give you a simple, 12-item informal scale that helps you discover the role anger plays in your life.

For the following 12 statements, indicate the extent to which each one describes you. Jot down one of the following responses for each statement: not at all like me, a little like me, or a lot like me.

1. My family and/or friends tell me I get angry too easily.

2. I feel my anger is excessive.

3. My anger has frequently gotten me into trouble in the past.

4. I get frustrated pretty easily.

5. I hold on to my anger longer than I should.

6. I hate waiting or being kept waiting.

7. Petty annoyances can make me fly off the handle.

8. I take criticism and disapproval badly.

9. Incompetence and stupidity in others makes me angry.

10. I get angry when traffic or lines don't move quickly enough.

11. Being treated rudely or unfairly makes me very angry.

12. In arguments, I'm usually the one who gets more angry.

For each time you responded "a lot like me," give yourself three points. For each response of "a little like me," give yourself two points. And for each response of "not at all like me," give yourself a zero. If you have fewer than 18 points, anger is not a major part of your life. If you have between 19 and 30 points, anger is affecting your life moderately. And if you have 31 to 36 points, anger is a definite presence in your life.

You may also want to get a second opinion. You may not be the best person to measure the length of your fuse, and a more objective evaluation couldn't hurt. Why not have someone who knows you well answer the quiz for you? You may not feel you have a problem with your anger, but the people closest to you may have a different opinion. Who knows? They may even see you as less angry than you see yourself. Compare your score with the score your loved one gives you and talk about any major discrepancies in scoring (but try not to get angry while you do so).

The Pros and Cons of Anger

Anger, just like anything else, isn't all good or all bad: It has many pros and cons. The following sections explain those for you, so that you get a clear picture of anger and the effect it may have on your life.

Looking at the positives of anger

Anger can be a highly distressing emotion that results in all kinds of negative consequences. Yet among the other possible stress emotions (upset, depression, grief, anxiety, and so on), anger remains the most popular and the most common. And not without reason. Anger has some appeal:

✔ **Anger is activating and mobilizing.** When you're angry, you feel as if you're doing something about what's triggering your stress. You feel there is a response you can make, a way of expending energy toward resolving the distressing situation. It can get you to take action and do something about the problem.

✔ **Anger makes you feel powerful.** Anger can make you feel like you're in charge, even when you aren't. When you tell someone off, you feel stronger and more in control. Anger allows you to express yourself in a forceful way.

✔ **Anger often gets results.** By becoming angry, as opposed to remaining calm and pleasant, you may get what you want. Many people are intimidated by anger and are more obliging when confronted with it than they normally would be.

✔ **Anger is often a respected response.** We often interpret anger as standing up for ourselves and not letting others take advantage of us. And other people may see it the same way. Our anger may be labeled as assertive, strong, and confident.

Examining the downside of anger

Although your anger does have its upside, the downside of anger far outweighs any positive benefits. Besides being emotionally distressing and making you a prime candidate for a black eye, anger can give you other things to worry about.

Anger can make you sick

When you're angry, your body reacts much the same way it does when you're experiencing any other stress reaction. Your anger triggers your body to take a defensive stance, readying you for any danger that may come your way. (Check out Chapter 2 for more on this response, known as fight or flight.) When your anger is intense and frequent, the physiological effects can be harmful. Your health is at risk. And any or all of those nasty stress-related illnesses and disorders can become linked to excessive anger.

Anger can break your heart

Recent research now indicates that your heart (or, more accurately, your cardiovascular system) is particularly vulnerable to your anger and its negative effects. In his book *Anger Kills*, Duke University researcher Redford Williams describes a number of possible ways hostility can negatively affect your cardiovascular system. I highlight a few of the study findings here:

✔ **When potentially hostile individuals were angry, they had larger than normal increases in blood flow to their muscles (suggesting an exaggerated fight-or-flight response).** They also experienced an increase in their levels of important stress hormones, such as adrenaline and cortisol, which can have negative effects on the cardiovascular system, as well.

- ✓ **Potentially hostile individuals with higher levels of blood cholesterol were found to secrete more adrenaline than those individuals with lower levels of cholesterol.** For these individuals, the linkage between higher adrenaline secretions and higher cholesterol levels means they have a greater likelihood of arteriosclerotic plaque buildup.

- ✓ **People who scored high on measures of hostility tended to have fewer friends.** This lack of strong friendships means a weakened social support system. Being able to talk to someone about what's stressing you can lower your blood pressure — and having no one to talk to certainly doesn't do anything to help you. Research has shown that socially isolated individuals excreted higher levels of stress hormones in their urine than those who had strong support systems.

- ✓ **Hostile individuals typically don't take good care of themselves.** They tend to engage in a number of destructive health behaviors, including smoking, drinking, and overeating. All of these behaviors can have negative effects on the cardiovascular system.

Anger can break other people's hearts

When you're angry, you're probably not a whole lot of fun to be with. Even worse, your hostility and aggression can be downright destructive. Your anger affects those around you — the people you live with, work with, and interact with. Anger can strain and damage your relationships with your partner, spouse, children, friends, and coworkers. Together, anger and hostility can lead to conflict, mental and physical abuse, breakups, and divorce. Because of your anger, you may endanger your chances for career advancement or even lose your job. Anger tends to escalate, as well. The other party involved often becomes angry, too. When you're angry, you may do something or say something you regret later on, which can lead to other stress emotions, such as guilt, shame, upset, and depression.

Funny, you don't look like a Type A

Remember all that hoopla about the Type-A personality and how stress-producing it could be? The typical Type A was the hurried workaholic, attempting to get more and more done in less and less time. The good news is that recent research has poked some holes in this picture and suggested that some of those Type-A traits may not be as harmful as we once thought. What research does show, however, is that the most toxic traits in the Type-A pattern are hostility and anger. Working hard, by itself, probably won't give you that heart attack. But if you're angry, mistrusting, and cynical, you may want to change your ways.

Anger can shorten your life

Research shows that your life can actually be shortened by anger. Psychologist John Barefoot measured the hostility levels of 118 law students. Then, he tracked these individuals for 25 years. He found that nearly 20 percent of those who scored in the upper quarter of the hostility scale had died by the age of 50. In comparison, he noted a death rate by the age of 50 of only 5 percent for those who scored in the lowest quarter of the scale.

Understanding when and why anger is appropriate

Does this mean that all of your anger is inappropriate or destructive? No, not at all. In fact, in measured doses and expressed in the right way, anger can be appropriate and effective, helping you take action, solve problems, or better deal with the situation at hand. Anger clearly has a place in your emotional repertoire. But a big difference exists between feeling annoyed or somewhat angry for a brief period of time and having strong feelings of anger that simmer for hours. When it's intense and prolonged, anger can result in incredible amounts of stress and damage to your overall well-being. Understanding how you create your anger and knowing how to reduce that anger are the keys to anger control. The next section provides suggestions for doing exactly that.

Tempering Your Temper

Anger is not an automatic reaction beyond our control, even though it may feel like that at times. Instead, anger is a response that can be managed. So, before your next outburst of rage and fury, take a look at some of these anger-reducing strategies and tactics. Who knows? They just may save you from a nasty argument, an upset stomach, costly litigation, or worse.

Keeping an anger log

The first step in managing (and ultimately eliminating) much of your stressful anger is knowing what it looks like and where it comes from. A simple anger diary, or anger log, can help you identify those times when you are angry and give you the information you need to begin feeling less angry.

Simply enter in your log (a small notebook, a piece of paper, a file on your laptop — whatever works for you) the times when you became angry and what triggered your anger. Also, rate the level of your anger using a simple ten-point scale, where a rating of ten means "very, very angry," five means "moderately angry," and zero means "not angry at all." Also rate on a ten-point scale the importance of the situation or event that triggered your anger. Rate as a one, two, or three triggers of "minor" importance; rate as four, five, six, and seven situations of "moderate" importance; and rate as eight, nine, or ten events or triggers that you judge to be of "major" importance.

Take a look at the example in Table 12-1:

Table 12-1	Rating Your Anger	
What Happened?	*Importance*	*My Anger Level*
My child spilled juice on the couch.	3	6
I missed my train by one minute.	2	5
My boss blamed me for a mistake made by my coworker.	4	7
My computer crashed, and I lost the last hour's work.	3	8

Checking your stress balance

Find out if your anger is excessive and inappropriate by checking your stress balance. Just compare the level of your anger with the importance of the anger-producing situation. Use a ten-point scale, where ten means "incredibly important" and zero means "not at all important." Insert that rating next to your description of the distressing situation. You're "in balance" when the two numbers match; chances are your level of anger is appropriate and functional. But if your anger level is higher than the importance of the situation, you're likely overreacting. And if your level of anger is way up there (eights, nines, or tens), you may be experiencing rage and hostility rather than garden-variety anger.

Using the examples in Table 12-1, the juice spilled on the couch is probably an importance level of three; missing the train, a two; being unfairly blamed, a four; and losing data because of a computer crash, a three. In each case, the person is overreacting and off-balance.

Becoming Mindful of Your Anger

Being off-balance can indicate that you're caught up in automatic, often distorted, thinking. You need to re-group, detach from your feelings and thoughts, and become centered. One of the best ways to do this is to become more mindful. This means becoming more aware of your feelings as just feelings, and your thoughts as just thoughts. But first you need to interrupt the process of being angry. You need to step back. There's some truth to that old saying, "When you get angry, count to ten before you do anything." This is a good start, but you can find even better ways of detaching.

Breathing mindfully

Start by focusing on your breathing for a minute or two. Try the simple breath-counting exercise I suggest in Chapter 6. Wherever you are — standing or sitting; in bed, on the bus, or in your car — pay attention to the rhythm of your breathing. Notice your breath as you inhale: the way it feels in your nostrils and the way your abdomen rises as you take in air. Breathe a little more slowly and a little more deeply than you normally would, but still try to keep your breathing as natural as you can. When you exhale, exhale through your slightly parted lips, noticing the slight swooshing sound you make. Silently count "one" when you exhale, "two" when you exhale a second time, and so on until you reach ten. Then count backward from ten to one and repeat the process. With each exhalation, try to relax more deeply, letting go of any muscle tension in your body.

Mindfully detaching

When you're feeling more centered, the next step is to become aware of your thoughts and feelings in a non-judgmental, non-critical manner. This means becoming an observer of your inner experience. You want to become an accepting, compassionate onlooker who is genuinely curious about your thoughts and feelings but isn't locked into them or controlled by them. We tend to see our thoughts and feelings as Truth. We think:

> "If I feel this way, or if I'm having these thoughts, they must be valid, true representations of what's going on, and they should be listened to and reacted to."

But not necessarily. As you discover in Chapters 10 and 11, your thoughts and feelings can be a biased product of your history, experiences, parents, and even genetic make-up. Your anger can reflect insecurities, worries, fears, and a host of other psychological dynamics that you're probably not even aware of. The good news is, with a little time, practice, and direction, you can figure much of it out, fix your thinking, and change your feelings. The first step, however, is becoming aware of your inner experiences — your thoughts and feelings — and your behavior — your angry reactions. Your anger log can help you do this. Assessing your stress balance gives you perspective, and mindfully detaching gives you even more distance and objectivity. Now you're in a better position to explore and change the ways in which you create your anger.

Modifying Your Mindset

Most often, your thoughts and perceptions are what make you angry.

Thoughts like "I was angry because that idiot cut me off in traffic" or "Missing my train made me angry" suggest that an outside event or circumstance is what caused you to feel anger. But the reality is that these situations are only potential triggers for anger. Like your other stress emotions (anxiety, upset, frustration, and so on), your anger is largely self-created. Your thinking — your perceptions and interpretations — play an important role in creating (and ultimately reducing) your stress.

Thinking about your thinking

See if you can identify your anger-producing thoughts. Ask yourself, "What could I be saying to myself to make myself angry?" Take a look at Table 12-2 and try to complete it with your own experiences.

Table 12-2	Your Angry Thoughts and the Experiences That Triggered Them
Situation	*My Automatic Thoughts*
My son spilled juice on the couch.	"The couch is ruined! He should have been more careful! How could he have been so careless? He knew he wasn't supposed to bring food into the living room!"
I missed my train by one minute.	"This is awful! This always happens! Now my whole day is ruined. I hate this!"

Writing down these anger-producing thoughts helps you get a clearer picture of what you're saying to yourself to make yourself angry about a particular situation. By getting in touch with this thinking, you're now in a good position to begin changing that thinking, thereby reducing your anger.

Finding and fixing your thinking errors

If your level of anger is excessive or prolonged, you're probably making at least one thinking error. Examine your automatic thoughts and see if you can find any thinking errors. (If you're rusty on what I mean by the term thinking error, take a quick look at Chapter 10.) Although just about any of the thinking errors can result in some form of anger, the two that most often trigger an anger response are unrealistic demands and can't-stand-it-itis.

Expecting the expected

Your expectations play an important role in determining your level of anger. Having unrealistic expectations about your world and the way other people should think and act, as well as demanding that they be more like you, adds to your anger level. If you expect everyone else to be honest and fair, you'll probably wind up feeling more than a little angry most of the time, because your expectations won't be met. Expectations are accompanied by "shoulds" and "shouldn'ts"; when you create demands that are unrealistic, you end up judging the person who doesn't act the way you think they should.

Am I suggesting that you become a complete cynic? Not at all. If anything, becoming more trusting is a better way of feeling less angry and less hostile. Becoming realistic in your expectations doesn't mean becoming cynical and untrusting. Not everyone out there is selfish, nasty, and only out for themselves. But other people see things differently and have priorities different than yours. At times, they'll do things you wouldn't do. Expect the expected, given the world we live in. The following exercise helps you assess the extent to which your expectations are in line with reality.

Would you ever expect any of the following situations to happen? Answer yes or no.

At some point in the not-too-distant future:

- ✔ Someone will cut you off in traffic.
- ✔ Somebody you know and care about will disappoint you or treat you unfairly.
- ✔ You'll just miss catching your bus or train.

✔ Your computer will crash at a critical time.

✔ Someone in front of you in the express checkout line will have more than the specified ten items.

✔ Someone will play music incredibly loudly and disturb you.

✔ Someone will push his or her way onto your already crowded elevator, even though it's totally full.

Answering "no" to more than one or two of the above suggests that your expectations of the world (and the people who live there) are not totally realistic. You're probably in for some surprises — and some anger.

Lengthening your fuse

No one likes frustration. But, unfortunately, frustration is an integral part of your life. When faced with a frustrating situation, you may find that you overreact too quickly, becoming too angry too fast. If so, your fuse is way too short. One way of better tolerating frustration is to "do the opposite." This technique may sound a little far-fetched, but it really works.

For example, suppose you're having trouble falling asleep. Try *not* to fall asleep, and you may be surprised by how quickly you fall asleep. Therapists call this approach paradoxical intention, and it can help you overcome some of your excessive anger. Try some of the following suggestions:

✔ **Find a longer line.** If waiting in line triggers your anger, the next time you find yourself waiting in line, try moving to an even longer line.

✔ **Stay in a slower lane of traffic.** If you get angry when you're stuck in a stalled line of traffic, see if you can find a slow line the next time you're driving.

✔ **Pick the most inept sales clerk.** The next time you need some help to purchase something, see if you can spot the newest, most inexperienced, and most inept salesperson.

Now, when you're in these unusually difficult situations and you find your anger level rising, do the following:

1. **Practice some deep breathing to relax your body.**

2. **Repeat to yourself, "This is not the end of the world. I want to get a handle on my anger. This is only a hassle. I can cope with this."**

And indeed you can.

Recognizing the anger two-step

The anger two-step works like this:

✔ Step 1: It starts when someone criticizes, rejects, or otherwise disapproves of you. You personalize this, feel bad about yourself, and put yourself down, feeling discounted, diminished, or disrespected.

✔ Step 2: Automatically, and generally unconsciously, you get angry at the disapproving individual, criticizing or disapproving of him or her.

The upside of this psychological reversal is that you feel better, for a while. Feeling angry is often an easier emotion to live with than feeling bad about yourself. The anger, however, is still misguided, and it can be destructive. Being aware of this emotional dance is your first step in replacing it with better ways of coping.

Using your coping self-talk

When confronted with a potentially anger-provoking situation, you can either say things to yourself that make you angry or say things to yourself that reduce or even eliminate any anger that may have been triggered. By consciously and explicitly talking to yourself, you have a powerful tool that can help you regulate your anger.

Here are some useful examples of anger-reducing self-talk. Choose the ones that best fit your situation and try coming up with some of your own.

✔ Is this really worth getting so angry about?

✔ My getting angry is not going to help anything.

✔ People can look at things differently than I do. They always have, and they always will.

✔ Don't take this personally.

✔ Let it go. It's not worth the emotional effort.

✔ I really don't have to feel angry about this if I choose not to.

✔ Relax. Take a deep breath. Hold it. And let it all out.

✔ Other people have different priorities.

- ✔ Just because someone says something, that doesn't make it true.
- ✔ How would Mr. or Ms. Mental Health handle this?
- ✔ Stay calm, stay cool.
- ✔ Don't go for the bait.
- ✔ People have the right to be wrong. And often they are.
- ✔ Don't judge the person. Judge the behavior.
- ✔ Will I remember this in three years? Three months? Three hours?

To vent or not to vent? That is the question

Are you better off expressing your anger or keeping it in? Popular psychological wisdom suggests that when you're feeling angry, you should get it all out, releasing that pent-up hostility. Punch that pillow, wallop that punching bag, smash those dishes. You'll feel better afterward. Right?

Maybe not. As author Carol Tavris comments in her important book, *Anger: The Misunderstood Emotion*, "Expressing anger makes you angrier, solidifies an angry attitude, and establishes a hostile habit." Recent clinical studies have shown that *emotional catharsis* (the active expression of anger and hostility by physically releasing anger) can work against you. Researchers found that when people acted out their anger in this way (hitting or punching something), they felt more aggressive afterward, not less aggressive. Worse, by giving people permission not to control their feelings, the people experienced more episodes of aggressive behavior in general. Does this mean you shouldn't express your anger? No. It just means you may need to find better ways of doing it.

The following sections provide some answers to common questions about venting your anger. Take a look at the suggestions I offer here. They may help you get control of your own anger.

Can I at least yell?

Yelling doesn't appear to help reduce your anger. Screaming "You're a stupid jerk and I hope you rot in hell!" to someone who has just done you wrong clearly has a lot of emotional appeal. And it may even feel pretty good in the short run. However, it may not be the best thing for your health and overall stress level. When you yell, your body becomes stressed. Your heart rate increases. Raising your voice, and certainly yelling, can lead to an increase in blood pressure, as well. In some individuals — Type-A personality types, for example — the increase in blood-pressure levels may be even greater. Yelling can have psychological effects, as well. In one study of 535 women, yelling, screaming, and lashing out resulted in greater feelings of low self-esteem. Because in most cases the yelling did little to resolve the problem, the women felt — and were seen — as being out of control rather than taking charge and acting competently. You can be sure that yelling — and feeling out of control or incompetent — doesn't elevate your sense of self-worth.

Should I suppress my anger?

Anger can be destructive when it steeps and simmers within you. Keeping your angry feelings inside of you, and keeping those feelings fresh by re-angering yourself over and over, is not the best choice. However, the long-standing belief that suppressed anger is the mother of just about every psychosomatic disease, from ulcers to constipation, may be ill-founded. A big difference exists between letting all of your angry feelings spew forth in an uncontrolled manner and packaging it so your message will express your feelings but not trigger World War III. And, of course, an even better option is to resolve the conflict or fix the situation that is triggering your anger, reduce your anger level, or both.

Rehearsing your anger

Often, you may become angry because you're caught off guard, and your gut reacts before your head has a chance to evaluate the situation a little more sensibly. One effective strategy for combating this irrational response is to anticipate which situations and circumstances may trigger your anger and plan ahead. Before the situation occurs, rehearse what you'll say and how you want to feel. You can always identify upcoming situations in which you know that your chances of becoming angry are high. These situations may be just before you're about to discuss a point of disagreement or conten-tion with someone, and you know that the person will be less than receptive or downright opposed to what you have to say. You may be dealing with a client, a coworker, a relative, or the sales clerk at the local shopping mall.

When you can, anticipate the situation, imagine it occurring, and then imag-ine what you'll say and how you'll act. Your goal, of course, is not to go ballis-tic or become excessively angry. Choose the words you think will work best. Also, imagine that the other person is getting angry and is close to getting you angry in turn. Use your coping self-talk. Imagine telling yourself to calm down, to not go for the bait, and to keep your anger level low. Rehearse this situation several times in your head. Chances are, when the situation does materialize, you'll be much better prepared to handle it.

Doing an emotional replay

Okay, for whatever reason, you were unable to rehearse or get ready for that situation. You were caught off-guard, and the situation resulted in an undesirable show of anger. All is still not lost. A useful technique in reducing future anger is something I call emotional replay. Here's how it works:

1. **At some point after you've had an experience or encounter where you felt and maybe expressed excessive anger (this could be an hour later, or maybe even days later), replay that situation in your mind.**

   This time, instead of seeing yourself becoming angry, imagine yourself responding in a calmer, more controlled manner. You're imagining the same situation, but your response is the one you want it to be.

2. **Try to get in touch with the kind of thinking and interpretation that may generate this less-angry state. Use your coping self-talk.**

   If you can, jot down some of these thoughts and beliefs and see if you can use them earlier in the anger sequence — like before you get angry. Examples of this kind of adaptive thinking include the coping self-talk described earlier in this chapter, such as "Is this really worth getting so angry about?" Your coping self-talk can help you see things differently.

Becoming an actor

Although your anger control may not be the world's best, you probably know one or two people whom you admire for their calmness and coolness under fire. The next time you're confronted with a potentially anger-provoking situation, try to see the situation through their eyes. Imagine how they would look at this. What would they say to themselves? How would they react?

By immersing yourself in their character, at least briefly, you can try to look at situations as they would. You role-play with a script, but instead of using your own, you choose the script of an anger role model, someone you feel has something to teach.

Being discreet and choosing your moment

Managing your anger doesn't mean letting it all out in some hostile manner, but nor does it mean keeping it in and letting it aggravate you. Being assertive and discreet means packaging and expressing your anger in a way that doesn't send your physiological system into orbit and doesn't result in you throttling someone — or finding yourself being throttled. The fact that you're angry doesn't mean you have to say your piece in that moment of emotional heat.

Most often, you're better off if you wait. Choose a time when your anger is reduced and the other person is in a better mood.

Breathing your anger away

When you're angry, your body is probably running in high gear. Your heart rate and blood pressure are up, and just about all the other measures of physiological distress are elevated, as well. You can speed up the process of dissipating your anger by adding some physical strategies to your psychological bag of tricks. Relaxing your body is a good place to start. And because you can always find time to breathe, a deep-breathing exercise can be an effective way of lowering your body's level of physiological arousal and can make reducing your anger an easier job.

The next time you find yourself getting angry, follow these steps:

1. **Take a deep breath, inhaling through your nostrils.**

   Hold that breath for three or four seconds.

2. **Slowly exhale through your slightly parted lips.**

   Let a wave of relaxation spread from the top of your head, down your body, to your toes.

3. **Wait a little bit and then take another deep breath.**

   Repeat the process.

You'll soon feel more physically relaxed and less angry.

Looking for the funny part

Humor can be an excellent tool to help you diffuse your anger. If you can find something about the anger-triggering situation to make you laugh or at least bring a smile to your face, you can be assured that your anger will be lessened and possibly even eliminated. The following sections offer two ways of creating humor.

Blow things up

Exaggeration is a great way of diffusing a potentially stressful situation, robbing it of much of its impact. Try using the blow-up technique. Here's how it works: Suppose, for example, that you find yourself standing in line at the Bureau of Motor Vehicles waiting to renew your license. The line is moving slowly. Very slowly. You can feel your stress level creeping higher. Now, introducing a touch of exaggeration, imagine that it will take forever to reach the front window. You picture your family coming to visit you on Sunday afternoons, bringing many of your favorite snacks. You strike up strong friendships with others in the line. You talk of taking vacations together. You start planning your five-year reunion . . .

Try some therapeutic fantasy

A humorous fantasy can help you reduce and diffuse your anger. Here's what I mean. Imagine that you're a passenger in a taxicab, and you notice that the cab driver is driving much too quickly for your liking. You also notice that your anger level is creeping skyward. Before you yell at him, strike him, or blow some internal gasket, imagine this improbable scenario:

> You tell him that he's driving too fast, and he immediately slows down and, with a sheepish look on his face, turns to you and says, "You're absolutely right! What could I have been thinking? I'll slow down immediately. In fact, I won't charge you for this ride, to make up for my unsafe and insensitive behavior. I'm sorry. This will never happen again."

By imagining this or another unlikely outcome, you can create a different mindset that is less angry and more accepting of the foibles and failings of others. Then, calmly tell him to slow down.

Revenge is sweet, but forgiveness is less stressful

We've always given lip service to the value of forgiveness, but the reality has always been more lip than actual forgiveness. Psychologically, holding onto a grudge is always easier than forgiving the source of our anger for whatever he or she did. But the long-term effects aren't positive at all.

In a study conducted recently at Hope College, in Holland, Michigan, psychologists explored the effects of forgiveness on people's stress levels. They looked at their levels of stress when they were in a non-forgiving mode and compared those stress levels to when the same people were in a forgiving mode. The amount of stress was considerably greater when the subjects were entertaining revenge rather than forgiveness.

Forgiving for small indiscretions is usually no real problem. The major transgressions are the ones that are harder to swallow. You can reach a point of forgiveness by trying to understand where the other person is coming from, looking at his or her background, family history, and specific factors that may have played a role in his or her actions.

For some acts, forgiveness may be unrealistic. The best you can hope for in these situations is some form of acceptance. It's done. You can't change it. So try to move on. Maybe the best revenge truly is living well.

Chapter 13

Worrying Less

In This Chapter

▶ Identifying your worries

▶ Understanding why you worry

▶ Controlling your worries

*E*verybody worries at some time or another. In fact, worrying can be a good thing. You *should* worry about some things in your life. Worrying is healthy and appropriate when it motivates you and leads you to attempt to resolve a problem in a productive, adaptive manner. If you're worried about an exam, you may study harder. If you're worried about your health, you'll probably go see a doctor.

Some people, however, worry far more than they have to, and in turn they do very little to effectively resolve their worries. For these people, much of their stress takes the form of *excessive worry*. This inordinate and often useless worrying can rob people of much of life's joy and interfere with their day-to-day functioning. And if a person's worrying becomes chronic, it can result in a wide variety of stress-related conditions and disorders. Controlling and managing your worries becomes an essential part of managing your stress.

In this chapter, you figure out how to identify your worries and understand why you worry the way you do. You also discover better ways of managing and minimizing much of your worry.

Do You Worry Too Much?

In this section, I provide a brief, ten-item self-assessment that helps you determine whether you're worrying too much. Simply indicate to what extent each of the statements below describes you ("not at all like me," "a little like me," or "a lot like me").

1. Worrying is a major source of stress in my life.

2. After I start worrying, I find it difficult to stop.

3. People who know me well tell me that I worry too much.

4. I have trouble getting to sleep or falling back to sleep because of my worrying.

5. I often think of worst-case scenarios when I worry about a problem.

6. I frequently become anxious and worry about things that could happen but usually don't.

7. I have a great deal of difficulty coping with uncertainty.

8. I worry more than I should about small stuff.

9. When I worry, I usually just upset myself more, rather than try to resolve my worry.

10. Sometimes I literally worry myself to the point of sickness.

Answering more than a few of these statements with "a lot like me" suggests that your worrying is excessive and may be contributing greatly to your overall stress level.

Don't Worry, Be Happy. Yeah, Right!

If you're worried, your family members and friends may have given you some of the following advice. You may have even recommended one or more of these tidbits yourself:

"Don't worry so much."

"Stop being such a worrywart."

"Just keep positive thoughts in your mind."

"Everything generally turns out okay."

"You've just got to believe in yourself."

If you're a worrier, you know how difficult it is to stop worrying. Being told these tidbits of advice, however well-meant, does little to curb the distressing and seemingly unending list of things you find to worry about. In fact, sometimes, actively trying not to worry about something actually causes you to worry more. Trying to stop your worrying is much like me asking you not to think of a pink elephant. Of course, the moment you read those words, you think of a pink elephant.

We worry even when we're not aware that we're doing it. We worry in our sleep and at various levels of conscious awareness. Worrying can be an automatic response that can become persistent and seem out of control. Fortunately, a number of tools, strategies, and techniques really *can* help you worry less, and when you *should* be worrying, know how to worry productively. Your first step in controlling your worry is knowing what's worrying you.

Identifying Your Worries

When you change something, it's important to have a good idea of what you want to change. You need to know what your worries are — what they look like and what they sound like. Identifying your specific worries may take a bit of practice, but the results are worthwhile. Becoming aware of your worries and concerns gives you a starting point that can provide you with a focus for your change efforts. The exercises that follow give you lots of real-life material to work with as you master your new worry-management tools.

Creating a worry list

Maintaining a simple "worry list" will give you a clearer picture of what your worries look like. Try it now. Get a pencil and piece of paper, or your computer, tablet, or cell phone, and jot down your current worries.

Next to each worry, rate your *worry level*, the degree to which this worry distresses you. A one, two, or three indicates that you're feeling only a minor degree of stress about this situation. A four, five, six, or seven means you're feeling a moderate level of distress, and an eight, nine, or ten means you're experience a great deal of stress because of this worry.

My worry	*My Worry Level*
Job security	8
Mother's health	8
Possible IRS audit	8
Condition of the car	6
Money for kids' college	8
Squeaky front door	4
Hair loss	10
Fence that needs repair	6
Upcoming meeting at work	8
Gift for Aunt Harriet	5

Identifying your worries is only the beginning. You want to know how to manage and minimize these worries. Much of the rest of this chapter shows you how to do just that. But before jumping to those sections, you may want to spend another minute or two checking to see whether you've left out your less-obvious concerns — your hidden worries.

Spotting your hidden worries

You may think that identifying your worries is a cinch because they seem to be always on your mind, filling your thoughts, triggering your anxiety and upset, and robbing you of life's enjoyment. You *feel* worried, but you aren't sure what exactly you're worried about. This can happen in several ways:

✔ **You're worrying about multiple problems at the same time.** Your worries shuttle between the first and third concern, then back to the second, and so on. The cumulative worry doesn't allow you to focus on one particular worry, so you get overwhelmed by having too many worries.

✔ **The worry is there, but at an unconscious or subconscious level. Although you may not be consciously aware of a particular worry, the emotional component — some anxiety, upset, or anger — is still with you.** This is often the case when you find yourself in a "bad mood." The feelings are there, but you aren't sure where they came from. The worry has no focus.

✔ **You've displaced your worry.** You may be distressed by a "background" worry that you're unable to resolve. When a second worry enters the picture, you may displace your distress onto this new worry.

Here are some life areas to consider, and some questions to ask yourself, to help you uncover some potentially hidden worries:

Social worries

✔ Am I worried about some negative interaction that has happened to me in the past?

✔ Am I worried about what other people will think of me in upcoming social interactions? Am I fearful of rejection and disapproval?

✔ Am I worried I won't know what to say or do in some future social situation?

✔ Am I worried that I don't have enough friends?

Family and relationship worries

- ✔ Am I worried about my current relationship?
- ✔ Am I worried about not having a relationship?
- ✔ Am I jealous and worried about another person threatening my relationship?
- ✔ Am I worried about ending up alone?
- ✔ Am I worried about my children?

Health worries

- ✔ Am I worried about the state of my health?
- ✔ Am I worried about some condition or disorder that hasn't been diagnosed?
- ✔ Am I worried that even though I am well now, I might get sick in the near future?

Money worries

- ✔ Am I worried that I won't have enough money to take care of myself and my family?
- ✔ Am I worried about the amount of money I owe?
- ✔ Am I worried that I might lose the money I have?

Work worries

- ✔ Am I worried that I might lose my job?
- ✔ Am I worried that my bosses don't think I'm doing a good enough job?
- ✔ Am I worried that my colleagues don't think well of me?
- ✔ Am I worried that I couldn't find another job if I left this one?

Hopefully at this point you have a clearer picture of what your worries look like. Your next step is understanding why you worry the way you do.

Understanding Your Worries

While some worry is appropriate and useful, much of your worry is excessive and maladaptive, creating much more stress than is appropriate. In this section I discuss the differences between these two kinds of worry and the reasons you worry in unproductive ways.

Comparing productive and unproductive worry

Worries can be productive, helping you manage your life and reduce your stress. On the other hand, worrying can result in unnecessary fear, anxiety, and upset. Understanding the differences between these two forms of worrying — productive and unproductive — is an important step on your path to managing and ultimately minimizing your worrying. Here are some criteria to help you figure out which category your worrying falls into.

Unproductive worry

Unproductive worry displays the following characteristics:

- ✔ It imagines all sorts of unlikely outcomes.
- ✔ It assumes that one bad outcome will cascade into a series of even worse outcomes.
- ✔ It worries about events far into the future that don't need a solution right now.
- ✔ It assumes that your worrisome thinking is valid and reflects the realistic truth.
- ✔ It assumes that your negative feelings are accurate measures of the importance of the worry.
- ✔ It rehashes negative experiences in the past.
- ✔ It demands that you have control over just about everything in your life.
- ✔ It refuses to accept that negative experiences are part of life.
- ✔ It makes the approval of others an overly important need.
- ✔ It accepts only perfect, or near perfect, solutions to problems.

Productive worry

Here's what makes this kind of worrying adaptive and functional:

- ✔ It helps you solve a problem or resolve a situation.
- ✔ It doesn't demand certainty.
- ✔ It's not overwhelmed by emotion.
- ✔ It turns a worry into a problem to be solved.
- ✔ It explores appropriate ways of finding a solution to a problem.
- ✔ It doesn't get stuck in evaluating unrealistic outcomes.

✔ It defers those worries that can't be solved until a future point in time.

✔ It's not long lasting and can be ended in a relatively short period of time.

✔ It accepts that loss and tragedy are a natural and expected part of life.

Some examples

The following examples further illustrate the difference between productive and unproductive worries.

Unproductive worry: Worrying about whether that 5 p.m. flight will crash.

Productive worry: Worrying about how early you should leave home to catch a 5 p.m. flight.

Unproductive worry: Worrying that the headache you've had for two hours is a brain tumor.

Productive worry: Worrying about finding a good doctor you can see on a regular basis.

Unproductive worry: Worrying about how you'll fare in your job evaluation next December.

Productive worry: Worrying about what information you need to complete a project at work.

Unproductive worry: Berating yourself for failed attempts to lose weight in the past.

Productive worry: Worrying about the best way to lose weight.

Discovering why you worry unproductively

Now that you have a better understanding of what unproductive worry looks like, you want to know why you worry the way you do. Here are the major reasons people worry in ways that produce excessive distress.

✔ You believe (mistakenly) that worrying is the right thing to do and the best way to make sure that a concern or fear doesn't happen in the future. You're afraid that if you don't worry about the problem, that problem will somehow get worse.

✔ You can't stand uncertainty. An inability to tolerate uncertainty is probably the most important reason people worry. You feel you must know for certain what is going to happen.

✔ You "what-if." You come up with lists of bad things that might happen even though there is little chance that any of these outcomes will come to pass.

✔ You "catastrophize and awfulize" by choosing to focus on the *worst* possible outcomes that could result from your what-if-ing.

✔ You believe that your thoughts are facts — that they represent "the truth" and should always be listened to.

✔ You believe that your feelings are facts — that if you feel a certain way, that feeling must reflect the justification for your worrying.

✔ You have trouble tolerating discomfort and feel you must avoid it as much as possible.

✔ You equate your abilities, traits, and performances with your self-worth. If you fail, you feel you are a failure, so you over-worry about failing or falling short.

✔ You equate your self-worth with other people's approval. Much of your worrying is fear that you might not get that approval or, if you already have it, that you might lose it.

Controlling and Stopping Your Worrying

Understanding why you worry will only get you so far. Now you need useful solutions to your worrying problems. The rest of this chapter takes you to that next level, giving you the tools you need to change how you worry and help you start to worry less (and, at times, not at all).

Writing about your worries

You'd be surprised that by spending just a few moments writing about your worries, you can weaken their power. Recent research findings reported in the *Journal of the American Medical Association* show that writing about stressful and worrisome experiences can reduce stress-related symptoms.

By writing down your worries, you begin to feel that you're more in control of them. Much of your worrying goes on in a vague, ill-defined manner. Sometimes you aren't even quite sure what you're worrying about. By committing your worries to paper, you're dealing with them in a more direct way. Instead of floating around out there somewhere, they're now in a concrete form, recorded forever.

You don't have to write volumes. In the study cited in *JAMA*, patients wrote for only 20 minutes a day for three consecutive days, and about half of them experienced positive effects that seemed to last for months.

Scheduling your worries

When you have a major worry, you quickly discover that the worry can be forceful and insistent. One way of combating this is, oddly enough, to do your worrying at designated times. Build worrying into your day. Call this your *worry time.* Whenever you sense that your worries are creeping into your mind, remind yourself that it's not yet your worry time and that the worrying will have to wait. Jot down this worry in a worry diary, notebook, or day planner that you use for other appointments. Assign yourself a time to worry. Start with 20 minutes. It could be during a coffee break, just after lunch, or on your trip home after work. If you find that 20 minutes is too much time, cut back by five minutes until you find your optimal worrying period.

The value of this approach is that it provides you with a sense of having addressed the worry. You'll be able to worry about whatever is bothering you — but only at a specified time. This approach allows you to feel more comfortable not worrying (or at least worrying less) for the rest of your day. Elsewhere in this chapter you can master more complex ways of reducing your worries.

To practice this scheduled and concentrated form of worry control, start with a smaller worry and work up to your most distressing concerns. From your worry list, choose a worry that is manageable and not overwhelming. Choose items from your list that are not triggering higher levels of worry. To start, stay away from the eights, nines, and tens and after a while move up to your more formidable worries.

Having a place to worry

You may need a *worry corner* — a place or places where you go to worry (either productively or unproductively). You then restrict your worrying to these special places as much as possible. These places become associated in your mind with worrying. In the same way that having a worrying time gives you permission to defer your worrying until a specific time, having a worry place gives you permission not to worry in places that are associated with more positive aspects of your life. It shouldn't be your bed, because you don't want to associate sleep or sex with worrying. It shouldn't be at the dining-room table when you're having dinner with the family. Try to make this place a tad uncomfortable, and not a place where you'd like to spend a great deal of time. It can be the bathroom at work or a stairwell. It literally can be a corner. Find a corner in one of the rooms in your home that is infrequently used. Stick a stool there. Make that your place of worry. When you find yourself starting to worry in other places, gently remind yourself that this is neither the time nor the place to worry.

I have two places where I worry, both productively and unproductively. The first is while I'm in the shower. While lathering up, I use that time to worry. When I turn off the faucets, I try to turn off the worries. The second place I worry is on my commute to work. With not much else to do, I find that I can usefully worry while sitting on the subway or bus. By the time I get to my office, I often feel a sense of greater closure on a particular problem.

Thinking Straighter, Worrying Less

Worrying is a process that starts when you perceive an event, situation, or circumstance as potentially dangerous or threatening. You think about that situation — at times unconsciously and automatically — and, depending on what you say to yourself about that situation, you create varying degrees of emotional stress. If your self-talk is positive and sensible, your stress level will be lower.

On the other hand, if your self-talk is negative and irrational, you cause yourself to feel excessive worry. This worry manifests itself not only emotionally but also physically, producing all of the symptoms that characterize the fight-or-flight response. And the fight-or-flight response can result in even more worry.

In this section, I discuss the relationship between your thoughts and your worries, and more specifically the connections between particular thought distortions and worry. I give you the resources to replace your distressing thought patterns with more worry-resistant thinking.

Remember that feelings and thoughts aren't facts

We're at the mercy of that chaotic discussion in our heads that we call thinking. Too often, though, much of that thinking and feeling is the product of less-than-stable psychological dynamics, such as our insecurities, fears, and vulnerabilities. This host of triggering thoughts can send us into a mental spiral, often with stressful results. The problem is that we believe that most of our thoughts are on the mark. We also believe that if we're feeling something — any emotion — then this emotion is an accurate response that should be felt and acted upon. As I discuss elsewhere in this chapter and in Chapter 10, our cognitive distortions, also called thinking errors, are just that: distortions and errors. If we listen to them and accept them as the truth, we find ourselves sinking deeper into the quicksand of worry.

Stop feeding your worries

Just because you have a worry doesn't mean you have to keep feeding that worry with more negative rumination. As I discuss in Chapter 6, you can cultivate mindfulness and develop the skill of detaching from your worry, becoming more accepting of what is and less judgmental or fearful.

We give our worries too much power by ruminating about what has happened in the past or may happen in the future. If you can stop this process, you can feel less stress. Mindfulness can help you do just that. It allows you to detach, stepping away from your worry without feeding or escalating it. With mindfulness, you can begin to notice the worry and be aware of the feelings it creates without adding to your distress. Don't try to fix it, avoid it, deny it, or come up with any answers. Get in touch with the feelings the worry may have created. Experience those feelings with a degree of curiosity, acceptance, and kindness. You'll find that although the problem may still exist, you've found a way of living with that problem. And if the problem is solvable, you're in a better place emotionally and cognitively to deal with it and come up with a solution.

Cultivate acceptance

In life you'll face many negative experiences that you'd rather not deal with. But you *do* have to confront some of those experiences — not only death and taxes but also illness, accidents, job loss, financial instability, sexual difficulties, problem children, and difficult in-laws. You have lots to worry about: Real problems do exist (although often our biggest problems are the ones we never thought to worry about). Much of our worrying is an attempt to either make the situation go away or make our feelings about the situation go away. In other words, our worries are often our attempts to fight reality. You figure that if you fight hard enough, you'll win. Alas, too often we have little control over our universe and other people within it. The worrying itself becomes the problem. Sometimes it's better to accept a situation rather than fight it mentally by worrying. The good news is, acceptance doesn't mean you can't solve your problem or discover a better way of coping with it. (See Chapter 6 for tips on cultivating acceptance.)

Correcting Your Thinking Errors

If your worrying is excessive, chances are your self-talk and thinking are somewhat out of whack, which means that you're probably making one or more of the thinking errors I describe in Chapter 10. The following sections outline the specific thinking errors that can cause excessive worrying. I also discuss how to avoid those errors. Each of these thinking errors can add to your anxiety level, make you worry more than you should, and make your worrying more stress-producing.

Minimizing your what-ifs

Even on the calmest day, some people can find a host of things to worry about. Chronic worriers can take just about any situation and find something to worry about. They dissect every potentially dangerous or threatening situation and ask themselves, "What if . . ." Here are some examples of things chronic worriers worry about:

- What if that twinge in my shoulder means I'm having a heart attack?
- What if the plane crashes on my upcoming flight?
- What if my taxi driver is on drugs?
- What if this pimple turns out to be cancer?
- What if there's a snowstorm the day my daughter gets married?

You get the idea. One way of minimizing your what-ifs is knowing just how likely it is that they will actually happen.

Assessing the odds

Just about every nasty, scary, threatening event you could imagine has some chance of happening. However, for many, if not most, of these feared occurrences, the chances are really very slim. Few of us are good at estimating the odds that something will happen. Do you know the chances of your airplane crashing or being hijacked, or the odds that you're developing a brain tumor or contracting some strange disease? The odds are incredibly low. If you replace "Is it likely?" with "Is it possible?" you'll notice that most things are possible — even though many of the things you worry about aren't likely. Often, you worry about the wrong things. You worry about getting rare diseases or dying in horrible ways. The irony is, you worry less about not putting on your seat belt, going to your doctor for a regular checkup, or having an accident in the kitchen, all of which have a greater chance of causing you grief than the things you do worry about. Perhaps a better way of looking at the odds is looking at the chance that something *won't* happen, rather than the odds that it will. Here are some odds of bad things *not* happening:

> Not dying in a flood – 99.9966667%
>
> Not dying in an earthquake – 99.9992418%
>
> Not dying in a lightning strike – 99.9988085%
>
> Not dying in a tornado – 99.9983333%
>
> Not dying in a tsunami – 99.9998%
>
> Not dying in an air-travel accident – 99.995%
>
> Not dying due to drowning – 99.9888168%
>
> Not dying in a fire (includes smoke) – 99.9103943%
>
> Not dying by firearm assault – 99.6884735%
>
> Not dying in a motor-vehicle accident – 98.9795918%
>
> Not dying by stroke – 96.5517241%
>
> Not dying of cancer – 85.7142857%
>
> Not dying of heart disease – 83.3333333%

Realizing that Murphy's Law is wrong

Remember Murphy's Law: "If anything can go wrong, it will." Well, even though this may seem like an accurate description of what happens in your life, it isn't. The reality is, most things that can go wrong in fact don't go wrong. We remember well when things go awry, but we tend to forget when things go off without a hitch.

Cutting out your catastrophizing and awfulizing

Worriers are consummate catastrophizers and awfulizers. They are constantly vigilant, on the lookout for horrendous problems and imminent disasters. This vigilance in and of itself can be stressful, not to mention emotionally and physically draining.

And even if a feared event does happen, will it always result in catastrophic results like the following?

- ✔ If I lose my job, I'll wind up in a box on the street!
- ✔ If I fail the test, my life will be totally ruined!
- ✔ If I don't get into that college, my career is in the toilet!
- ✔ If I don't meet my deadline, they'll cancel the whole project!
- ✔ If I'm late, they'll never talk to me again!

Probably not. Whenever you emotionally exaggerate the importance of a situation (by saying, for example, "This is the worst thing that could ever happen!"), you can be sure that your stress level will rise accordingly. You can quickly turn something small that warrants some concern into a major catastrophe that elicits significant stress. Yes, I realize that sometimes things don't work out. You may fear losing your job, and you may even actually lose your job. But even when the worst happens, you'll cope. Life will go on. You may not forget the catastrophes, but you will probably come to accept them.

Getting perspective

As I discuss in Chapter 3, assessing your stress balance can be a useful tool in helping you determine if your worrying is excessive. It can help you get perspective.

To find out whether you're "in balance," start by writing down a current worry. Now rate the *relative importance* of that worry on a ten-point scale, where one represents a minor worry and ten is an important worry. For example, suppose your worry is, "I'm worried that the gift I gave a friend for her birthday wasn't fancy enough." In the bigger scheme of things, this is a relatively small problem and probably warrants something like a one or two (or maybe a three if you're mentioned in her will). But probably not much more.

Now, rate the *amount* of worry you're experiencing using a similar ten-point scale, where one represents very little worrying and ten represents an incredible amount of worrying. Now check your balance by comparing the importance of the worry with your level of distress. Most of the time, the ratings should be at about the same level; if so, you're probably thinking straight and looking at your worry in an appropriate way. If your worry level is *greater* than your rated level of importance — for example, worrying at an eight level about a problem that's only a two — you may be looking at the problem in a distorted way, perhaps creating more stress for yourself than is necessary.

If your worry level is *lower* than your rated level of importance, you may not be concerned enough about the problem (such as saving money for your kids' college tuition). Alternatively, you may just have great coping skills. (You're losing your hair, but you accept that.)

Watching out for conclusion-jumping

We often come to a conclusion without having all (or at times any) of the evidence. Consider these worry-making interpretations:

- ✔ "Everyone seems to be avoiding me, probably because I'm going to be laid off!"
- ✔ "She hasn't returned my call yet, so she must not like me!"
- ✔ "This headache means I have a brain tumor!"
- ✔ "Because I did poorly on this last test, I'll never get into a good school!"
- ✔ "I'll never find anybody who wants to be with me!"

Could you be right? Sure. Are you right? Probably not. Ask yourself:

- ✔ "Do I really have any solid evidence that my worry is true?"
- ✔ "Could I convince a jury of my peers that my worry makes sense?"
- ✔ "If a good friend said this same thing to me, would I support her negative conclusions?"
- ✔ "Have I jumped to conclusions in the past and later found out I was badly mistaken?"

Coping with uncertainty and lack of control

Alas, our world is filled with uncertainty. And when we're uncertain, we feel out of control. A sense of not having control can easily trigger stress. We would like to have control over the unpleasant and unsettling events in our lives, but frequently we can't. We cause ourselves to feel far more stressed than we have to. Becoming more comfortable with uncertainty and lack of control is an essential part of your program of stress management.

The first step in becoming more comfortable with not having control is recognizing the extent of your control.

Take a moment to complete this little exercise. Use this simple point scale:

> 0 = No control
>
> 1 = A little control
>
> 2 = Lots of control

To what extent can you control the following events or circumstances?

Situation	My degree of control over this situation
Traffic	_____
Other people's personalities	_____
The weather	_____
The speed of elevators	_____
Crime	_____
Street noise	_____
Stopping people from acting like idiots	_____

You get the point. We can be incredibly limited when it comes to controlling our world and those who live in it. So, the next time you find yourself in a potentially stressful situation, ask yourself, "How much control do I really have in this situation?" If your answer is "not much," ask yourself a second question: "Then why am I making myself so stressed?" Sometimes, just acknowledging that you have no control can reduce your level of worry. Because you can't change it, maybe you can accept it. Worrying won't help.

Watching out for self-rating

One of the more important sources of distress and worry in people's lives is *self-rating*. You self-rate whenever you equate the way you value yourself (your self-worth) with your performance, your societal status, your achievements, your looks, your smarts, or any other trait or ability. You also self-rate when you tie the approval of others into your own feeling of self-worth. Worrying enters the picture when you're uncertain about whether you have what you feel are the necessary ego-maintaining qualities, or when you feel that you might lose the approval of those around you. To recognize whether your worrying is the result of self-rating, ask yourself the following questions:

- ✔ Am I overly worried about what others will think of me?
- ✔ Am I overly concerned about not doing well?
- ✔ Do I feel that my worth depends upon my job title?
- ✔ Do I feel that too much of my self-worth is tied to how others see me?

Going to yourself for advice

One of the quirks of being human is that we seem to be terrible at dealing with our own problems, but we're usually pretty good at solving other people's problems. Why not use this bit of psychological irony as a tool to help you worry less?

Imagine that someone is sitting in a chair opposite you. He or she has come to you for advice. For whatever reason, this person values your opinion and guidance. Even more strangely, he or she has the same worry you have. Restrain yourself from your first impulse — throwing your hands up in frustration — and reach deeply into your storehouse of wisdom. You may find that you come up with some wonderful ideas. You're an incredible solution finder. Now share these ideas with yourself.

Becoming a problem solver (rather than a worrier)

After you recognize that you're a worrier, you need to know how to shift from worry mode to problem-solving mode. When you're in problem-solving mode, you adopt a different mindset. It begins with detaching from fears, uncertainties, perfectionist tendencies, and all of the distorted thinking and emotional over-reacting described in previous sections. As radical as this may sound, switching to problem-solving mode doesn't necessitate a brain transplant or major personality overhaul. It means becoming more mindful (see Chapter 6). You need to re-center, slow down mentally and emotionally, and rely on that side of you that is more accepting, objective, and reasonable.

Using your coping self-talk

People who worry too much tend to be somewhat limited in generating options, alternatives, and solutions to potentially stressful problems. This is mainly because their fears and anxieties limit their ability to think outside the box and come up with more creative ideas. They continue to worry in unproductive ways. Instead, you want to begin talking to yourself in more adaptive ways. You can ask yourself a number of questions to help clarify your worries, and you can give yourself good advice and direction. This coping self-talk will help guide you on your road to managing and minimizing your troublesome worries. Sometimes, writing down your answers can be an effective aid in this process. It slows you down and helps you focus your thinking. From the list below, choose the bits of coping self-talk that seem most relevant to you.

- ✔ "What exactly am I worrying about?"
- ✔ "Do my emotional reactions (anxiety, upset, anger) fit the importance of the problem?"
- ✔ "Is my thinking here out of line? Am I making some thinking errors?"
- ✔ "Stop what-if-ing and catastrophizing and awfulizing."
- ✔ "Don't assume the worst will happen."

✔ "I can cope with this!"

✔ "Don't make this a bigger deal than it really is."

✔ "I'm being a worrywart! Do I always want to be a worrywart?"

✔ "Realistically, what is the worst that can happen?"

✔ "Is all this worrying helping me in any way?"

✔ "I *will* be able to figure out ways of coping with this."

✔ "On my zero-to-ten scale of importance, how important is this, really?"

✔ "In three years (three months, three weeks, three days), will this still be important to me?"

✔ "Is this problem really an emergency or crisis, or can I worry about it at a more appropriate time?"

✔ "Can I change this, or is it better for me to work to accept this?"

✔ "If I choose to address the problem, what are the next steps?"

✔ "What advice would I give a friend who had exactly the same worry?"

✔ "What am I afraid of?"

✔ "Is there another way, a more sensible way, of looking at this?"

✔ "Am I looking at worst-case scenarios?"

✔ "How likely is it that what I'm worrying about is really going to happen?"

✔ "How would someone else (a good friend or a role model, for example) look at this problem?"

✔ "How would someone who is more of an optimist look at this?"

✔ "What are some alternatives and solutions that I may have missed?"

Escaping Your Worries

Sometimes you feel like a prisoner of your own worries. You've done the work outlined in previous sections, you know the worries are misguided and unproductive, but you still can't shake them. Sometimes, not dealing with them, at least at that moment, is the answer. Here are some ways to get some distance from your worries.

Getting distracted

Worrying about something while you're doing something else at the same time is difficult, especially if that other thing demands your attention. This means that if you're having trouble turning off a persistent and nagging worry, try to find some way to distract yourself. This strategy makes particular sense if, in fact, you can't do very much to fix or resolve the situation or circumstance you're worrying about. Your distraction could be watching TV, watching a funny or engrossing movie, reading a good book, cooking something you like, gardening, doing carpentry — any involvement that can hold your attention and take you away from your worry.

Sometimes the distractions can be even less obvious. You can distract yourself by window-shopping, people-watching, remembering the details of a favorite vacation, or simply getting into some kind of idle conversation with a neighbor, a store clerk, or the person next to you in line. Anything that can take your mind off your worry will work.

Going for a walk

One of the frequently overlooked ways of coping with worry is to go for a walk. A brisk walk is even more effective. When you're walking, you're distracted, and you're releasing physical stress and tension — all terrific antidotes to stress.

Working up a sweat

Try worrying next time you're jogging, rowing, swimming, lifting, climbing, hitting a golf or tennis ball, or doing any other form of exercise or sport. It's not easy. After about ten minutes of working out on the stationary bicycle or treadmill at my gym, I find it hard to concentrate on anything. Part of the positive effect comes from the physical relaxation that often follows physical exertion. With your body is more relaxed, your mind slows. Also, your body may be secreting endorphins, hormones that are known to have stress-reducing effects. The bonus: Not only can you control your unwanted worrying, you can also stay in shape at the same time.

Talking about it

We feel better and worry less when we've had an opportunity to talk to someone about those things that are bothering us. When we can get our worries out on the table, it gives us some perspective, and with this perspective can come greater feelings of control and hope. You need, of course, someone to tell your worries to. This person could be a family member, a friend, or simply an understanding and sympathetic listener. Some of my best therapy sessions have resulted not from my brilliant insights but from just letting my clients talk about their worries.

STRESS BUSTER

Worry harder!

One way of making your worry time and worry corner even more effective is to worry harder during those times. Research supports the notion that if you worry intensely for a brief period of time (say, 15 or 20 minutes), you may actually reduce your need to worry at other times of the day — at least for that particular worry. This doesn't mean that you will never worry about that problem again. However, you will probably find that you worry about it less at other times.

The key word here is intensity. When you worry in your usual way, you worry inconsistently. You have worry lapses, you distract yourself, or you avoid thinking about certain negative scenarios. To get the therapeutic benefits of concentrated worrying, your worrying has to be constant and focused so that you become satiated with worry and get tired of worrying. In other words, you worry yourself out. By immersing yourself totally in a worry for a fixed period of time, you actually make it less likely that you will worry about that problem, at least for a while.

Humoring yourself

Humor is a marvelous antidote to worry. The problem is, when we're worrying, we're usually in no mood to joke. The following sections provide two of my favorite ways of using humor to diffuse a potential worry.

Exaggerate

Exaggeration can be a useful tool in helping you reduce your worrying. Suppose, for example, that you're worrying about an upcoming presentation you have to make at work. Try imagining that, as you start your presentation, the audience begins to throw tomatoes and other assorted produce. A colleague comes to the front of the room and announces that this is the worst presentation he has ever heard in his professional life. The boos and foot-stomping are deafening.

Or how about this: You're worried that you may flunk your upcoming exam. Imagine that you not only flunk the exam but that your grade is so low it is entered into *The Guinness Book of World Records*. No college ever accepts you, and you live in a cardboard box on the street for the next 20 years. Mothers parade their children in front of your box, warning, "See what happens when you don't study!"

Hopefully a wee smile may help give you some perspective on your worry.

Play sitcom

Using this technique, you imagine that your worry is the theme for a favorite sitcom episode. It could be *Modern Family, Two and a Half Men,* a *Seinfeld* or *30 Rock* rerun, or any show you enjoy. Imagine that one of the characters on the show is entrenched in your worry. But the other cast members manage to look at this worry in a less serious, more playful way. Looking at your worries through their eyes will, hopefully, dilute it and give you some emotional distance.

Relaxing your body and calming your mind

When you're relaxed, you'll probably find that worrying is much harder to do. When your body is relaxed, your mind slows down, as well. Why not use this fact to help you control your worrying? The next time you notice that you're worrying, begin using one or more of the relaxation techniques described in Chapters 4 and 5, or try one of these relaxation methods:

- ✔ **Abdominal breathing:** Simple changes in your breathing patterns can result in significant reductions in your level of tension. You not only induce a more relaxed physical state, but you also create an effective source of distraction from your worries. As you breathe deeply, try saying the word "relax" to yourself every time you exhale.

- ✔ **Progressive muscle relaxation:** By tensing and relaxing various muscle groups, you have a systematic way of reducing muscular tension in all parts of your body. After you get the hang of this approach, try the "quickie" version described in Chapter 4.

- ✔ **Imagery:** Imagine yourself in a place you associate with positive feelings and absolutely no worries, such as the beach you visited on your last vacation. Take yourself there using all of your senses; imagine what you might see, hear, smell, feel, and even taste.

The more relaxed you are, the less likely you are to worry.

Trying some positive imagery

Often, when you worry, you really don't allow yourself to take the worry to a positive (and often more likely) conclusion. One method of reducing your worry is to use something called positive imagery.

When you use positive imagery, you form a mental picture of that worry, including as much detail as you can — what you see, what you hear, and so on. Then imagine a positive resolution to your worry. All goes relatively well.

For example, if you have a presentation to give, imagine that as you approach the podium you are feeling calm. You feel remarkably at ease. You start a little nervously, but very soon you find your stride and the presentation goes swimmingly. You even begin to enjoy the process a little. You finish and hear appreciative applause. Several of your colleagues come up to you and tell you what a nice job you did. You feel great!

You don't have to go overboard with the positive nature of your imagery. Just make it more positive than your worries would suggest. Chances are, your revised image of what will happen may be a lot closer to what actually happens. Trust me.

In a pinch, try this

This approach may sound a bit strange, but it can be highly effective in helping you turn off those unwanted and intrusive worries. It's a variation of the "stop" technique I describe in Chapter 5. Here's how it works:

1. **Whenever you sense that some recurring, unwanted, and distressing worry is ruminating in your thoughts, become conscious that you are fretting about that worry.**

2. **Pinch yourself on your wrist or some other part of your body. At the same time, yell the word "stop" silently inside your head.**

3. **Replace that worrisome thought with a pleasant thought.**

   The pleasant thought could be a happy memory or a pleasant image. Hold that pleasant thought for 20 or 30 seconds and then go about your usual business.

   Repeat this sequence if the distressing worry returns.

You may need some time before you weaken the troublesome worry. But stick with it!

Chapter 14

Reducing Interpersonal Stress

· ·

In This Chapter

▶ Communicating more effectively

▶ Developing assertiveness

▶ Dealing with difficult people

· ·

*Y*our relationships and interactions with others can be a major source of joy and satisfaction. Unfortunately, your involvement with others can also be a major source of stress. Whenever you ask people where most of their stress comes from, they almost always answer "other people." The "others" may be family members, people at work, or just some incredibly rude so-and-so who is giving you a hard time, because he or she got up on the wrong side of the bed that morning. And unless you're hiding in a cabin in rural Montana, it's likely that you may run into someone very soon who will try to push your stress button.

Minimizing your interpersonal stress means having the tools, strategies, and tactics that allow you to navigate the prickly world of other people. This chapter shows you how you can make your interactions and involvement with others far more satisfying and certainly far less stressful.

Developing Stress-Reducing Communication

Your ability to communicate affects your relationships with family, friends, co-workers, bosses, clients — everybody, in fact. Ineffective communication can contribute to everything from having an unhappy marriage to losing your job, from a so-so social life to a lousy sex life. And that usually means more stress in your life. Unfortunately, when you're feeling stressed, your ability to communicate deteriorates. Alas, you probably haven't been taught how to communicate effectively. You're taught how to drive a car and how to solve equations. Your cell phone, camera, and DVR come with instruction manuals.

But when it comes to communicating with others, you may need some guidance. The following sections offer some suggestions and strategies that can increase your communication smarts and help you minimize the interpersonal stress in your life.

Become a good listener

The fact is, poor listeners have more stress in their lives. If you're a poor listener, your relationships are probably not as satisfying and effective as they could be. Good listeners have more friends and better marriages, function more effectively at work, and, as a result, usually have less hassle, friction, and conflict in their lives. Whether you're a terrible listener or a good listener, the following are some ways that you can become a better listener.

Make a mental commitment

The next time you're in a situation where someone is talking and you feel it is important that you truly listen, make a mental commitment to do just that. Listen. Make it a priority. Put effort and energy into your listening. Don't be distracted. Don't look at your watch. Don't yawn. Don't look around. Don't daydream. If it's too noisy where you are, ask the speaker to join you in a quieter spot. Pretend that there will be a test on what the other person is saying and that your score will go on your permanent record.

Look like you are listening

A good listener does more than just stand there without saying anything. You should be an active listener. Acknowledge verbally and non-verbally that you are listening by responding with a nod, a facial expressions, a raised eyebrow, an "oh really," an "I see," or anything else that gives the speaker the idea that you're still conscious. If you're far away from the speaker, move closer. Lean slightly toward the person speaking. Look the other person in the eye. And uncrossing your arms and legs suggests a more open, verbally-receptive stance.

Timing, timing, timing

If "location, location, location" is the formula for success in real estate, in stress-reducing communication, the formula might be "timing, timing, timing." *When* you say something is just as important as *how* you say it. For example, your child comes home far later than you would like. Your child knows this. You can have a heated discussion extremely late at night when both of you are emotionally ready for a fight, or you can leave it for the next day when you can more calmly (and effectively) present your dissatisfaction. Should you find yourself in an argument or heated disagreement, try to stop yourself and defer the interaction to another time when, hopefully, cooler heads will prevail. "Let's discuss this further tomorrow, okay?" Better timing usually means less stress.

Are you a good listener?

Most of us think we are good listeners. Most of us also think that we have a great sense of humor, that we look terrific, and that we are wonderful drivers. Maybe yes, maybe no. The next time you're talking to someone, monitor yourself; notice whether you're truly listening and paying attention to what the other person is saying. Better yet, ask friends and family members if they think you're a good listener. You can also ask them about your driving, your looks, and your sense of humor.

Give some feedback

One effective technique that helps ensure that you are listening and that gives the speaker a real sense that you are actively following his every word is to reflect back or comment on bits of what you hear. For example:

> Speaker: "My job is getting worse. I'm there now till all hours. I'm beginning to hate it."

> You: "Yeah, it must be hard not having enough time for you and your family."

This response shows the other person not only that you're listening but also that you're empathetic and can relate to what he or she is saying. Even if your feedback is off the mark, it allows the speaker to modify his or her remarks and clarify his thoughts and feelings, which is similar to what therapists may do in their sessions. The feedback may be as simple as paraphrasing the speaker's words in your own words. For example:

> Speaker: "I'm at the office now from 8 to 8 at night! It seems like I'm there all the time!"

> You: "8 to 8. That's a lot of hours to be at work."

This kind of active listening encourages the speaker to share more of his or her thoughts and feelings with you. It creates a feeling of connectedness.

Understand the importance of validation

An important part of effective interpersonal communication is the process of *validation*. Too often the communication process becomes derailed when one or both parties feel they are not being heard. One person feels that he is trying to express his thoughts and feelings, but the other person's response fails to convey understanding. A nasty cycle can be created in which each side, trying to get his or her viewpoint across, argues more loudly and heatedly, trying to overpower the other side. Without validation, it becomes much harder to resolve an interpersonal issue or disagreement. High levels of invalidation and/or low levels of validation can be associated with higher distress levels. You can end up with two people doing their own thing with little or no recognition of what the other person is thinking or feeling.

When you validate someone, that person feels that you're not only listening to them but also *understanding* and *accepting* what they're saying. Sometimes the validation is pretty simple: looking directly at the person and nodding your head. It may involve some simple phrases — "I hear what you're saying" or "I know what you mean."

At a more involved level, validation can mean that you put what the other person is saying into your own words:

> "What I hear you saying, Beth, is that you feel angry at me because I don't want your parents staying with us for three weeks."

But authentic validation goes beyond this. It tells the other person that you not only hear what he or she is saying but also understand why he or she feels that way. It recognizes that, from their perspective, their thoughts and feelings make sense.

> "I totally see why you would like to spend that time with them. You haven't seen them for a while and you miss them. It makes total sense."

Validation does *not* imply agreement. Just because you see and understand where another person is coming from doesn't mean that you necessarily agree with that person. Sometimes you may not totally understand where the other person stands. Asking some questions in a gentle, accepting way can elicit more information. And even receiving a more complete understanding of how the person is looking at this issue doesn't ensure that you'll agree with that person. You may now want to express your feelings and describe how you see the issue.

> "I feel like I would have to act like a host for three weeks, and frankly your mother can be difficult. She talks all the time and rarely listens. I feel worn out after two days with her."

Hopefully, Beth will recognize and validate her husband's thought and feelings. The resolution? Beth and her husband may not find a perfect solution or even a good option. ("What about asking them to come for two weeks? I could live with that.") The important point here is that the process of respective validation creates a climate of mutual support. The spiral of stress is slowed and hopefully weakened. Both parties feel less anger and less resentment when they feel the other person genuinely understands and is empathetic and sympathetic to their position and viewpoint. Validation usually means less stress.

Listening can be good for your health

Not only are you being polite when you listen, but you may also live longer. In his book *The Language of the Heart*, psychologist James Lynch finds that the act of listening actually lowers your blood pressure. He looks at blood-pressure levels in hypertensive patients and finds that patients' blood-pressure levels drop dramatically when they are listening to someone else.

Don't "one-up" the speaker

When someone else is talking, don't immediately begin formulating your own verbal comeback. Wait to start formulating your replies. Mentally rehearsing your wonderful story while the other person is telling his guarantees that you hear little of what the other person is saying. While most everything someone tells you can remind you of something that happened to you, resist, at least for that immediate moment, the urge to tell an even funnier joke or a better story. Withhold, for a while at least, that brilliant repartee. Do not interrupt. Don't put the other person down. Don't debate. Don't go for a win. In short, don't "one-up" the speaker.

Hold off on giving advice

Often, when others talk, they are talking about what is going on in their lives. They may be confiding in you and sharing some concern or problem. Upon hearing of a problem or predicament, your natural instinct is to give some advice. Men especially have difficulty not coming up with solutions and suggestions. However, while your ideas may be terrific and right on the mark, it may be that the speaker isn't looking for your well-intended advice and would really just like to express his feelings. You can always get back to the person later and ask him whether he'd like to talk some more and listen to some of your ideas.

Practice listening

Think of a person in your life whom you care about and with whom you are not a great listener. Purposefully plan to listen carefully to that person every time you speak with her. Remember the guidelines that I describe in this section, and monitor yourself as to how you are doing. Practice listening with this person until you recognize your improvement. Then find another person to add to your list of people to listen to better, and so on.

Another way of honing your listening skills is to practice listening to something you find boring. Usually you don't have to wait long before such an opportunity presents itself. It can be a less-than-scintillating presentation at your next business meeting or some fellow committee member going on and on about a trivial point. It may be a television program outlining economic growth in the newly created province of Kalikistan. Force yourself to listen and pay attention to what is being said. You may find that you get much better at listening over time.

It's your turn to talk

Listening, of course, is only one part of the communication process. Sometimes you have something to say. What you say and how you say it make a big difference in the amount of stress you experience. Some communicational guidelines can help make what comes out of your mouth less stressful for you and for the people you care about.

Use "I" statements

One sure way to escalate any interaction into a stressful confrontation is to start blaming or finding fault. For example, you find yourself becoming more than a little annoyed as you have to wait (yet another time) for a friend. Now, you can say:

> "You're never on time! Can't you get your act together?!"

This approach can put the other person on the defensive. She may feel attacked and feel the need to protect herself. Rather than start with a blaming "you," start with an "I." Here's what I mean:

> "I feel that when you come late, you don't care that much about me. I get annoyed and angry. I'd like it if you could try to be on time."

This approach allows you to express your feelings and tell the other person what you would like her to do differently, but in a non-attacking, non-hostile way. Following is a model, or template, to help you reframe your blaming.

Start with:

> "When you do . . ." (describe the other person's behavior)

Then say:

> "I feel . . ." (describe how this behavior affects you)

And finish with:

> "I'd prefer . . ." (describe what you would like to see happen)

Practice some damage control

What does come out of your mouth, and certainly the way it comes out, reflects how you're feeling at the time. If you have a particularly bad day at work, you may not come home feeling all warm and fuzzy. You may feel angry, or upset, or worse. And should you be greeted by any new demands or frustrations, your reactions may be less than delightful. You're in danger of both feeling and spreading a good deal of stress. A little damage control is needed. Two suggestions:

- ✔ **Warn others.** As soon as you recognize that your mood has headed south and has real toxic potential, share that information with those around you. Let them know what you're feeling and warn them what to expect. Try the following:

  "Hon, it's been a rotten day all round. I'm in a foul mood and not really fit for human company. I probably shouldn't be taken seriously for at least another hour. It's nothing you've done. Give me a little time and I should be my old wonderful self again."

  The funny part is, once you have delivered this message, it's less likely that you will, in fact, interact negatively with those around you.

- ✔ **Make amends.** Should you screw up and manage to stress out everyone in sight, all is still not lost. As quickly as you can regain your emotional equilibrium, let the target of your negative fallout know that you're sorry, that it wasn't him or her who triggered your emotional overreaction, and that you'll work hard to make sure it doesn't happen too often.

  A little damage control up front can avoid a lot more stress down the road.

Look for a pattern

Rather than complaining about every little bit of negative behavior, wait until you have collected a number of incidents of such behavior. And then complain. For example, suppose you're upset because a friend appears not to be listening to you when you're talking, although you work very hard to listen when she talks. You can express your feelings to her the next time you find her not listening, or you can handle it a better way. After you have noticed that the behavior persists, bring it up at a time when you and she are not upset, angry, or defensive. Then raise it as a more general issue (using the "I" statement). Should the pattern continue, express your feelings again — but at the right time, expressing even more strongly your displeasure at her behavior.

Discovering What It Means to Be Assertive

Are you assertive or non-assertive in your interactions with others? Becoming effectively assertive in your interpersonal relationships can result in much less emotional distress. Whenever you act non-assertively, you generally end up feeling more anxious and tense than you would like. You may also feel angry and resentful about not expressing your true feelings. You may feel frustrated at not getting what you feel you should have. You can feel victimized, pushed around, and taken advantage of. You feel less in control and less hopeful that you can achieve what you would like to achieve. Your self-esteem is lowered. You feel less positive about yourself and about how others see you. And those times when you do act assertively, you may feel guilty or anxious, worrying about any repercussions of your behavior. Any or all of the above, of course, produces a good deal of stress. Fortunately, finding out how to become more comfortably assertive is something that can be mastered relatively painlessly. The first step is knowing just how assertive or unassertive you are.

How assertive are you?

In the following list, I outline several of the behaviors and traits of unassertive people. Read each statement and rate yourself on the extent to which that statement applies to you: "not like me," "a little like me," or "a lot like me":

- ✔ I'm very uncomfortable expressing my needs and wants.
- ✔ I hate confrontations and arguments.
- ✔ I have trouble asking for help or a favor from others.
- ✔ I find it hard to ask people to return things they have borrowed from me.
- ✔ When people ask a favor of me, I find it hard to say no.
- ✔ I'm uncomfortable receiving compliments and praise.
- ✔ In social situations, I usually let others do the talking.
- ✔ Expressing feelings of caring and affection makes me uncomfortable.
- ✔ I find it hard to ask someone who is annoying me to stop.
- ✔ Maintaining eye contact when I'm talking to others is difficult for me.
- ✔ Returning a purchase to a store makes me very uncomfortable.
- ✔ I have a lot of trouble speaking up in a group or in a meeting.

> ✔ I become anxious when I'm in a conversation with people I don't know well.
>
> ✔ I feel that I am not assertive enough.
>
> ✔ Others who know me have said that I am not assertive enough.

Looking at your ratings, how many fall into the "a lot like me" category? If more than one or two do, it suggests that you may want to explore further the role that non-assertiveness plays in your daily dose of stress.

Following, I present four scenarios that can help you identify your interactive style. Circle the response that best reflects how you might react:

1. You've ordered dinner in a fairly nice restaurant — a big steak, in fact. You like your steak on the rare side, and you tell your waiter of your preference. The steak arrives far more well-done than you like. You:

   a. Smile, say thank you, and finish as much of the steak as you can, unhappy with every bite.

   b. Tell the waiter that he is a complete idiot and that he needs a hearing aid, and yell this loudly enough so that everyone in the restaurant hears you and secretly wishes you dead.

   c. Politely explain that the steak is not the way you would like it, and ask him nicely for another.

   d. None of the above. I would _____.

2. You're in a taxi, and the driver is driving far too quickly for your comfort. You begin to feel nervous. You:

   a. Grin and bear it, while mentally listing your heirs.

   b. Call the cab driver a reckless imbecile, while banging on the partition with your foot.

   c. Calmly ask the driver if he would please slow down.

   d. None of the above. I would _____.

3. You're in the middle of your dinner when the telephone rings. It's someone who wants to know if you're interested in switching your telephone service. He drones on and on. You:

   a. Listen for the entire 20-minute spiel and agree to sign on.

   b. Tell him you'll be back in a second, and put the receiver in a sock drawer while you return to finish your dinner.

   c. Interrupt the caller, saying politely that you aren't interested, and then hang up.

   d. None of the above. I would _____.

4. You're patiently waiting for a sales clerk to serve a customer next to you. Another customer shows up and stands on the other side of the customer being served. Though you were there first, the newcomer seems oblivious to your presence. He quickly hands his purchase to the clerk before you have a chance to blink. You are not happy. You:

   a. Say and do nothing.

   b. Grab the man by his lapel and throw him to the ground.

   c. Firmly, but politely, tell the sales clerk and the other customer that you were there before he was and that you would like to be served first.

   d. None of the above. I would _____.

In each of the above scenarios, you can respond in four very different ways:

✔ **You can respond *passively*** and keep your honest feelings and thoughts to yourself, or express them in a self-effacing, apologetic manner so that the other person doesn't take you seriously (the first of the answer choices). This response shows that you don't consider your own needs to be important and you feel that the needs of others always come first.

✔ **You can respond *aggressively*** by directly expressing your anger or expressing it in more subtle, passive-aggressive ways (as in my somewhat exaggerated second choices). With this response, you disregard the other person's rights and feelings. You want to win, but at any cost.

✔ **You can respond *assertively*** with the third answer choices. You stand up for yourself, expressing the way you truly feel. You are considerate of other people's feelings. You don't attack or blame, but nor do you become meek and withdraw.

✔ **You can respond with the fourth choice.** This form of response can be a combination of the first three. It can be part passive and part assertive, or some other mixture of interactive styles.

Not too hot, not too cold — just right

Acting assertively means knowing how to express your opinions, wants, and feelings in ways that don't compromise the rights of others or demean others. When you assert your own needs, you don't let others take advantage of you, nor do you feel guilty. Being assertive is more than returning a broken toaster or telling a waiter to take back your undercooked steak. Often, being more assertive means being able to express positive feelings to someone, to express affection and caring. Being assertive also means being able to give and receive positives, be they compliments, thank-yous, or other expressions of praise and gratitude. You are not meek, you are not aggressive, and you do not blame and resent. You feel good about your actions. And you feel less stress.

Examples of assertive behavior

To help you get a better picture of what assertive behavior is, I list some assertive responses to common situations.

✔ **Refusing a request:**

- I'm sorry, I can't drop that package off for you.

- That's not a good time for me.

- I'm sorry, but I really don't want to do that.

✔ **Being given some unwanted advice:**

- I really don't want your advice right now.

- Thanks for your help, but I'll be fine.

✔ **Expressing disapproval:**

- I don't like what you're doing.

- I would like you to stop that.

✔ **Expressing a compliment:**

- I think you're doing a fantastic job.

- I think you look terrific.

✔ **Receiving a compliment:**

- It's nice of you to say that.

- Thank you.

What assertive behavior is not

An old cartoon shows an office door with a sign on it reading, "Assertiveness class in session. Don't knock; just barge in." Back in the '70s there was great interest in the topic of assertiveness. A flood of books hit the shelves telling us that we could now say "no" with impunity, and to stand up, speak up, and go get what we want. Assertiveness training courses flourished, and the streets were filled with course graduates all too eager to express their thoughts and feelings. While most people got the point of being more assertive, many others missed the point and interpreted being assertive as permission to express all their pent-up aggression and hostility.

Assertiveness is not:

- ✔ Simply getting what you want
- ✔ Disregarding the rights and feelings of others
- ✔ Acting belligerently or antagonistically
- ✔ Being aggressive or hostile
- ✔ Making fun of others
- ✔ Walking around with a chip on your shoulder
- ✔ Dominating, demeaning, or humiliating others

Becoming More Assertive

Looking around at those you know, you may be tempted to make a judgment on whether you are assertive, and you may think that you were born that way. Actually, there is some truth to this. You do come into this world with some hard wiring that predisposes you to be assertive or non-assertive. Your parents, other people, and your life experiences also contribute to how you interact with others. However, should you lack any or all of these influences, you can still become assertive. With a little time and some effort, you can readily see yourself becoming more assertive — and less stressed.

Ten ways to stay permanently non-assertive

1. Never say no to anyone and avoid confrontations at all costs.

2. Always put the needs of others ahead of yours.

3. Feel guilty whenever you do something that you want to do.

4. Believe that your feelings don't matter, that only other people's feelings matter.

5. Believe that you're selfish if someone is unhappy with your decisions or actions.

6. Believe that being wrong or making a mistake is something to always be avoided.

7. Always do what people in authority tell you to do.

8. Believe that you're not as smart or as competent as other people.

9. Believe that it's not polite to disagree or express a contrary opinion.

10. Never accept a compliment without putting yourself down in some way.

Observing assertive behavior

Following are some guidelines on how to become more assertive:

- ✔ **Watch others.** Notice how and when others act assertively. Pay special attention when you're with people you admire for their assertiveness skills.

- ✔ **Watch yourself.** Keep a brief record of when you do and don't act assertively. Nothing fancy — just make some notes to yourself.

- ✔ **Start small.** Start by working on situations where you feel only minimal or moderate amounts of anxiety. Work your way up to the harder stuff. Don't expect immediate changes. Becoming more assertive means changing years of behaving otherwise. Learning new ways of thinking and behaving takes a little time.

- ✔ **Cut yourself some slack.** Don't be too hard on yourself if you act non-assertively. Figure out what you did wrong and try not to let the same thing happen the next time.

Watching how you say things

It's not just the words; it's also how you say them. While the words may be wonderfully assertive, the manner in which you deliver your message, and your body language, may be saying something that is other than assertive. Ask yourself:

- ✔ Am I speaking in a loud, clear voice?
- ✔ Am I mumbling when I'm talking, or garbling my words?
- ✔ Am I looking at the person I'm talking to?
- ✔ Am I fidgeting while I'm talking?
- ✔ Am I sitting or standing straight when I'm talking?
- ✔ Am I shouting or yelling?
- ✔ Is my tone sarcastic and demeaning?

The next time you get an opportunity to work on your assertiveness, pay attention to any or all of the above. When you're acting assertively, your non-verbal behavior is congruent with your message. All of you is saying the same thing.

Saying "no" (oh, so nicely)

Many times, a simple and direct "no" or other assertive response is totally appropriate and should be your option of choice. You need no further explanation or discussion. However, sometimes straight assertion is a little cold and may be taken as somewhat off-putting. Some tact and packaging may be required.

Here are some examples:

Situation: Friends sitting next to you in a theater are talking during the movie.

> Direct assertion: "Would you please be quiet?"
>
> Packaged assertion: "Guys, keep it down. I can't hear anything."

Situation: A co-worker asks you for help.

> Direct assertion: "No, I can't do it."
>
> Packaged assertion: "I'd like to help, but I really can't now."

Situation: You are interrupted while you're talking.

> Direct assertion: "Don't interrupt me when I'm talking."
>
> Packaged assertion: "Hang on. I'm not finished yet."

Situation: Being asked out for dinner by an acquaintance. (You don't want to go.)

> Direct assertion: "No, thank you."
>
> Packaged assertion: "Thank you for the offer. But I really can't."

If you're caught off guard and find yourself tongue-tied, you can always defer your answer:

> "I'll have to look at my schedule. I'll get back to you."

It's also useful to have one or two wonderful excuses at your fingertips.

> "I really can't. My nephew is coming into town that weekend."
>
> "I'm sorry, but we already have a dinner invitation for that night."

Sometimes a convenient excuse or white lie works and is the appropriate response. That may sound as though it's a violation of the principles of assertion, but sometimes the other person's feelings may be more important to you than to say, "No way. I just don't want to." Remember, discretion is often the better part of assertion.

Starting nice and working your way up to nasty

I have always liked the strategy of escalating assertion when dealing with more difficult situations. Using this approach, you start as politely and as courteously as you can and then move up the assertion ladder, rung by rung. Should you find yourself nearing the end of that ladder with little hope of success, you may need to venture into the realm of more forceful behavior. Here's what I mean.

Suppose that you're enjoying a particularly good book. You become aware that your silence has been disrupted. Your next-door neighbor has turned up his television set to a highly disturbing level. It is loud. Very loud. You are very annoyed. You could let the incident go, but because this is not the first time this has happened, you decide that a little assertive behavior is required. You determine that escalating assertion is the way to go. Table 14-1 gives an illustration of how you might proceed.

Table 14-1	Escalating Assertion with a Noisy Neighbor
Your Mood	*The Action You Take*
Mr. or Ms. Nice Guy	A polite note under his door
I'm a little miffed	A courteous but firm phone call
I'm ticked off	A personal visit with strong eye contact
No more Mr. or Ms. Nice Guy	Wall-banging; verbal threats
The gloves are off	The police; the super; lawyer's letter
Nuclear war	Lawsuit; you blast your own TV
Defeat	Earplugs

Start modestly and hope that you can resolve your issue before you get to the end of your list. The key to escalating assertion is being in emotional control, which means working to not let your anger or upset overwhelm you and get you to do something you may regret later.

Talking like a broken record

Persistence pays at times. By repeating your request again and again, like a record with a scratch (remember LPs?), you often find that you get what you want. Consider this interchange. You purchase a lamp that works fine for the first day, but after that you begin to hear some crackling in the socket that leaves you feeling a little leery of turning it on. You decide, rightfully, to take it back.

> You: "This lamp doesn't work properly. I think the wiring is defective. I'd like a refund."
>
> The store clerk: "Do you have a sales receipt?"
>
> You: "No. However, you can see by the box that the item was purchased here."
>
> The clerk: "We don't do refunds without receipts."
>
> You: "That may be, but I would like my money back."
>
> The clerk: "I can't do that."
>
> You: "I would very much like my money back."
>
> The clerk: "But we almost never give a refund without a receipt."
>
> You: "I really would like my money back."
>
> The clerk: "Okay, but just this one time only."
>
> You: "Thank you."

As you can see, nothing brilliant is going on here. Basically you wear down the other person. You are firm and repetitive. The tone of your voice doesn't vary. You stay on target. You are a Johnny (or Jeannie) one-note. This technique works best when you stick to a single sentence that you repeat again and again. Does this approach work every time? Nope. But by sticking to a consistent and unwavering demand, you find that in more instances than you may imagine, you get what you want.

Trying a little "fogging"

This technique is a nicer version of the broken record but includes some of the same ideas. Fogging recognizes that you may care about the other person's feelings or that the other person may have a valid point or be asking something reasonable of you, but that you would like to decline. The following example makes fogging clearer.

The "good girl" syndrome

Women, in particular, face additional pressures to remain non-assertive. Culturally and historically, women have been taught to be "other-oriented." Women are taught that they should be passive, submissive, and compliant. They are told, "Be nice, and people will like you," "Never be the center of attention," and "Don't look too smart." And while these messages are less strong these days, they still exist. Growing up with these early socialization messages lodged in women's psyche, life becomes even more complicated given the multiple roles that women now assume. More often than not it is women who take the lion's share of child-raising responsibilities. Women are seen as primarily responsible for taking care of things at home, even if they work a staggering number of hours at an outside job. And should a parent get sick or require time and attention, you can guess who gives most of her time and attention. Couple this with a non-assertive mindset, and the stress can become enormous.

You're asked to donate money to a charity that you feel has merit, but you have decided that it's not one that you want to add to your give-to list. The fund-raiser is well-meaning but persistent. Using the broken record approach seems a little harsh. You opt for fogging:

> The fund-raiser: "It's a great cause. It helps a lot of people."
>
> You: "I know it's a good cause. I don't want to donate to another charity at this time."
>
> Fund-raiser: "You don't have to give a huge amount. Anything will do."
>
> You: "I realize that. But I'd rather not make a donation at this time."
>
> Fund-raiser: "Why don't I put you down for $30? That's not an awful lot."
>
> You: "I know it isn't. I'd rather not make a donation."

Though it may sound much like the broken record strategy, it is a softer interaction. You are actively listening to the other person, paraphrasing or feeding back some of what he is saying. You appreciate his point of view, and you may in fact be quite sympathetic, but you still want to stick to your guns. It's the perfect technique when you're solicited for donations, membership on committees, volunteer positions, or reasonable favors that you want to decline.

Coping with Difficult People

Believe it or not, some people can be ill-mannered, grouchy, and nasty and appear to lack many basic interpersonal skills. They lose very little sleep over giving you a hard time. Sooner or later — and probably sooner — you will run into one of these types. You may have to bring out the bigger guns. More sophisticated strategies and tactics are required to spare you this unwanted and avoidable stress. The following sections outline what you need to do.

Stay calm

When you're seething and little puffs of smoke are coming out of your ears, the chances of effectively reacting to a difficult situation are not the best. Your first strategy should be to get yourself into a more composed, relaxed state. By relaxing your body at the first hint of conflict, you give yourself the best chance of responding well in a difficult situation. Some simple breathing exercises (see Chapter 4) should do the trick. I like using some Rapid Relaxation exercises in these situations. The following is what you can do to stay calm:

> Inhale deeply through your nostrils, and at the same time press together your thumb and forefinger on one hand. Hold that breath for four or five seconds and then exhale fully through your slightly parted lips. As you're exhaling, let go of the tension in your hand and let a wave of soothing relaxation spread from the top of your head to the tip of your toes. Repeat one or two times until your body feels more relaxed.

Focus on the issue

When you're expressing a grievance, problem, or dissatisfaction, too often you express your feelings in global, vague ways. Consider the following statements:

> "Why can't you be nicer to me?"

> "You're never there when I need you!"

> "You're inconsiderate!"

> "I wish you weren't so lazy!"

"I wish you would try harder to be a better friend!"

"I need more respect from you!"

It may be quite clear to you what you mean; it may be less clear to the person you are talking to. The typical response uttered by the other person is, "What are you talking about?" Usually anger and more than a smidgeon of defensiveness are attached.

Try to focus on specific behaviors that can be directly addressed. Try to shy away from global generalizations and broad judgments. For example, some of the dissatisfaction voiced earlier in this section can be restated in more specific and understandable ways:

"I would like it if you could talk with me more and listen better."

"Could you keep your phone on when you're away so I can reach you if I have to?"

"I'm upset because you didn't invite me to go shopping with you."

"I would like you to put your dirty clothes in the hamper."

"I would like it if you could call me more often. Sometimes I feel I do most of the calling."

"I don't like it when you say I'm not good at anything."

Avoid kitchen-sinking

Kitchen-sinking describes what you do when you lump a bunch of grievances together and throw them at the other person all at once. For example, a parent may express his or her anger to a child in the following way:

"You can't do anything right! You never take the garbage out, clean your room, get up on time, or finish your homework!"

This grievance may or may not be accurate, but expressing these complaints all at once usually ensures that the reaction is defensive and probably hostile.

If you have more than one beef, grievance, or issue, express them one at a time. And use the "I statement" approach rather than blaming and putting the other person on the defensive.

Don't be a labeler

When we have a gripe about someone (or even about ourselves), we tend to use simple, often one-word labels. We like labels. They simplify things. Unfortunately, they over-simplify things. People are not easily classified by a single descriptor. At some point, everyone does something that can be construed as lazy, selfish, mean, silly, and just about every other derogatory adjective you can come up with. Table 14-2 illustrates how labels can be destructive, and how we take a single act or bit of behavior and turn it into a permanent character trait.

Table 14-2	A Look at How Labels Can Distort a Situation
The Label	*The Behavior*
You're a slob.	You didn't pick up after yourself.
You're lazy.	You didn't do your homework.
You're stupid.	You didn't know the answer to my question.
You're inconsiderate.	You didn't invite me to go shopping with you.
You're selfish.	You didn't ask me if I wanted some of your popcorn.

Watch the "never" and "always" traps

Statements with the words "always" and "never" usually are forms of exaggeration that distort what is happening and misrepresent the other person's behavior. They become traps that put the other person on the defensive and make it harder to resolve the potential conflict. Perhaps some of these statements sound familiar:

"You never do anything right!"

"You always manage to hurt my feelings!"

"You never consider how someone else might feel!"

"Everything you do turns out badly!"

Try to avoid these global characterizations. Whenever possible, catch yourself when you hear these words forming in your mind and replace them with less provocative descriptors. In their place, try substituting "often," "too much of the time," "a lot," or "usually."

Hit above the belt

When you have a strong difference of opinion, and when your anger level is high, you may just want to hurt the other person. Sometimes you fight dirty and place a punch below the belt. These are accusations or statements about the other person that trigger some aspect of personal vulnerability. Usually the criticism or complaint is something the person cannot change or finds it difficult to change. Some examples:

"If you were prettier, our sex life might be better!"

"Why can't you be smart like your brother?"

"If you would lose 40 pounds, I wouldn't be yelling at you!"

Rarely does the other person respond with, "Gee, you're right! I see your point!" Rather, the person may get back at you with his own below-the-belt zinger. The argument escalates and gets nastier. More stress is created.

While some below-the-belt comments are clearly intended to hurt, other comments may not be intended to "get you." You may have areas of sensitivity that are clear to you but not to others. If a comment hurts or upsets you, and you feel it is below the belt, let the other person know this.

Stop personalizing

A store clerk yells at you, your boss is in a foul mood, a friend is angry with you — any or all of these situations can trigger a good deal of stress. However, any stress that you feel is greatly magnified when you believe you may be the reason for that other person's anger or upset. But you may not be. You may not have done or said anything that would merit the emotional outburst by the other person.

You personalize when you mistakenly assume that your personality or behavior triggered negative reactions in others. If you've been around for any length of time, you quickly learn that everybody has an opinion, and usually a strong one, about everything. And, more often than not, they are negative opinions that these people will happily share with you. When you personalize, you fail to distinguish between opinion and fact. You assume that because people say something or voice a criticism, they are right. Sometimes they are right, but often they are not. Remember, other people may have problems. Many have disordered personalities and other forms of emotional dysfunction. Most are probably under too much stress, and certainly all have priorities that are different from yours. So before you become too distressed, stop and ask yourself, "Am I really the one at fault here?"

Curb your "should" statements

One of the fastest ways of creating interpersonal stress is to use unhealthy "should" statements. As I discuss in Chapter 10, unhealthy "shoulds" are really demands. When used in an interpersonal situation, these "shoulds" insist that others be more like you want them to be. They are really "musts" and "have-tos" that are inflexible and don't tolerate non-compliance. Some examples:

> "People *should not* be late!"

> "People *should* understand my point of view!"

> "Others *should* treat me fairly!"

While these statements can seem pretty reasonable, what makes them less reasonable is the speaker's mindset, which implies a strong demand and insistence, as in "You absolutely *must* treat me fairly!" The expectation is often unrealistic. Other people will always think and act in ways they "shouldn't." They look at their world differently. Maybe they shouldn't, but they do. Accepting this as a starting point can give you some psychological distance. Healthy "should" statements are more flexible, recognizing that others may see the world and our needs differently. To start eliminating many of the unhealthy "shoulds" in your interpersonal interactions, try substituting the phrase "It would be better if . . ." or "I would prefer it if . . ." This can act as a cue, making you more aware of the kinds of "shoulds" you're using.

Have a dress rehearsal

Interpersonal conflict and unnecessary stress most often result when we're caught off guard. Take some time to plan what you want to say to the other person. Sometimes being caught unprepared is unavoidable. Many times, however, you can see it coming and have a chance to ready yourself for the interaction. Do some role-playing. Imagine what you might say and also imagine how the other person might react. Then imagine how you might respond. But go further than this. Also imagine that the other person becomes hostile and difficult. See yourself coping with this situation. Imagine yourself being calm, assertive, and in control. Play with different scenarios until you feel that you're ready for just about anything.

Following are some scenarios to mentally rehearse:

- ✔ You're quite unhappy about some things a coworker has been doing lately, and you want to make it clear that you would like it to stop.

- ✔ You know that a friend is going to ask you for a favor, one you definitely don't want to grant.

- ✔ You have to ask someone to do something that you know is going to make her angry.

Practice may or may not make perfect, but it certainly will reduce your stress.

Lose the battle, win the war

Hardly a week (a day? an hour?) goes by without someone doing or saying something that has button-pushing potential. Your life has no shortage of opportunities for conflict. You may be one of the many people who feel that they have to respond to every slight, insult, imposition, and provocation that comes their way, which can keep you very busy and highly stressed.

While this head-on style should have a place in your repertoire of interpersonal skills, and while sometimes direct confrontation may be the way to go, sometimes avoiding conflict is the option of choice. Where is it written that you must respond to anything that comes your way? Sidestep, let it go, look the other way, keep your mouth shut. The trick is knowing when to act and when to retreat. It means not treating these encounters as though they are all of equal importance. It means choosing your battles wisely, and choosing to lose the less-important battles so you'll be a winner in the longer run. The following is a tool that will help you decide whether you want to fight that battle or let it go.

Use the "stoplight" technique

Using this technique, you put any conflict or disagreement into one of three groups: green-light interactions, red-light interactions, or yellow-light interactions.

You don't have to worry about the green-lighters. They are all the positive interactions you may have; you want as many of these as you can get. On the other hand, red-light interactions are encounters, issues, or situations where you feel something must be done. You must say or do something to deal with the situation.

Yellow-light issues are interactions that fall between the two. These are negative, but not so bad or distressing that they warrant red-light status. Yellow-light items can be let go, avoided, or given the blind eye. Consider the following borderline situations:

Circumstance	*Red-light or Yellow-light? (R or Y?)*
Someone jostles you in a crowd	_____
You're interrupted when you're talking	_____
Someone cuts you off in traffic	_____
Your waiter is slow in serving you	_____
The person in front of you in line is taking too long to pay for her purchase	_____
People are talking during a meeting	_____
Somebody says something stupid	_____
You're treated impolitely	_____

In each of these situations, you have the choice of responding to the situation or ignoring it. Sometimes you might consider one or more of these incidents as "red-lighters." I'm suggesting, however, that you start to put more of these kinds of incidents into the "let it go," yellow-light category. Spare yourself the stress. Are you being unassertive? Not really. Save the emotional energy for the more important stuff.

Just because something goes into a yellow-light category now doesn't mean it can't later be given red-light status. When my son forgot to take out the garbage, I let it go. When it happened a second time, I didn't let it go. Similarly, when the painter didn't show up when he promised, I decided yellow-light. The second time he messed up, red-light.

Chapter 15

De-Stress at Work (And Still Keep Your Job)

● ●

In This Chapter

▶ Identifying your work stress

▶ Understanding why your workday really starts the night before

▶ Taking the stress out of commuting

▶ Building stress management into your workday

▶ Creating a stress-resistant workspace

▶ Bringing less stress home with you

● ●

Stress is a major problem in the workplace. Here's what the scorecard looks like:

✔ A 2012 survey by the American Psychological Association found that two in five employed adults (41 percent) feel stressed out during the workday. This percentage is higher than was reported in a similar 2011 study (36 percent).

✔ Less than half of employees (46 percent) are satisfied with the growth and development opportunities offered by their employers.

✔ A similar 46 percent are dissatisfied with the employee-recognition practices of their employers.

✔ Less than half of employees feel that they are adequately compensated for what they are doing.

✔ Less than half of respondents feel that their jobs give them flexibility in terms of where, how much, and when they work.

If you feel that your job is stressful, you're not alone. Too many workers report that their job is a major source of stress in their lives. The specific sources of work stress can be job insecurity, low pay, impossible clients, a terrible boss, dreadful coworkers, ridiculous deadlines, nasty office gossip, or lost time with family members. So before you're a candidate for a job-burnout seminar (and certainly before you do something you may regret later), read this chapter. You find out how to regroup, get a grip, and minimize your stress at work.

Reading the Signs of Workplace Stress

Some people thrive on the adrenaline rush they get from diving into the "challenges" they face at work. But if you're not stimulated and feel that you're drowning instead, then work stress may be the problem. See if you recognize the signs of work stress. Check off the symptoms that describe you while you're at work:

_____ You're often irritable.

_____ You have trouble concentrating.

_____ You're tired.

_____ You've lost much of your sense of humor.

_____ You get into more arguments than you used to.

_____ You get less done.

_____ You get sick more often.

_____ You care less about your work.

_____ You struggle to get out of bed on workday mornings.

_____ You have less interest in your life outside of work.

At some point in their professional lives, most people will check off one or two of these items. However, if you feel that items on this list *consistently* describe you, or if you feel they have become a major source of distress in your life, you may want to seek professional help. Start by making an appointment with your family physician.

Some things are getting better

Lest you think the workplace is nothing but stress, here's a bit of good news. The 2012 survey by the American Psychological Association cited in the introduction to this chapter also found the following positives:

✔ The percentage of workers whose employers provide sufficient opportunities for them to be involved in decision making, problem solving, and goal setting at work is up significantly from last year (60 percent vs. 53 percent).

✔ A higher percentage of employees report that their employer provides sufficient opportunities for internal career advancement compared to last year (40 percent vs. 35 percent).

✔ A significantly higher percentage of employees feel motivated to do their very best for their employer (72 percent vs. 66 percent).

Knowing What's Triggering Your Work Stress

All right, so you're stressed at work. One of the key steps in managing your work stress is knowing where the stress comes from. Simply check off any of the items below that you feel are a major source of your stress:

- ____ Work overload (too much to do)
- ____ Work under-load (too little to do)
- ____ Too much responsibility
- ____ Too little responsibility
- ____ Dissatisfaction with career/job choice
- ____ Dissatisfaction with current role or duties
- ____ Poor work environment (noise, isolation, danger, and so on)
- ____ Long hours
- ____ Lack of positive feedback or recognition
- ____ Job insecurity
- ____ Lousy pay
- ____ Excessive travel
- ____ Limited chances for promotion
- ____ Discrimination because of gender, race, religion, age, disability, or sexual orientation
- ____ Problems with the boss or management
- ____ Problems with clients
- ____ Problems with coworkers
- ____ Office politics
- ____ A grueling commute

You have others? Jot them down:

_____

_____

_____

Researcher Robert Karasek and his colleagues at the University of Southern California found that the two most stressful aspects of a job are:

- ✔ **Lots of pressure to perform.** Tight deadlines, limited resources, production quotas, severe consequences for failing to meet management's goals — any or all of these can result in a highly pressured work environment.

- ✔ **A lack of control over the work process.** Stress often results when you have little or no input regarding how your job should be done.

Making Positive Changes to Control Your Workplace Stress

Pinpoint your stress triggers at work and then ask yourself to what extent you can remove or at least reduce the impact of that stress. In some cases, you don't have the ability to eliminate some of the sources of stress at work. You may have little control over whether you keep or lose your job. You may dislike what you're doing but feel you can't change jobs. Getting the boss transferred may take some doing, and asking for a raise the day after the company announces downsizing plans may not be in your best interest. What you can change, however, is you. You can manage your stress and reduce its consequences by applying some of the ideas in this section.

Overcoming SNS (Sunday-night stress)

As the weekend winds to an end, you may find yourself dreading Monday morning. The real culprit is Sunday night and your anticipatory anxiety. The irony here is that most often, when you get to the office and spend a couple of hours on the job, your stress level actually lowers. You stop worrying about what your work problems might be, replacing those concerns with distracting involvement and action. You find that the reality is less distressing than your negative anticipation. The trick is figuring out how to cope with the night *before*. Take in these tips:

- ✔ Get to bed a little bit earlier Sunday night. (Many people find that their Sunday-night sleep is their worst sleep of the week.)

- ✔ Avoid eating that late-night heartburn special, which is guaranteed to keep you up 'til Wednesday.

- ✔ Plan something relaxing and enjoyable that you can look forward to on Sunday night — rent a movie, curl up with a good book, or take a bubble bath.

- ✔ Try not to schedule something you dislike as the first thing to do on Monday.

- ✔ If possible, make Monday a day with a lighter workload.

- ✔ Plan something you can look forward to on Monday. (How about lunch with a friend?)

Starting your workday unstressed

Getting to your job in reasonable condition is half the battle. By the time you open your office door (if you have one), you don't want to feel as if you've already fought (and probably lost) several minor skirmishes. Get a leg up on your work stress. Hit the ground running. Start your day the night before. Here's how:

- ✔ **Go to bed.** Not getting enough sleep the night before can be a real stress producer. Your stress threshold is lowered. You're more irritable and find it much harder to concentrate. People and situations that normally wouldn't get to you, now do. Arriving at work tired is a guarantee that this isn't going to be one of your better stress days. (If getting to sleep is a problem, take a look at Chapter 9.)

- ✔ **Get up a tad earlier.** Getting out of bed even a few minutes earlier in the morning can give you enough of a safety net so that you don't find your-self rushing, looking for something at the last minute, and racing out the door with a powdered donut in your hand. Don't add to your stress by running late.

- ✔ **Eat breakfast.** To manage your stress, getting off on the right nutritional foot is important. When you wake up in the morning, as many as 11 or 12 hours have passed since you last ate. Your body needs to refuel. You may feel fine skipping breakfast, but studies show that people who don't eat a reasonable breakfast more often report feelings of fatigue and more stress later in the day. (If you don't know what to eat for breakfast, check out Chapter 9.)

- ✔ **Work out before you shower.** If you can manage it, getting some physi-cal exercise before your workday starts can put you ahead of the game. Hitting the stationary bike, working the stair climber, or even walking briskly around the block can throw you into gear and get you ready for your day. Studies show that even short periods of exercise can speed up your heart rate, increase the amount of oxygen to your brain, and release endorphins, which can exert a calming effect. You're ready for anything your job might throw at you.

- ✔ **Check your schedule.** When you get to the office, spend the first part of your morning organizing your day. Knowing that you're in control of what will get done reduces any uncertainty and anxiety. An important part of this is becoming more organized and managing your time effec-tively. (You may want to take a look at Chapters 7 and 8.)

Generally, most people feel that Monday is the most stressful day of the week. Studies show that you're more likely to have a stroke or heart attack on Monday morning than at any other time during the week.

Calming your daily commute

I remember all those years I commuted to my teaching job about 40 minutes out of the city. I had a "reverse commute." I headed out of the city to the hinterlands, while most other people traveled toward the city. While on the train, I read my newspaper, drank my coffee, relaxed, and had a good old time. Most people have a very different experience. They either battle for a seat (if they're lucky) on a crowded train or sit in stop-and-go traffic for what seems like an eternity. Far from fun, commuting can be a major stressor. Following are some tips to help you reduce the stress of coming from and going to work:

- **Practice some "auto" relaxation.** Try this simple technique while you're caught in traffic or even while stopped for a red light: Using both hands, squeeze the steering wheel with a medium-tight grip. At the same time, tense the muscles in your arms and shoulders, scrunching up your shoulders as if you're trying to have them touch your ears. Hold that tension for about three or four seconds. Then release all of that tension, letting go of any muscle tightness anywhere in your body. Let this feeling of relaxation spread slowly throughout your entire body. Wait a few minutes and do it again.

- **Beat the crowd.** Often, leaving a little earlier or a little later can make a big difference in the quality of your commute. You may get a seat, you may find that the traffic is less congested, and you may find that what was horrific yesterday becomes a lot more endurable.

- **Amuse yourself.** Commuting can seem like a joyless endeavor. You can, however, make your time in your car (or on the subway, bus, or train) productive, entertaining, or at least pleasant.

  Personally, my favorite pastime when I find myself stuck in traffic or sitting on the subway is daydreaming. I relish the opportunity to mentally veg and let my mind wander. Of course, I can also choose from other, more socially redeeming diversions. Have some interesting reading material in your pocket or purse whenever you go out. It can be an amusing little paperback, your e-reader, or an article you've cut out or downloaded but haven't yet found the time to read.

  You can also turn to your digital device for solace. These days the selection of music, video, audio books, and podcasts is incredibly wide. When I'm not daydreaming, I'm plugged into my smartphone learning Spanish. I find these found moments just perfect for a short lesson.

Minimizing your travel stress

Your business travel may be more than getting to and from work. You may spend a lot of time on trains or planes. To many, the idea of travel may seem glamorous. Flying to Paris, Rome, or even Cleveland for work may sound like an adventurous outing, an escape from the stress of the office. But be careful what you wish for. Yes, a little travel can be a welcome change of pace. But travelling a lot is stressful. Just ask anyone who spends many hours in the air each month. A study by the World Bank Group found that nearly 75 percent of respondents said their stress levels were high or very high because of their business travel.

Here are some traps to watch out for and some ideas to help you tame that road-warrior distress:

- ✔ **Bad eating habits**. You can more easily control what and when you eat when you're at home. Sitting in business class (if you can swing it) tempts you with all kinds of wonderful yet not terribly healthful goodies. It can be hard to say no. A study by the Mailman School of Public Health at Columbia University found that those who travel more are more prone to obesity than those who travel less. And, as you know, when you're overweight, you're prone to a host of weight-related risks such as higher blood pressure, diabetes, and elevated cholesterol. The trick is to pre-think what you're going to eat *before* you get into that tempting situation or pick up that restaurant menu.

- ✔ **Little exercise.** Business travel can be pretty sedentary. Obviously sitting on the plane for hours is confining. Get up and walk around from time to time, do some static exercises, and stretch on the flight. Even when you get off the plane, you may have little time for physical activity. Seasoned travelers have figured out how to build some exercise into their travel plans. These days you can find a health club, spa, or gym in every major hotel. Many hotels have exercise videos available. Even if you didn't bring your sneakers, the hotel can often provide you with work-out clothes.

- ✔ **Poor sleep**. While some travelers swear they sleep best in a hotel, many more find that the quality of their sleep is worse. One obvious culprit is jet lag that finds you tossing and turning at 4 a.m. Another is the late nights spent entertaining clients. It may also be getting used to a new bed. A survey conducted by Westin Hotels and Resorts found that 55 percent of frequent business travelers experience sleep deprivation, and

22 percent experience some form of sleep disruption or insomnia. If you can arrive at your destination a day or two earlier, this will help your body adjust. Try not to burn the candle at both ends. Get to bed as early as you can. Watch the alcohol and the caffeine. Some people swear that taking melatonin helps, but the jury is still out on its efficacy. Set your watch for the new time. This will help you adjust psychologically to the change. Drink water both during and after the flight to avoid dehydration. Take a hot bath before you go to bed. Finally, sometimes earplugs and an eye mask can help reduce distractions.

De-stressing during your workday

One of the secrets of effective stress management at work is finding ways to incorporate a variety of stress-reduction techniques into your workday. By using these methods on a regular basis you can catch your stress early — before it has a chance to turn into something painful or worrisome.

Take a look at these surefire strategies to help you nip that stress in the bud:

Cut muscle tension off at the pass

A day at work is usually a day filled with problems, pressures, and demands, with little time to think about your newfound relaxation skills. Your stress builds, and much of that stress takes the form of tension in your muscles. Drain that tension before it becomes more of a problem using some of the techniques I describe in Chapters 4 and 5. This may include trying some relaxed breathing, rapid relaxation, differential relaxation, meditation, imagery, or one of the many other relaxation techniques presented in these chapters. Some potential relaxation opportunities include the following:

- When you finish a phone call
- When someone leaves your office and closes the door
- When you find yourself in a boring meeting

Collect some mileage points

Get up and walk away from your desk — get some coffee or water, or make copies. Walk around a lot, and at lunch be sure to get out of the office and take a quick stroll.

Stand up when you're on the telephone — or, at least some of the time you're on the phone. Walk around. This gives your body a chance to use different sets of muscles and interrupts any buildup of tension.

Stretching and reaching for the sky

For many of you, your days are characterized by long periods of sitting at a desk or stuck in a cramped work area, punctuated only by trips to the coffee or copy machine. Other folks are on their feet all day. In either case, stretching is a great way of releasing any tension that has accumulated in your muscles. Here are some of my favorite ways of stretching:

The cherry-picker

This stretch works well for your shoulders, arms, and back. Sit in your chair, with feet flat on the floor, or stand in place. Raise both of your arms over your head and point your fingers directly toward the ceiling. Now, pretend to reach and pick a cherry on a branch that's just a little higher than your right hand. Stretch that hand an inch or so, and then make a fist. Squeeze for two or three seconds. Relax your hand. Do the same with your left hand. If cherries aren't your thing, consider apples.

The pec stretch and squeeze

This move is good for relieving tightness in your pectoral and deltoid muscles and upper back. Sitting at your desk, or standing up straight, put both of your hands behind your head with your fingers interlaced. Bring your elbows back as far as you can. (See Figure 15-1.) Hold that tension for five to ten seconds, release the tension, and then do it a second and third time. Find various times in your day when you can repeat this stretch.

Figure 15-1:
Unwind a bit with the pec stretch and squeeze.

Illustration by Pam Tanzy

The leg lift

This stretch relieves tension in your quadriceps (in the thighs) and strengthens your abdominal muscles. Sitting in a chair, lift both of your legs straight in front of you. At the same time, curl your toes toward you. (See Figure 15-2.) Hold that tension for five to ten seconds and then let your feet fall to the floor. Repeat two or three times, and at other points in your day.

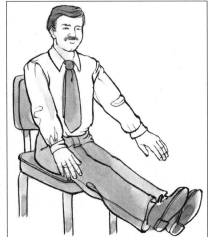

Figure 15-2: The leg lift works your quadriceps and abdominal muscles.

Illustration by Pam Tanzy

The upper-back stretch

This stretch is great for relieving any tension in your upper back. Put your fingertips on your shoulders, with elbows out to the side. Raise your elbows until they are in line with your shoulders (see Figure 15-3). Now bring your elbows forward until they touch or almost touch each other. Hold that position for five to ten seconds and then let your arms fall comfortably to your side. Repeat two or three times, and also at different times in your day.

Tennis (ball) anyone?

When you find that your bodily tension is over the top (better yet, try this before you get to that point), pick up a tennis ball or other soft ball, squeeze it for eight to ten seconds, and then slowly release all the tension in your fingers and hand. Let that feeling of relaxation spread out to the rest of your body. Repeat several times throughout the day.

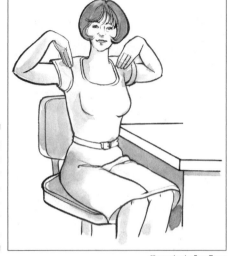

Illustration by Pam Tanzy

For more stretching ideas, take a look at *Fitness For Dummies*, 4th Edition, by Suzanne Schlosberg and Liz Neporent (Wiley), which has dozens of great ways you can stretch and release muscle tension.

Creating a stress-resistant workspace

You may not be able to control every single aspect of your job, but you probably have the power to control your personal work area. Your workspace can (literally) give you a pain in the neck, straining your muscles and tiring your body. The culprit may be an awkwardly placed computer monitor, uncomfortable seating, poor lighting, or simply a totally cluttered desk that's hiding that memo you remember writing and now urgently need. Your life is stressful enough as it is. You don't need your workspace adding to your daily dose of stress. This section shows you a few ways to make your workspace a lot more stress-resistant.

Organizing your desk

How can a neater desk reduce stress? Well, because the source of many types of stress comes from a feeling of being out of control, of being overwhelmed. When your work area looks like a battlefield, you feel the tension growing. And when you can't find that report you need, your stress level soars even higher. By organizing your files and piles, you get a sense (perhaps mistakenly) that there is some order in all the chaos. So, at the end of your workday, straighten things up. Doing so takes only a few minutes, but the rewards are large.

Does your desk look like a wreck?

Your desk can cause you stress. Yes, that polished piece of mahogany (laminated particleboard?) can be your enemy. Take this short true or false quiz to see if it's time to de-stress your desk.

1. When new employees first see your desk, they ask if your office has been vandalized recently. True or false?

2. Your desk smells funny. You distinctly remember leaving half a tuna sandwich under some folders last month, but you haven't seen it since. True or false?

3. If you had to find an important memo on your desk in the next hour, and let's say your job depended on it, you would be better off spending that time calling a headhunter. True or false?

Answering "true" to any of these statements suggests that too much of your stress may be desk-induced.

Lights! Sound! Action!: Creating a more pleasant workspace

Here are a few ways to take some of the stress out of your workspace. I realize that your employer may not be entirely supportive of all of your (or my) stress-reducing efforts. I also realize that if you share a tiny cubicle with three others, it may be hard for you to burn incense, move in a couch, or install a multi-speaker stereo system and personal video player. Nevertheless, see what you can do with some of the following ideas:

- **Soothe yourself with sound.** If you can orchestrate it, listening to calming music at your workspace can unruffle your feathers. Your MP3 player or radio can be the source of relaxing music. Classical music, especially Bach and Mozart, works nicely. If these composers are too highbrow, try one of the "lite" radio stations.

  Recent studies at the University of California found that listening to Mozart, particularly the piano sonatas, can significantly improve a person's ability to reason abstractly. Not only do stress levels go down, but IQ goes up. On the other hand, listening to Philip Glass or Metallica didn't enhance anything.

- **Lighten up.** Although I'm sure that a naked, 300-watt bulb dangling from your office ceiling can provide you with more than enough light, you want more than "just enough light." The right lighting in your workspace can reduce eyestrain and make your environment a more pleasant place to work. Go for soft and indirect lighting. Just make sure you have enough light.

✔ **Create visual resting spots.** Give your eyes — and your mind — a break. At regular intervals, look away from your computer screen or paperwork and focus on a distant object to "stretch your eyes." You can also create visual relief in your office by adding a few interesting objects. For example:

   • Strategically place one or more photographs of those you care about to bring a warm glow to your heart. Better yet, have the picture include a scene — a vacation, a gathering — that reminds you of a happy experience.

   • Place a plant or flowers in your workspace to add an air of beauty and relaxation to your workday. Some plants (such as English ivy and spider plants) are even said to help clean the air of indoor pollutants — an added bonus!

   • Hang some artwork that you find calming and peaceful.

✔ **Be scent-sible.** Fill a bowl with green apples to add a relaxing scent to your office. From time to time I sprinkle a little aftershave on top of the papers in my waste bin. Hey, call me crazy. Be careful, though. Many people are scent sensitive and may be allergic to your favorite smells. If you share your workspace, ask before you sprinkle.

✔ **Have more than one dumbbell in your office.** Keep a set of weights or mini barbells in your office. In a spare moment or two you can rip through a set of reps and feel a bit more relaxed. Alternately, keep an elastic stretcher in your desk that you can use for both your arms and legs.

✔ **Keep a toy chest.** What's an office without a few toys? (Balls that knock into each other . . . a game on your computer . . . that peg-jumping triangle game . . .)

✔ **Don't get tied down.** One of those headsets that attaches to your telephone can free up your hands to do other things, such as look through your e-mail, lift those weights, or play that computer game. The better ones are wireless and let you really move around your office so that you can file, play Nerf basketball, or rearrange your books in order of their color.

Becoming EC (ergonomically correct)

Your desk or workspace can cause stress for other reasons besides disorganization. The problem is, your body wasn't designed to sit and work in one place for long periods of time. When you sit in a stationary position, your muscle groups contract. The blood flow to these muscles may become reduced, resulting in oxygen-deprived muscles. This can lead to pain, strain, muscle aches, and fatigue.

Here are some suggestions that can help you avoid that ergonomic pain in the neck:

- **If you spend long periods of time typing at your computer, where and how you sit becomes important.** The height of your chair in relationship to your keyboard and monitor are important variables to consider in avoiding excessive muscle tension and fatigue in your shoulders, neck, and upper back. You don't want to be straining your neck while looking at your monitor. Adjustability is the key. If your chair or table is too high or too low, replace it. Better yet, find an adjustable chair and table. Seat heights should range from 15 to 22 inches, depending on what your dimensions look like.

- **You should also have some padded support for your lumbar (lower back) region.** The backrest should be full-length, extending some 18 to 20 inches higher than the seat of your chair. If your lower back isn't supported sufficiently, consider a lumbar roll — a cylindrical pillow that fits nicely in the small of your back.

- **Your keyboard should be approximately at elbow level when you're seated.** When using your keyboard, make sure your fingers are lower than your wrists. To avoid repetitive-stress injuries (such as carpal tunnel syndrome), you may want to consider an ergonomically designed keyboard that reduces the strain on your wrists. You should also consider a support for your wrist when you're using your mouse.

- **Having a foot rest is a good way of taking some of the strain off your legs and back, especially if you're short.**

  A study carried out by AT&T on its telephone operators found that switching to easily adjustable tables and chairs resulted in a significant reduction in reported discomfort, particularly in the back, shoulders, and legs.

- **Not all writing instruments are ergonomically equal.** Find a pen that is particularly comfortable to work with. The grip should not result in your fingers becoming easily fatigued.

- **If you spend a lot of time on your feet, finding the correct footwear becomes a necessity.** If you find you have to trade some style for greater comfort, go for the comfort.

Listen to your mother: Sit up straight!

Sometimes your stress comes from the most unlikely of places — your chair, for example. Sitting improperly for long periods of time can result in bodily fatigue, tension, and, ultimately, pain. Sitting actually puts more pressure on your spinal discs than does standing. When you slump or hunch forward, the pressure is even greater. Sit back in your chair with your spine straight. Your lungs now have room to expand, and you place less strain on your back. You may find that you have to invest in a more supportive chair. Spend the bucks — a good chair is well worth the money.

Managing your work time

Having too little time is often cited as a major work stress. In the current economy, time-related stress is magnified by having fewer people to do the same amount of work. Deadlines introduce even more stress. If getting organized is near the top of your list of stress reducers, time management is way up there as well. Chapter 8 describes a number of effective ideas and strategies to help you manage your time. Here are some work-related time-management highlights:

- Work with lists and calendars.
- Prioritize your tasks.
- Batch your e-mails and phone calls.
- Divide and conquer by breaking larger tasks into smaller parts.
- Don't over-commit.
- Delegate when you can.

Nourishing your body (and spirit)

What goes into your mouth from 9 to 5 (or from 8 to 7) can make a big difference in your stress level. Eating the wrong foods, or even eating the right foods in the wrong amounts or at the wrong times, can make it harder for you to cope with the stress in your life. Also, when you eat poorly, your body doesn't work as efficiently as it should. Low levels of blood sugar can result in feelings of anxiety and irritability. Poor eating habits can also leave you unnecessarily fatigued. Over-eating during the workday can leave you lethargic and sleepy. All of this means that you're not in the best position to handle all the pressures and demands you must face at work. Here are some ideas and suggestions that can help make what you eat an ally in your battle against stress, and not the enemy.

Do lunch (with a difference)

Although the days of the three-martini lunch are gone, you can still find the harried worker overloading his or her plate with the kinds of food that ensure a high stress level for the rest of the day. Some suggestions for powering up your body (and not creating a meltdown) for the afternoon:

✔ Never skip lunch — no matter how busy your day gets.

✔ Eat less at your midday meal — no seconds.

✔ Eat stress-reducing foods. (Chapter 8 tells you what they are.)

✔ Don't drink any alcohol.

✔ Skip dessert.

Make your lunch break a stress break

Lunchtime isn't only about eating; it's a great time to work on lowering your stress. Try to get out of your work environment at lunch. Even if the outing is as simple as going for a walk around the block, go. Better yet, find a park, library, waterfront — anything relaxing — that can put you (however temporarily) into a different frame of mind. Find your lunchtime oasis.

The coffee-free coffee break

The caffeine in two cups of coffee can increase your heart rate by as much as 15 beats per minute. It can also make you irritable and nervous. So forgo that third or fourth cup of coffee (and donut). Instead, eat something that adds to your body's ability to cope, such as a:

✔ Cup of low-fat yogurt.

✔ Cup of fruit salad.

✔ Handful of mixed nuts.

✔ Piece of chocolate (one piece!).

✔ Piece of fruit.

✔ Cup of herbal tea.

✔ Glass of water (You need to hydrate!).

✔ And, if you must have that nth cup of coffee, at least try going the unleaded (decaffeinated) route.

Work it out

If you can swing it, one of the better things to do on your lunch break is to hit the gym or health club. Many are conveniently located near work sites. Work up a sweat, take a shower, and then have a quick but nourishing bite to eat.

Avoid the (jelly) beans

Many people remember Ronald Reagan for his significant accomplishments, and rightfully so. What I remember, however, are those jars of jelly beans strategically positioned in his office. While they are admittedly colorful, having gobs of candy at hand may not help you with your stress. A sugar fix energizes you in the short run but leaves you flagging later in the day. You're better off avoiding this and any other candy. If you need a pick-me-up, try to choose something from the list in the nearby sidebar.

Taking Advantage of Company Perks

These days, larger companies and organizations offer a number of services and benefits that can help reduce your stress level. If you're not aware of such perks, ask around or check with your HR office to learn more. Here are some possibilities that might be available to you.

Gyms and health clubs

Exercise is an important source of stress reduction. The tough part is actually *getting to* the gym or health club. Convenience and accessibility make this more likely to happen. If it's close, you're more likely to show up. Many employers have workout facilities right on their premises. This makes it easier for you to show up before work, during your lunch hour, or after work. Even on the coldest, rainiest day, you can manage to take the elevator to the building's health club and get a workout.

Many companies and organizations that don't have exercise facilities on their premises offer corporate discounts at nearby gyms or health clubs.

Flextime

Trying to fit your busy schedule into someone else's can be a major source of work stress. A number of work settings give employees the option of determining which hours they want to work rather than the normal "nine to five." This may take the form of working a condensed week or working a regular week but starting work and leaving work at a preferred hour. The clear benefit to employees is greater control over their time and more flexibility balancing work with home and family. The result is that employees working on a more flexible schedule report being more satisfied with their work experience and less stressed.

Working from home

Many employees feel that their work stress is lessened when they're allowed to work from home even for a small part of their week. The good news is, more and more companies are allowing their employees to work one or more days a week at home. Given the rapid developments in technology, working on your computer or phone at home might not be a negative for the company. Again, the clear advantage for the employee is flexibility and greater control over one's time. The result is increased job satisfaction, higher autonomy, less work-family conflict, and less stress.

Employee assistance programs

Most large employers now offer a variety of personal services. This can range from exercise and weight-loss programs to personal and financial counseling (even stress management!). The individual needs don't necessarily have to involve the workplace. You may need help dealing with your aging parents, overcoming substance abuse, handling a crisis, or addressing legal concerns. And of course you may need help with issues at work. Often employers contract with third-party companies that manage the service. Confidentiality is assured, and your boss need not know what you're up to.

Coming Home More Relaxed (And Staying That Way)

You've had a long, long day. You're tired and dragging your tush. The last thing you want to do is take your work stress home with you. Consider these guidelines to make sure you arrive home in better shape than when you left work:

- **After work, work out.** If early mornings or lunchtimes are impractical times to hit the gym or health club, consider exercising right after work. Take out your frustrations and worries on the stair climber or in a step class. Not only is this mode of venting healthier, you'll still have your job in the morning!

- **Leave your work at work.** One of the more common stress traps is to take your work-related stress and spread it around so that the other parts of your life become stressful. I'm sure you have enough stress at home without importing more stress from your work. If you find that you absolutely have to take work home, be very specific about what you want to accomplish and how much time you want to spend doing it.

Never take work home routinely. And try not to go to work on the weekends unless it's absolutely necessary.

Ah, home sweet home! But is it? Even if your ride home has been relatively non-stressful, opening your front door can lead to a whole new set of challenges. Walking straight into these stressors can catch you off guard and put you into a foul mood. When you get home, be sure to build in a short period of relative quiet — say 15 or 20 minutes — that can help you make the transition into your second world.

All work and no play . . .

When your job is stressful, you may need something positive to look forward to. It can be a quiet dinner at home with family, a night out with friends, a restaurant dinner, a movie, or a concert. It can be as simple as sitting on your couch and catching up on your favorite TV series. It just has to be something that adds a measure of contentment to your life.

An upcoming vacation can also provide a source of positive excitement. Planning that trip can (hopefully) be part of the pleasure. Finding out where to go and what to do can be involving and satisfying. Your trip need not be a long vacation; it can be a mini-vacation where for a day or two you get away. Weekends are especially important times for you to recharge and introduce positive experiences into your life.

Following are some suggestions for low-stress work-home transitions:

- ✔ Take a relaxing bath or shower.
- ✔ Have a drink (one will do).
- ✔ Sit in your favorite chair and simply veg.
- ✔ Listen to some relaxing music.
- ✔ Read a chapter from a good book.
- ✔ Work out.
- ✔ Take a relaxing walk.

If, when you open your door, chaos descends, and it's clear that none of these activities are even remotely possible, you may want to consider implementing some of these relaxing segues before you reach home. I find that sipping a latte and doing the crossword puzzle at the local coffee shop near my home works for me. You can take that walk or spend a few minutes in a local park (with a good book?) before you open your door. You are now ready to cope with the chaos.

Chapter 16

Maintaining a Stress-Resilient Lifestyle

In This Chapter

▶ Building in stress management

▶ Insulating yourself from stress

▶ Getting involved

▶ Learning to have fun

Managing your stress is a little like managing your weight. In the beginning, you're enthusiastic and, with much gusto and determination, you start dropping those pounds. Weeks (or maybe only days) later, your enthusiasm begins to wane. You're even gaining back any weight you may have lost.

Your attempts at stress reduction can easily fall victim to the same fate. Staying motivated and finding the time to practice your stress-management skills is not that easy. You may also find that, even though you now have the right tools, you rarely use them. This common situation is much like belonging to a health club and never going. On most days, especially your busier ones, time flies by, and you don't consider doing anything that even slightly resembles stress management.

This chapter shows you how to avoid many of the pitfalls that often derail your attempts to manage your stress over the long haul. But there's more: Effective stress management means more than having the right stress-reducing tools and techniques. Stress management means knowing how to balance the pressures and demands in your life with positive satisfactions, personal pleasures, and a lifestyle that insulates you from the negative effects of stress. This chapter shows you how to create that balance and how to use these positives to enhance your overall stress resilience.

Making Stress Management a Habit

One of the keys to successful stress management is turning your stress-reducing skills into habits. By integrating some bits of behavior into your daily life, you can reduce your dependence on motivation and pure grit. Think of a habit like brushing your teeth. Rarely do you ask yourself, "Do I feel like brushing my teeth today?" No, you simply brush your teeth (or at least I hope you do). This behavior — brushing your teeth — has become a habit. You repeat this behavior day in and day out, with little effort or resistance on your part. This is what you need to do with your stress-management behaviors. The following sections provide some suggestions for making stress management a habit — one of your better ones.

Making use of found moments

Sometimes, the situation you're in makes you a prisoner of the moment. You can't escape. You have to be where you are, and, to make things worse, you don't have much to do while you're there. You may be waiting in line at the grocery store or (gasp!) at the Bureau of Motor Vehicles. Why not capitalize on these situations and turn them into opportunities to bring some stress management into your life? Sneak in a little relaxed breathing, meditation, rapid relaxation, imagery, coping self-talk, or any of the many other stress relievers I discuss in this book. Many of the stress-management methods in these chapters work quite well, even if you have only a minute or two.

Knowing where to find these moments

When to use your stress-management skills isn't always obvious. Take a look at Table 16-1 for some potential times to use these skills, along with some suggestions of relaxation techniques you may want to use. If you want to find more detailed information on the relaxation techniques listed in the table, turn to Chapters 4 and 5.

Table 16-1   Places to Practice Your Stress-Management Skills

Place	Relaxation Method to Try
Sitting in a boring meeting	Diaphragmatic breathing
Riding a bus, train, or taxicab	Guided imagery
Flying in an airplane	Meditation
Riding an elevator or escalator	Rapid relaxation
Getting your hair cut	Autogenic suggestion

Place	Relaxation Method to Try
Sitting in the dentist's chair	Progressive muscle relaxation
Taking a bathroom break	Deep breathing
Lying in bed, as you fall asleep	Personal imagery

While you're waiting, exhale

Having to wait for somebody or something is one of the better opportunities you have to build some stress relief into your day. Rarely a day goes by in which, at some point, you don't find yourself having to wait. Here is just a partial list of those all-too-common waiting opportunities. Try to take advantage of these opportunities in your own life.

- ✔ Waiting at a stoplight
- ✔ Waiting for an elevator
- ✔ Waiting in traffic
- ✔ Waiting for a train or bus
- ✔ Waiting for the microwave to cook your food
- ✔ Waiting on hold on the phone
- ✔ Waiting in your doctor's office
- ✔ Waiting for a TV commercial to be over
- ✔ Waiting for a file to download
- ✔ Waiting in line at the supermarket
- ✔ Waiting for your turn at the ATM
- ✔ Waiting in line anywhere

Relaxed breathing, deep breathing, imagery, meditation, and rapid relaxation, and other "instant de-stressers," are some of the short, fast, and effective ways of taking the edge off your stress whenever you find yourself waiting.

Using a "stress dot"

A *stress dot* is nothing more than a sticker to remind you to keep stress management an active part of your life. Stress dots can be useful tools in triggering your memory. To create a stress dot, look at your local office-supply store for very small circles of brightly colored sticky paper. (About ⅛-inch in diameter should do it.) Or you can make your own stress dots by cutting small circles out of anything with an adhesive back. Place this dot in a strategic spot, so that it becomes a cue or prompt and can signal you to do something stress-relieving.

Here are some places that may work for you:

- ✔ The face of your watch
- ✔ Your watchband
- ✔ Your steering wheel
- ✔ Your refrigerator door
- ✔ Your computer
- ✔ Your keyboard
- ✔ Your e-reader or tablet
- ✔ Your pen
- ✔ Your coffee cup
- ✔ Your cell phone
- ✔ Your television set
- ✔ A light switch

Remembering Your Ps (Prompts) and Cues

In life, sometimes you need a little reminding. You need someone or something to nudge you to do things. In your younger days, your parents probably filled this role. (And what a fine job they did!) These days, however, you may find that you have to do your own reminding. This section provides you with some ways you can remind yourself to use your new stress-management tools. All you have to do is use your stress prompts and stress cues.

The idea here is to use naturally and frequently occurring behaviors — your prompts and cues — as reminders. The sight of my front door reminds me that I need to take out my keys. Getting into a car triggers me to fasten my seatbelt. These behaviors are automatic. I don't have to think about them much. The same principle can help you build in ways of managing your stress. Whenever you're presented with a prompt or cue, follow it up by doing an instant de-stresser exercise — deep breathe, meditate, use some imagery or rapid relaxation, and so on.

Here are some common stress prompts and cues to get you started:

- Ending a phone call
- Looking at your watch
- Shutting your office door
- Stopping at a stop sign
- Listening to your telephone messages
- Turning off your computer
- Turning off your TV
- Turning off a light

Making an appointment with yourself

When you schedule something, you're more likely to follow through with it. You almost always show up for appointments with your doctor, your dentist, your lawyer, your accountant, your dinner date, and the person who cuts your hair. So why not use that same principle for other things in your life, like managing your stress? Try some of the following suggestions:

- **Schedule regular times during the week when you will do something to manage your stress.** Make Thursdays Lunch-with-a-Friend Day. Schedule Monday and Wednesday evenings as health club times.

- **Make your coffee break a stress break.** Set aside a few minutes mid-morning and mid-afternoon to drain some of that accumulating tension from your mind and body.

- **Commit part of each lunch hour to some stress-reducing activity.** Go to the gym or try meditating in a nearby park for 20 minutes.

- **Designate specific chunks of time during your week as times when you do the kinds of activities you normally wouldn't.** While these activities will be specific stress-management techniques, they can also be activities that are diverting and relaxing — listening to music, taking in a film, going for a swim, and playing squash or tennis.

Logging in once in a while

Try this suggestion for at least an entire day. On your laptop, tablet, or smart-phone, or simply on an index card or scrap piece of paper, make a note of when you did something to reduce your stress. Be brief, making sure that your record-keeping doesn't add to your existing stress level. Table 16-2 shows some sample entries.

Table 16-2	A Sample Stress-Management Log	
Time	*Where*	*What I Did*
9:30 a.m.	Bedroom	Meditated for 15 minutes
10:20 a.m.	Kitchen	Practiced deep breathing
Lunchtime	On the street	Did some stretching
3:30 p.m.	In the car stuck in traffic	Did some rapid relaxation
4:30 p.m.	Waiting for the elevator	Practiced relaxed breathing

You get the idea. You may find that by monitoring your stress-management attempts, you'll become more conscious of doing them and of doing them more often. Try it.

Becoming a freelance, unpaid, stress-management guru

The topic of stress frequently comes up in conversation, and if it doesn't, you can always bring it up yourself. When you do, you may find that most people have a great interest in your stress-management activities. People will ask you how you handle your stress. Tell them. In fact, show them. One of the best ways of mastering something is by teaching it to others. Teach a friend or interested listener one or more of your favorite stress-management techniques. You'll begin to feel somewhat proprietary about these tools and, as a result, feel more motivated to use them yourself.

Finding Your Oasis (Sand Optional)

To effectively manage your stress, you need a place where you can escape the pressures and demands of everything going on around you. In fact, you need several such places. Ideally, these should be places that are quiet, peaceful, and relaxing. These places become your oases — your places of refuge in a stress-filled world. Places like this usually aren't that easy to come by. A wood-paneled study or a Zen garden may only be wishful figments of your imagination. The reality is, the place you use as an oasis may be your bathroom or your bedroom. But these can just as easily serve as places you retreat to when your soul needs a little peace and tranquility. Continue to add to your list of peaceful places. Your oases don't need to be magnificent. All you need is a place where, for at least a small part of the day, you won't be disturbed. In the following sections, I start you off with some suggestions.

Creating an inner sanctum

Try to create a space within your home that you really like to spend time in. Have at least one feel-good room or an area that is emotionally welcoming. Your private corner can be anyplace — maybe a window seat, a warm kitchen, an inviting bedroom, or a cozy study — where you can close a door and feel hidden away from it all, where you feel unhurried and unhassled. This place is your inner sanctum, a space within a space to which you can retreat when the world outside feels less than hospitable, a place where you can sit, read, write, think, meditate, or just daydream. Designate this space as somewhere that you don't worry, pay bills, answer the phone, or do anything else that could even remotely increase your level of stress. The rewards of having a quiet retreat are immense.

Taking a bath

The bathroom may be the only room in your house where you feel like you can lock the door and be alone. One of the many things you can do in a bathroom is take a bath. A hot bath is a wonderful place to relax and totally let go. Stretched out and surrounded by warmth, in a bath you can give yourself permission to relax. Adding some Epsom salts or essential oils can make your bath even more pleasurable, especially if you're feeling tense or achy. Introducing some soft lighting, gentle music, and a soothing drink can make this place feel like heaven.

Enjoying a walk in the park

Most communities have wonderful parks where you can stroll aimlessly, taking in the activity around you or becoming lost in your own thoughts and images. In the larger parks, you can often find yourself quite alone, one of the few places where there is no one else around. But the park doesn't have to be large. Some are no more than a small patch of grass, a few trees, and a bench or two. When I can, I find that walking through the park on my way to my office or coming home after work is a wonderful way of mellowing out and disassociating from my busy day.

Jogging, bicycling, or inline skating in the park are great ways of combining exercise with a sense of solitude. You can bring headphones or, better yet, simply enjoy being alone with your thoughts.

Seeking sanctuary

We tend to think of houses of worship as religious sanctuaries, places for prayer. And, of course, they are. But churches and temples can also be visited for non-religious forms of expression. You can reflect, meditate, or simply lose yourself in reverie. They are quiet and often softly lit — ideal settings in which to be alone. Many churches and temples are quite majestic and sweeping in their architecture, inspiring and revitalizing even the most tired spirit. And, except for during midnight mass and Yom Kippur, your chances of finding an empty pew are excellent.

Becoming a lobbyist

Many hotels, especially some of the older ones, are wonderful buildings that can be a treat to spend time in. You won't be alone here, but chances are you won't be bothered. Although many people are coming and going, don't be surprised if you find a comfortable chair situated in a relatively quiet part of the lobby.

Losing yourself in the shelves

Bookstores, especially the larger ones, can be marvelous places to sit, write, and escape the pressures all around you. I consider my local bookstore my personal library. It's a great place to escape to a quieter mode. The catch? It can be a madhouse on weekends. On good days, however, the unhurried, not crowded floors, lined with wonderful books, become an inviting setting to which you can retreat.

And don't forget the public libraries. Libraries, especially the larger ones, are great places to spend an hour or more in relative solitude. Large tables, vast spaces, and enforced quiet all contribute to an ideal place to work, think, and imagine.

Accentuating the Positive(s) with Stress Buffers

When you think of reducing your stress, most often you think of ways of eliminating, or at least minimizing, the negatives in your life. Get rid of as many of those unpleasant pressures and demands as you can, and your life will be much less stressful. However, creating a lifestyle that is truly stress-resilient means not only eliminating the negatives but also finding and building in positive sources of satisfaction and pleasure that compensate for the negatives you haven't been able to eliminate. I call these your *stress buffers*. They include a wide range of activities, involvements, and commitments that bring positive feelings to your life.

One of the keys to creating a stress-resilient lifestyle is living more than a one-dimensional life. This means looking at your lifestyle and figuring out what's missing. Complete the following quiz to determine whether your lifestyle is providing you with the stress buffers that are important in helping you resist the negative effects of stress. Respond to the following statements with "very much," "so-so," or "not really":

✔ I have family I can rely on when I need to.

✔ I have friends I can talk to when problems arise.

✔ I have friends I enjoy spending time with.

✔ I have hobbies and/or interests I enjoy.

✔ I look forward to certain activities during the week.

✔ I get satisfaction from the work I do.

✔ I find my life satisfying and involving.

✔ My spiritual beliefs give me support and comfort.

✔ I enjoy meeting new people.

✔ I like trying new things.

✔ I take a vacation regularly.

✔ I enjoy nature and the outdoors.

✔ I frequently do things that are fun.

✔ I have an adequate income.

✔ I do things for others who are less fortunate.

The following sections discuss various stress buffers and show you how they can help you lead a more fulfilling, multi-dimensional life.

Connecting with Others

Having people in your life you can talk to, complain to, cry with, and laugh with — not to mention go see a movie with — represents an important stress buffer in your life. Connecting with family members and friends becomes one of the more important ways you can insulate yourself from stress and strengthen your ability to cope.

Family: The ties that bind

Although at times your family may seem like the source of much of your stress, for most people, family members can be an important source of caring and emotional support. After all, few other people in your life know you as well and stand by your side when the chips are down. Being with family and sharing memories of times past can provide you with a sense of being part of something larger, something that feels warm and comforting. Family events such as birthdays, anniversaries, marriages, christenings, and bar and bat mitzvahs all bring with them a sense of repeated experience and family reunion and provide you with a sense of emotional connectedness that can buffer you from stress.

However, as you well know, maintaining family ties and holding on to those good feelings takes some effort. Make the time to be with those you care about. Work at making these relationships positive and satisfying. It's worth it.

Some research data verifies what seems intuitively true — that being in a good marriage can have stress-reducing benefits. A study conducted by Pamela Jackson, Ph.D., a sociologist at Indiana University in Bloomington, Indiana, found that, in supportive marriages, the amount of stress experienced by spouses in troubling times was significantly less than that reported by individuals in less-supportive relationships. These individuals were less likely to become depressed when their lives became highly stressful. Other research supports these findings. It appears that being in a harmonious marriage results in fewer psychological and biological signs of stress.

You need a Monica, a Rachel, or a Chandler

When you ask people what they value most in life, near the top of that list, right under family, is friends. Most of us regret, or will come to regret, that we neglect our friendships at the expense of other, often less-rewarding activities. We wish we had spent more time with friends, called them more often, and worked harder to maintain and nurture our friendships.

Your friendships are probably your most important stress buffers. Friends provide company for you, bring you pleasure, and help relieve feelings of loneliness. Good friends listen to your problems, give you guidance, and support you emotionally. They are your therapists.

People with a strong social support system report experiencing less stress and are better able to cope with the stress they do feel. Studies show that friendships can insulate you from the effects of stress.

 Having friends can lower your blood pressure, improve your immune system, and even increase your life span. In one research study of some 7,000 women conducted over 17 years, the researchers found that those women who had few friendships had a higher risk of dying from all kinds of cancer. Having good friends, it appeared, was even more protective than being in a marriage. Another study found that among patients with coronary heart disease, those individuals who were neither married nor had close friends were more likely to die in a five-year period than were those who were married, had a close friend, or both. It seems that having friends and family can reduce the destructive effects of stress on your body.

Doing Something, Anything

Finding satisfaction in a hobby or interest is an important way of reducing your stress. Any hobby — whether it's collecting beer cans or stuffed animals, doing some bird-watching, or whatever else suits your fancy — can be absorbing and diverting. The fact is, it really doesn't matter that much what you do. It's a big mistake to reject or abandon a hobby because you think it's unworthy or less esteemed by others. The fact that you're doing something is what counts. Leave your ego out of it.

I have a friend who collects baseball cards. He can spot a Mickey Mantle rookie card at 30 paces. He visits the card shows, chats with the dealers and other buyers, and generally seems to have a fine old time. He looks forward to arranging his new acquisitions, merging and purging with obvious glee. Though I have little interest in collecting these cards, I must admit that I'm a little envious of the pleasure and sense of satisfaction my friend feels about these 2x3-inch colored squares of cardboard.

For him, and for countless others, having a hobby or pastime is an incredibly positive experience that provides joy and interest and acts as a stress buffer, insulating them from much of their daily worries and hassles. When you're engrossed in a hobby or pleasurable pastime, the time seems to fly by, and, often, you're with others who share your interest.

But what about you? Ask yourself how you spend your spare time and if any activities or involvements could add to your life.

Joining the group

Every community has groups and organizations that can put you together with like-minded people. By sharing a common interest, you establish a natural bond that can transform your relationships with others in the group from mere acquaintanceships to good friendships. Here are some groups you may want to consider joining:

- Your local church or temple
- Your child's school (attend PTA meetings, be a class parent, organize a fundraiser, serve on safety patrol)
- Your neighborhood association
- A special interest group (a book group, a nature group, a music group, a political group, a singles group, and so on)

Learning a thing or two

You have numerous opportunities to attend classes on something you find interesting. Can't think of where to go? Here are some suggestions:

- Local universities, colleges, and community colleges, which often have non-credit continuing-education programs
- The Y
- Language schools
- Arts and crafts schools, which offer classes on everything from scrapbooking to painting and photography
- Cooking schools
- Writing centers
- Aerobics groups
- Dance schools
- Music schools

Getting in the game

Or, consider getting involved in a sport or game. Lest you've forgotten, here's a short list of the more popular offerings:

- Bridge
- Tennis
- Golf
- Poker
- Mah-jongg
- Bowling
- Lawn bowling (why not!)
- Billiards
- Swimming
- Gymnastics
- Ice skating
- Baseball or softball
- Basketball
- Volleyball
- Hockey
- Bingo
- Scuba diving

Where to sign up? You can start with the local Y or check out the bulletin boards at your gym. I found an equally matched tennis partner by looking at the "players wanted" board at my neighborhood tennis courts. And, of course, you can always search online.

Find your community online

The Internet can be a marvelous tool to help you connect with people who want to do the same thing you want to do. With a little searching, you can locate websites that ask you to enter your interest (bingo, bongos . . .) and tell you where to go to pursue your interest. Sites such as meetup.com will put you in touch with others who share your interests. My wife, an avid folk dancer, wanted to join up with others who also enjoyed folk dancing. Sure enough, she looked online and found existing groups and the names of people who wanted to start groups.

Accomplishing something

Sometimes just getting something done is stress relieving. It doesn't have to be big things. Small accomplishments can often produce impressive emotional payoffs. They can take the form of self-maintenance tasks, errands, or any simple chores. Here are some suggestions. You can add your own ideas.

- Calling back some friends
- Fixing something
- Cleaning something
- Going shopping
- Cooking a meal
- Going to the cleaners
- Writing in a journal
- Re-arranging your closet
- Straightening a room
- Getting your hair cut
- Washing the dishes
- Folding and putting away laundry
- Taking the dog for a walk

At first blush, many of these activities may seem like *work*. Yet once you start and finish any of these tasks, you may be surprised at just how pleased you are and how good you feel. The trick is just jumping in and starting.

Becoming a volunteer

One of the better stress buffers is becoming a volunteer. You can start small. Help out at your local library, church, or synagogue. Help those who are housebound, or be a mentor to a child in the school system. You have no shortage of ways to help others. If you're short on ideas, take a look at the list of volunteering suggestions in Chapter 11.

Getting a pet

Having a pet is a marvelous way of combating your stress. Convincing data shows that pets can indeed reduce your stress and serve as important sources of emotional comfort. The presence of a pet in the room can put you at ease, evoke feelings of caring and tenderness, and provide you with a companion. Pets can lower your blood pressure, make you feel more relaxed, and distract you from your own day-to-day worries and concerns. And because they don't complain, have opinions to disagree with, or know how to operate the television remote, pets trigger less conflict and friction than do the people who live in your house. As a bonus, they can even take care of any roach or rodent problems.

Cultivating calm with gardening

How many times have you heard of a gardener going ballistic? In fact, some scientific literature documents the positive, stress-buffering effects of gardening. Gardening is now widely thought of as a form of therapeutic intervention in many medical and psychiatric settings. Author and gardener Linda Yang points out that the word "paradise" comes from the Greek "paradeisos," meaning "private park of kings" — where peace and beauty dwell amid fruit trees and flowers.

Working in a garden can be satisfying. You can find something soothing and peaceful about potting a petunia or tending to a tomato. Why? Because you're in control. The pace is your own, with no one telling you what you're doing wrong or giving you a deadline. It's just you and nature. Your garden doesn't need to be extensive. It can be a small terrace, a shared plot of ground, an indoor herb garden in the winter months, or simply several houseplants that you water and prune. A flowerbox works well, too — the effects are the same. A few square yards of paradise can bring a large measure of tranquility to your life.

Getting in the kitchen

I'm not a particularly good cook, but I do enjoy the process. I find it involving, creative, and incredibly relaxing. Maybe it's the kitchen or my love of eating, but I find tinkering with a recipe to be very satisfying. Baking is especially comforting because of the wonderful aromas that emanate from the oven. Eating the end result is great fun, too. Of course, this may not be the most exciting idea for you if you already spend hours in the kitchen supplying the rest of your family with sustenance. In that case, making reservations may be your idea of a good way to relieve stress.

Becoming a bookworm

Ah, the joys of a riveting pot-boiler, seething romance, or faithful classic. Reading a good book is one of the more pleasurable ways of reducing your stress. Whether you're lying in bed, lying on the beach, or curling up in your favorite chair, reading can slow your pulse, lower your blood pressure (it's been proved), and distract you from the cares and worries around you. Reading can transport you to another world.

But reading provides more than distraction. It can also stimulate your mind and your imagination. It can enrich your experience, giving you new information, ideas, and interests. It can even have social benefits. Join a book group, and reading puts you in touch with others who share your interests.

Books are relatively inexpensive, portable, and incredibly convenient. You can read on the train, plane, waiting for a salesperson or your dentist, or any other time you find yourself with some moments to spare.

These days, if you're short of time and can't get to the bookstore, you can use your computer or tablet to order or download a book. You can find virtually (no pun intended) any book online and have it sent to you or download it to your e-reader, often at a greatly reduced price. Turn off your TV set. Read a book.

Remembering to enjoy the little things

When we think of the things that bring us pleasure in life, we usually come up with the big stuff: getting that job promotion, taking that dream vacation, winning the Nobel Prize. You tend to overlook the smaller satisfactions and enjoyments that happen regularly. For me, having that first cup of coffee in the morning, reading the newspaper, and walking by the park on my way to the subway are very enjoyable. In and of themselves, these events are no big deal, but they add up, and together they contribute to a broader positive picture. Here is a list of some simple pleasures that can add to the quality of your life:

- The smell of newly cut grass
- Hand-written letters
- Spring rain
- New snow on a moonlit street
- The smell of the air after rain
- The fragrance of someone's perfume
- The warmth of the sun

✔ The sound of rustling leaves in the fall

✔ The smell of burning wood

✔ The sound of children laughing

✔ The crackling of an open fire

✔ The smell of freshly baked cookies

✔ The sound of birds chirping in the morning

✔ Sunrises and sunsets

✔ Completing a task

Getting out of the house

When was the last time you did one of the following?

✔ Went out for dinner

✔ Went to a movie

✔ Went dancing

✔ Saw a play

✔ Heard a concert

✔ People-watched

✔ Went to a nightclub

✔ Strolled in the park

✔ Went shopping just for fun

✔ Explored a new neighborhood

✔ Saw a dance performance

✔ Went to a sports event

✔ Had lunch with friends

✔ Went to a museum

✔ Went to an art gallery

Take the time to find joy in the little things and to explore some new avenues — and reduce your stress while you're at it.

Regrouping and Getting a Grip

Vacations are a wonderful way of regrouping and regaining some perspective on your life. That two-week vacation in the mountains or at the ocean can be glorious. The trouble is, by about 3 p.m. on the Monday of your return, you're ready for another vacation, which unfortunately, is now 50 weeks away. Rather than depending on that major vacation to provide you with a timeout, you're better off scheduling some minor or mini-vacations that you can scatter throughout the year.

Try building in more frequent, shorter trips and vacations. These can take the form of half days away, day trips, sleepovers, weekends, and long weekends. Think of your time away as a safety valve that needs to be opened from time to time. The trick is to evenly distribute these getaways throughout your year, before the pressure builds.

Pre-schedule time away

The most common reason people give for not getting away is not having enough time. They would love to get away, but something always comes up. But if you wait for that perfect time, you may wait forever.

Start by assuming that no perfect time will ever arrive for you to get away. But make a commitment to getting away anyway. Rather than reacting to an imposed schedule, create a time-away schedule early on that ensures that you actually follow through with your plans. Build in some getaway time, and make it a higher priority in your life. Sit down with your calendar and block out some major time periods and some smaller time periods when you plan to be away. Spread out the dates to cover various times of the year so that you don't have to find the time — it's already scheduled.

Build a getaway file

If you're going to escape, you need to know where to escape to. Isn't it amazing how little you know about getaways even a few hours away from home? Begin collecting information about places you can escape to. Start with the wonderful books on local travel at your bookstore. You can find books describing all kinds of trips, places to stay, and things to do and see. Include in your file favorite places friends have told you about, articles from newspapers and magazines, and brochures. You can also explore the unlimited possibilities of the Internet, and perhaps keep a virtual folder of bookmarked travel sites. Create two categories: one for shorter, one- or two-day trips, and a second for longer trips. The websites, books, articles, and brochures themselves can encourage greater interest and excitement and give you some new ideas about where to go and what to do.

Take a mini-vacation

For an escape to be short, you have to be able to get there in an hour or less. The plan is to get away from your home for a few hours or a full day and return the same day. Even without a car, you can get out of town. If you live in a major city, you can find day excursions via public transit to places and sites away from where you live. You may be amazed at what there is to see and do — all in a day or less.

One of my favorite short trips out of the city is a visit to a state park and forest about an hour away. In the middle of the park is a lake where you can rent canoes and small sailboats by the hour. I usually bring a picnic. It serves as a wonderful day away.

Here are some other ideas you may want to try:

- ✔ **Check into a hotel or spa.** A night or two in a nice hotel can be energizing. Weekend rates are usually a lot cheaper than weeknights, too. Pretend you're a tourist. Or, if you'd rather, you never have to leave the hotel at all. If you want to get out of town, a health spa can be just the thing to revitalize your tired juices.

- ✔ **Take a hike.** Hiking in natural surroundings can have a soothing, calming effect. The views can be spectacular. On a hike, you won't find any elevators, fax machines, or computers. And you may see animals besides pigeons, squirrels, rats, and roaches. Many routes allow you to park your car and follow a trail that brings you back to your starting point. Organizations such as the Sierra Club are not only a good way of obtaining information about hikes but also can put you into contact with other people if you're short of company.

- ✔ **Take your bike.** Although I'm sure you can bike somewhere in your neighborhood, finding a less congested road or a new vista may have greater appeal. After you get out of town, you'll find many bicycle trails and open roads that offer great scenery and little traffic. If you don't already have one, a bicycle rack for your car is a terrific investment.

✔ **Look for water.** If you live near a body of water — and it doesn't have to be large — a day by the water can be a wonderful escape from the congestion and confusion of your usual day-to-day life. Even if the water is too cold for swimming, strolling on a beach or a promenade above the water can be marvelously relaxing. Many people forget about the shore during the off-season, but this is a mistake. In the spring, fall, and winter months, the beaches are beautiful and also wonderfully empty.

✔ **Pick some fruit.** One of my family's favorite outings is to visit one of the many farms about an hour or so away from where we live. Depending on the season, we pick apples, blueberries, strawberries, or raspberries. Then we go home and figure out what to do with them. Pies are the simplest project, but we have recently ventured into the world of jams and jellies. Many of the farms offer other perks, such as horseback riding and the wonderful taste of freshly pressed cider.

✔ **Stay in a country inn.** Small country inns and out-of-the-way bed and breakfasts provide the ideal contrast to the bigness and busyness of the city. You're away from the boring motels and hotels that dot the thru-way. Meandering through country roads and byways, you can find that unique, one-of-a-kind hideaway that will not only provide you with a bed but also feed you with home-cooked specialties.

On the other hand, if you live in the country, going into the city and taking in the sights, maybe seeing a show, and people-watching can be a refreshing change of pace.

Other places you may consider visiting include the following:

✔ Botanical gardens

✔ Nature conservatories

✔ Mansions and estates open to the public

✔ Public gardens

✔ Country auctions

✔ Vineyards

✔ County fairs

Living Mindfully in the Present

When you think about it, much of the stress you experience comes from either getting upset about things that have happened in the past or worrying about what will happen in the future. You worry about what you did or didn't say to a difficult boss or irritating coworker, or agonize about that upcoming meeting or deadline. The present, alas, gets lost in the shuffle, as does any enjoyment you could be experiencing. In Chapter 6 I place much value on becoming mindful of the present. If you can train yourself to live in the present, focusing on what is happening to you right at this moment, your life can be much less stressful. You may also find that your life slows down, and time passes less quickly.

Life in the present, however, can be pretty ordinary. Everyday experiences may be nothing to write home about. Yet valuing this ordinariness can add satisfaction to your day. For example, eating a meal is a routine thing to do. But instead of automatically rushing through it, try to approach your eating with a different mindset. (Refer to Chapter 6 for suggestions for mindful eating.)

Here are some additional "ordinary" things you do that can become satisfying and valued. Try adopting a mindful approach to each or all of these:

- ✔ Taking a shower
- ✔ Walking to work
- ✔ Eating a treat
- ✔ Drinking a cup of coffee
- ✔ Getting dressed
- ✔ Brushing your teeth
- ✔ Making your bed
- ✔ Listening to music
- ✔ Doing some exercise

Your goal here is not accomplishing anything (though this may be a benefit). Your goal is just the *being* there and the *doing*. By turning these tasks and chores into mindful ones, you can have a different experience.

You may think that focusing only on the present moment should be pretty easy. But it's not. Your mind finds it difficult to stay in the present. Your past and your future are like magnets, pulling your attention away from what you're doing right now. But if you can overcome the distractions and focus on what is happening in the present moment, you find that you're less distressed about things going on in your life and that you feel more relaxed and less tense.

In a wonderful section of Jon Kabat-Zinn's *Wherever You Go, There You Are: Mindfulness Meditation in Everyday Life*, the author describes how he mindfully cleaned his kitchen stove with the help of a Bobby McFerrin album. The result was fairly poetic, with the rhythms of cleaning and scrubbing mingling with singing, dancing, and a general total involvement in what is normally seen as a mundane, forgettable task. Any activity can be done mindfully.

Doing your laundry, washing the dishes, making the beds, vacuuming the rug, opening a can of soup, even eating — all of these can be done more attentively, with greater awareness of every aspect of the task.

Try eating with chopsticks once in a while. If you're not in the habit of eating with chopsticks, it will slow down the eating process and get you to pay more attention to what you're eating and how you eat it. If you're looking at a chunk of meat, cut it up into edible bites first. As a bonus, you'll eat less — and weigh less — if you make this a habit. If chopsticks aren't your thing, try eating with your other hand. This trick slows you down equally well.

Taking Your Fun Seriously

Ask yourself when you last did something that was pure fun. When was the last time you just played? Or did nothing? Sometimes, doing nothing or having fun is just what the doctor ordered. It may seem sinful and decadent, and you may feel your guilt level rising just thinking about it, but taking time to do nothing really is an important part of your stress-management program. Playing or goofing off can distract you from your problems. It can give you time to regroup and regain some equilibrium. You return to your world refreshed and ready to jump back into the fray.

"That's great," you respond, "I've spent half of my life playing around and goofing off, so I must be well on my way to being totally stress-free." Not quite. I'm not talking about the time you spend avoiding, procrastinating, and otherwise neglecting all those things you would be better off doing. The secret of stress-reducing goofing off and play is goofing off or playing at the right time. It means building in play time and time for yourself with nothing to do.

For example, you can see that a project you've been working on for weeks will be finished later that day. That evening you can do any number of things — paint the house, reupholster chairs, or clean out all the clutter from your basement. What you'd really like to do, however, is watch the ball game. Do it. And don't feel guilty.

Be careful not to equate playing games with having fun. If your golf swing or backhand is causing you grief, or if your weekly bridge game leaves you feeling homicidal, you may not be having lots of fun. Fun means thoroughly enjoying yourself. Remember, your stress level should go down, not up.

Part V
The Part of Tens

Ever wonder how your job ranks on the stress scale? Head to www.dummies.com/extras/stressmanagement for a free bonus list of ten super-stressful jobs and find out whether your job is one of them.

In this part . . .

- ✔ Ever notice how some people just don't seem to get stressed out? Discover the top ten habits of effective stress managers and ways you can put those habits into practice in your life.

- ✔ Despite your best efforts to live mindfully, stay organized, and manage your time, life happens. Even happy occasions can quickly become fraught with stress. Find out the ten most stressful life events and what you can do to minimize their impact on your stress level.

Chapter 17

Ten Habits of Highly Effective Stress Managers

In This Chapter
▶ Taking care of your mind and body
▶ Making strong interpersonal connections

The following qualities are, I think, the most important skills and behaviors for reducing stress and creating stress resilience. How many of these describe you? If you can't check off all (or any!) of the items, don't worry — you can change old habits and learn new ones. Managing your stress is not a magical process. It's about mastering new behaviors and finding new ways of looking at yourself and your world.

Knowing How to Relax

You need to know how to let go of tension, relax your body, and quiet your mind. There is no one right way to relax. For some people, meditation, focused breathing, and imagery may be the favored path. Others may prefer a more active approach, with techniques such as progressive muscle relaxation. If you're a little rusty on how to use these tools, take a look at Chapters 7 and 8.

Attaining a state of greater relaxation need not be limited to formal approaches. Any activity that distracts you from the stressors of your world can be relaxing. It can take the form of a hot bath, a stroll in the park, a cup of coffee (decaffeinated), or a good book or favorite TV program. All can provide a relaxing escape from stress.

Eating Right and Exercising Often

The foods you eat can play an important role in controlling your stress levels — or making them worse. When you're under stress, you tend to be far less vigilant about what goes into your mouth. You should be eating foods that reduce your stress. Unfortunately, you're probably craving foods that aren't on anybody's list of healthy choices — sugary foods, fatty foods, and salty foods (not to mention caffeine and alcohol). And even if you manage to eat the "right" foods, chances are, if you're under stress you will overeat or, at times, under-eat.

Eating the wrong foods can affect how well you deal with stress. Your body needs a balanced, healthy diet to maximize your ability to cope. This means giving your body the right nutrients that supply you with adequate reserves of vitamins, minerals, and other essential elements. And don't forget the liquids. Your body needs to be adequately hydrated. See Chapter 9 to get more specific recommendations about which foods best prepare you to cope with stress.

And don't forget about exercise. Engage in some form of physical activity regularly — at least twice a week and, when possible, more often. It can be participating in a sport or working the treadmill. Your exercise regime doesn't have to be fancy or over-done. Walking whenever you can is one of the more overlooked forms of exercise. If you belong to a health club or gym, even better. The secret of exercise is building it into your life — scheduling it. And make it convenient. If you can find a gym near your home or where you work (or even *at* work), that's great. The chances of your showing up there are now far greater. Just do it!

Getting Enough Sleep

Getting enough sleep is a key element in managing your stress. Too little sleep can leave you tired and drained of energy. Your body and mind aren't prepared to tackle stress. Most people do well on seven or eight hours per night, but individual needs vary. You can usually tell if you're getting enough sleep if you wake up rested and can get through the day without feeling tired. If you're unsure about how much sleep you need, experiment on the weekend or on vacation, gradually lengthening your sleep time and seeing how much better you feel. By the way, getting *too much* sleep (more than eight hours) may not be so good for you, either.

Basic sleep hygiene can help. Try to get to bed at a consistent time, leaving you enough hours of sleep before you hear your alarm. Before bed, don't get overstimulated by exercise or an argument with your partner or spouse. Keep the room dark and cool. Stay away from large meals just before bedtime. Avoid stimulants like smoking or caffeinated drinks. Reserve the bedroom for sleep (and sex) if at all feasible.

For many, getting to bed isn't too difficult. It's the "falling asleep" part that's problematic. If this is your problem, peruse Chapter 9, where I describe useful ways of getting more Zzz's. And while sleeping pills and alcohol may work in the short run, they're *not* recommended as part of a long-term solution.

Not Worrying about the Unimportant Stuff

Know the difference between what's truly important and what isn't. Put things into perspective. Many — if not most — of life's stressors are relatively inconsequential. One good way of putting things into perspective is asking yourself, "On a scale of one to ten, how would I rate the relative importance of my stressor?" Remember that eights, nines, and tens are the "biggies" — major life problems such as a serious illness, the loss of a loved one, a major financial loss, and so on. Your fours, fives, sixes, and sevens are problems of moderate importance — a lost wallet, a broken-down car, or a broken water heater. Your ones, twos, and threes are your minor worries or stressors — you forget your wallet, your watch battery dies, or you get a bad haircut.

Now, rate the level of worry and distress you feel *about* that stressor. Again, use a similar ten-point scale, where ten represents "a great deal of distress" and one is "only a very small amount of distress."

Compare the two numbers. If the amount of stress you're experiencing is larger than the importance of the stressor, you're probably overreacting. If this is the case, take a look at the "thinking errors" I describe in Chapter 10 and begin changing how you think.

Not Getting Angry Often

Anger is a stress emotion you can largely do without. Knowing how to avoid becoming angry and losing your temper is a skill well worth mastering. Learning how to control the expression of your anger can also spare you a lot of grief and regret. Much of your anger comes from various forms of distorted thinking. You may have unrealistic expectations of others (and of yourself!) that trigger anger when they aren't met. Your anger may arise from low frustration tolerance, where you exaggerate your inability to cope with discomfort. You may be "catastrophizing and awfulizing" or creating some "can't-stand-it-itis." Chapter 12 can help you with this.

Being Organized

It's important to feel a sense of control over your environment. A cluttered and disorganized life leads to a stressed life. Getting organized means developing effective organizational strategies and tools. For many, clutter is the prime culprit. For others, the lack of an organizational strategy becomes the roadblock — where did I file that file? Fortunately, many useful ideas can help you reverse disorganizational challenges. Chapter 7 gives you those skills.

Managing Time Efficiently

Know how you spend your time and how you waste your time. Learn to use time effectively. Be in control of your schedule. A good place to start is creating and using organizational lists. By combining to-do lists and your calendar (paper or digital), you have a powerful organizational tool to help you gain control over your time. To know where your time goes, you may try keeping a simple log, tracking how you use your time. Doing this for even a few days gives you a good picture of what needs to be changed. Chapter 8 provides you with more specific direction.

Having a Strong Support System

Don't neglect the meaningful people in your life. Spend time with your family, friends, and acquaintances. Have people in your life who listen to you and care for you. If you find that your social support system is a little thin, consider ways of meeting others. These days, you have no shortage of places to meet others who would like to meet you. The activities can include joining a book group, playing a sport, hiking, walking, or biking, to suggest but a few. Going online can make this process much easier. Your local church or synagogue can also bring you into contact with people who share your values and goals. And don't rule out a volunteer experience; you can help others and meet new friends.

Living According to One's Values

Examine your values and goals, assessing whether they truly represent who you are and where you want to go in life. Pursuing values that aren't reflective of the kind of life you want can lead you to an unhappy and stressful place. Ask yourself, "What do I want to get out of my life? What is truly important to me?" Chapter 11 helps you explore these questions and gives you a number of ways of clarifying and articulating your important wants and goals.

Having a Good Sense of Humor

Laugh at life's hassles and annoyances. Be able to laugh at yourself, and don't take yourself too seriously. And remember that bit of wisdom, "He who laughs, lasts."

Chapter 18

Ten Events That Trigger Stress

. . . .

In This Chapter

▶ Weathering life's storms

▶ Understanding how joyful events can become stressors

. . . .

Stress, like beauty, is often in the eye of the beholder. What may be incredibly stressful for you may be a minor irritation for someone else, and perhaps not stressful at all to a third person. It is largely your perception and interpretation of a situation or event that make that event or situation stressful. However, certain events tend to be viewed as highly stressful by most people, most of the time.

What follows is a list of ten events, experiences, and circumstances that people feel are the most stressful. Although this list is taken from my own clinical experience, I don't expect you to agree with most of my choices. You may be surprised, however, to see events that you normally think of as positive — getting married, having a child — listed as stress-producers. But they are. Major life changes, even good changes, are usually stressful.

Losing a Loved One

Surely nothing can be more devastating than the death of someone you very much care about. The loss of your spouse, your child, a close relative, or a very good friend can result in an overwhelming amount of stress. And this stress can last for a very long time. This tragedy comes at the top of just about everyone's list.

Experiencing a Major Illness or Injury

No surprise here, either. I'm not talking about a sprained ankle, the flu, or a case of the measles. The kinds of illnesses and injuries that trigger high levels of stress are the ones that are painful, debilitating, and long-lasting. Life-threatening illnesses and injuries are certainly among the most stressful. Chronic diseases and conditions often lead to chronic stress.

The stress may come from physical pain or from the psychological distress of worrying about the course of the illness or injury — and grieving the loss of what once was, as well as the loss of future hopes and dreams. At times, the stress may come from the more mundane — the difficulties of simply trying to get through the day.

Divorcing or Separating

That relationships can and do end is hardly news. Divorce and separation are commonplace. Everyone knows someone who has been affected in some way by a failed relationship. The prevalence of marital break-ups (more than 50 percent of marriages in the United States end in divorce) may make you think, "No big deal. It happens all the time." Unless, of course, yours is the relationship that's ending. Then you realize just how stressful this experience can be. Should there be children in the relationship, the distress is far greater.

Studies show that people who suffer through a divorce report far more stress-related signs and symptoms than do those who stay married. It can take a very long time to regain your emotional equilibrium, and for your stress level to return to something resembling normal.

Having Serious Financial Difficulties

Money may or may not be the root of all evil; lack of money, however, is almost always the root of much stress. Your particular financial woes may stem from a salary far too low to meet your needs, a once two-income family becoming a one-income family, or a job change or layoff that results in less money coming in. Or, the stress may be triggered by your expenses. A bigger-than-expected mortgage, that wrap-around sound system, unexpected medical bills, or your kid's college tuition may leave you wondering and worrying about how you're going to pay for all of this. And if you think you can't, you're under stress.

Losing a Job

Losing your job often results in the expected stress of not having enough income to maintain your lifestyle. But the stress can be more complicated. Many people tend to tie up their egos with what they do for a living. Being out of work can seem like a failure, which can leave you feeling less worthwhile as a person. Thrown into the package may be the additional anxiety of whether you can find a comparable job that pays enough and quickly enough to meet your financial obligations. Put all of this together and you have a recipe for stress.

Getting Married

Saying "I do" doesn't seem to be such a distressing process. Yet making that important decision and backing it up with a serious commitment can trigger a great deal of upset and anxiety. It's probably the most important decision you will make in your lifetime. Then, you have to make so many plans. The details can be overwhelming: deciding when to have the wedding, choosing where to have it, finding a caterer and florist, hiring the band, booking a limo . . . the list seems endless.

And then you have the family interactions with not only your own delightful relatives, but also this new set of virtual unknowns. Congratulations!

Moving to a New Place

This winner is deceptive. You may think of moving as a relatively low-level stress, worthy of 35th place on this list. Yet moving can be incredibly stressful. First, you have the practical considerations: looking for a new place, hiring movers, finding the time and energy to pack up everything, only to turn around and unpack it all at the other end.

Then there are the psychological questions: Will I like the new house or apartment? What about my old friends? Will I make new friends? If you have children, you often have the added stress of getting them comfortable with a new school and new friends. Oh, and did I mention the mortgage?

Fighting with a Close Friend

A fight or serious disagreement with a good friend that ends the relationship can be highly stressful. The process of fighting or arguing is painful enough in itself, but the residual feelings of anger, upset, and loss can be terribly distressing. You have a void in your life — someone who was a companion, confidant, and sounding board is no longer there. All of this can be very painful.

Having a Child

This, you would think, is a blessing, not a stress. And I trust it is a joyful, happy time in your life. But this blessing does not come without other concerns. The birth process itself can be painful. The health of the mother and the new baby can be worrisome. With a new child come added financial responsibilities, and, sometimes, the birth means one less paycheck. You have concerns about how to parent — will you be able to take care of this brand new person when you get him or her home? And if the new arrival has siblings, you may have concerns about their reactions to their new brother or sister. Not to mention the sleep thing. Sleep? What's that?

Retiring

Retirement is probably the most deceptive source of stress. You think of retirement as a time of prolonged rest and relaxation — a chance to do all those things you've wanted to but couldn't. Stress? Where would the stress come from? Well, going from a rather involved, well-defined lifestyle to one of endless options can be stressful. You may find that after a honeymoon period, you begin to get a wee bit bored. You may miss friends and coworkers. You may realize that spending so much time with your spouse is a little harder than you imagined. Away from your job title, and the accepted definition of your duties and responsibilities, you may feel less sure of yourself and have some identity issues.

Be careful what you wish for. I hear even the Garden of Eden had some stress.

Index

• A •

ABC model of stress, 30–31, 189–190, 191
abdominal breathing, 54, 55
acceptance
    cultivating, 259
    of differences in people and techniques, 46
    mindful, 113–116
activity. *See also* exercise
    daily physical, 171–173
    performing mindfully, 335
    prioritizing to reach goals, 216–217
    scheduling, 319
    stress buffers, 323, 325–326, 328, 331
addiction to stress, 22
adrenalin, 27, 28
advice, giving
    to others, 275
    to self, 264–265
aerobic exercise in morning, 175
air traffic controller, talking like, 208
alcohol
    relaxation, 72
    sleep, 179
Alidina, Shamash (author)
    Mindfulness For Dummies, 167
all-or-nothing thinking, 199
altruism, 224–226, 229, 328
amends, making, 277
anger
    appropriateness of, 237
    avoiding, 341
    breathing away, 247
    changing thoughts leading to, 240–244
    emotional replay, 246
    managing, 237–238, 246–248
    measuring, 233–234
    mindfulness of, 239–240
    negatives of, 235–237
    positives of, 234–235
    rehearsing, 245
    suppressing, 245
    venting, 244–245
Anger Kills (Williams), 235
Anger: The Misunderstood Emotion
        (Tavris), 244
anger two-step, 243
apps for time management, 150
aromatherapy, 84–85, 307
Aromatherapy For Dummies (Keville), 85
arthritis and sleep, 181
asking for opinion on stress level, 36
assertiveness
    aggression and hostility compared
        with, 281–282
    assessing, 278–280
    escalating, 285
    examples of, 281
    fogging, 286–287
    observing, 283
    overview, 278, 280–281
    persistence, 286
    practicing, 282–287
    of women, 287
attention and mindfulness, 98, 111–112
audio instructions, finding and
        downloading, 47
autogenic training, 65–66
automatic thoughts
    described, 75
    as hidden, 194–195
auto-pilot behavior, 101, 108
avocados in diet, 163
avoiding
    anger, 341
    conflict, 293
awareness. *See also* mindfulness
    concept of, 97, 98
    creating, 110–111
    lack of, and stress, 99
    of time, 140
awfulizing. *See* catastrophizing and
        awfulizing

• B •

back muscles
  relaxing, 63
  stretching, 303, 304–305
backing up computer files, 135
ball, squeezing, 304
bananas in diet, 163
Barefoot, John (psychologist), 237
baskets for organizing paper, 134
bath, taking, 321
A Beautiful Mind (movie), 104
bed and breakfast stay as mini-vacation, 335
bedroom
  sound-proofing, 178
  uses of, 177
behavior patterns, communicating
    about, 277
belief, power of, 227–228
belly-button balloon breathing, 58–59
Benson, Herbert (cardiologist and
    researcher), 86, 89, 227
bicycling, 172, 322, 333
bills
  electronic, 130
  paying, 149
biofeedback, 95–96
black-and-white thinking, 199
blowing up technique. *See also*
    exaggeration
  to diffuse stress, 224, 247–248
  for worry, 82–83
blueberries in diet, 163
Bodian, Stephen (author)
  Meditation For Dummies, 2nd Edition, 89
body scanning exercise, 53–54
breakfast, importance of, 165, 166, 299
breaks from work
  limiting, 152
  practicing skills during, 319
  scheduling, 149
  uses of, 310
breathing
  anger, 247
  belly-button balloon, 58–59
  changing patterns for, 54, 57–60
  complete or Zen, 57–58
  emergency, 60

evaluating, 56
experimenting with ways of, 56–57
falling asleep, 182
hypnosis, 95
meditation, 89–90
mindful, 107–108, 239
posture, 59
problem patterns for, 55
as replenishing soul, 56
sleep, 181
snapping wrist to stop unwanted
    thoughts, 78
stress-effective, 57
while waiting, 154
worry, 269
yawning, 60
broccoli in diet, 163
Broken Heart Syndrome, 18
broken item, getting rid of, 127
brown rice in diet, 163
Buddhism and mindfulness, 97, 98
buddy
  practicing techniques with, 47, 126
  working out with, 175
bulk, buying in, 153
burnout at work, 12
business travel, 301–302
buttocks muscles, relaxing, 64
buying
  in bulk, 153
  less, 137–138
  time, 159–160

• C •

caffeine, 310
candle, burning, 85
can't-stand-it-itis, 196–197
carbohydrates, complex and simple, 162, 168
cardiovascular system and anger, 235–236
caregiving issues for women, 13
catalogs, canceling, 130
catastrophizing and awfulizing
  described, 75, 195–196
  examples of, 221
  falling asleep, 183
  worry, 256, 261–262
categorizing item for organization, 128

catharsis, emotional, 244
causes of stress, 25
chair for computer use, 308, 309
change
  acceptance, 114
  public commitment to, 157
  roadblocks to, facing and overcoming, 45–47
  stress from, 10–11
chest breathing, 55
childbirth, 346
children
  marital separation or divorce, 344
  move to new place, 345
  stresses of parents, 21
cholesterol level, 20, 236
chopsticks, eating with, 336
circulatory disease, 17
clarifying values and goals, 212–215
class, attending, 326
classical music, soothing, 83–84, 306
climbing stairs, 171, 173
cloud service, storing document with, 132
clutter
  disorganization from, 119
  excuses for, 120–121
  fooling self with, 123–124
  hoarding, 125
  managing expectations for, 124
  motivation to clear away, 122
  roadmap to clear away, 123
  techniques for dealing with, 125–127
cognitive distortions. *See* errors in thinking
Cohen, Sheldon (researcher), 19
colds, resistance to, 19
commitment to listen, 272
communication
  "I" statements, 276–277
  listening skills, 272–276
  overview, 271–272
communication technology-related stress, 14
community service, 224–226, 229, 328
commuting to work, 300
comparativitis, 199–200
compassion and mindfulness, 99
complete breathing, 57–58
computer files, organizing, 134–135
conclusion, jumping to, 199, 220, 263

conflict, dealing with, 288–294
Congreve, William (playwright), 83
consignment, selling on, 126
cooking
  as stress buffer, 329
  as substitute for stress eating, 165
coping self-talk
  for anger, 243–244
  described, 207–210
  for worry, 265–266
cortisol, 18, 27, 28
counting sheep, 184
country inn stay as mini-vacation, 335
Crohn's disease, 18
cue
  to break stress-eating cycle, 165
  to consider time management, 143–144, 152
  to practice skills, 317–319
Culp, Stephanie (organizational expert), 134
cultivating
  acceptance, 259
  optimism, 220–222

• D •

daily physical activity, increasing, 171–173
daily stress
  described, 14–15
  journal or log for recording, 41–44
daily task, mindfulness for, 108–110
dating clutter, 126
day planner, 146–147
death
  leading causes of, 16–17
  of loved one, 343
delayed sleep-phase disorder, 181
delegating task, 137, 158–159
delivery service, taking advantage of, 160
desk, organizing, 305–306
detaching
  from anger, 239–240
  from stress, 110–111
  from worry, 259
diabetes and sleep, 181
diaphragmatic breathing, 54, 55
diet
  breakfast, importance of, 165, 166, 299
  business travel, 301

diet *(continued)*
  eating mindfully, 108–109, 167–168
  eating out, 169–170
  effect on mood, 162
  importance of, 339–340
  low-stress foods, 162–163
  overview, 161
  snacks, 168
  stress-eating cycle, 164–167
  during workday, 309–310
difficult people, coping with, 288–294
difficult situation, escalating assertion
  in, 285
digital information, safety of, 132
dining out, 169–170
disapproval, fear of, 75, 156
discrimination at work, 12
disorganization
  clutter, 120–127
  frustration resulting from, 117, 122
  hoarding, 125
  identifying forms of, 119
  recognizing, 118–119
displaced worry, 252
distance from stressor, creating, 111
distorted thinking. *See* errors in thinking
distraction
  breaking stress-eating cycle, 164–165
  mindfulness compared with, 99
  minimizing for time efficiency, 150–154
  reading as, 330
  from unwanted thoughts, 78–79
  from worry, 266–267
distress, defined, 22
divorce or marital separation, 344
documents
  filing system for, 131–134
  scanning, 135
drinking liquids, 166, 178
dry mouth, 26
DVDs for exercise, 174

• *E* •

eating mindfully, 108–109, 167–168
80/20 rule, 149
elastic band, snapping to stop unwanted
  thoughts, 78

electronic devices
  managing and minimizing interruption
    from, 150–151
  workout material for, 174
electronic files, organizing, 134–135
Ellis, Albert (psychologist), 30, 203
email, managing, 135–136
emergency breathing, 60
Emmons, Robert (psychologist), 217
emotional catharsis, 244
emotional eating, stopping, 164–167
emotional reaction. *See also* anger; worry
  controlling, 341
  described, 29–30
  facts compared with, 103
  mindlessness, 102–104
  procrastination, 155–156
  recording and rating level of, 43–44
  to scents, 84–85
  thought as creating, 187–191
  thought compared with, 192–193, 258–259
emotional reasoning, 201–202
emotional replay technique, 246
emotional support for decluttering, 126
employee assistance program, 312
employment. *See* work
encryption, 132
endorphins, 170
epidemic of stress, 9–10
ergonomic workspace, 308
errands, combining, 149
errors in thinking. *See also* catastrophizing
  and awfulizing
  black-and-white or all-or-nothing, 199
  can't-stand-it-itis, 196–197
  comparativitis, 199–200
  conclusion-jumping, 199, 229, 263
  coping self-talk, 207–210, 243–244,
    265–266
  emotional reasoning, 201–202
  estimating odds, 260–261
  filtering, 202
  as hindering optimism, 220–221
  leading to anger, 241–244
  magnifying and minimizing, 203
  mind reading, 199
  overgeneralizing, 198–199, 220
  personalizing, 201, 291

self-rating, 205–206, 221, 264
should-ing, 203–205, 241–242, 292
what-if-ing, 197–198, 255, 260
worry, 260–266
escalating assertion, 285
eustress, defined, 22
evaluating breathing, 56
exaggeration
to cope with worry, 82–83, 268–269
to diffuse stress, 224, 247–248
with "never" and "always," 290
excessive worry, 249
exclamation mark behavior, 205
exercise
after work, 313
to break stress-eating cycle, 164
business travel, 301
as daily activity, 171–173
health clubs and gyms, 173–174, 311
importance of, 340
motivation for, 174–175
overview, 170
sleep, 178
solitude, 321–322
to stop worrying, 267
as stress buffer, 327
at work, 307, 311
before workday, 299
expectations and anger, 241–242
expectations for results
changing thoughts and feelings, 210
decluttering, 124
hypnosis, 94
managing, 47
meditation, 90
mindfulness, 108
expressing gratitude, 217–220
eyes, visual resting spots for, 307

● **F** ●

face muscles
hot towel for, 71–72
massaging, 69–70
relaxing, 62
smiling to detach from stress, 110
failure, fear of, 75, 156
faith, 227–228
falling asleep, 181–184

family. *See also* children; parents
delegating tasks within, 159
as stress buffer, 324
worry about, 253
fantasy, therapeutic, 248
fear of disapproval or failure, 75, 156
feedback when listening, 273
feeding worry, 259
feeling, thought compared with, 192–193
feet
footwear for spending time on, 308
massaging, 69
relaxing muscles in, 63
Feuerstein, Georg (author)
Yoga For Dummies, 2nd Edition, 72
fighting dirty, 291
fight-or-flight response, 25–27, 29, 30
filing system
for electronic files, 134–135
for paperwork, 131–134
filtering, 202
financial difficulty, 253, 344
fish in diet, 163
Fitness For Dummies, 4th Edition
(Schlosberg and Neporent), 305
flextime, 312
focusing on issue in conflict situation,
288–289
fogging, 286–287
folder, organizing computer files with, 135
food. *See* diet
foot rest, 308
forgiveness, 248
found moment, 316–317
friends
hostility, 236
loss of relationship with, 346
practicing techniques with, 47, 126
as stress buffers, 324–325
working out with, 175
fruit
in diet, 163
picking, 334
frustration, dealing with, 242
fun, taking seriously, 336
fused thinking, 104
future, constructing optimistic, 222
Future Shock (Toffler), 10

• G •

games
  for exercise, 174
  as stress buffers, 327
gardening, 172, 329
gastrointestinal disease, 18
gauge for measuring stress level, 36–37
getaway file, creating, 332–333
ghrelin, 180
goals
  clarifying, 212–215
  constructing optimistic future, 222
  reaching, 215–217
"good girl" syndrome, 287
good stress, 22
Goodman, Joel (director of HUMOR
    project), 223
gratitude, expressing, 217–220
grazing (eating frequent smaller meals), 166
group, joining, 326
grouping
  items for organization, 128–129
  tasks for time efficiency, 149
grudge, holding, 248
guided imagery
  for falling asleep, 182
  for quieting mind, 79–81
  for worry, 269
gut check on stress level, 36
gym, joining, 173–174, 311

• H •

habit, stress management as, 316–318
hand, massaging, 69
handle item once rule, 127
hassle, daily, 14–15
head, relaxing muscles in, 62. See also face
    muscles
headache, 20
headset for phone, 307
The Healing Power of Doing Good (Luks), 229
health. See also illness
  friendship, 325
  listening skills, 275
  stress affecting, 16–20
  stress related to, 10
  worry about, 253
health club, joining, 173–174, 311
heart disease, 17, 235–236
heartburn and sleep, 180
heat, turning down at night, 179
Helicobacter pylori (H. pylori), 19
helping others, 224–226, 229, 328
hidden thoughts, 194–195
hiking, 333
Hirsch, Alan (researcher), 84
hitting below belt, 291
hoarding, 125
hobbies, 325–326
holding breath, 55
home
  exercising at, 174
  stress related to, 12–13
  transition from work to, 313–314
  working from, 312
hostility and cardiovascular system, 235–236
hot towel for relaxation, 71–72
hot tub for relaxation, 71–72
hotel stay as mini-vacation, 333
humor
  to cope with worry, 268–269
  importance of, 222–224, 342
  to manage anger, 247–248
hypnosis
  described, 91–92
  induction of trance, 92–93
  moving into deeper state of, 93–94
  waking up from trance, 94–95
hypothalamus, 27, 28

• I •

"I" statements, 276–277
icons, explained, 5
identifying
  sources of worry, 251–253
  stress-producing thoughts, 192–193
Iknoian, Therese (author)
  T'ai Chi For Dummies, 72
illness. See also health
  anger, 235
  cardiovascular and circulatory, 17,
    235–236

disturbed sexual performance, 20
experiencing, 344
gastrointestinal, 18
immunological, 18–19, 223
muscle tension, 17
imagery
for falling asleep, 182
positive, 269–270
for stopping unwanted thoughts, 79–81
for worry, 269
immune system, 18–19, 223
impulse buying, 121
infertility, 21
inflammation and heart disease, 17
injury, major, experiencing, 344
in-line skating, 172, 322
inner sanctum, creating, 321
insomnia, 180–181
Internet, saving time using, 153
interpersonal stress. *See* relationships
interruption, minimizing for time
     efficiency, 150–154
irritable bowel syndrome, 18

• J •

Jackson, Pamela (sociologist), 324
job. *See* work
job loss, 345
journal
for anger management, 237–238
for gratitude, 218–219
for recording stress, 41–44
for recording stress practice, 319–320
for recording use of time, 140–142
for worry list, 251, 256
junk mail, discarding, 130

• K •

Kabat-Zinn, Jon (researcher), 105, 335
Karasek, Robert (researcher), 297
Keville, Kathi (author)
Aromatherapy For Dummies, 85
keyboard, placement of, 308
kindness, acts of, 224–226, 229
kitchen-sinking, 289

• L •

labeling
contents of containers, 128
people, 290
lack of control
coping with, 263–264
at work, 297
The Language of the Heart (Lynch), 275
late meal, eating, 177, 180
laughter
to cope with worry, 268–269
importance of, 222–224, 342
to manage anger, 247–248
learning by teaching, 2
leg muscles, relaxing, 63
Leg-lift exercise, 67, 304
leisure time
amount available, 10
looking forward to, 313
as stress buffer, 325–331
leptin, 180
library sanctuary, finding, 322
life at home, stress related to, 12–13
life experience as source of distressing
     thoughts, 74
lifestyle management. *See also* diet;
     exercise; sleep
cues and prompts to practice
     skills, 317–319
fun, taking seriously, 336
overview, 2, 315
place to relax, 320–322
present moment, being in, 98, 105, 107,
     334–336
stress buffers, 323–331
stress management as habit, 316–318
vacations, 332–334
light
turning off at night, 179
in workspace, 306–307
liquid in diet, 166, 178
list of worries, 251, 256
listening skills, 272–276
lists for time management
described, 145
importance of, 342

lists for time management *(continued)*
  master to-do list, 145–146, 149
  tips for making, 148–149
  will-do-later list, 147
  will-do-today list, 146–147
lobby sanctuary, finding, 322
log
  for anger management, 237–238
  for gratitude, 218–219
  for recording stress, 41–44
  for recording stress practice, 319–320
  for recording use of time, 140–142
  for worry list, 251, 256
longevity and anger, 237
loss
  of friendship, 346
  of job, 345
  of loved one, 343
  of weight, 18
Luks, Allan (researcher), 225, 229
lunch
  importance of, 165–166, 310
  practicing skills during, 319
Lynch, James (psychologist)
  The Language of the Heart, 275
Lyubomirsky, Sonja (psychologist), 217

• M •

magnifying, 203
mailing lists, getting off of, 130
management of stress. *See also* lifestyle
    management; mindfulness; practicing
    techniques; relaxation
  habits to cultivate, 339–342
  resources for, 11
  stress buffers, 323–331
management of stress response, 34
management of stress triggers, 32–33.
    See also mindfulness; thoughts
mantra, 89, 90
marital separation or divorce, 344
marriage, 324, 345
masking noise for sleep, 178–179
massage, 68–70
master to-do list, 145–146, 149
mattress, importance of, 177
meals. *See also* nutrition

big or late, 166, 177, 180
  cooking, 165, 329
  grazing (frequent small), 166
  preparing ahead of time, 153
  at restaurant, 169–170
measuring stress level
  gauge, 36–37
  gut check, 36
  stressor-identification scale, 40–41
  stress-symptom scale, 37–39
medical conditions and sleep, 180–181
medication for sleep, 179
meditation
  benefits of, 86–87
  breathing for, 89–90
  challenges of, 87, 90
  described, 86
  frequency and duration of, 90–91
  mantra for, 89, 90
  mindfulness compared with, 99, 100
  preparation for, 87–88
Meditation For Dummies, 2nd Edition
    (Bodian and Ornish), 89
meetup.com website, 327
melatonin, 302
memory and scent, 85
"mental health" days off from work, 12
menu weakness, 169
messages, responding to, 150–151
milk in diet, 163
mind, turning off
  to sleep, 182–183
  techniques for, 76–78
  worry, 256–258, 270
mind reading, 199
mind-body connection, 52
mindfulness
  of anger, 239–240
  benefits of, 104–106
  breathing, 107–108, 239
  components of, 98–99
  cultivating acceptance, 113–116
  described, 97–98
  detaching from worry, 259
  developing skills of, 106–112
  eating mindfully, 108–109, 167–168
  evaluating as potential tool, 100
  living in present, 98, 105, 107, 334–336
  myths about, 99–100

recognizing mindlessness, 100–104
simple exercise for, 106
Mindfulness For Dummies (Alidina), 167
mindlessness
  auto-pilot, operating on, 101, 108
  dangers of, 102–104
  multi-tasking, 102
  recognizing, 100, 108
mineral supplement, 167
mini-meditation, 91
minimizing, 203
mini-vacation, 333–334
moderation in eating, 170
Moen, Phyllis (researcher), 225
moment, being in, 98, 105, 107, 334–336
Monday morning stress, 299
money, worry about, 253, 344
monitoring stress, journal or log for, 41–44
morning exercise, 175
motivation
  to clear away clutter, 122
  for physical activity and exercise, 174–175
  for time management, 156–157
moving to new place, 345
multi-tasking, mindless, 102
Murphy's Law, 261
muscle pain and sleep, 181
muscle tension
  ergonomic workspace, 308
  massage, 68–70
  progressive relaxation, 61–65
  recognizing, 53–54
  as symptom of stress, 17
  at work, 302
music, soothing, 83–84, 306
"musterbation," 203

napping, 180
National Association for Holistic
    Aromatherapy, 85
neck muscles
  massaging, 69
  relaxing, 62–63
Neporent, Liz (author)
  Fitness For Dummies, 4th Edition, 305

nighttime routine, 177–181
"no," saying, 284–285
noise
  minimizing distraction from, 151
  sleep, 178–179
non-acceptance, acceptance compared
    with, 115–116
non-assertive behavior, 282. *See also*
    assertiveness
non-judgmental, being, 98
non-reactive, being, 99
nonverbal communication, 272
nutrition
  breakfast, importance of, 165, 166, 299
  business travel, 301
  eating mindfully, 108–109, 167–168
  eating out, 169–170
  effect on mood, 162
  importance of, 339–340
  low-stress foods, 162–163
  overview, 161
  snacks, 168
  stress-eating cycle, 164–167
  during workday, 309–310
nuts in diet, 163

• *O* •

observing assertive behavior, 283
oils, types of, 85
one step at a time, taking, 45
one-minute body scanning exercise, 53–54
one-month rule for DVR items, 153
one-upping speaker, 275
online bill paying, 130
online services, 153
opinion on stress level, asking for, 36
optimism, cultivating, 220–222
opting out of junk mail, 130
oranges in diet, 163
organizational skills. *See also* time
    management
  being proactive, 137
  buying less, 137–138
  clearing clutter, 120–127
  for desk, 305–306
  importance of, 341

organizational skills *(continued)*
  for paper and information, 129–136
  for personal space, 128–129
  recognizing and identifying
      disorganization, 117–119
Ornish, Dean (author)
  Meditation For Dummies, 2nd Edition, 89
overdoing exercise, 175
overgeneralizing, 198–199, 220
The Overworked American (Schor), 10

paperwork
  disorganization of, 119
  organizing, 129–135
  sampling of, keeping, 127
parasympathetic nervous system, 65
parents
  effects of stress on children, 21
  as sources of distressing thoughts, 74
  stresses for, 13
Pareto principle, 149
password, 132
Payne, Larry (author)
  Yoga For Dummies, 2nd Edition, 72
penalty for not completing task, 157
perception in stress, 187–189
perfectionism, 75, 155
performance
  effect of stress on, 22
  sexual, 20
  at work, 297
peristalsis, 18
persistence and assertiveness, 286
personalizing, 201, 291
perspective, putting things in, 262, 341
pet, as stress buffer, 328–329
philosophy of life
  cultivating optimism, 220–222
  express gratitude, 217–220
  helping others, 224–226, 229
  sense of humor, 222–224
  spirituality, 227–228
  values and goals, 211–217
phone call
  headset for, 307
  responding to, 150–151

physical activity, adding to day, 171–173.
      See also exercise
physical signs and symptoms of stress,
      15–16, 27–29, 52–53
picture, taking of item with sentimental
      value, 127
pinching to stop worry, 270
pituitary gland, 27, 28
place
  moving to new, 345
  to practice skills, 46, 316–317, 320–322
  to worry, 257–258, 268
play time, taking seriously, 336
playing sport, 172–173
podcasts, 154
positive imagery, 269–270
posture and breathing, 59, 309
potassium in diet, 163
practicing techniques. *See also* lifestyle
      management
  anger management, 240–244, 245–248
  assertiveness, 282–287
  autogenic training, 65–66
  breathing, 57–60
  coping self-talk, 207–210, 243–244,
      265–266
  coping with difficult people, 288–294
  finding place for, 46, 316–317, 320–322
  found moments, 316–317
  guided imagery, 79–81
  hypnosis, 92–95
  listening, 275–276
  massage, 68–70
  meditation, 86–91
  mindfulness, 106–112
  progressive relaxation, 61–65
  roadblocks to, 45–47
  scheduling time for, 319
  stretching, 67
  thought stopping, 76–77
  time management, 145–154
  at work, 302–305
  worry management, 256–258, 260–270
prayer, role of, 227
present moment, being in, 98, 105, 107,
      334–336
pre-sleep mode, 183
pressure to perform at work, 297

prioritizing
  activities, 157
  daily tasks, 148
  items for usage, 129
problem solving compared with
      worrying, 265
procrastination, 155–157
productive worry, 254–255
progressive relaxation
  falling asleep, 182
  practicing, 61–64
  quick version, 64–65
  worry, 269
prompt
  to consider time management, 143–144, 152
  to practice skills, 317–319
protein in diet, 162
psychological signs and symptoms of
      stress, 16, 17, 29–30, 74
psychoneuroimmunology, 18–19
public commitment to change, 157

• *Q* •

questionnaire
  on anger, 233–234
  on assertiveness, 278–280
  on extent of control, 263–264
  to measure stress, 37–41
  on stress buffers, 323
  on values and goals, 212–215
  on workplace stress, 296
  on worry, 249–250
quiet place, finding to practice techniques,
      46, 316–317, 320–322

• *R* •

random acts of kindness, 226
rating scale
  stressor-identification, 40–41
  stress-symptom, 37–39
reading, as stress buffer, 329–330
Reality Test, 204–205
recession, U.S., 11
recipients for clutter, 126
recording in log. *See* log
recording TV program for later viewing, 153

refocusing thoughts to fall asleep, 183
reframing with humor, 223
rehearsing
  anger, 245
  conflict situation, 292–293
relationships. *See also* family; friends
  anger, 236
  assertiveness, 278–287
  communication, 271–277
  coping with difficult people, 288–294
  divorce or separation, 344
  marriage, 324, 345
  overview, 271
  as stress buffers, 324–325
  worry about, 253
relaxation
  autogenic training, 65–66
  biofeedback, 95–96
  breaking stress-eating cycle, 165
  breathing away tension, 54–60
  conflict situation, 288
  falling asleep, 182, 183
  hypnosis, 91–95
  importance of, 339
  as increasing stress, 67
  laughter, 223
  massage, 68–70
  meditation, 86–91
  mindfulness, 105
  progressive relaxation, 61–65, 182, 269
  specific skills for, 51
  stretching, 67
  three-minute energy burst, 71
  in traffic, 300
  visualization, 79–81
  worry, 269
The Relaxation Response (Benson), 89
religious belief, 227–228
remembering. *See also* prompt
  to be mindful, 98
  password, 133
resignation, acceptance compared
      with, 114–115
restaurant, eating at, 169–170
results, expectations for
  changing thoughts and feelings, 210
  decluttering, 124
  hypnosis, 94

results, expectations for *(continued)*
  managing, 47
  meditation, 90
  mindfulness, 108
retirement, 346
revenge, 248
reward for completing task, 156–157
rice in diet, 163
roadblock
  to change, 45–47
  to time management, 155–157
rubber band, snapping to stop unwanted
    thoughts, 78

• *S* •

safety of digital information, 132
salad bar, eating from, 169–170
sampling of important papers, keeping, 127
sanctuary, finding, 322
scanning document, 135
scent, soothing, 84–85, 307
scheduling
  organizational tasks, 137
  priority goals, 216–217
  tasks, 122
  technique practice time, 319
  time, 145–150, 156
  vacation, 332
  worry, 82, 257, 268
Schlosberg, Suzanne (author)
  Fitness For Dummies, 4th Edition, 305
Schor, Juliet (author)
  The Overworked American, 10
scrunch progressive relaxation
    exercise, 64–65
self-downing, 75
self-motivation, 156–157
self-rating, 205–206, 221, 264
self-talk, coping
  for anger, 243–244
  described, 207–210
  for worry, 265–266
Selye, Hans (researcher), 22, 24
sense of humor
  to cope with worry, 268–269
  importance of, 222–224, 342
  to manage anger, 247–248

sensual dimension, adding to
    visualization, 81
separation, marital, 344
serotonin, 162
sex, for relaxation, 71
sexual harassment, 12
sexual performance, 20
shaking off tension, 71
shame and decluttering, 122
shifting work time to avoid distractions
    and interruptions, 152
shopping without buying, 138
shoulder breathing, 55
shoulder muscles
  massaging, 69
  relaxing, 62–63
should-ing, 203–205, 241–242, 292
showering to relax, 70
signs and symptoms of stress
  in children, 21
  illness and disease, 16–20
  physical, 15–16, 27–29, 52–53
  psychological, 16, 17, 29–30, 74
  on relationships, 20–21
  stress-symptom scale, 37–39
  at work, 296
simple pleasures, 330–331
sitcom technique, 269
skating, in-line, 172, 322
skipping breakfast, 165
sleep
  business travel, 301–302
  falling asleep, 181–184
  going to bed earlier, 176–177
  importance of, 340
  need for, 176
  overview, 175–176
  routine for, 177–181
  work stress, 298, 299
sleep apnea, 181
sleeping pills, 179
smiling to detach from stress, 110
snacking, anti-stress, 168
snapping wrist to stop unwanted
    thoughts, 78
soaking in tub to relax, 71
social worry, 252
software for time management, 150

sound machine, 84, 178–179
sound-proofing bedroom, 178
spa visit, 333
space, organizing, 128–129
speaker, one-upping, 275
spirituality, 227–228
sport, playing, 172–173
squeezing tennis ball, 304
stairs, climbing, 171, 173
statements, electronic, 130
stimulant, hidden, and sleep, 179
stomach muscles, relaxing, 64
stoplight technique, 293–294
stopping unwanted thoughts
    at bedtime, 182–183, 184
    techniques for, 76–78, 86–91
    worry, 256–258, 270
storage, furniture and containers
        for, 127, 128
storing password, 133
stress. *See also* management of stress;
        signs and symptoms of stress; stress
        buffers; stress triggers
    ABC model, 30–31, 189–190, 191
    automatic response to, 25–27, 30
    balance between good and bad, 34
    causes of, 25
    defined, 23–25
    as self-created, 187–191
    as stimulus and response, 36
stress balance, 193–194, 238, 262
stress buffers
    activity, 325–326, 328, 331
    cooking, 329
    family, 324
    friends, 324–325
    gardening, 329
    overview, 323
    pets, 328–329
    reading, 329–330
    simple pleasures, 330–331
    sports, 327
stress dot, 317–318
stress triggers
    defined, 25
    events, experiences, and circumstances,
        343–346
    examples, 1

frequency of, 30
managing, 32–33
number of, 32
rating importance of, 43
recording, 42
workplace, 297
stressor-identification scale, 40–41
stressors. *See* stress triggers
stretching
    to relax, 67
    at work, 303–305
Successful Time Management For Dummies
        (Zeller), 139
sugar at work, 311
suggestion
    hypnotic, 92
    power of, to induce physiological
        change, 65–66
Sunday-night stress, 298
supplement, vitamin and mineral, 167
support system, 126, 324–325, 342. *See also*
        friends; relationships
suppressing anger, 245
survival potential of stress, 25–27, 29
sweet potatoes in diet, 163
sympathetic nervous system, 27–28
symptoms. *See* signs and symptoms
        of stress

• T •

T'ai Chi For Dummies (Iknoian), 72
talking. *See also* coping self-talk
    about stress-management activities, 320
    about worry, 267
task
    accomplishing, 328
    breaking into smaller steps, 148–149
    delegating, 158–159
    hiring someone for, 159–160
    penalty for not completing, 157
    performing mindfully, 335–336
    reward for completing, 156–157
    for wait times, 154
Tavris, Carol (author)
    Anger: The Misunderstood Emotion, 244
teaching, learning by, 2

techniques. *See* practicing techniques; *specific techniques*
technology-related stress, 13–14
temperament and worry, 74
tennis ball, squeezing, 304
thoughts. *See also* catastrophizing and awfulizing; worry
  ABC model of stress, 30–31, 189–190, 191
  anger management, 240–244
  automatic, 75, 194
  black-and-white or all-or-nothing, 199
  can't-stand-it-itis, 196–197
  changing, 33
  comparativitis, 199–200
  conclusion-jumping, 199, 220, 263
  coping self-talk, 207–210, 243–244, 265–266
  dangers of mindless, 102–104
  distraction from, 78–79
  distressing, 73–74
  emotional reasoning, 201–202
  facts compared with, 102–103
  feelings compared with, 192–193, 258–259
  filtering, 202
  hidden, 194–195
  as hindering optimism, 220–221
  imagination, using to stop unwanted, 79–81
  magnifying and minimizing, 203
  meditation to stop unwanted, 86–91
  mind reading, 199
  negative, 75
  overgeneralizing, 198–199, 220
  personalizing, 201, 291
  self-rating, 205–206, 221, 264
  should-ing, 203–205, 241–242, 292
  sources of, 74–75
  stopping unwanted, 76–78, 182–183, 184
  stress as self-created, 187–191
  stress balance, 193–194
  turning off, 76–78, 182–183, 256–258, 270
  what-if-ing, 197–198, 255, 260
three-minute energy burst, 71
three-month rule for keeping reading material, 126
thriving on stress, 22
time management
  activity to spend less time on, 143
  activity to spend more time on, 142
  being mindful of time, 140

buying time, 159–160
cues and prompts, 143–144
delegating task, 158–159
disorganization, 119
importance of, 342
lists for, 145–150
log of time spent, 140–142
minimizing distraction and interruption, 150–154
psychological roadblocks to, 155–157
questioning use of time, 144–145
recognizing problem with, 140
software and apps for, 150
at work, 309
timing of conversation, 272
Toffler, Alvin (author)
  Future Shock, 10
tolerating frustration, 242
tombstone test for clarifying values and goals, 212–213
total scrunch progressive relaxation exercise, 64–65
towel, hot, for relaxation, 71–72
toy chest for work, 307
trance
  deepening, 93–94
  induction of, 92–93
  waking up from, 94–95
transition from work to home, 313–314
travel for work, 301–302
Triage Method of Clutter Control, 126
trying
  to fall asleep, 182–183
  techniques, 46
TV time
  minimizing, 152–153
  physical activity during, 171
Twist stretching exercise, 67
Type-A personality, 236, 244–245

• *U* •

ulcers, 19
uncertainty
  coping with, 263–264
  fear of, 75
unproductive worry, 254, 255–256

• V •

vacation, 332–334
validation in communication, 273–274
values
   actualizing, 215–217
   clarifying, 212–215
   living according to, 211–212, 342
vegetables in diet, 162
venting anger, 244–245
videos for exercise, 174
visitor, minimizing interruption from, 151
visual resting spots for eyes, 307
visualization
   falling asleep, 182
   positive imagery for worry, 269–270
vitamin supplement, 167
volunteering to help others, 224–226,
   229, 328

• W •

waiting, use of time spent, 154, 317
walking
   to escape worry, 267
   to exercise, 171, 172
   to relax, 321–322
   at work, 302
"warm and heavy" suggestion in autogenic
      training, 65–66
warning of bad mood, 277
water, mini-vacation by, 334
weight gain
   business travel, 301
   lack of sleep, 180
   stress, 18
weight loss, 18
what-if-ing, 197–198, 255, 260
Wherever You Go, There You Are
      (Kabat-Zinn), 335
white lie, 285
white-noise machine, 151, 179
will-do-later list, 147
will-do-today list, 146–147
Williams, Redford (researcher)
   Anger Kills, 235
wise sayings, collection of, 229–230

women
   assertiveness of, 287
   home-related stress for, 13
   work-related stress for, 12
   yelling and self-esteem of, 245
work
   commuting, 300
   eating during workday, 309–310
   employee benefits, 311–312
   ergonomic workspace, 308
   identifying best time for, 148
   leaving behind, 313
   lighting at, 306–307
   minimizing distraction and
         interruption, 150–154
   organizing desk, 305–306
   statistics on stress at, 295
   stress related to, 11–12, 295–296
   stress triggers, 297
   stretching at, 303–305
   Sunday-night stress, 298
   time management, 309
   transition to home from, 313–314
   travel for, 301–302
   worry about, 253
workaholic traits, 236
working out at health club or gym, 173–174
World Privacy Forum, 130
worry
   aromatherapy for soothing, 84–85
   assessing, 249–250
   avoiding, 341
   at bedtime, 184
   blowing up, 82–83
   correcting thinking errors, 260–266
   cultivating acceptance, 259
   cultivating optimism, 220–222
   described, 73–74, 249
   distraction from, 266–267
   hidden, 252–253
   humor to cope with, 268–269
   identifying sources of, 251–253
   music for soothing, 83–84
   place for, 257–258, 268
   productive, 254–255
   relaxation, 269
   scheduling, 82, 257
   sound machines for soothing, 84

worry *(continued)*
  thoughts and, 258–259
  trying to stop, 250–251
  turning off, 76–78, 256–258
  unproductive, 254, 255–256
  varying intensity of, 268
  writing about, 256

Yang, Linda (author and gardener), 329
yawning, 60

yelling when angry, 244–245
yoga, 71–72
Yoga For Dummies, 2nd Edition (Feuerstein and Payne), 72

• Z •

Zeller, Dirk (author)
  Successful Time Management For Dummies, 139
Zen breathing, 57–58

Apple & Mac

iPad For Dummies,
5th Edition
978-1-118-49823-1

iPhone 5 For Dummies,
6th Edition
978-1-118-35201-4

MacBook For Dummies,
4th Edition
978-1-118-20920-2

OS X Mountain Lion
For Dummies
978-1-118-39418-2

Blogging & Social Media

Facebook For Dummies,
4th Edition
978-1-118-09562-1

Mom Blogging
For Dummies
978-1-118-03843-7

Pinterest For Dummies
978-1-118-32800-2

WordPress For Dummies,
5th Edition
978-1-118-38318-6

Business

Commodities For Dummies,
2nd Edition
978-1-118-01687-9

Investing For Dummies,
6th Edition
978-0-470-90545-6

Personal Finance
For Dummies,
7th Edition
978-1-118-11785-9

QuickBooks 2013
For Dummies
978-1-118-35641-8

Small Business Marketing Kit
For Dummies,
3rd Edition
978-1-118-31183-7

Careers

Job Interviews
For Dummies,
4th Edition
978-1-118-11290-8

Job Searching with
Social Media
For Dummies
978-0-470-93072-4

Personal Branding
For Dummies
978-1-118-11792-7

Resumes For Dummies,
6th Edition
978-0-470-87361-8

Success as a Mediator
For Dummies
978-1-118-07862-4

Diet & Nutrition

Belly Fat Diet For Dummies
978-1-118-34585-6

Eating Clean For Dummies
978-1-118-00013-7

Nutrition For Dummies,
5th Edition
978-0-470-93231-5

Digital Photography

Digital Photography
For Dummies,
7th Edition
978-1-118-09203-3

Digital SLR Cameras &
Photography For Dummies,
4th Edition
978-1-118-14489-3

Photoshop Elements 11
For Dummies
978-1-118-40821-6

Gardening

Herb Gardening
For Dummies,
2nd Edition
978-0-470-61778-6

Vegetable Gardening
For Dummies,
2nd Edition
978-0-470-49870-5

Health

Anti-Inflammation Diet
For Dummies
978-1-118-02381-5

Diabetes For Dummies,
3rd Edition
978-0-470-27086-8

Living Paleo For Dummies
978-1-118-29405-5

Hobbies

Beekeeping
For Dummies
978-0-470-43065-1

eBay For Dummies,
7th Edition
978-1-118-09806-6

Raising Chickens
For Dummies
978-0-470-46544-8

Wine For Dummies,
5th Edition
978-1-118-28872-6

Writing Young Adult Fiction
For Dummies
978-0-470-94954-2

Language &
Foreign Language

500 Spanish Verbs
For Dummies
978-1-118-02382-2

English Grammar
For Dummies,
2nd Edition
978-0-470-54664-2

French All-in One
For Dummies
978-1-118-22815-9

German Essentials
For Dummies
978-1-118-18422-6

Italian For Dummies
2nd Edition
978-1-118-00465-4

Available in print and e-book formats.

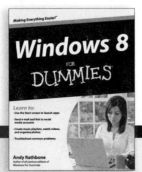

Math & Science

Algebra I For Dummies,
2nd Edition
978-0-470-55964-2

Anatomy and Physiology
For Dummies,
2nd Edition
978-0-470-92326-9

Astronomy For Dummies,
3rd Edition
978-1-118-37697-3

Biology For Dummies,
2nd Edition
978-0-470-59875-7

Chemistry For Dummies,
2nd Edition
978-1-1180-0730-3

Pre-Algebra Essentials
For Dummies
978-0-470-61838-7

Microsoft Office

Excel 2013 For Dummies
978-1-118-51012-4

Office 2013 All-in-One
For Dummies
978-1-118-51636-2

PowerPoint 2013
For Dummies
978-1-118-50253-2

Word 2013 For Dummies
978-1-118-49123-2

Music

Blues Harmonica
For Dummies
978-1-118-25269-7

Guitar For Dummies,
3rd Edition
978-1-118-11554-1

iPod & iTunes
For Dummies,
10th Edition
978-1-118-50864-0

Programming

Android Application
Development For
Dummies, 2nd Edition
978-1-118-38710-8

iOS 6 Application
Development For Dummies
978-1-118-50880-0

Java For Dummies,
5th Edition
978-0-470-37173-2

Religion & Inspiration

The Bible For Dummies
978-0-7645-5296-0

Buddhism For Dummies,
2nd Edition
978-1-118-02379-2

Catholicism For Dummies,
2nd Edition
978-1-118-07778-8

Self-Help & Relationships

Bipolar Disorder
For Dummies,
2nd Edition
978-1-118-33882-7

Meditation For Dummies,
3rd Edition
978-1-118-29144-3

Seniors

Computers For Seniors
For Dummies,
3rd Edition
978-1-118-11553-4

iPad For Seniors
For Dummies,
5th Edition
978-1-118-49708-1

Social Security
For Dummies
978-1-118-20573-0

Smartphones & Tablets

Android Phones
For Dummies
978-1-118-16952-0

Kindle Fire HD
For Dummies
978-1-118-42223-6

NOOK HD For Dummies,
Portable Edition
978-1-118-39498-4

Surface For Dummies
978-1-118-49634-3

Test Prep

ACT For Dummies,
5th Edition
978-1-118-01259-8

ASVAB For Dummies,
3rd Edition
978-0-470-63760-9

GRE For Dummies,
7th Edition
978-0-470-88921-3

Officer Candidate Tests,
For Dummies
978-0-470-59876-4

Physician's Assistant Exam
For Dummies
978-1-118-11556-5

Series 7 Exam
For Dummies
978-0-470-09932-2

Windows 8

Windows 8 For Dummies
978-1-118-13461-0

Windows 8 For Dummies,
Book + DVD Bundle
978-1-118-27167-4

Windows 8 All-in-One
For Dummies
978-1-118-11920-4

 **Available in print and e-book formats.**

Take Dummies with you everywhere you go!

Whether you're excited about e-books, want more from the web, must have your mobile apps, or swept up in social media, Dummies makes everything easier .

Dummies products make life easier!

- DIY
- Consumer Electronics
- Crafts
- Software
- Cookware
- Hobbies
- Videos
- Music
- Games
- and More!

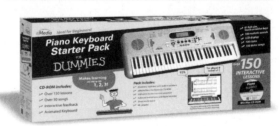

For more information, go to **Dummies.com®** and search the store by category.

FOR
DUMMIES
A Wiley Brand